African Creeks

Race and Culture in the American West
Quintard Taylor, Series Editor

African Creeks

Estelvste and the Creek Nation

Gary Zellar

University of Oklahoma Press
Norman

Library of Congress Cataloging-in-Publication Data
Zellar, Gary.
African Creeks : Estelvste and the Creek Nation / Gary Zellar.
p. cm. — (Race and culture in the American West series ; v. 1)
Includes bibliographical references and index.
ISBN 978-0-8061-3815-2 (hardcover : alk. paper)
1. Creek Indians—Mixed descent—Georgia. 2. Creek Indians—Government relations.
3. Blacks—Relations with Indians. 4. Indian slaves—Georgia. 5. Africans—Migrations.
I. Title.
E99.C9Z45 2007
973.04′0597385—dc22

                                                                      2006026247

African Creeks: Estelvste and the Creek Nation is Volume 1 in the Race and Culture in the American West series.

The paper in this book meets the guidelines for permanence and durability of the Committee on Production Guidelines for Book Longevity of the Council on Library Resources, Inc. ∞

1 2 3 4 5 6 7 8 9 10

In memory of Dad,
a history lover and grower of corn and roses,

and for Mom,
seed sprouter and gardener extraordinaire

By ignoring such matters as the sharing of bloodlines and cultural traditions by groups of widely differing ethnic origins, and by overlooking the blending and metamorphosis of cultural forms which is so characteristic of our society, we misconceive our cultural identity . . . we dread to acknowledge the complex, pluralistic nature of our society, and as a result we find ourselves stumbling upon our true identity under circumstances in which we least expect to do so.

Ralph Ellison, *Going to the Territory*

Contents

List of Illustrations   xi

Acknowledgments   xiii

Introduction   xvii

1   "Eating from the Same Pot":
African Creek Slavery   3

2   "Like a Terrible Fire on the Prairie":
African Creeks and the Civil War   41

3   "To Do More Than the Government Has Seen
Fit to Do": Reconstructing Race in the
Creek Nation   77

4   "Times Seem to Be Getting Very Ticklish":
African Creeks and the Green Peach War   115

5   "The Strong Vein of Negro Blood":
Creek Racial Politics and Citizenship   161

6   "If I Ain't One, You Won't Find Another
One Here": African Creek Identity, Allotment,
and the Dawes Commission   194

7   "A Measure So Insulting as This":
Jim Crow in the Indian Country   231

List of Abbreviations   259

Notes   261

Bibliography   307

Index   329

Illustrations

Photographs

Silas Jefferson   146

Silas Jefferson, with Creek chief Locha Hacho   147

Study of Creek freedman boy   148

African Creek woman and child at their
homestead in the Creek Nation   149

"Cotton Picking Time" in the Creek Nation   150

Old Creek Agency School and Baptist Church   151

Little River Colored Baptist School students   152

Tullahassee Mission ruins after December 1880
fire   153

Tullahassee Manual Labor School   154

James Coody Johnson, Seminole chief Halputta
Micco, and Okcha Hacho   155

Black family in the Creek Nation   156

African Creek school at Pleasant Grove   157

Island Smith   158

Paro Bruner   159

Emancipation Day flyer   160

Maps

Creek country in the East, before removal   9

Opothleyahola's exodus and Civil War battles   49

Creek country, 1866–1907   83

Muskogee township plat, 1899   223

Acknowledgments

I WOULD LIKE TO THANK MANY PEOPLE WHO helped me form an inchoate body of research into a manuscript. First, my heartfelt appreciation goes to Elliott West, my dissertation director at the University of Arkansas, for his patience, guidance, insights, and advice, and for laboring over many drafts and revisions of the dissertation, as well as providing research funds that made this study possible. Elliott was truly a dissertation director sent from heaven as well as a mentor and friend. I would also like to thank Daniel F. Littlefield, Jr., one of the pioneers in the study of African-Indian relations, not only for sharing his voluminous research files but also for sharing his hospitality during my extended research trip to Little Rock. His insights regarding Creek political and social life helped me focus my research and provided direction into uncharted territory.

As will become apparent from reading the notes accompanying the following pages, I am also deeply indebted to the scholarship of Angie Debo and her path-breaking studies, *The Road to Disappearance* and *And Still the Waters Run.* While some of Debo's analysis and interpretations have come under criticism lately, at the time she was writing, putting tribal peoples at the center of their own stories through the use of tribal records and oral histories was an act of scholarly courage. Her inclusion of African Creeks as legitimate actors in Creek history only underscores the essential justice and humanity of her work and helped guide me in this expanded study.

I would also like to thank African Creek informant Robert Littlejohn, Sr., for sharing valuable information and helping connect the dots. Celeste Johnson also shared valuable insights and suggestions. The late Napoleon Davis welcomed me as a guest at his Creek Freedmen's Memorial Shrine in Taft, Oklahoma, and provided me with information on the Loyal Creek claims as well as his family history.

I owe Jeannie Whayne, the chair of the University of Arkansas Department of History, a debt of gratitude for introducing me to agricultural and rural history as an analytical tool and for guiding me through the historiography of Southern history. I would also like to thank Willard Gatewood, distinguished professor emeritus, and one of the deans of African American and Southern history, for his guidance and support over the years and for providing me the opportunity to visit the National Archives in Washington, D.C., with a grant from the Gatewood Endowment. I am grateful to the members of the University of Arkansas Department of History Awards Selection Committee for honoring me with the 2002 Gatewood Fellowship, which allowed me to continue with the dissertation at a critical time.

I would like to honor the memory of the late Nudie Williams, who over the years unselfishly offered his knowledge of Indian Territory and Oklahoma history. Although his final illness and passing prevented him from seeing the dissertation through its last stages, he was there in spirit. I would also like to extend my appreciation to Charles F. Robinson II for joining the dissertation committee at the last minute and offering helpful critiques despite the limited time afforded him.

Kent Carter, Meg Hacker, Barbara Rust, and staff provided invaluable assistance in locating material in the immense holdings at the Ft. Worth National Archives. William Welge, the Oklahoma Historical Society archives director, helped guide me through OHS's huge and valuable holdings. Mike Todd, Phyllis Adams, and Tressie Neeley helped me locate material in the archives and manuscript collections at OHS. Melvina Heisch, the OHS director of historic preservation, provided access to valuable resources in the Preservation Office files. Chester Cowen, photographic archivist at OHS, and Lillie Kerr aided in finding and identifying photographs and making them available.

Special thanks go to Mary Jane Warde, historian, scholar, and friend, for offering her insights into Creek politics and social life, for steering me toward valuable manuscripts and other sources at the Oklahoma Historical Society, and for guiding me to the Angie Debo Papers. I am grateful to Lori N. Curtis, head of special collections and archives, and Milissa Burkart at McFarlin Library, University of Tulsa, for their help in rounding up photographs from the Alice Robertson Collection. I would also like to thank Sarah Irvin, the archivist at the Thomas Gilcrease Institute of American Art and History, for help in locating manuscript material.

Tom Sweeney generously allowed me to study A.C. Ellithorpe's diary as well as to consult other materials in his private collection at General

Sweeny's: A Museum of Civil War History, in Republic, Missouri. Alan Chilton and Arnold Schofield at the Ft. Scott National Historic Site in Ft. Scott, Kansas, alerted me to many First Indian Home Guard sources and generously supplied me with materials from their own files. Bob Knect of the Kansas State Historical Society provided me with valuable information on the Ellithorpe Collection as well as other materials in the KSHS archives. Andrea Cantrell, head of research services for Special Collections at the University of Arkansas Mullins Library, gave helpful advice on locating resources there and in other locations. Don Bateman, Beth Juhl, and Luti Salisbury, at University of Arkansas Mullins Library, all provided valuable assistance over the years in locating material. I owe Michelle Tabler, and the other members of the interlibrary loan staff at the Mullins Library, thanks for fielding and delivering innumerable requests for hard-to-find materials.

I would like to extend special appreciation to James William Dankert, esteemed scholar, artist, and friend for giving his time in researching the files of Chicago newspapers for various articles. And special thanks to Randye Jones (The Art of the Negro Spiritual Project) for calling my attention to "Five Creek Freedmen Spirituals" and for her efforts to bring the joy of this music to a wider audience. Also thanks to Lucy Zellar for tracking down the score, and Cassandra Volpe at the American Music Research Center for providing transcripts of the score and Hortense Love's accompanying notes.

Thanks are due to the people at the University of Oklahoma Press for making this book a reality. Charles Rankin, editor in chief, accepted the manuscript from an unknown scholar and patiently guided it through the initial stages. Director John Drayton's interest and support for the project confirmed my belief that the book "belonged" at the University of Oklahoma Press. Matthew Bokovoy, acquisitions editor, threw his enthusiasm into the project and provided support during the initial revision process. Editors Steven Baker and Melanie Mallon both lent their expertise in getting the manuscript into its final form, and I am grateful for Melanie's careful reading and editing of the manuscript, which helped clarify key issues and avoid redundancies. Thanks also to Bill Nelson for creating three of the maps that appear in this book. I would also like to thank the two anonymous reviewers for their critiques and suggestions, which helped identify strengths in the manuscript and areas in which clarification was necessary.

Finally, I would like to thank my family for their encouragement and support. Lucy Zellar encouraged me along the way and proofread the final draft. Brooke Zellar deserves my heartfelt appreciation for being a wonderful and caring mother to our children. Special love and appreciation go to my daughter, Violet, and my son, Garrison, for their understanding, love, and patience. And to my mother, Charlotte Zellar, I cannot describe how important her unwavering support, encouragement, and unconditional love have been to me during the years it took to complete this study. To my late father, Leonard Zellar, and my stepmother, Mary Lloyd Zellar, I also owe special love and appreciation for their support over the years. I would like to dedicate the manuscript to the memory of my father, Leonard "Lou" Zellar, for instilling in me a love of history and learning and encouraging me to "go to the bone" to find answers to historical questions, or at least to discover new possibilities, and to Mom, for always being there.

Introduction

IN FALL 1879, WILLIAM O. TUGGLE, a private agent for the Creeks, visited the Indian Territory, collecting information to present a convincing case to Congress regarding some Creek claims for payment, which the Creeks had been pressing for since before their removal to the West. Tuggle was no dewy-eyed liberal reform advocate; he was a Southern Democrat from Georgia, a self-described "unreconstructed rebel." Nonetheless, Tuggle had come to admire Creek accomplishments, and he speculated on the future of the evolving multiracial society he saw in the Creek country:

> What a strange medley of people are here in the Indian Territory, Caucasians, Mongolians or Indians, Africans and several new breeds manufactured by judicious crossing! If there is any virtue in mixing blood here's a fine opportunity to try the experiment—Copartnership between Shem, Ham and Japheth, with the possibility that Shem and Ham will finally have a rich store of experience while sagacious Japheth will take care of the finances of the firm.[1]

These sons and daughters of Ham, former slaves and free blacks of the Creek Nation, were known as Estelvste, a Creek phrase that means "black people." They had lived among the Creeks since the first Spanish entradas through the Creek lands east of Mississippi during the early sixteenth century. They spoke the same language, ate the same foods, held the same worldview, and shared kinship ties with the Creek people. Once a part of Creek society, African Creeks played key roles in all major events in its history. During the eighteenth and early nineteenth centuries, some successfully integrated into positions of influence. By the first decades of the nineteenth century, most African Creeks provided the slave labor that enabled leading Creek families to accumulate wealth and power. African Creeks also acted as cultural brokers, interpreters, preachers, warriors, and negotiators as Creeks responded to intrusions into their native lands in Georgia and

Alabama and endured tribal divisions, the bitter Red Stick War, removal to Indian Territory, and the trauma of the Civil War.

African Creeks entered the post–Civil War era holding and exercising full political, legal, and economic rights as citizens in the Creek Nation. As one of the unheralded success stories of the Reconstruction era, African Creeks held offices in all branches of the Creek constitutional government and participated freely and energetically in its fractious political life. They established themselves as a stable class of yeoman subsistence farmers, ranchers, traders, and merchants on the Creek communal lands. With their equal share of tribal funds, they established schools that rivaled or even surpassed those in the neighboring states. Yet despite these promising beginnings, by 1910 the "sons of Japheth" had seized control of the "finances of the firm" and divested the Estelvste of their land, excluded them from political life, and socially ostracized them with Jim Crow laws in the new state of Oklahoma. This startlingly rapid decline in the African Creek position illuminates larger issues of national and western development—the destructive effects of a national ideology of progress and of pressures for cultural consolidation in a nation transformed by civil war. The story of the Estelvste is a disturbing but revealing illustration of an important but understudied aspect of American race relations during a crucial stage in their evolution. It lays bare the forces working to erode cultural traditions underlying the "copartnership between Shem, Ham and Japheth," and by extension, it tells of the nation choosing a future with no place within it for truly multiracial societies.

The Creeks had not consciously created a multiracial society on the racial frontier in the Indian Territory, but traditions of diversity and inclusion had its roots as far back as the Mississippian era among the southeastern Indians. This tradition continued as Creek culture adapted to the changes wrought by Euro-American colonization, dispossession, war, and finally allotment and Oklahoma statehood. Race consciousness and racism certainly permeated some parts of Creek society and poisoned relations between the Estelvste and Creek Indians, leaving a legacy that has yet to be resolved. But throughout Creek history, race and the building of a racial hierarchy was less important to the Creeks than the building of a Creek community that recognized the significant role that individual Estelvste played in Creek society. To ignore that reality would only diminish the Creek ability to deal effectively with the enormous changes swirling around them.[2] African Creeks forged a community identity within the confines of the Creek cultural milieu, and what follows is a narrative history that describes the people and events as well as the social and political developments that contributed to the building and sustaining of African Creek community identity. I hope that this study contributes something positive to the emerging body of work on African-Indian relations done recently by scholars such as Barbara Krauthamer, Tiya Miles, Kevin Mulroy, Celia E. Naylor-Ojurongbe, Claudio Saunt, Circe Sturm, Murray Wickett, and others.[3] I owe a tremendous debt to scholars who pioneered research in this field—Kenneth Porter, Daniel F. Littlefield, Jr., and Theda Perdue—and hope that this work will point the way for further, and much needed, research in the field.

African Creeks

1

"Eating from the Same Pot"
African Creek Slavery

THERE IS A CREEK ORAL TRADITION that an African ship ran aground on the Shell Islands off the Alabama coast many years before contact with Spanish explorers and their African compatriots in the sixteenth century. According to the eighteenth-century Creek narrators, the marooned African sailors lived among them for the rest of their lives and left descendants who could be identified by their coarse hair texture. Although the southeastern American Indian archeological record has yet to yield definitive evidence of direct contact, some historians and archeologists consider a pre-1492 Africa-to–North America transit likely, although the extent of the contact is debated. The first recorded contact between Africans and the southeastern Indians began when several black members of Hernando de Soto's expedition deserted and found refuge in the various Indian chiefdoms they encountered during their entrada through the Southeast in 1540.[1]

The people and polities Soto encountered, and in which the Africans found refuge, were Mississippian cultures, different in political structure from the Creeks of the historic period, but from which the Creeks inherited language and other major cultural traits. The Mississippian cultures began to form around AD 800–1000 in the Southeast, and some had reached the height of their development when they met Soto and his men. They were a communal people who lived in towns ranging from two dozen families to several thousand inhabitants, knit together in an intricate web of kinship and clan relationships. They built elaborate mound and plaza complexes that served as centers for their ritual and ceremonial lives. Their towns, in turn, were organized into chiefdoms in which hereditary chiefs, their kinship circle, and selected elites ruled a socially stratified society. The Coosa paramount chiefdom, one of the richest and most extensive that Soto and his entourage spent an extended time in, linked various chiefdoms that stretched some four hundred miles from southeastern Tennessee into east-central Alabama and was possibly one of the largest Indian polities in North America at the time, containing as many as thirty-five thousand people. Given its extent, Coosa was most likely a culturally diverse collection of peoples who spoke a variety of Muskhogean dialects as well as other southeastern Indian languages.[2]

Rich fields provided the Coosas and other Mississippians with their principal food source—corn. Archeologists and ethnohistorians see the Mississippians' commitment to intensive maize agriculture as the key to their development as complex societies. Indeed, much of their religious, political, and ritual lives were directed toward harnessing communal energies and negotiating the balance of forces, both temporal and spiritual, necessary to ensure the fertility of their fields and bring order to their world.[3]

The Mississippian societies were kinship-oriented matrilineal cultures that charted descent from their mothers and owed their primary allegiance to their mothers' clan relations. Although Soto and his men encountered women in leadership positions, and archeologists have uncovered evidence of women being buried in high-status graves, men and women had strictly defined gender roles in Mississippian societies. Men would help clear farm fields and aid in the planting, but women were generally in charge of farming. They cultivated communal cornfields interspaced with beans, squash, pumpkins, and sunflowers from which they produced an agricultural surplus they stored for later use. Mississippians also gathered various wild foods.

Women produced household goods and cared for children. Men provided meat and hides through hunting and acquired other prestige goods through trade and raiding. Indeed, warfare and raiding were important features of Mississippian life, through which men earned status as well as material goods. Men also built houses, ceremonial buildings, traps, and canoes and did the labor associated with hunting and fishing.[4]

Mississippian warfare practices accounted for a form of slavery in the southeastern societies. Captives taken in war or raiding not only added to a warrior's prestige but also fortified a chiefdom's population. Although the Spanish did not mention the presence of slaves during their stay in Coosa, they did observe slaves at work in the fields in neighboring chiefdoms, and the same situation probably prevailed in Coosa. Slaves were considered "people without kinship," a particularly repugnant notion in a kinship-based society, but adoptive practices were probably in place, particularly for captive women and children, wherein slaves could eventually find a place in society. Adoptive practices could also apply to foreigners who voluntarily came among them, if evidence from the later historic period is any indication. The Coosas likely recognized the slave–master relationships that existed in the Soto expedition, and given the Spaniards' conduct while in Coosa—freely plundering food, seizing women, and holding the chief himself hostage while pillaging and terrorizing their way through the province —the Coosas probably viewed the African slaves among the Spanish as potential allies. Another Creek oral history from a later period recounts that while the Indians feared and distrusted the Spanish, they were more familiar with the Africans on the expedition. Why this would be so is not clear: there were indeed many cultural similarities between the forest peoples of West Africa and the southeastern Mississippians, but most of the African slaves on the expedition were thoroughly acculturated domestic slaves who spoke Spanish and had converted to Christianity. What is more, not all the Africans on the expedition *were* slaves, as skin color or African origins did not automatically imply slave status. In any case, it is no wonder that African slaves on the expedition could see advantages in escaping bondage, not to mention the hazards and deprivations of expedition life, to live in a prosperous chiefdom like Coosa.[5]

Soto's chroniclers reported that in some cases, "the flight of these men was the result of an affection for women." One African slave from the expedition "eloped" with the "Lady of Cofitachequi," a young woman from an elite ruling family in the Piedmont area of the Carolinas. The two were reported to be "living together as man and wife" when the expedition left the area in June 1540. Indian informants told members of Tristain de Luna's 1559 expedition that another fugitive, Johann Biscayan, a literate African slave, escaped and lived with the Coosas for eleven or twelve years. Robles, another African slave, also stayed behind, but under slightly different circumstances. Described by his owner as "a fine Christian and a good slave," Robles was too ill to travel (the type of illness is unknown) and was not expected to survive the journey back. The Coosas gladly accepted him into their care, and later accounts verified that he did survive. These first encounters between Africans and the forebears of the Creeks, then, reveal no apparent aversion based on skin color.[6]

The hopes of a stable future among the southeastern Indians was compromised by something else the Spanish, and probably the fugitives, introduced into the Southeast—Old World contact diseases against which the Indian people had no immunity. Historians and ethnographers are still debating what impact the epidemics had on the Mississippian chiefdoms' decline, and some attribute the decline to the Spaniards' destructive challenge to chiefly authority and other long-term trends that characterized many of the chiefdoms. Perhaps for a combination of reasons, then, powerful chiefdoms like Coosa collapsed, and in their place "coalescent societies" began to form by the seventeenth century, out of which grew the southeastern Indian tribes known during the historic period, among them a grouping of towns and tribal peoples that English traders called Creeks.[7]

After the collapse of the chiefdoms, the hierarchical political structure and social stratification gave way to a more decentralized and egalitarian political system of voluntary town alliances forged in response to the continued European intrusion and the opening of trade in deerskins and Indian slaves that began in the seventeenth century. Groupings of allied towns along the Coosa, Tallapoosa, and Alabama river watersheds in present-day Alabama became known as the Upper Creeks because of their proximity to the upper trading path, which extended into the interior from South Carolina. Along the Flint and Chattahoochee river systems in western Georgia were associated towns called the Lower Creeks because of their location on the lower trading path. By the 1750s, the two groupings of towns became known as the Creek Confederacy. Two important features of the Creek town alliances were their flexibility and diversity. The towns in the confederacy were free to join with other towns in negotiating agreements, to remain neutral, or to act independently of one another. Decisions in the towns were made by consensus, in which each male member of the town had a voice at the town councils, presided over by the town chief, or *micco*. Indeed, throughout their history, Creeks identified more with their individual towns than with the wider confederacy because the mother towns contained the public square, where town councils were held and where the annual purification and renewal ceremony known as the *poskita* (busk), or green corn ceremony, was held each summer, after the first corn crop ripened. In addition to its flexibility, the confederacy was distinguished by its linguistic and ethnic complexity. Over a dozen different languages were spoken, most of them eastern Muskhogean dialects, along with other non-Muskhogean languages such as Yuchi, Natchez, and Shawnee. Other Muskogean tribal peoples, such as the Alabama, Kosati, Tuskegee, and Hitchiti, among others, also joined the Creek Confederacy.[8]

While the Mississippian hierarchical political structure disappeared, other elements of the earlier southeastern cultures remained intact. They maintained their matrilineal kinship-oriented social structure, and indeed, kinship-clan networks became more important than ever in the post-Mississippian world as a way to bring order and stability to Creek communities. They also continued their commitment to maize agriculture and gathering wild foods and medicines. Other social mechanisms survived, such as reciprocity and redistribution of material goods, which attached social significance to the exchange of material goods and discouraged the accumulation of material wealth. The division of labor between men and women survived and indeed was integral to the bipolar worldview by which the Creeks categorized and balanced their world.[9]

Hunting and warfare practices were adapted to meet the challenges of the European colonial market systems that increasingly wound their way into the southeastern Indian lands by the end of the seventeenth century, through the British from the north and east, the Spanish from the south, and the French from the west. Indeed, exigencies of trade, particularly the traffic in Indian slaves, led to defensive and predatory alliances among various towns and tribal groups to protect themselves from slave raiders and to deliver captured slaves to European traders, particularly the British. The trade in Indian slaves tapered off after the Yamasee War in 1715 and was replaced by the deerskin trade as the principal way to acquire European trade goods. The Creek involvement in the Indian slave trade, besides solidifying town alliances, imprinted the practice of treating people as commodities for trade purposes, if not for the bounty of their excess labor. It undoubtedly brought African and Indian peoples together in various ways: as adversaries, as potential commodities, or even as potential allies or family members.[10]

Extended contact between Africans and Creeks began when English settlers brought black slaves into South Carolina during the later part of the seventeenth century, and South Carolinians opened their brisk trade with the Creeks and other Indians in the interior. Because Spanish Florida offered a more secure haven for runaway slaves from the English colonies, the number of Africans finding their way into the Creek country at first remained low. Beginning in the late seventeenth century, Spanish colonial authorities had issued proclamations offering freedom to "any *negro* of Carolina" willing to convert to Catholicism. The Spanish organized the fugitive slaves into military settlements and provided them with land, tools, and rations in exchange for their service in protecting the colony. British treaties, furthermore, contained provisions for return of fugitive slaves fleeing to the Creek country, and Creeks generally cooperated with British colonial officials in returning slaves, if it suited their purposes. It usually did, given the substantial rewards for returning fugitive slaves. One historian estimated that rewards equaled nearly two-thirds the amount Indian hunters could earn in a year in the deerskin trade. The British also used threats to enforce the fugitive slave agreements. Being cut off from British trade goods for harboring fugitive slaves posed a serious dilemma for the Creeks. While both the Spanish and the French offered trade goods, and the Creeks played the one European power off the other effectively, British items were considered vastly superior. British colonial authorities, furthermore, were concerned with more than fugitive slaves. Fearing collusion between blacks and Indians in the southern borderlands, they wanted to keep free blacks and slaves out of the Indian backcountry altogether. Regulations governing the Indian trade barred English traders from keeping slaves or employing free blacks.[11]

Nonetheless, some Africans and African Americans did come to live in the Creek country in the years before the American Revolution. In some cases, Creeks refused outright to return the fugitives, ignoring both the potential rewards and possible British trade sanctions. For one thing, as Alan Gallay has written, "a runaway slave who 'discovered' a party of Indians was more likely to be treated as a free agent," than was a runaway captured by Indians outright. And if a runaway was fortunate to find his own way into a Creek "peace town," he or she was more likely to be given sanctuary.[12]

The living conditions that runaways found in the Creek country contrasted sharply with slavery as it evolved on the English colonial plantations that bordered the Creek lands, and there is scant evidence of Creeks owning slaves as chattel in the years before the American Revolution. African

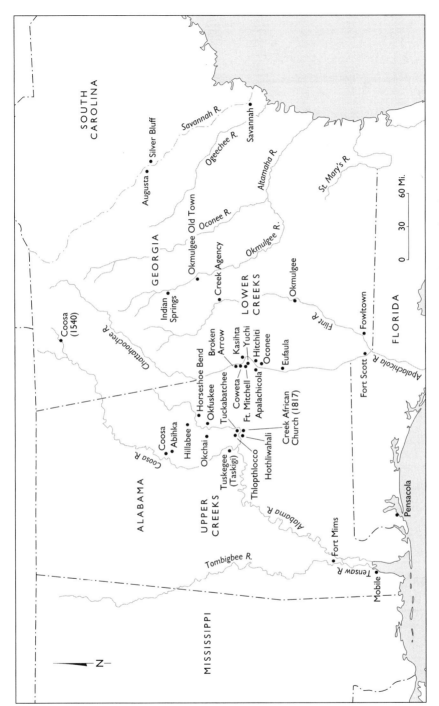

Creek country in the East, before removal (present-day state lines).

9

refugees were frequently adopted into clans and absorbed into the Creek community. Those held as slaves were slaves in the Creek Indian sense, which could be compared to the kinship slavery found in traditional West African societies. This type of servitude offered considerable latitude in living and work arrangements. Slaves were not bound to a plantation work schedule but worked the Creek communal agricultural lands without supervision, built houses, or became domestic servants. Most important, whites, blacks, and Indians alike were held as slaves and could become members of a clan through adoption. Furthermore, slave status was not inherited. No matter what the status of the parent, when a Creek slave married a Creek woman, the children born to that union were considered citizens of the tribe. As Kathryn Holland Braund has written, "Clan affiliation was more important than skin color. Creeks of any race were identified by their mother's clan, not their skin color." Though the overwhelming number of black people in the Creek Nation at this time were male runaway slaves who married Creek women, and their children could claim clan legitimacy and inheritance through their mothers, the black women who came into the Creek country probably were adopted directly into clans more frequently to ensure that the children belonged to a matrilineage.[13]

Other deeply embedded Creek cultural practices regarding social and political coercion affected the reception that the runaways received and the contours of servitude that developed among the Creeks during this early period, calling into question whether the patterns of obligation and duty implied in the European master-slave relationship can even be compared to Creek society. As Claudio Saunt has written, Creeks manifested a deep fear of the slave regimens observed on English plantations and were afraid that their own towns would be contaminated through contact with the oppression they observed there. On the plantations they saw African and Indian people bound in iron chains, signifying the ultimate power to coerce, an utterly alien concept to Creek traditions of dispersed authority. And while involvement in the deerskin trade and diplomacy with Europeans had altered traditional attitudes toward accumulation and redistribution of material goods, most Creeks saw little need to use coerced labor as means to accumulate wealth, and thus the work of the African "servants" was probably channeled into traditional subsistence patterns, or used in some form to facilitate the deerskin trade.[14]

The African and African American peoples who came into the Creek country, whether as runaways, free blacks, or slaves, brought skills that made them valued members of the Creek community. Familiarity with the deerskin trade and skills such as blacksmithing, carpentry, and gun and trap repair lessened dependence on Euro-American trade goods. As Euro-American cultural and territorial pressures increased, perhaps the most important skills the African Americans brought were cultural. Their ability to speak and understand English as well as comprehend the nuances of Euro-American cultural attitudes was a great aid to the Creeks. As the contact with white settlers increased, so did the role that African Creeks played as cultural brokers in the Indian, white, and black cultural equation that emerged in the southern borderlands.[15]

Besides acting as cultural brokers between Euro-American and Indian cultures, cultural affinities between African cultures and those of the southeastern Indians may have played a role in the reception that African peoples received in the Creek country. By the 1720s most of the slaves coming into South Carolina (and after 1751 into Georgia) were coming directly from Africa, and those coming from the forest regions of West and central Africa shared many cultural traits with southeastern Indians. Some of the African cultures were matrilineal, kinship and clan–based societies that practiced a riverine-swidden type of agriculture and had town-based political structures similar to the Creeks. Both cultures embraced a holistic religion and worldview that did not separate the secular from the sacred, including a reverence for natural elements, animal spirits, and deceased ancestors. Furthermore, cultural practices like reciprocity and the redistribution of material goods were common in West African cultures and folktale archetypes, and storytelling as a means of transmitting traditions was common in both societies. A great deal of hybridity appears in the tales collected from both African Americans and Creek Indians in later years that suggests cross-cultural transfer. Creeks likely adopted African dance and musical forms from the Africans that came among them. Dances and songs that featured stylized depictions of warrior deeds and heroes of the past as well as everyday life in comedic and dramatic forms served a ritual and an entertainment function in both cultures. All these elements, then, would have made Africans seem more familiar to the Creeks and would have smoothed the transition from being considered strangers to being absorbed into the Creek community.[16]

In the years between 1750 and the beginning of the American Revolution, developments in the southern borderlands had an effect on the number of African American slaves and free blacks coming into the Creek country. South Carolina was by this time thoroughly entrenched as a slave society with a black majority. Georgia abandoned its earlier restrictions on slavery in 1751, and the slave population there skyrocketed. More Euro-American colonists and African Americans were close to the Creek lands than ever before. After Florida was transferred to British control under the terms of the Treaty of Paris in 1763, and Spanish protection for runaways was cut off, the Indian lands west of the Proclamation line became a more alluring destination for fugitive slaves.[17]

The largest group of Africans in the Creek country before the American Revolution were slaves held by the English and Scottish traders. In the years immediately before the American Revolution, white traders married to Creek women began to establish commercial plantations on the Indian lands to replace the shrinking profits in the deerskin trade. In violation of colonial regulations, the traders brought increasing numbers of slaves into the backcountry to work their plantations or assist them in the Indian trade. They used their wives' claims to a share in the Creek commonwealth to stake out what amounted to privately arranged land cessions. Some Creeks objected to this use of tribal lands, seeing their fear of contamination by the English patterns of coercion becoming manifest. Another objection was traders' slaves selling vegetables and produce from their gardens. Such competition interfered with an important source of income for Creek women, who supplied produce for the frontier exchange economy from their own gardens. Also, some Creeks objected to the damage done to their fields and gardens by the traders' free-ranging livestock, although some Creeks had begun keeping livestock themselves in limited numbers as insurance against the declining deer population. In 1772, the Upper Creeks in council resolved to keep the traders from establishing any more plantations. But despite the restriction, the trend continued and would take on a new life in the years after the Revolution.[18]

But the Creeks' objection was to the traders' uses of slave labor rather than to the slaves themselves. The traders' African slaves were in frequent contact with the Creeks, and thus many of the slaves learned the language and were well aware of conditions in the Creek country that offered possibilities for fugitive slaves seeking to flee the increasingly coercive slave regimes developing in South Carolina and Georgia. The information was readily transferred through slave communication networks, and many would take advantage of the possibilities of being absorbed into the Creek community over the coming years.[19]

One of the principal traders doing business with the Creeks was George Galphin. Galphin employed a black slave, known as Ketch in the Indian trade, as one of his most trusted servants. Ketch's relationship with Galphin had more facets than simply master and slave. For one thing, his sister Mina was one of Galphin's many "wives." He also worked in the deerskin trade for Galphin, using his bilingual skills to arrange trades with the Creeks. A towering figure, Ketch was a familiar face in the Lower Creek settlements. His intimacy with the many sides of the cultural equation in the Southern borderlands made him a valuable broker. In fact, the Lower Creek town chiefs asked specifically for Ketch to carry important communications between them and Galphin or colonial authorities. Besides interpreting important talks between the Creeks and the British and carrying out trading assignments for Galphin, Ketch herded cattle and practiced carpentry. He helped build the first cabin at Galphin's trading post on the Ogeechee River and aided Galphin in setting up cattle drives into West Florida after Spain ceded Florida to the British in 1763. After George Galphin died in 1782, Ketch fled into the Creek country, taking his many skills with him. He lived for many years there as an "Indian Negro" in the years after the American Revolution, before emerging from Creek society during the Creek removal to live out his life on the Alabama plantation of the cross-cultural Indian trader Thomas S. Woodward.[20]

Ketch might have brought more than trade goods into the Creek country from the Galphins' trading post. With Galphin's help, African American slaves and free blacks established the first African Baptist church in the Americas at Galphin's settlement in Silver Bluff, on the Georgia–South Carolina border, in the years immediately before the American Revolution. David George, one of the founders of the Silver Bluff Church, was also one of Galphin's slaves who worked in the Indian trade. George had fled a cruel master in Virginia in the early 1760s, ducked into the Creek country, and was captured by a Creek chief known as the Blue Salt King of Cusseta. George worked for Blue Salt King for about five months: "I made fences, dug the ground, planted corn, and worked hard, but the people were kind to me." The chief then received word from George's Virginia master that there was a reward for George's return. After George caught wind that Blue

Salt King had accepted some "rum, linen, and a gun" for his return, he fled farther into the interior and lived among the Natchez for several years. While living there under the Natchez chief Jack, George was hired by one of Galphin's subordinates to work in the deerskin trade. After about five years of working in the interior and making many five hundred-mile journeys to Galphin's Silver Bluff settlement, George asked Galphin to allow him to work at Silver Bluff. Galphin agreed, and it was there that George was converted and organized the Silver Bluff Baptist Church, housed in Galphin's mill house, with several other of Galphin's slaves, among them George Liele, Jesse Peter (Galphin), and Henry Francis (who was said to be part Indian and African). While there is no record that the Silver Bluff Church organized missionary activities into the Creek country, the Silver Bluff settlement was a major entrepôt for trade into the interior, and the Galphins' slaves were intimately involved in both the Indian trade and in organizing the Silver Bluff Church. The American Revolution disrupted Galphin's Indian trade and the activities of the Silver Bluff Church, scattering the church's adherents. Other African American slaves were funneled into the interior by the British as "gifts" to the Creeks for cooperating with the British war effort, and some of the "king's gifts" were probably converted Baptists that came forward when missionary efforts began in the Creek country in the early nineteenth century.[21]

The years of the American Revolution marked a turning point in African and Creek relations and in the slave system that was developing. The number of African Americans living in the Creek country increased dramatically with the wartime disruptions. Slaves fled Loyalist and Patriot plantations alike in South Carolina, Georgia, and the Floridas for safety with the Indians. The Creeks also raided white plantations and rounded up black slaves as captives.[22]

In previous times, the Creeks would have perhaps adopted, ransomed, or sold most of the blacks coming into their country, but several developments during and immediately following the war ordained that most runaways coming into the Creek country would remain slaves. The war's disruptions brought the final death blow to the deerskin trade, which had been faltering for many years, and the Creeks looked to other sources of income to acquire trade goods. Some began stock raising or commercial agriculture operations, enterprises in which slave labor could be employed profitably. As Creeks became involved in commercial agriculture, for the first time,

AFRICAN CREEKS

several leading Creeks became slaveowners. The war and the demise of the deer-skin trade also affected the white traders and the flow of black slaves into the Creek country. Some Loyalist traders left the trade and the country altogether as exiles to England or Scotland. Others turned to a more intensive commitment to commercial agriculture, but because they had scant knowledge of agriculture, the Indian traders "depended heavily on the agricultural expertise of their black slaves."[23] These Loyalists severed all ties with their white communities in the new United States and exiled themselves into the Creek country, along with their families, slaves, and stock. They established plantations and trading outposts. The influx of these "Indian countrymen" with their slaves accounted for the largest number of black slaves coming into the Creek country. Also during this period, several offspring of the white trader–Indian marriages came of age and began to play important roles in tribal politics and government. Alexander McGillivray and William McIntosh were the most famous and influential of these mixed-ancestry leaders. They, along with other cross-cultural families, were primarily responsible for the growth of plantation agriculture and the slave system in the Creek country as well as a reorientation of tribal politics.[24]

Slavery under some of these Creek families closely resembled Euro-American chattel slavery. As adoption of slaves and runaways into Creek clans became less common, some of the cross-cultural families began securing titles to slave property and made slave status hereditary. They also built separate slave quarters and supervised their slaves' work regimen. But evolving concurrently was a hybrid system in which the slaves were raised on a basis of near equality within Creek kinship groups, which included African, Indian, and Euro-American elements. Within this system, Africans and Creeks shared work duties, dinner tables, hearths, and kinship. Creek family names such as Grierson (Grayson), McGillivray, McIntosh, Perryman, Durant, Barnard, and Cornel, and later variations in spelling, would become common surnames for African Creek families that signified kinship ties as well as a master-servant relationship. Kathryn Holland Braund has described one variety of slavery that developed in the Creek country during the late eighteenth and early nineteenth centuries as a patron-client relationship, a variety of kinship slavery. Slaves provided for their own upkeep and rendered their patrons a share at harvest or butchering time. Creek patrons provided a kinship link for their client slaves that was perhaps a halfway adaptation, allowing that African Creeks were part of the community but still dependent on their patrons. Although Creek women and their matrilineages were considered superb subsistence farmers, they benefited from the African Creek knowledge of more intensive agricultural techniques brought from West Africa or learned on white plantations. Creek slaveholders could then more easily make the transformation to commercial agriculture. Whether the agricultural enterprises included raising livestock, cotton, or corn for the market, it meant closer contact with Euro-American culture. The African Creeks' skills as interpreters came to the fore in particular in this commercial realm. As J. Leitch Wright has said, "even thoroughly acculturated" Creeks depended on their black slaves to help them assess Euro-Americans' motives.

While some Creeks definitely began to consider slaves as property, under the patron-client system, servitude was mitigated by the possibility that the relationship could include kinship ties and recognition as a family member. Some Creek slaveholders did adopt the practice of buying, selling, or trading slave families as a unit. An unspoken rule appears to have developed that prohibited selling African Creek families with generational ties in the nation to anyone outside the nation without the slaves' consent. Under these conditions, African Creeks developed stable families that spanned many generations. Thus, while avenues leading to adoption and full citizenship for African Creeks narrowed considerably, Creek cultural attitudes mitigated the harshest effects of slavery.[25]

Another form of slavery developed during this period. The growth of a class of slave hunters and traders had its roots in the earlier Creek war-captive culture and involvement in the Indian slave trade. Creek slave hunters provided the early plantations in South Carolina and the Caribbean Islands with American Indian slaves in the early eighteenth century, before the arrival of large numbers of slaves from Africa. Diminishing profits in the deerskin trade and a slave-labor shortage in the Southern borderlands after the American Revolution combined to make slave catching and trading a profitable enterprise for Creek hunters. U.S. Indian intercourse laws were less strict than British colonial regulations for bringing black slaves into the Indian country. Consequently, a brisk trade developed, complicated by disputed titles to slaves who had come as runaways, war captives, or king's gifts into the Creek country. Some of these title disputes continued throughout the duration of slavery in the Creek Nation and were resolved only by the Civil War.[26]

In the years after the American Revolution, American settlers poured into the Southern borderlands, pressuring the Creeks and other Indian peoples for land. The plan of the new nation was to convince Creek men to give up hunting as their primary occupation and to convert them into yeomen farmers who would then voluntarily sell their excess lands to American settlers. In 1796, to put the plan into effect, President George Washington appointed Benjamin Hawkins U.S. Indian agent to the Creeks and superintendent for the tribes south of the Ohio River. Hawkins first established the Creek Agency at Coweta Tallahassee, a Creek town on the Chattahoochee River on the eastern edge of the Creek country, and he took up his work with missionary fervor. Hawkins established a model farm and a blacksmith's shop at the agency and attempted to instruct the Creeks in the civilizing benefits of "regular husbandry," the mechanical arts, and spinning and weaving. Hawkins wanted the Creeks to abandon their communal fields and tried to convince them to establish private land holdings. Hawkins's particular concern was that some Creeks failed to "properly manage their slave property." He reserved his highest praise for those Creeks, mostly from cross-cultural families, who employed slave labor in commercial agriculture operations. Hawkins later moved his headquarters farther east to a location on the Flint River, where he established a much larger plantation operation that included saw and grist mills, a tanyard, a hatter's shop, a boot and shoemaker, a tinsmith and cooper, and a cabinetmaker and wheelwright.[27]

As part of the civilization plan, Hawkins accepted the application of two Moravian missionaries, Burkhard Peterson and Johann Christian Karsten, to come into the Creek country in the latter part of 1807. Hawkins himself was not a religious man; Peterson generously described him as "a skeptic." He doubted the effectiveness of missionary activity in inducing the Creeks to adopt the yeoman farmer lifestyle, but both men were skilled artisans, and Hawkins allowed them to come into the Creek country as "mechanics," not as missionaries. While Creeks and African Creek slaves showed some interest in tinsmithing and metalworking, Peterson and Karsten's religious activities got off to a slow start. Almost a year passed before anyone came forward to hear about Christianity.[28]

Peterson and Karsten had little luck with Creek Indians. The missionaries pronounced that their encounters with development-minded Creeks like William McIntosh, Peter McQueen, Alexander Cornells, Timothy Barnard, and others were completely unsatisfactory from a spiritual viewpoint.

The Creeks appeared to be more interested in commerce than in spiritual matters, and when pressed about their understanding of religious questions, their typical response was, "Yes, I know." Cornells elaborated on the Creek attitude: "You white people have the Old Book from God. We Indians do not have it and are unable to read it. But I have heard much of it from our Old Chiefs, the same Word of God of which you spoke here. The Indians know it without a book; they dream much of God, therefore they know it." Among other, less-acculturated Creeks, the missionaries ran into the same indifference to Christian doctrine, which was compounded by there being no Creek concept for the doctrine of original sin, which the missionaries found central to conveying an understanding of Christianity. An earlier encounter between the English traveler and chronicler John Pope and town chief Little Prince of Broken Arrow illustrates the Creek distance from even the idea of a being known as the devil. When Pope asked Little Prince about the existence of the devil, Little King replied contemptuously to Pope: "There is no devil. God Almighty is too much a gentleman to keep bad servants about him."[29]

The missionary activities did attract the attention of one of Hawkins's slaves, a man named Phil, who was literate and had undergone a prophetic religious awakening. Phil had earlier caused quite an uproar in the Creek community with fiery apocalyptic preaching, which upset one of the Creek slaveowners because he said it made his slaves "sullen and crazy." Nonetheless, Hawkins agreed that the missionaries could proselytize in their spare time as long as it did not incite the Creeks or interfere with carrying out the civilization program.[30]

Phil took up his preaching activities once again, although forbidden to do so by Hawkins, pitching in with a fervor that alarmed the gentle Moravians. He told the missionaries that he had heard God speak to him, telling him to go to the desert and pray. He found a secluded spot in the woods where he prayed and fasted and brought some African Creeks with him. Peterson reproved him for "misleading the Negroes" with false sermons and prayers, but Phil angrily replied that he had perfect wisdom and understood the word of God better than the missionaries did. After this confrontation, Phil advised African Creeks to turn away from the missionaries' meetings and began to hold services at his cabin. He pronounced his master, Agent Hawkins, "irredeemable" and began a campaign against the white blacksmith at the agency, whom he declared judgment against as a murderer. Up to this point, the missionaries had kept Phil's preaching activities in confidence, but Phil's public declarations and activities could not be concealed, and Mrs. Hawkins had Phil tied to a tree and given fifty lashes for insolence, disobedience, and "meddling in affairs of white people" at the agency. After Phil's punishment, he was forbidden to attend religious services, and African Creeks once again returned to the Moravians' meetings, saying they had no part in the black prophet's behavior.[31]

Peterson and Karsten's missionary efforts ended with the outbreak of the Red Stick War in 1813. Their lack of success with Creek Indians was offset in part by the inroads they had made among African Creeks. The African Creeks' ability to understand English as well as the cultural context of the Christian message aided the missionaries' efforts, and some African Creeks had probably been converted earlier, through contact with the African Baptist church at Silver Bluff, before coming into the Creek country. Accepting the Christian message, however, posed a dilemma for African Creeks. On the one hand was the often heard objection of slaveowners everywhere, that the Christian message, no matter how it was fashioned, was essentially a liberating theology that led slaves to disobedience. This was the objection most often voiced by the Creeks who more readily adopted the chattel slavery system.[32] On the other hand, many Creeks objected to Christianity because of its corrosive effect on Creek traditions, the ideas and practices that were responsible for the social fluidity and the lack of racial antipathy that African peoples experienced in the Creek Nation. Despite this dilemma, the African Creeks continued to provide fertile ground for Christian missionary activity, opening an avenue that eroded Creek traditions while providing a place to form an African Creek community identity.[33]

Besides driving the Moravian missionaries from the nation, the Red Stick War showed the increasingly important part African Creeks played in Creek affairs. The war's causes were a complex mixture of cultural, economic, social, and diplomatic issues, and the African Creek place in the Creek socioeconomic world figured in all these issues. Plantation operations, so fondly encouraged by Hawkins and worked with slave labor, represented the epitome of white cultural intrusion and were special targets for the Red Stick insurgents. The Red Sticks urged Creeks to abandon Hawkins's civilization program and return to the old ways, prevent further erosion of traditional cultural practices, and wrest control of tribal affairs from the emerging class of propertied Creek elites, who were increasingly adopting Hawkins's civilization program. The Red Sticks counted the plantation slaves as potential allies, however, and many of the slaves joined the insurgents. African Creeks played a major role in the Red Sticks' attack on Ft. Mims at the war's outset. "Indian Negroes" who had run away from the fort provided inside information on the layout and the number of defenders there. They also prodded their Indian allies to renew their attacks after enthusiasm seemed to be flagging. African Creeks were later among the most tenacious defenders at the Battle of Holy Ground. After a combined force of white frontiersmen and Choctaw warriors overran the fortified settlement, African Creek warriors aided in covering the retreat. One of the leading Upper Creek Red Stick chiefs, Tustenuggee Emarthla, or Jim-Boy, was said to be part African. Most African Creeks found that their best interests lay with the Red Sticks. African Creek slaves, however, provided essential information on troop movements to both sides in the conflict. They helped defend Ft. Mims, and it was said that the fort was overrun by the insurgents in the first place because those in charge of the fort ignored intelligence related by slaves, who had warned them of an imminent attack. Black slaves were also used as guides and interpreters for the white troops dispatched to the Creek country after the attack on Ft. Mims.[34]

With the signing of the Ft. Jackson Treaty in August 1814, which officially ended the hostilities, the Creeks were forced to cede 14 million acres of their former domain. The Upper Creek towns had been devastated, and more than three thousand Creeks had been killed. The remaining Red Sticks, along with a sizable number of African Creeks and runaway slaves from neighboring white frontier settlements, fled to Florida. There the African Creeks and other runaway slaves found a precarious refuge in maroon communities or Seminole settlements. White troops, aided by friendly Creeks, pursued them relentlessly. They assaulted and destroyed the maroon stronghold known as the Negro Fort, on the Apalachicola River in Florida in 1816, and plunged into Florida once again in 1817–1818, setting off the First Seminole War on the pretext that the Red Sticks who relocated to Florida were harboring runaway slaves. Both Creek and white slave traders and hunters made regular forays into Florida in pursuit of slaves, making claims on the black inhabitants of the maroon and Seminole settlements.[35]

As the Second Great Awakening began to take shape in the years following the Creek War, missionary activity ignited religious revivals throughout the frontier areas. In November 1817, the Baptist Board of Foreign Missions sent two missionaries attached to their Mississippi association, Rev. Thomas Mercer and Benjamin Davis, to the Creek country. Arriving at Tuckabat-chee, the missionaries consulted with Big Warrior (Tustenuggee Thlocco), the head chief of the Upper Creeks, and gained his approval to preach and establish a school. They baptized William, one of Big Warrior's slaves, and ordained him as a preacher. They then moved on to Alexander Cornells's settlement fifteen miles east, where they preached to a mixed congregation of Creeks, whites, and African Creeks. The next day, November 12, 1817, they baptized seven African Creeks, four men and three women, and the seven came together to establish the first Christian church in the Creek country, the Creek African Church, with a man named Charles as the pastor and another African Creek named Tyler as deacon. The missionaries said that Charles had a "happy faculty for communicating his ideas, both in Creek and English," and, further, that "these Negroes were raised among the Creeks and received their knowledge of Christianity from a religious slave who belonged to Col. Hawkins, the former agent." The religious slave was, no doubt, the black prophet Phil.[36]

The period between the end of the Red Stick War and removal to the Indian Territory was an unsettling time for the Creeks. Tens of thousands of white settlers poured into the Creek land cessions following the Creek and First Seminole wars. By 1820, eighty-five thousand Euro-Americans and forty-two thousand African Americans, most of them slaves, had settled or were squatting on Creek lands. This avalanche created pressure for yet more land cessions and for finally extinguishing altogether the Creek title to their lands east of the Mississippi.[37]

In the face of the mounting pressure from Euro-American settlers, the Creeks were weakened by internal dissensions and preoccupied with re-building and recovery from the devastation of the Red Stick War. As part of the effort to appear more acculturated, William McIntosh directed the first written Creek law code in 1818. The laws contained a milder, Creek version of the black codes that restricted slave and free African American life in the surrounding states.[38] Law 20 discouraged intermarriage between African and Indian partners through abrogating inheritance rights of their mixed Creek-African offspring, but the law did not prohibit such marriages out-right.[39] Under Law 21, slaves were forbidden to accumulate personal prop-erty or own livestock: "Slave(s) shall not raise property of any kind. . . . If the

Master does not take it from them, the lawmakers shall, and they may do as they please with the property." Significantly, "lawmakers" were new tertiary chiefs drawn from the various towns who owed their allegiance to the new national council and to William McIntosh rather than to their towns or clans. By creating this new body of enforcers, McIntosh extended the coercive power of the Creek National Council, and his own influence, considerably. A committee of four was also "appointed to receive runaway Negroes," pay out rewards to slave catchers, and collect restitution from slaveowners for the nation's trouble in apprehending fugitive slaves. This provision no doubt was inspired by McIntosh, who was heavily involved in the slave trade himself. Law 22 allowed manumission without restriction. This law was more in accord with Creek tradition but ran counter to the trend in neighboring states and territories, where Euro-American courts and legislatures were making manumission increasingly more difficult.[40]

The laws apparently were written mainly to assuage white fears. The Creeks' traditional liberality in dealing with their slaves upset the increasingly coercive slave regime being imposed throughout the South. Despite Law 20, unions between Creeks and Africans continued; indeed, it was said that African men made attractive partners because they were better providers, being less reluctant to take up farming. In parts of the Creek country, the traditional relaxed attitude toward slaves and slavery still held sway, and the laws had little effect on the daily lives of African Creeks, particularly in the Upper Creek settlements. African Creek slaves continued to accumulate farming and carpentry tools, spinning wheels, household goods, and other kinds of personal property. They also kept poultry flocks, cattle, and horses; stored quantities of corn and rice; and cultivated peach orchards. Even McIntosh's slaves were among those busily gathering property, as later claims for property losses would show.[41]

Christian missionaries resumed their cultural intrusion in the Creek Nation during the early 1820s. The Methodists, led by William Capers and Isaac Smith, gained permission from the Lower Creek chiefs in 1821 to establish a school for teaching English, agriculture, and mechanics at Asbury Mission, on the Chattahoochee River. The Baptist board followed up on their mission work, abandoned at the outbreak of the First Seminole War, and established Withington Mission among the Upper Creeks near Tuckabatchee in 1822, headed by Reverend Lee Compere. Although African Creeks provided translators and interpreters for the schools, there is no indication that any of their children attended the classes. While the agreements of 1821–1822 were unclear, the Creeks apparently refused to allow Capers and Compere to preach, but the two nonetheless found people who wanted to hear them. As with the earlier missions, the first people to come forward for the preaching were African Creeks. Earlier, Creek chiefs had tolerated a measure of proselytizing, but during the 1820s, internal and external pressures, as well as cultural and political tensions, led to no tolerance for compromising Creek culture.[42]

Many African Creek faithful were whipped publicly for attending prayer meetings. Although Compere was shocked and angered by the brutality of the punishments, Creek informants had warned him that such punishments would be carried out if he allowed the African Creeks to hear the preaching. Wealthy Creek slaveholders echoed the often heard complaint of Euro-American slaveholders across the South, that preaching to slaves gave them fanciful notions of equality or liberation. The Upper Creek chiefs Opothleyahola and Tuskeneehau, however, said the whippings were motivated not by fear of slave disobedience, but by the effects that preaching would have on traditional Creek practices, which were rapidly eroding under the onslaught of white intrusion on the remaining Creek lands. Tuskeneehau told Compere's only Indian convert, John Davis, "if they allowed the black people the liberty then the Indians would go to hear the preaching, and the Kings of the Towns would lose their authority." The Creeks also resented the missionaries pressing them to leave their ancestral lands and move west of the Mississippi.[43]

John Crowell, the Creek agent, opposed missionary activities and felt they were causing unnecessary friction in the tribe. Although Crowell recognized the positive effects that mission schools had in acculturating the Creeks, he dismissed the religious component of the mission schools, saying, "preaching is fudge." He also told Capers that his primary objection to the preaching was the effect that preaching had on African Creek slaves, which he felt made them insubordinate.[44]

While more Creeks were coming to recognize the necessity of adopting a measure of the Euro-American civilization program, most Creeks, from both Lower and Upper towns, opposed any further land cessions and were adamantly against removal. In their 1824 council, the Creeks decreed that anyone who agreed to sell or exchange even one foot of Creek land would be sentenced to death. Despite the decree, McIntosh and his followers willingly signed the 1825 Treaty of Indian Springs. Under the terms of the treaty, they exchanged most of what remained of the Creek lands in the East for lands west of the Mississippi. American negotiators had promised McIntosh and his party protection from reprisal and rewarded them handsomely for their cooperation. But the guarantee proved as worthless as earlier agreements pledging to protect Creek lands from white intruders after a party of one hundred or more antitreaty Creeks descended on McIntosh's plantation in April 1825 and executed him and several of the other signers.[45]

Following the executions, the United States brokered an amnesty for the McIntosh faction and made arrangements for their emigration to the West. The treaty party, now led by William McIntosh's half brother, Roley, selected lands near the junction of the Grand, Verdigris, and Arkansas rivers in the Indian Territory. African Creeks Cow Tom and William McIntosh (one of Roley McIntosh's slaves) accompanied the scouting party and advised their owners on the suitability of the land surveyed. Creeks associated with the McIntosh party began their removal in 1828, and by 1833 this first emigration was over. The twenty-five hundred Creeks and African Creeks making the journey accounted for less than 10 percent of the Creek Nation, and an overwhelming number of those traveling west came from the Lower towns associated with the McIntosh faction. From this part of the nation, however, came some of the wealthiest planter families, who owned the largest number of slaves. The first immigrants included 498 slaves and 13 free African Creeks, more than one-third of the African Creeks in the nation. They contributed greatly to rebuilding the Creek Nation in the West, clearing the land on which the Creek plantations blossomed, building the cabins, tending the crops, and after a time, putting up the first churches.[46]

Events moved rapidly toward the total removal of the Creeks after the McIntosh party left for the West. In 1830 Andrew Jackson signed the Indian Removal Act, and then even the antitreaty Creeks led by Opothleyahola realized that the time had come to submit to the inevitable. In March 1832 Opothleyahola and the other Creek chiefs traveled to Washington and signed the Treaty with the Creeks, 1832. In the treaty, the Creeks ceded all their lands east of the Mississippi for a tract west of Arkansas and were given $210,000 in educational and agricultural annuities and other payments. The Creeks were given a choice of removing to the West or selecting individual allotments in their former domain. Free African Creeks, as citizens of the tribe, were also allotted reservations under the treaty and given the opportunity to remain in the East. The allotment process, however, proved to be an enormous fraud as American settlers freely plundered the Creek's land and their improvements. Accordingly, the Creeks had little choice but to emigrate.[47]

An 1832 census of the tribe in the East showed that there were 445 slaves among the 14,142 Upper Creeks, 457 slaves among the 8,552 Lower Creeks, and fifty-five free blacks in the nation. B. S. Parsons, the U.S. agent counting the Upper Creeks, observed that the free blacks "seem to be in every way identified with these people . . . the only difference is the color." The situation seemed similar for the African Creek slaves. For some, their emigration calls into question whether they were actually slaves at all; several parties composed entirely of African Creek slaves made the trip using their own resources.[48]

Between 1834 and 1837, the greatest number of Creeks, African and Indian, made the trek west and joined the McIntosh Lower Creeks, already settled in the Arkansas-Verdigris river valley. The Upper Creeks, led by Opothleyahola, settled farther south, primarily along the branches of the Canadian River, separated from the Lower Creeks by forty miles of prairie.[49]

Geography was not the only thing separating the Creeks. Tensions still remained between tribal factions, roughly fractured along the lines of the treaty and antitreaty parties. Opothleyahola was a major voice among the Upper Creeks and as before retained more of the traditional Creek culture. They still kept communal fields, and few of them bothered to learn English. One early visitor to the Upper Creek North Fork settlement on the Canadian said there was a large African Creek community there, and half of them claimed to be free blacks. The Upper Creeks held fewer slaves, and the slaves themselves judged their status more benign than that of the Lower Creek slaves.[50] There were substantial slaveowners among the Upper Creeks, however. Opothleyahola was one of the largest slaveholders among the Creeks and developed a large plantation of over two thousand acres on the north fork of the Canadian with slave labor. Some Lower Creeks, on the other hand, more readily adopted Euro-American culture. More of them spoke English, and they were well on their way to abandoning communal fields for separate land holdings during their first years in the new land. The cross-cultural families, the McIntoshes, the Perrymans, and the Marshalls, to name but a few, carved prosperous plantations out of the "howling wilderness" using slave labor.[51]

The Lower and Upper Creeks each selected their own principal chiefs after settling in the West. Roley McIntosh served as the Lower Creek principal chief until he retired in 1859. The principal chief's office rotated among several Upper Creek leaders over the years, but Opothleyahola retained a powerful influence. The division continued until 1840, when a general council was created to unite the two divisions. African Creeks helped build a council house at High Spring, later known as Council Hill, about midway between the Upper and Lower settlements. Roley McIntosh was named principal chief of the entire nation. While the creation of the council went a long way toward bringing the Creeks together, political control still remained centered in the various towns and in the hands of the town councils and town chiefs.[52]

Missionary activities began in the Creek country west of the Mississippi in the early 1830s, after the McIntosh Creeks settled at the fork of the Arkansas-Verdigris rivers. John Davis, who emigrated to the West in 1829, gained Roley McIntosh's consent to began preaching for the Baptists with the aid of a few African Creeks. The Creek agent disapproved, however, fearing that it might ignite a replay of events in the East and impede further removal efforts. The Presbyterians, hiving out from their nearby Union Mission in the Cherokee country, were the first to constitute a church among the Creeks in the Indian Territory. Once again, the African Creeks were the first to come forward, providing "black exhorters" to preach to mixed congregations. And once again, they were the first persecuted. Despite Roley McIntosh's consent, some Creek slaveowners opposed the missionary work among their slaves and whipped them for attending meetings. The Methodists were also busy with the new arrivals. Several of the converts from the Asbury Mission began proselytizing among the Creeks, among them a young Creek Indian named Sam Checote, who would later serve as principal chief. The church the Methodists established in 1831 primarily comprised African Creeks. They also established a day school and continued their activities, which were mainly successful among the African Creeks.[53]

In summer 1832, the Baptists sent a missionary to the Creek country to aid John Davis. David Lewis and his family arrived in the Creek Nation in August 1832; and shortly thereafter, Isaac McCoy, the noted Baptist missionary, Indian advocate, and surveyor and explorer, joined Davis and Lewis. With three African Creeks, Jake, Henry, and Murrell, the missionaries es-

AFRICAN CREEKS

tablished the Muscogee Baptist Church on September 9, 1832. The church was located five miles north of the Arkansas River and fourteen miles northwest of Ft. Gibson, on the outskirts of the Creek settlement. In a short time the congregation at the church grew to sixty-three members—forty-two African Creeks, twelve Creeks, and four whites—and those attending the Sunday services soared to more than three hundred, among them Jane Hawkins, one of Chief William McIntosh's daughters. Lewis and Davis had a schoolhouse built with an adjoining cabin for Lewis and his family. Lewis described the buildings as "cheap, economical, plain and as strong as any for a thousand miles around." After John Davis moved to the southern side of the Arkansas River in early 1833 to start another church, Lewis, left without an interpreter, hired an African Creek man for the job, at fifty dollars a year. Lewis said that the man was a very good interpreter, "very acceptable among the Indians and a very pious man and a good preacher." Lewis does not give the man's name and only mentions that he was John McIntosh's slave and a blacksmith by trade. He was most likely an African Creek known as Blacksmith Jack. The school Lewis established was a source of discouragement for the young minister because although he boasted thirty "scholars" at one period, the students attended irregularly and were as reluctant to learn English as Lewis was to gain a command of Creek.[54]

Lewis's mission fell apart in late 1834 under circumstances that caused a great deal of ill-will among the Creeks toward the missionaries. According to McCoy, Lewis apostatized, reportedly got an Indian woman pregnant, and left the Creek country without making arrangements for the child. But during his stay he had made inroads, principally among the African Creeks, and had established Sabbath schools for African Creek children. Charles Kellum succeeded Lewis in 1837. From his base in the adjoining Choctaw Nation, where the chiefs were more accepting of Christianity, Kellum described the Creeks as "very hostile to preaching." Indeed, they had expelled all missionaries from the nation that year. Accordingly, Kellum had to wait a year before beginning his work in 1838 in the Creek Arkansas settlements. Thousands of Upper Creeks arrived in the West that year, and cultural and political tensions between the two factions were high. Even though the Upper Creek settlements were reported to be more opposed to preaching than the Lower Creeks were, Kellum ministered for a year in the Upper Creek North Fork settlements and operated a school there for a time. Kellum described North Fork as a heathen stronghold and despaired of making any headway. In the summer, during the traditional Creek *poskita* (green corn) ceremonies, the parents emptied the schools so the children could attend the festivities. Although it shook Kellum's Christian sensibilities to the marrow to hear people "howling like wolves and beasts of the forest" and to imagine wild dancing throughout the night, the Creek's native worship (minus the dancing) probably had more in common with the fervor shown at evangelical camp meetings on the frontier than Kellum cared to admit.[55]

After returning to the Arkansas settlement, Kellum ran into opposition from Chief McIntosh, who now said that the preaching spoiled his slaves. McIntosh told Kellum that when he sent his slaves to work, they would sit under a tree and read "the book"; therefore, "no more preaching in the Nation." Kellum was offered the opportunity to preach among the Indians if he would sign an agreement that stipulated he would not preach to the slaves. But Kellum refused to sign any such agreement, and the official door to missionary activity was closed. Kellum still maintained a school at the building put up by Lewis, which he now named Ebeneezer Station. But continued hostility from some of the Creek leaders, the Creek agent, and white traders made his work difficult. In addition, Kellum had financial problems. No money was forthcoming from the Baptist Missionary Society, and the Creek agent withheld the education annuity promised in the 1832 treaty. The African Creek slaves sustained Kellum, providing him with food, money, and friendship. Blacksmith Jack told Kellum, "Bro Kellum when u'se in a strait, come stay (with us) and eat. All I have is the Lords." Despite the injunction against preaching, Kellum held midnight meetings and continued to find more adherents among the African Creeks. By early 1840, Kellum asked to be relieved. But, before leaving the Creek country, he ordained two "black brethren," Jake and Blacksmith Jack, to carry on the work.[56]

Two years later, when Kellum returned, he reported that a revival led by Jake and Jack had drawn one thousand Creek, African Creek, and white worshippers. At the meetings, Jake would preach in the morning in English, and Jack would sermonize in Creek in the afternoon. One hundred had been baptized the previous Sabbath, Jack reported, most of them promising young Indians. For the first time, Indians began to outnumber African Creeks at the services. Jane Hawkins, Chief William McIntosh's daughter, and one the largest slave-holders in the nation, opened her home for meetings. Even the Creek agent James Logan, who had previously objected to preaching, praised the results of the African Creek ministers' activities. He said that there was nary a jug of whiskey to be found in the nation. There were also frequent meetings in the Arkansas district, and Benjamin Marshall, the largest slaveholder in the nation, encouraged his slaves to attend. Marshall claimed that his slaves doubled in value when they became religious. Kellum reported that at North Fork, "that Hell upon earth," hundreds of converts flocked to the meetings nearly every night. During this transitional period, as more Creek Indians began attending the Christian meetings, it was said the Indians preferred African Creek preachers over the white missionaries, even though the Creek agent and the white missionaries tried to convince them otherwise. Indeed, the white missionaries were troubled with the way that some of the "black exhorters" were interpreting Christian doctrine to include traditional Creek beliefs. For example, the missionaries frowned on the Creek custom of holding camp meetings throughout the night, similar to the poskita ceremonies. In the Creek meetings, one could hear African American spirituals sung in Creek and New Testament scripture translated into Creek by African Creek preachers. One African Creek preacher was even criticized for leading new converts astray in the other direction by embracing Old Testament dietary laws and telling adherents that eating catfish was unclean.[57]

The fervor in the Upper Creek settlements farther south on the Canadian River came at a cost, however. According to the Choctaw missionary Sidney Dyer, there was but one person in the community who "feared God, an old colored brother named Jesse." Jesse had been a member of the African Creek Church in the old Creek Nation, and he had converted a Creek Indian named Joseph Island, Island's brother William, and the village fiddler, Harry Island, who was an African Creek. Harry Island, born in the Old Creek nation before the Red Stick War, would recount his conversion many times over the years as he became a respected preacher, interpreter, and leader in the African Creek community. He called all his acquaintances to his cabin and proclaimed his conversion, smashed his fiddle, and foreswore whiskey. Harry's conversion allegedly caused "much stirring of the spirit in the village." Whiskey shops closed down, and locals proclaimed that they had never seen a change so dramatic. Brother Jesse and the Islands continued their meetings, which drew a number of adherents, among them fourteen other members of the African Creek Church that had been established in old Creek country. Since the church now contained a number of Creek Indian members, it was decided to change the name to the Tuckabatchee Church.[58]

The stirring also attracted the attention of the traditionalist Creek chiefs who announced that anyone attending the meetings of the "praying people" would be whipped. The penalties were carried out, the first victim being Juba, an elderly free African Creek, who was beaten nearly to death by a group of Creek lawmakers. But Jesse, Harry Island, and another African Creek preacher named Billy (Hawkins) kept the revival going in the Canadian district despite the persecution. Jesse received fifty lashes from an almost apologetic group of lawmakers in February 1845. The African Creek preacher submitted without struggle, which, according to Jesse, puzzled his tormentors.[59]

Following Jesse's whipping, the persecutions abated and finally ceased altogether. In late 1845 Creek agent James Logan reported that he had received a petition signed by several leading Creeks asking that missionaries be allowed to return to the nation and open schools. He also mentioned that the "children of color" attended Sabbath schools with Indian children. Chilly McIntosh, Chief Roley McIntosh's nephew and the head warrior (or general) of the nation, had been converted at one of the meetings in 1844, where he was seen "weeping like a child." Chief McIntosh and other leading Lower Creeks all had joined some church by 1848. But Opothleyahola and many of the other Upper Creek leaders held to the old ways. In reference to the value of Creek religion versus the missionary's message, Opothleyahola reportedly said, "A man will much more surely get to heaven by worshiping the brass plates than in any other way." The brass plates were revered sacred objects, which, according to Creek belief, were given to the Tuckabatchee Creeks by the Master of Breath for safekeeping. The plates signified the link between the divine and the earth and were still used in the poskita ceremonies. Tuckabatchee Micco, an Upper Creek town chief, asked Gen. Ethan Allan Hitchcock (Hitchcock was sent to the Indian Territory to investigate frauds in Indian provisioning contracts in 1842) to please explain to him why the black people among them insisted on holding prayer meetings despite the persecutions. Hitchcock, of course, had no ready answer, but curiously their conversation was translated by an African Creek interpreter, who probably felt the time was not propitious to provide an answer either.

Hitchcock had just visited a prayer meeting in North Fork, and he described the mélange of people attending and the melding of cultures experienced at the meeting. Having stated his position, Opothleyahola withdrew his objections to missionary activities, and the Creek Council mandated full toleration for missionary activities in 1848 as long as they had approval of the council. Soon thereafter, the Methodists received permission, and a contract, to open a boarding school, which they named Asbury, in the Canadian district. The Presbyterians followed, opening the Tullahassee Manual Labor School and Mission in 1850. The school was located near the fork of the Arkansas and Verdigris rivers on the eastern edge of the nation. It was at Tullahassee where a whole generation of Creek leaders in the post-Civil War era received their training. The mission also played an important part in African Creek education in later years.[60]

The days of persecution were over for the "praying people." The Christian missionaries had won their forty-year cultural battle, with African Creeks in the vanguard. A white minister from Arkansas, visiting the Presbyterian mission at Coweta in 1848, marveled at the idea that "Europe should be speaking to America through Africa," where African Creek Robert Johnson translated his sermon for the Creek Indian congregation. Yet, up until that time, the congregation would have been principally African Creek rather than Creek Indian. From this point on, more Creeks began learning English in the mission schools, and there was less need for African Creek translators or interpreters.[61]

The African Creek experience in missionary activity was part of a larger role of cultural brokerage, a role that shaped, and would continue to shape, their place within the Creek communities. Its consequences could work both for and against these people who lived between two worlds. By facilitating the absorption of Euro-American culture, for instance, African Creeks indirectly cultivated attitudes antithetical to Creek racial tolerance and relatively benign slavery. These developments had enormous consequences, generally detrimental, for African Creek status and identity in the Indian nation. As Christian translators, interpreters, and preachers, African Creeks exercised power that was rarely accorded them in the traditional Creek square ground; but once they succeeded in transmitting the cultural message, native Creek translators and preachers replaced African Creeks. Although mixed congregations were still a normal occurrence until the Civil

War, and African Creek preachers continued to have an impact in the Creek Christian community, the African Creek power to influence events through this particular cultural avenue was diminished.

In other ways, however, their role as cultural brokers provided long term rewards. In the African Creek community, as in African American communities in the states, African Creeks organized their own churches, which became focal points for their communities. Slaves and free African Creeks alike were members, and the preachers from the churches became important leaders in the African Creek community. These congregations would provide continuity and stability during the difficult and disruptive times to come.[62]

A cultural dialectic had been evolving for some years, the development of a separate African Creek identity within the confines of Creek Indian culture. The tradition of cultural integration had absorbed Hitchiti, Tuckabatchee, Alabama, and Yuchi peoples into the Creek web. Those peoples had retained their languages and separate identities, and at times the "pure" Creeks held them at a cultural and political arm's length. Still, they were considered part of the tribe. That tradition persisted with the African Creeks, but it was complicated by the intrusion of Euro-American values and ideas regarding race, slavery, progress, and civilization.

Relations between African Creek slaves and the Creek Indians in the West were characterized by a fluidity that could not be equaled anywhere in the slaveholding South, particularly not in the neighboring states of Arkansas, Missouri, or Texas. For both slave and free African Creeks, the conditions found in the Creek Nation offered social, cultural, and economic opportunities not available to most African Americans living in the United States or even in the other Indian nations in the Indian Territory. But while living in relative geographic and cultural isolation from the coercive system that developed in the Southern states had its advantages, living on the racial frontier also had its hazards.

Except for those living on the plantations of a few of the wealthy Creek families, most African Creek slaves lived under conditions that bore little resemblance to those of slaves living in the Southern states. Although the Creek Council enacted a number of increasingly restrictive laws regulating African Creek slaves and free blacks in the years between their arrival in the West and 1860, the code that evolved was not nearly as restrictive as in adjoining slave states. As in the old Creek Nation in the East, the laws passed by the Creek Council in the West against slaves owning property and restricting movement and intermarriage were seldom enforced. In living arrangements, work schedules, family development, social integration, and mobility, African Creek slaves also enjoyed advantages over most slaves found on white plantations in neighboring states, or even in the adjoining Cherokee and Choctaw nations.[63]

Slave homes were portrayed as not much different from those of the average Creek Indian. Nellie Johnson, interviewed in the 1930s, described her family's cabin on Chief Roley McIntosh's holdings as "a big, nice clean log house . . . and everything around it look[ed] better than most renters these days." On the Mose Perryman plantation, located in the Choska bottoms along the northern bank of the Arkansas River, the cabins had clapboard roofs, puncheon floors, shuttle windows, and large stone fireplaces. Many African Creeks adopted traditional Creek architecture and built brush arbors on the sides of their cabins for use during warm weather. John Harrison, a former Perryman slave, recalled that his master cooked his own meals in the fireplace just like the slaves until he bought a cookstove just before the Civil War.[64]

Most Creek slaves were not confined to slave quarters in the sense of being under restriction or supervision. On some plantations, the slave's cabins were grouped close together, and as in other frontier settlements, the purpose was protection from hostile Indians or wild animal attacks, not necessarily for closer slave supervision. On Chief McIntosh's vast holdings along the Arkansas, a slave could locate a cabin anywhere near good water and rich soil.[65]

On plantations like Benjamin Marshall's, where hundreds of slaves worked to produce corn, cotton, wheat, and rice for export outside the Creek country, there was undoubtedly supervision of what was planted and a careful accounting made of the harvest. Most Creek slaves, however, had no overseer, nor even scant supervision from their masters. William Quesenbury, a white merchant from Arkansas, observed during a visit to the Creek country in the 1840s that among the Lower Creeks, "their negroes have to support themselves with clothing and food. To do this they are allowed the Saturday of every week, and after their master's crop is laid by in July, from that time until September, or harvest time" to tend to their own patches. Chief McIntosh, according to Nellie Johnson, left his slaves to manage planting and harvest and never bothered them except when he wanted some produce or livestock to sell. She said, "Old Chief just treat all the Negroes like they was just hired hands, and I was a big girl before I knowed very much about belonging to him." Other former Creek slaves recounted that the only slaves who had to work hard were those belonging to wealthy planters. Mary Grayson remembered that her father, Jacob Perryman, a slave on the Mose Perryman plantation, "worked the farm and tended to the horses, cattle and hogs." Her mother, Mollie Perryman, worked around Mose Perryman's house and cooked meals. Each African Creek slave family was responsible for part of the fields and worked the crops as if they belonged to them. Slaves were allowed to work their own patches in their spare time and keep whatever they earned from selling the produce. There were even instances recounted of masters borrowing money from their slaves. Thus, a modified patron-client form of slavery prevailed in some parts of the Creek country, particularly among the Upper Creeks, wherein the balance of the patron-client relationship was tipped heavily in favor of the client and calls into question whether the relationship can be classified as slavery at all.[66]

Creek slaves enjoyed considerable freedom of movement and latitude in arranging family life. Married slaves with different masters frequently lived together and raised their families with little concern from their masters over where they located as long as they rendered the master his due. William McIntosh and his wife Eldee (or Rhody) belonged to different masters, but they lived on the Mose Perryman plantation. Apparently, William traveled to work next door on the Daniel N. McIntosh plantation, where he worked training horses and tending other livestock.[67]

Under these circumstances, there was considerable communication among slaves on different plantations. They were allowed to visit one another freely and were frequently sent on errands beyond the confines of the nation. A trip to nearby Ft. Gibson or into the Cherokee or Choctaw nations was not unusual. Under these conditions, African Creek slaves formed wide-ranging communities and kinship ties, and they could communicate with each other freely and, if need be, quickly.[68]

Creek agriculture in the West, whether the subsistence farming done by most Creeks or production agriculture seen on the plantations of wealthy slaveowners, concentrated on corn and livestock. African Creek slaves raised corn as the staple crop and looked after extensive livestock herds. Indeed, cattle constituted a major source of wealth. On some plantations they also grew rice, and to a limited extent wheat, for export. Cotton was also raised, but primarily for home use. Although some of the larger plantation operations, such as Benjamin Marshall's, raised some for export, cotton was not a major crop until after the Civil War. They also raised vegetables, melons, and sweet potatoes and tended fruit trees, especially peach and cherry, which they had brought with them from the East. Scarcely a Creek home, African or Indian, was without some peach trees. The slaves supplemented their crops with wild nuts and berries that grew abundantly throughout the area. Most slaves tended their master's livestock and raised mainly hogs, chickens, turkeys, or geese for home use. There were notable exceptions, however. Jacob Perryman was allowed enough range land on the Perryman plantation to keep 10 "American horses" (as opposed to Indian ponies), 2 mules, 75 hogs, and 4 steers. Troy Steadham, who lived near the Creek Indian Agency, just west and south of the forks of the Arkansas and Verdigris, owned 150 head of stock cattle, 10 horses, 2 oxen, and 30 hogs, a considerable estate for anyone living in the Creek country at the time, slave or free. Toby Drew, who also lived near the Creek Agency, owned 10 horses, 100 hogs, 2 mules, and 9 steers. That slaves could accumulate such property is in keeping with the patron-client relationship, even though such accumulation of property was against the slave code, which was supposed to be still in force.[69]

Although the black codes also barred any African Creek, slave or free, from owning guns, the untamed character of the greatest part of the Creek country made such strictures impractical and unenforceable. Many African Creek slaves either depended on, or regularly supplemented their diets with, wild game that abounded in the area. The need to protect livestock from predators that roamed the countryside was an immediate concern that convinced some slaveowners to let their slaves keep guns. Whatever the reason, many African Creeks owned or at least had access to firearms and knew how to use them.[70]

African Creek slaves also played a key role in trade and merchandising. Many Creeks, particularly those who spoke little or no English, depended on their slaves to carry out their trading and commissary transactions with Euro-American traders. African Creeks not only bridged the language barrier for their owners but were also credited with the ability to understand Euro-American culture and thus arrange a more advantageous trade. Consequently, many white traders reversed the arrangement and began to employ African Creek interpreters at their stores.[71]

As in trade, so with the cultural and social life of the nation: Fostering and establishing Christianity in the nation allowed African Creeks a great deal of freedom of movement. Black devotees and preachers traveled some distance to attend church services, camp meetings, and revivals. African Creek slaves also participated in various more worldly pursuits. They joined in the traditional Creek intertown ball games as valued players and attended horse races, which were a popular pastime. Jacob Perryman no doubt entered his "American horses" in the races. Dances, called *bangas*, were also popular. Indians and blacks of both sexes intermingled freely on such occasions, dancing to fiddle music provided by African Creeks while imbibing illicit whiskey.[72]

Like the slaves, the free African Creeks lived under far fewer restrictions than free blacks in the surrounding slave states or other Indian nations. While the Creek codes imposed taxes on all free blacks living in the nation, forbade them to marry Creek Indians, and in some cases (but not all) denied them adopted citizenship, like the slave codes, the laws posed no great barrier to living an unrestrained life in the Creek Nation and were seldom enforced.[73]

From the first years in the new land, manumissions were common and were not restricted until the eve of the Civil War. Most of the free blacks were small farmers, ranchers, or laborers, but many took advantage of the unfettered atmosphere and established stores, trading posts, hotels, and wagon-train stations. Monday Durant, one of the most important and influential leaders in the African Creek community, owned a small store near the mouth of the Little River in the western reaches of the Creek country. Durant was described as "a large, strong man of fine physical proportions," who readily spoke Creek. Like his contemporary Harry Island, Durant was born in the old Creek Nation before the Red Stick War. He had begun preaching at a young age and organized a Baptist church in the Little River community in 1854. Durant would go on to be a leading figure in establishing Baptist congregations in the Creek country. He combined his church building, preaching, and mercantile activities with stock raising and ran several large herds of cattle, horses, and hogs on his ranch along the Canadian River.[74]

Sarah Davis was one of the leading free African Creek merchants who lived in the Creek Agency settlement. Davis was born among the Creeks in Alabama in 1799 and was formerly a slave of William McIntosh's daughter Rebecca; Davis accompanied the emigration party led by Ben Hawkins and John Sells to the Indian Territory in 1830. After Rebecca Hawkins emigrated to Texas, Davis was sold to D. N. McIntosh and worked as a house slave and servant for him. By 1853, she had earned enough money to buy her freedom as well as freedom for her two daughters, Elizabeth and Julia. She owned and operated a hotel and boarding house in the Creek Agency village, which also offered entertainment. Her seven-room establishment was frequented by travelers, traders, and Indian Agency employees and earned a reputation as a friendly, clean, and convivial place. The popularity of the place probably had as much to do with Sarah Davis's outgoing personality and the charms of her two daughters as with its being the only place within hundreds of miles where one could find a clean bed and hot meals, dancing, and music all under the same roof. Davis also claimed and improved a considerable number of acres north of the agency village toward the Arkansas River and established a thriving farm and ranch there with the help of her grandson, Joseph P. Davison.[75]

Other African Creek merchants included William Nero, who operated a store, livery stable, and wagon-train station in the North Fork settlement; Jake Brown, who ran a store in the Post Oak community, twelve miles from the Creek Agency; and Scipio Barnett, who owned a store near the Creek council ground at High Spring. Tobe McIntosh, a free African Creek with kinship ties to the McIntosh family, established a wagon-train business in the Creek Agency village that brought trade goods and people in from as far away as Ft. Smith, Arkansas, and Texas. Harry Island, the reformed fiddle player and whiskey drinker, parlayed his bilingual abilities into a job as an interpreter at one of the stores in North Fork. Since the Creek country had a shortage of skilled artisans of all kinds, free African Creeks with skills also found jobs as teamsters, blacksmiths, stonemasons, and carpenters.[76]

Other free blacks held some of the largest stock herds in the Creek Nation. Cow Tom was considered by many to be the African Creek chief in the Canadian District. As a former slave in the old Creek Nation, Tom had come West with his master in 1826, two years before the first immigration, to inspect the land to see if it was worth settling. After serving as a guide and interpreter for the U.S. Army during the Second Seminole War, Tom used the money he earned in the service to buy himself out. After his emancipation, Tom settled on the Canadian River on the southern boundary of the nation, about twelve miles west of North Fork Town. There he carved out an extensive ranch where he grazed four to five hundred head of cattle and claimed assets of nearly ten thousand dollars, making him one of the wealthiest African Creeks.[77]

Among the free African Creek women who were heads of households, the most common occupation listed was either farmer or stock raiser; in fact, they outnumbered the free African Creek men in these categories. This may be related to the traditional Creek matrilineal control of farming, although the tradition had transformed since removal as more Creek men became involved in farming. In any case, Caroline, Affey, Grace, Hope, Lydia, and Fanny Cornels were among the stock raisers. The next most common occupation for women was cook, and while this may imply some type of domestic service, no free African Creek women were listed as servants. Taken together 61.5 percent of free African Creeks made independent livings as either farmers, stock raisers, tradespeople, or merchants. And if the laborers listed in the farm households were family members and are added to the list, then the number would be above 70 percent—a stark contrast with free black populations in most states where the majority were either domestic servants or laborers.[78]

While both slave and free African Creeks were able to integrate themselves successfully into social and economic life in many ways, a darker side to life on the racial frontier was evolving. Slave life everywhere carried its measure of uncertainty and cruelty. For one thing, the Creek tradition of keeping families together and not selling them out of the nation changed in the West. Lucinda Davis, who described her experience of growing up a slave among the Upper Creeks in largely positive terms, was separated from her family at a young age and sold by her Lower Creek owners to her Upper Creek master, Tuskaya-hiniha. According to Lizzie Jackson, who also had an easygoing Upper Creek master, "Even if master was good, the slaves was bad off." Jackson later recalled slaves being sold even if they had families and were the best workers. Benjamin Marshall and some of the other aristocratic planters found the prices being paid for experienced field hands in the western cotton lands too much to resist and regularly sent slaves to be sold in the Paris, Texas, slave market.[79]

As Daniel F. Littlefield, Jr., has shown in his pioneering work on the African Creeks, the activities of Creek, Cherokee, and white slave hunters made life a living hell for some African Creek families in the West. The laxity in enforcing the slave and black codes favored the development of an independent and resourceful African Creek community. That same lax enforcement, however, also meant that slaves and free blacks could expect little protection from the illegal activities of the slave hunters. While most Creeks and their slaves understood and accepted the informal patterns of obligation and ownership, slave hunters readily took advantage of the situation to seize slaves who were living apart from their masters. Because many Creek slaveowners never bothered to secure titles to their slaves, slave hunters could manufacture titles or employ the fugitive slave laws to seize African Creeks. During the 1840s and 1850s, the slave-hunters, sometimes aided by unscrupulous Indian agents, roamed the Creek Nation nearly at will, seizing slaves and free blacks, mostly women and children.[80]

In the 1840s several hundred African Seminoles were located in the Creek country. They claimed freedom under Gen. Thomas S. Jesup's "freedom proclamation" issued during the Second Seminole War and resisted all attempts to return them to slavery. Creek slave traders made claims on a number of the African Seminoles, arising from their role in capturing "hostile" African Seminoles and their families during the Seminole wars. The controversy continued throughout the decade until a large group of African Seminoles, joined by several African Creek families, fled to Mexico in fall 1849. Most of the African Seminoles who remained behind were returned to slavery. At least thirty, however, remained in the Creek country and continued to live as free blacks until the Civil War.[81]

As the controversy over slavery and its extension into the territories rose to a fevered pitch in the 1850s, the seemingly anomalous condition of the African Creek slaves and free blacks drew the attention of concerned Creek slaveholders and proslavery advocates from neighboring states. These "concerned parties" agitated to have the blacks in the Indian Territory under stricter control. Proslavery politicians from the Southern states were anxious to prepare the Indian lands for true territorial status and eventually have them organized as slave states. Border newspapers in Arkansas were filled with alarming reports of the Indian lands harboring fugitive slaves and abolitionist missionaries. Following the trend toward harsher black codes being passed in the states, the pro-Southern planter aristocrats in the Creek Council passed laws that were more restrictive than their own in 1855. In 1856 they announced that no abolitionists would be hired as teachers in the Creek schools. Restrictions were also tightened on free African Creeks. Citizenship was denied to anyone born to a Creek mother who "had more than half African blood." This eliminated a whole class of African Creeks from citizenship, some whose families had lived in the nation for three generations as free blacks and had participated in the tribal annuity payments of 1857. In 1859 the treasurer for the Creek Nation, N. B. Moore, collected the taxes levied on free blacks in the nation, some of which had not been collected for many years. The tax, originally 25 cents a head, had risen to three dollars per head plus additional taxes on livestock, wagons, and tools.[82]

The fluid race relations among Creek and African Creeks were clearly becoming more restrictive. Integrative and inclusionary traditions that allowed an independent, self-supporting lifestyle were eroding with the arrival of Euro-American cultural values, the economic imperatives of commercial agriculture, and the looming sectional crisis in the United States over slavery. While the split in the Creek Nation between the treaty and antitreaty parties appeared to be healing during the years in the West, the division between the North and the South would draw the Creeks into fratricidal conflict. Old wounds reopened and divided the Creeks once again, and African Creeks found themselves at the center of the battle. In the course of the struggle, the African Creeks would redraw the boundaries of freedom in a way that would influence the outcome of political, social, and economic events for the African Creek community for the next fifty years.

2

"Like a Terrible Fire on the Prairie"
African Creeks and the Civil War

WHEN THE CIVIL WAR CAME, the freedom of action and independence African Creeks had fashioned on the racial frontier in the Creek country served them well. Nearly all able-bodied African Creeks served in either the First Indian Home Guard or the First and Second Kansas Colored regiments during the war. Indeed, African Creeks were the first black soldiers to fight for freedom, joining Opothleyahola's exodus to Kansas and fighting courageously at the battles of Round Mountain, Chusto Talasah, and Chustenahlah in the Indian Territory in November and December 1861. Once in Kansas, they were the first black soldiers mustered into the federal army, and they enlisted enthusiastically as soldiers in the First Indian Home Guard. Then, while on the Indian Expedition in summer 1862, they also became the first black soldiers in the federal army to participate in combat. They fought on the battlefields of the Indian Territory, Arkansas, and Missouri; left the fields, farms, and blacksmith shops of their masters as well as their own farms, ranches, and stores, and struck out to claim their freedom. Out of their years of displacement, suffering, and warfare, African Creeks redrew the cultural contours to suit the new parameters of freedom.

The sectional split between the North and the South over slavery translated into a civil conflict in the Creek Nation that had its own unique cultural and political origins. Although the Civil War in the Creek Nation had more to do with antagonisms between the treaty and antitreaty factions that arose during the removal era than with slavery, African Creeks found themselves at the center of the conflict, just as they had during the Red Stick War. But still, slavery, and the control of slave property, precipitated the first clashes in the Creek country, and Confederate sympathizers used the opportunity to exert more control over Creek affairs, which stretched tensions within the Creek community to the breaking point. The Civil War in the Indian Territory was a brutal affair that caught both civilians and soldiers in a maelstrom of destruction that destroyed, proportionally, more lives and property and created more refugees than in any Confederate or Union state. But out of these four terrible years, a bond was formed among the Creeks who "shared the road to Kansas"—whatever their skin color or town affiliation—that would be influential in shaping the postwar Creek community.[1]

As the 1860s dawned, some Creeks, particularly the wealthy planters who were busily developing a society and economy patterned after the white Southern plantation culture, were alarmed at what they saw as an increasing African influence in the tribe. Their reason for concern is revealed in the 1860 census, which reported 1,651 black slaves and 277 free blacks living among the Creeks. Altogether, African Creeks made up 14.3 percent of the tribe. What is more, the African Creek population had increased a healthy 23.7 percent since coming West. The Creek Indian population, on the other hand, had not adjusted so readily to the shocks of removal. Their population had declined dramatically—43 percent since removal. The free black population in the Creek country alone was greater than in neighboring Arkansas and nearly outnumbered those in Texas as well, and there is good reason to believe that the 277 free blacks counted was nowhere near an accurate count. Additionally, there were African Creeks with matrilineal kinship ties to Creek Indians enrolled in the tribal towns, even with the increasing restrictions on that important avenue to cultural recognition.[2]

As the sectional crisis deepened in the early months of 1861, secessionist politicians from the neighboring states and pro-Confederate former officials from the Indian Office, unlike most Union officials, saw the Indian Territory as an important resource. They also saw the Creeks' lax authority over their slave property and the abolitionist influence of some white missionaries as detrimental to the future success of the Confederate cause. Accordingly, they began a concerted campaign to convince the Creeks and other tribes in the Indian Territory to put their slaves under closer supervision and ultimately to side with the Confederacy.[3]

In the first act of the move toward an alliance with the Confederacy, the Creek Council, under the influence of the Confederate sympathizers, enacted a harsher series of laws designed to bring African Creeks under closer

AFRICAN CREEKS

control. The new laws that took effect in March 1861 included provisions that would confine slaves to their masters' lands, institute a pass-and-patrol system, and forbade slaves ownership of livestock or property or to hire out their labor. Under the new code, African Creek preachers were forbidden to preach before mixed congregations, and slaves could attend churches only within the immediate area of their masters' holdings. The new laws also instructed all free African Creeks to select a master by March 10, 1861, or face being sold to the highest bidder. Free blacks were told to dispose of all property before their return to slavery. Violations of the codes carried severe penalties for blacks or anyone aiding them in circumventing the laws. Tribal officers were appointed to oversee the free blacks' return to slavery, and the Creek Lighthorse, the tribal law enforcement body, was given authority to enforce the new code.[4]

The African Creeks were unnerved by these laws, yet, in the early months of 1861, there appeared to be little they could do to reverse the tide. Federal troops had been withdrawn from the outposts in Indian Territory in April and May, and nearly all the Indian agents were Southern Democrats who quickly proclaimed allegiance to the Confederacy. African Creeks were equally alarmed when Creek leaders, mostly from Lower Creek towns, signed a treaty with the Confederacy in July 1861, and then mustered two Creek Confederate regiments in the same month. The pro-Confederate Creek chiefs, Motey Kennard, Jacob Deerisaw, Echo Hacho, and Tuckabatchee Micco, joined by the wealthy Creek slaveholders Benjamin Marshall, James M. C. Smith, George Stidham, and the McIntosh half brothers, Chilly and Daniel N. (D. N.), now had additional power to enforce the new laws as well as to exert control over future developments.[5]

The African Creeks were not the only ones in the Creek Nation unsettled by the alliance with the Confederacy. Many Upper Creek leaders, who had counseled neutrality in the "white man's war," were driven into opposition after Confederate sympathizers signed the treaty. At a council held on August 5, Opothleyahola and other Upper Creek leaders, along with Coweta Micco from the Lower Creeks, repudiated the terms of the new treaty, declared the office of principal chief vacant, and elected Oktahasas Hacho (or Sands) their chief.[6]

The Confederate Creeks would maintain in later years that the split in the Creek country had more to do with intertribal antagonisms than with slavery. After all, less than 2 percent of Creeks owned slaves, and among slaveholders, 63 per cent owned fewer than five. Also, prominent leaders in the faction that would become known as the Loyal Creeks were slaveholders themselves and operated extensive plantations and ranches using slave labor. Opothleyahola, reputed to be one of the wealthiest people in the nation, farmed two thousand acres on the Deep Fork of the Canadian with twenty-five slaves. But the slaveholders that joined the Loyal Creeks were not tied to the institution, and when the time came to rid themselves of it, they did so.[7] The Confederate faction, on the other hand, was committed to slavery and the benefits of raising commercial quantities of cotton, corn, and livestock for sale outside the nation. Both the Confederate sympathizers and Opothleyahola's followers were intent on maintaining tribal sovereignty, about that there was no dispute. They disagreed, however, on whether the "new government" (i.e., the Confederacy) would provide better protection, or were less of a threat, than the "old government." While speaking to a delegation of Confederate Creeks sent to convince him to drop his opposition to the Confederate treaty, Opothleyahola said that they "were like some people who after having used an axe for a long time, see a new one and take it instead." Opothleyahola preferred the old axe.[8] Whether or not the old leader was claiming to guard Creek traditions or just wanted to stick by the old treaty is not clear, but the leaders in the Confederate faction clearly were determined to enforce compliance with the "new axe" and to use it to protect their interests—which included protecting their slave property. Although possibly not the controlling issue that split the Creeks, slavery complicated the picture and precipitated the first armed clashes in the Indian Territory. African Creeks played a pivotal role as cultural brokers during the conflict, expanding on their experience with freedom as preachers, interpreters, artisans, storekeepers, stock raisers, and farmers. And African Creeks exercised an option that few African Americans had in 1861: they took up arms and left the Creek country rather than give up the relative freedom they had come to expect.[9]

At first, those Creeks opposed to the treaty, mostly from the Upper Creek towns, merely separated themselves from the pro-Confederate faction, declared neutrality, and gathered in a camp on Opothleyahola's plantation at the headwaters of the Deep Fork of the Canadian River. There they hoped to remain neutral and unmolested. Such a withdrawal was in accord with Creek political traditions—when consensus could not be reached, the dissenting party withdrew from the public business of the tribe. But the possibilities of maintaining that position, surrounded by Confederate regiments mustered for war, were slim.[10] On August 15, Opothleyahola and Sands wrote to ask President Lincoln for help and reminded him that in the treaty, the government had promised, "should we be injured by anybody you would come with your soldiers and punish them. But now the wolf has come. Men who are strangers tread our soil. Our children are frightened and the mothers cannot sleep for fear. I well remember the treaty. My ears are open and my memory is good."[11]

The African Creek memory was good also. They recalled that Opothleyahola in earlier years had ordered African Creeks whipped for going to the "praying people." Now, despite his earlier orders, Opothleyahola reached out to forge an alliance with the Creek and Seminole blacks. He sent messengers into the slave settlements and free black enclaves throughout the Creek and Seminole country, bearing promises of freedom to all who joined him. Opothleyahola, in his role as emancipator, found willing allies in the African Creeks. Faced with a choice between slavery and freedom, they needed little convincing. They left their stores and blacksmiths shops filled with merchandise and tools, their farms with apple and peach trees laden with ripening fruit, and corn cribs full from the harvest. They abandoned ranches stocked with fodder and hay and brought what livestock they could. Some deserted the farms and plantations of their masters, a scene that would be repeated throughout the slave states in the coming years of struggle. Another scenario emerged that was peculiar to the racial frontier. Creek masters provided their slaves with wagons, horses, and provisions to sustain them on their journey toward freedom and with guns to protect themselves. Some Upper Creek masters joined the exodus as well.[12]

As many as five hundred African Creeks and African Seminoles, and an estimated five thousand Creek Indians and people from other tribes in the Indian Territory, collected at Opothleyahola's camp and other locations between August and November 1861. Most African Creeks came from the Upper Creek country in the southern and western parts of the nation. Others came from farther away, from the Arkansas district, near the Creek Agency and Tullahassee Mission in the eastern and northern parts of the nation.[13]

The story of Simon Brown illustrates how these changing conditions drove some African Creeks into active resistance and alliance with Opothleyahola. Brown was a slave of Hannah Brown, who lived near Tullahassee

Mission. Although Brown was a slave, in accord with the relaxed Creek attitude toward slavery, he lived and worked, earning wages, at Tullahassee Mission for the Robertson missionary family in the pre–Civil War years. He regularly made trips to Ft. Gibson and Park Hill in the Cherokee Nation on errands for the Robertsons, frequently traveling alone. In July 1861, Simon drove the wagon that carried the Robertsons into forced exile, out of the Creek Nation for the duration of the war. On this trip, Simon scrupulously followed the provisions of the new slave code and carried the Robertsons only as far as the boundary of the Creek Nation on the Verdigris River. From there, Simon bade his patrons goodbye and returned to Hannah Brown's plantation on foot.[14] No one knows what went through Simon's mind as he made his way back, but by November, the "trusted slave" fled the increasingly restrictive and oppressive atmosphere and brought his family to Opothleyahola's camp. He would later explain that he risked the journey and decided to join Opothleyahola because of "atrocities committed against Negroes by rebel troops."[15]

The expulsion of the missionaries from the Indian Territory also returned Robert Johnson to slavery. Johnson had interpreted for many years for various Presbyterian missionaries, beginning with R. H. Loughridge, who opened the Coweta Presbyterian Mission among the Creeks in the late 1840s. Johnson had been paying on his freedom from the wages he earned as an interpreter for the missionaries in the Creek and Seminole nations. After the missionaries were expelled, Johnson was without means and still owed seven hundred dollars to John Jumper, the Seminole chief (and Confederate leader), who had advanced the missionaries the money needed so that Johnson would not be sold out of the country. Unable to pay off the outstanding debt, Johnson was returned to slavery. Jumper employed Johnson as a body servant and took him wherever he went. Although Jumper never mistreated Johnson, the African Creek was used to making his own decisions and moving freely, and he chafed under close supervision. But Johnson would have to bide his time before making his dash for freedom.[16]

Free African Creeks also fled to Opothleyahola. The provision in the new law code that required them to sell their property and return to slavery prompted many to leave behind their lives of relative prosperity. Billy Hawkins, the free African Creek preacher from Post Oak, twelve miles west of the Creek Agency and just south of the Arkansas River, was ordained in 1857 by Evan Jones, the abolitionist Baptist missionary to the Cherokees. Hawkins regularly preached before mixed congregations at the Post Oak Baptist Church in the days before the new laws were passed. He also traveled freely to other churches and to camp meetings in the nation, and he had a thriving farming and ranching operation. It is unknown whether Hawkins had "selected" an owner, according to the code, but by September he and his family fled to Opothleyahola's camp for safety because he had "preached for the government" rather than stay silent.[17]

Gilbert Lewis, a slave of Kendell Lewis, lived on the Point, a peninsula of land jutting between the Verdigris and Arkansas rivers. He and his family left their home on the northeastern edge of the Creek country late in the fall and traversed the entire breadth of the troubled Creek Nation to reach Opothleyahola's camp. The country bristled with armed men—Creek, Choctaw, Seminole, Chickasaw, Cherokee, and Texan—all Confederate sympathizers. Yet the Lewises chanced the journey because "McIntosh would not allow the Negroes to remain at their homes in possession of their property." Kizzie Sells, at the time a slave of John Sells, had less distance to travel than the Lewis family did. Living at Little Deep Fork, close to Opothleyahola's camp, she abandoned her home in the middle of the night in August 1861, while Confederate troops were collecting slaves in the neighborhood and sending them to serve the rebels in the South.[18]

For various compelling reasons, African Creeks, slave and free, made alliances with Opothleyahola. Whether it was the promise of freedom extended, one year before Abraham Lincoln announced his limited emancipation plan, or to defend a certain kind of freedom already experienced by some, African Creeks actively resisted their enslavement in the most convincing ways available to them. Like Kizzie Sells and Gilbert Lewis, they spoke with their feet by abandoning their master's fields. Like Billy Hawkins, they spoke with their voices from the pulpits. They also spoke by taking up arms, becoming the first black community in America to organize armed resistance to the Confederacy.

The "fire eaters" among the Creek Confederates, D. N. McIntosh and James S. Smith, wanted to strike at Opothleyahola and his followers immediately after their repudiation of the Confederate treaty and were intent on "mak[ing] them feel our law." Others, including the Confederate commander of the Indian District, Col. Douglas C. Cooper, the former Choctaw agent, counseled patience as long as there were no armed demonstrations. Confederate Creeks worried that Opothleyahola and his followers would join with Kansas jayhawkers and move against them. Armed bands of Kansans had already raided south into the Indian country, and the fiery Kansas senator James H. Lane loudly and publicly proclaimed the need for Union forces to strike into the Indian Territory and blaze a trail into Texas.[19]

In the end, however, the principal reason that a combined force of Confederate Indians and Texans finally attacked the Loyal Creek party was their alarm and anger over the number of slaves fleeing to Opothleyahola. As early as September 11, D. N. McIntosh, the commander of the First Confederate Creek Regiment, told John Drew, the commander of a Confederate Cherokee regiment, "Negroes are fleeing to him [Opothleyahola] from all quarters—not less than 150 have left within the last three days," complained McIntosh. "This state of affairs cannot long exist here without seriously affecting your country. Therefore, [they] should be put down immediately."[20]

As Confederate hostility grew, Opothleyahola and the Loyal chiefs rebuffed further entreaties for negotiations, insisting that their intentions were peaceful. Opothleyahola maintained that the movement of people to and from his plantation were merely part of his efforts to establish a "cowpen" farther west along the Deep Fork. John Ross, the neutralist Cherokee chief who finally pragmatically threw in with the Confederates, sent his emissary Joseph Vann to Opothleyahola with a proffer of amnesty from Confederate commissioner Albert Pike in the first week of October. Pike offered amnesty for all Creeks under arms against the Confederate States and the so-called lawful authorities of the Creek Nation. The offer also contained the proviso that all fugitive slaves must be given up. When the Loyal Creeks rejected the offer, Motey Kennard and Echo Hacho wrote to John Ross, "Again they are causing our Negroes to run to them daily, greatly to the injury of many of our best citizens. . . . Therefore as soon as we are reinforced, which we daily expect, we shall proceed without further delay and put an end to the affair."[21]

The following week an Arkansas border newspaper reported that more than six hundred fugitive slaves from all tribes in the Indian Territory and neighboring states had fled to the protection of "Old Gouge, the insurgent chief." The same story said that help was on the way in the form of "a regiment of Texas troops" due to arrive on the scene in a few days. After a Confederate Creek scouting report informed D. N. McIntosh that a party of Opothleyahola's followers, which included "a large lot of Negroes," had

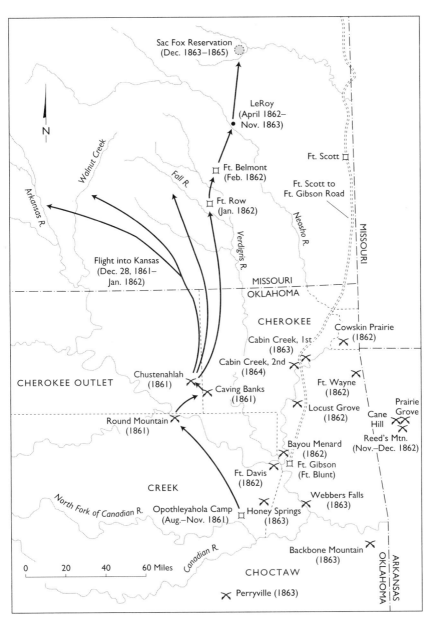

Opothleyahola's exodus to Kansas, and African Creek battles
in the Civil War, 1862–1865.

crossed the Deep Fork River and were moving northwest, McIntosh and the other Creek Confederates decided it was time to act. They told Col. Cooper that they intended to attack Opothleyahola and his party and that all free blacks captured would be "sold for the benefit of the Nation." All slaves not belonging to a Creek citizen similarly would be sold and all Creek slaves "shall be dealt with according to Creek Law," which could mean being put to death. Cooper still advised a negotiated settlement, but in case hostilities did break out, he notified the Creeks that slaves and property taken during the expedition belonged to the Confederate States of America. As appointed commander of all Confederate forces in the Indian Territory, he told the Creeks that all military operations within the Indian Territory would be his direction.[22]

That direction would take on a more threatening character when the Fourth (later designated the Ninth) Texas Cavalry crossed Red River and headed into the Indian Territory in the second week of October. On their way to a camp at North Fork, they received reports on the disposition of armed groups loyal to Opothleyahola in the area and readied themselves for action. While on a scouting and foraging mission about ten miles upriver from North Fork Town, a detachment led by Capt. Whatley reported an incident that augured what was in store for the Texans. "While moving to North Fork we were in camp when a small Negro Indian boy on a horse rode up. After some conversation with Capt. Whatley he rode away at a gallop, uttering a curious scream, terminating in something like the gobbling of a turkey, which the captain said was the Indian war whoop and meant mischief to us." Just what kind of mischief the young messenger meant to convey would soon become obvious as the Confederate troops clashed with the African and Indian allies.[23]

The Confederate expedition struck out toward the Loyal Creeks on November 14. When they arrived the following day at the main camp, now located at the Big Bend of the Deep Fork, they found it abandoned. The Loyal Creeks, no doubt alerted of preparations for an attack, had broken camp on November 5 and headed northwest. Oral history testimonies from Indian informants suggest that Opothleyahola planned to establish a "fort" on the site of old Ft. Arbuckle on the north bank of the Arkansas River, just east of the Red Fork (Cimarron River) to be closer to the anticipated relief from Kansas. If this is true, it means the Loyal Creeks' original intention was not to reach Kansas but to make a stand in the Indian Territory. The informants also said that Opothleyahola had earlier sent some African Creek slaves forward to prepare the site and to dig out some caves where the women and children could be protected if fighting broke out. This could possibly account for the "lot of Negroes" that D. N. McIntosh noted moving northwest from Opothleyahola's camp at Deep Fork in late October. In any case, the Confederates pursued the Loyal Creek party, determined to bring Opothleyahola and his followers to heel and reclaim their slave property. The Loyal Creeks, then, without aid from Kansas, and protecting the women and children as best they could, fought the first three battles of the Civil War in the Indian Territory.[24]

African Creeks and African Seminoles fought in the battles of Round Mountain on November 19, Chusto Talasah (Caving Banks) on December 9, and finally at Chustenahlah (Shoal Creek) on December 26. Col. Cooper estimated as many as "200–300 Negroes" were under arms in the battles. Charles Anderson, Jacob Bernard, Simon Brown, Harry Colonel, Redmon Colonel, Thomas Conner, John Coulter, Thomas Dobbins, Monday Durant, Jim Doyle, Ned Doyle, Joe Fife, Billy Hawkins, Gilbert Lewis, Morris McIntosh, Scipio Sancho, and Joe Sells were among those "able-bodied" men on the first exodus to Kansas, and its likely that they were among the first black men in America to raise arms against the Confederacy.[25]

At Round Mountain the Loyal Creek allies led the pursuing Confederates into an ambush as darkness fell on November 19 and then slipped away into the night to join the women and children sequestered in the caves. Following their defeat at Round Mountain, Texas cavalrymen grumbled about encountering "red niggers"—African Creeks—at the battle. The Loyal allies then moved northeastward into the Cherokee country, where Opothleyahola hoped to find support from conservative Cherokees troubled by the Confederate treaties. Cooper returned to the Confederate camp at Ft. Gibson, and after reprovisioning, the Confederates set out again on November 29, bent on imposing their law on the Loyal party.[26]

On December 5, a Confederate Cherokee scouting party found once again that their task might be more difficult than they had imagined when they came upon a group of armed African Creeks and Creek Indians. The Cherokee scouts boldly identified themselves as "soldiers of the South" and ordered the party to halt. In response, one of the blacks "reprimed his gun," then, "spoke back impudently" before continuing on. The Confederates, outnumbered and outgunned, decided to withdraw rather than confront the African and Creek allies. On December 9, at the Battle of Chusto Talasah the blacks once again "spoke back impudently" and joined their Loyal allies in a battle that raged for four to five hours along Bird Creek before Cooper ordered his troops to withdraw. At the Battle of Chustenahlah on December 26, however, fought near present-day Tulsa, the Confederate pursuers finally overwhelmed the Loyal allies, killed an undetermined number of armed men (Confederate reports said 250, a wild exaggeration) and captured 160 women and children as well as the bulk of the livestock and provisions carried by the refugees. The Confederates also captured twenty African Indians, most of them women and children. The surviving refugees, without food, clothing, shelter, or even shoes, plunged on to Kansas through a freezing winter storm, suffering horribly from hunger and cold along the way, and many died of exposure. Thirty-five hundred Creek refugees along with approximately two thousand more Indians from other tribes eventually reached their destination.[27]

The Loyal refugees reached Kansas during the first weeks in January in wretched condition. They were initially strung out in different locations for twelve miles along the Verdigris River valley in the southeastern corner of the state. Frostbite, hunger, and disease were rampant. One of the first doctors on the scene, U.S. Army surgeon A. B. Campbell, reported performing over one hundred amputations within a few days. Campbell also said pneumonia, consumption, and "inflammatory diseases of the chest, throat, and eyes" associated with exposure were common among the refugees. Few had provisions for even the rudest shelters and instead slept on the frozen ground with piles of prairie grass for bedding. Shoes were unknown, and food and clothing were in equally short supply. Refugees wandered the camps, naked in the freezing temperatures, searching for food and clothing for themselves and their families. At the direction of Gen. David A. Hunter, the commander of the District of Kansas, the U.S. Army subsisted the refugees from January through February 15, 1862. Gen. Hunter had been following developments in the Indian Territory with great interest and had even tried to raise a regiment of Kansas Indians to aid the Loyal Creeks during the late fall of 1861. He doubled his efforts after the refugees appeared in Kansas.[28]

The Indian Office took over the job of subsisting the refugees on February 15. The Southern superintendent for Indian Affairs, William S. Coffin, worked with scant resources and juggled the books to come up with a daily ration that cost thirty cents per refugee per day. Cutting coffee and sugar from the ration brought the daily cost down to fifteen cents per day. Refugees were allowed one pound of flour weekly. Not only were the rations meager, but the food itself was barely fit to eat. Most of the flour provided was wet and spoiled. Indian Office officials tried to give refugees bacon that had been condemned by the U.S. Army at Ft. Leavenworth, Kansas, as suitable for making soap but not for human consumption. Most of the refugees, even in their starving condition, rejected the bacon, saying it was not "fit for a dog to eat." For shelter the army provided condemned tents and unfitted canvas.[29]

But the Indian Office did not provide subsistence for the black "slaves" among the refugees. African Creeks were expected to get subsistence *from* their Indian patrons, but African Creeks actually got subsistence *for* the Indians. African Creek interpreters were intimately tied into the supply and subsistence system because Indian Office agents in charge of dispensing the subsistence needed interpreters. African Creek interpreters helped compile the lists of refugees and their families for the issuing agents and then were on hand to see that the subsistence was fairly distributed. African Creek interpreters were also in demand to help provide medical services. A. V. Coffin, the Indian Office's doctor for the refugees, said it was necessary to leave medicines with the interpreters to administer because the Indians would trust no one else. Accompanied by African Creek interpreters, Coffin also attempted to instruct the Indians in "sanitary and healthful practices." African Creeks were more willing than the Indians to consent to smallpox vaccinations, as later mortality figures would show.[30]

As the weather warmed that spring, the over one thousand Indian pony carcasses littering the banks of the Verdigris near the camps began to rot, compounding the already pestilent conditions. Superintendent Coffin was forced to relocate the refugees. The appalling stench and the threat to the refugees' health needed no translation, but the logistics of moving the refugees required interpreters. With the aid of the interpreters, by April, the refugees were moved into camps along the Neosho River thirty miles north, outside LeRoy, Kansas.[31]

Indian Office officials observed that the Indians not only shared their camps with blacks but also "treat[ed] them as their equals." Surgeon Campbell counted fifty-three African Creek slaves and thirty-eight free African Creeks in the Creek camps in February 1862. G. C. Snow, the Seminole agent, counted sixty African Seminoles among the refugees when they first arrived in Kansas, and one hundred more joined them later. Snow observed that most African Seminoles claimed to be free, were intelligent, and spoke English. He also said they knew how to do common work on the farm, "but, it is evident that they have not been brought up to labor like those among the whites." Snow does not say in exactly what way the African Seminoles were different, but if their earlier history is any indication, then the bally-hooed notion in the Southern press that Negroes were naturally subservient could be laid to rest. More African Creeks and Seminoles eventually made their way to Kansas as the first wave of refugees abandoned their homes in the Creek country during the winter of 1861–1862. The total number rose to near five hundred by the early spring of 1862. Snow's comment would be echoed by other white observers who came in contact with the African Indians during the Civil War years. These onlookers saw a significant difference in the way that African Creeks and other African Indians carried themselves when compared with African Americans from the states. The African Indians were more independent and shared cultural traits with the Indians that made their ways seem strange to African Americans and Euro-Americans alike. Richard J. Hinton, a *New York Times* correspondent in Kansas since the days of "Bleeding Kansas," was not at all put off by the African Indians and described African Indian slaves this way: "They are more on an equality with their owners. I can tell the runaway Negro from the Indians from any other. He looks and acts more manly. These Negroes mostly own something—horses, cows, hogs, etc.; have patches of land to cultivate, and in various ways have been able to cultivate self-respect above their fellows in the states." Hinton added: "Nearly every male adult slave among them owns some kind of gun" which would make them, along with their other qualities, good soldiers.[32]

The African Creek role as cultural brokers took on another dimension as the African and Indian allies proclaimed their willingness to return to the Indian Territory as a Union volunteer regiment. Almost immediately after their arrival in Kansas, the refugee chiefs Opothleyahola and Halleck Tuste-nuggee sent a letter to President Lincoln, promising to "sweep the rebels before us like a terrible fire on the prairie" if provided with the means to do so.[33] Gen. Hunter, in cooperation with Indian Office officials, began to enroll recruits in January. But Kansas political rivalries, and a jurisdictional battle between the Interior and War departments, delayed organizing the unit. In the midst of the political struggle, Hunter was reassigned to the South Carolina Sea Islands in March 1862. At his new post, he began his much publicized, but unsuccessful, attempt to muster a regiment of black soldiers. Finally, in April 1862, the War Department granted the Indian Office authority to raise two Indian regiments. Recalling the experiences that drove them to Kansas, the African Creeks and African Seminoles eagerly enlisted. A Kansas newspaper reported the blacks "would stick to the Indians through thick and thin and wished to go back to fight." An African Creek was quoted as saying that he wanted "to return to shoot his master, who is secesh."[34] When the First Indian was officially mustered into the federal army in May 1862, twenty-five to thirty African Creeks were in the regiment, the first black soldiers officially mustered into the Union army during the Civil War.[35]

When the recruits were enrolled and mustered, white officers determined, among other things, the recruits' "complexion." The descriptions ran the gamut in the First Indian. "Red" and "Indian" usually described the Creek Indians, but several recruits who later rose to prominence in the African Creek community shared this description as well. "Dark" was an amorphous description that could be applied to most Creeks and those African Creeks who had generational ties to the tribe. Many of those described as black or Negro had Indian names. Most of the African Creek recruits were listed as black, yellow, or African. The descriptions can be clearly seen on the muster rolls. So, when army officers enrolled the African Creeks on April 29 and mustered them on May 22, they operated far in advance of the policies approved by President Lincoln, but they conformed to the conditions found on the racial frontier.[36]

The First Indian comprised ten companies, the minimum needed for a regiment. Creek Indians served as officers in seven companies, including Tuckabatchee Hacho, Opothleyahola's nephew, and Tulsey-Fixico—two leading voices among the Upper Creek towns. Halleck Tustenuggee and Billy Bowlegs, war leaders in the Second and Third Seminole wars, led the two Seminole companies in the unit, and Joneh (Keptene Uchee, or Little Captain) led a company of Yuchi Indians.[37] White regimental officers were appointed to command the regiment and oversee its operations. Robert W. Furnas, a free-soiler from Nebraska, was given command of the regiment and appointed colonel. He brought his aide-de-camp, Stephen H. Wattles, and his friend Andrew Holladay. Wattles was commissioned a lieutenant colonel, and Holladay was appointed the regimental surgeon. A. C. Elli-thorpe, who left Chicago to answer the Union's call, received a lieutenant's commission and served as one of the most active junior officers. William A. Phillips, one of John Brown's chief supporters in Kansas, also played an active role in the unit and served as a lieutenant.[38]

Though their numbers were few at this early stage, the blacks in the First Indian were an essential element in the triracial unit. African Creeks served as interpreter-soldiers and provided a cultural bridge between the Creek soldiers, who spoke little or no English, and the white officers in the unit. Their duties went beyond merely translating orders. They served as negotiators, clerks, orderlies, modern medicine men, soldiers, and scouts.

The first action seen by the blacks in the First Indian as well as the first combat experienced by regularly mustered blacks in the federal army dur-ing the Civil War came on the ill-fated Indian Expedition in summer 1862. The ostensible purpose of the expedition was to clear the Indian Territory north of the Arkansas River of rebel troops so that the Loyal Indian and African refugees in Kansas could return home. Perhaps the larger goal of "blazing a trail into Texas," or at least beginning that effort, also figured into the detailing of six thousand white troops to the expedition to aid the First and Second Indian Home Guard regiments in the operation.[39]

After months of preparation, the Indian Expedition finally headed south on June 25, 1862. The soldiers in the First Indian were ready to "sweep the rebels before them." The white troops assigned to the expedi-tion were less enthusiastic. White and Indian troops set up separate camps and marched in separate details from the beginning of the expedition. Lt. Luman Tenney, from the Second Ohio Cavalry, visited the Indian camp and witnessed a traditional Indian ball game, which he found quite interest-ing, but some white soldiers expressed their "disgust" at the "primeval customs" seen at the Indian camp. They were also surprised to see blacks with the Indians and remarked on how they "mixed freely" with one an-other. While most white soldiers kept their social distance from the blacks and Indians, the officers had to keep in close communication with the men under their command. Col. William Weer, the commander of the expedi-tion, issued orders that stated, "whenever a detail of Indians is made from the Brigade for any duty whatever, the necessary number of interpreters and guides will [be] named to accompany each detail." "Interpreters" invariably meant African Creeks, as they were frequently the only soldiers in camp who spoke both Creek and English.[40]

The Indian and African allies routed the Confederates at all three important engagements during the expedition. At Locust Grove on July 3, 1862, Wattles and Ellithorpe led the First Indian in a surprise attack on a rebel encampment just outside the hamlet of Locust Grove in the Cherokee country. The action captured Cherokee Confederate Gen. Stand Watie's entire supply train, killed an estimated 50 rebels, and captured 116, including the Confederate train's commander, Col. J. J. Clarkson. The white troops detailed to support the Indians refused to join the attack, however. They felt that the element of surprise had been lost after Col. Weer, reportedly in a drunken stupor from a night of "visiting the jug," careened noisily out onto the open prairie beneath the enemy camp in his ambulance while the troops were forming for the attack. It was said that the only shot fired in anger by the white federal troops at the Battle of Locust Grove succeeded in seriously wounding surgeon Holladay.[41]

The next day, however, the white troops claimed credit for the victory, plundered the captured supplies, and later tried to blame the Indians for the mischief. Most of the troops spent the national holiday celebrating with whiskey. In their drunken revelry, the white troops, who had sat on their hands at Locust Grove, decided to "throw a few shells over the Indian camp as a test to see how they would handle the fire of the big guns." They laughed when the Indians fled into the brush for protection. The incident only aggravated existing tensions between the white and Indian troops, which steadily worsened as the supplies dwindled, the heat rose, and the availability of good water dried up. In the following week, the African and Indian allies scouted the area, and Lt. Ellithorpe led 250 soldiers on another dawn attack, this time at Sand Town Ford. No white troops were present this time to take credit or to alert the enemy, and once again the African and Indian allies succeeded in stampeding the rebels. Meanwhile, the thousands of white troops contributed to the demise of the expedition by staying in camp, consuming the dwindling rations, and swilling whiskey in the hundred-degree heat before staging a mutiny, arresting Col. Weer, and returning to Kansas on July 18. The Indian troops were left behind to guard the retreat of the white troops and hold the area, if possible. Both Ellithorpe and Phillips reported that their men were eager to stay and defend the area, despite meager rations and unrelenting heat. Maj. Phillips led the newly organized Cherokee Third Indian Home Guard, made up of further desertions from Drew's Confederate regiment, and a contingent of the First Indian on yet another successful and well-executed surprise attack against the rebels at Bayou Menard, just west of Ft. Gibson, on July 25 and succeeded in pushing the demoralized rebels south of the Arkansas River.[42]

Although Stand Watie and Albert Pike, the Confederate commander for the Indian Territory, had pronounced the Confederate cause as good as lost in the area, the Union Indian Expedition was disintegrating. In a startling lack of foresight, the captured Confederate supplies, including bacon, flour, and other food, had been packed off to Ft. Scott. With supplies exhausted, and little hope of getting any with the white troops gone, Col. Furnas became alarmed at being completely cut off. He was no doubt relieved when he received orders to fall back, and he ordered a retreat to Kansas at the end of July. Furnas later tendered his resignation to secretary of war Edwin Stanton and stated his reasons:

> I have always doubted the propriety and the policy of arming and placing in the field Indians. . . . All communication has been through interpreters, all of whom are ignorant and uneducated Negroes, who have been raised among the Indians and possess to a great degree their peculiar characteristics. The commander has but little assurance that orders are correctly given . . . or understood.[43]

For Col. Furnas, who had stayed in camp most of the time issuing orders, using the African Creeks as middlemen was a problem because they identified with the needs of the Indians. But the field officers, Maj. John Ritchie of the Second Indian Home Guard and Majs. Ellithorpe and Phillips of the First Indian, saw the Indian–African alliance from a different perspective—in action against the rebels—and they judged it successful. The principal problem with the Indian Expedition was the white volunteer regiments assigned to the expedition and its commanding officers. As two special Indian agents detailed to the expedition wrote from the field, "Such protection as the white man had recently given to the Indian Territory would ruin any country on earth."[44]

After their return to Kansas in August, many blacks and Indians in the First Indian went back to the refugee camps around LeRoy rather than report to the regimental camp near Ft. Scott.[45] Counseled by Opothleyahola to stay in their camps at LeRoy, approximately three hundred of the nine hundred able-bodied in the First Indian refused to march when Gen. James G. Blunt ordered them into Missouri at the end of September. The soldiers and their leaders felt betrayed by the white troops on the Indian Expedition, and they felt that ordering them into action in the white man's country violated the agreement to serve only as home guards in the Indian Territory.[46]

Those who did obey Blunt's marching orders found that Lt. Col. Wattles had succeeded Furnas as commander of the First Indian, and additional white officers were attached to their companies, which according to Wattles had the Indian officers' approval. Blunt felt the additions were necessary to improve discipline and to aid in keeping the company books and accounting.[47] The reorganization also included assigning African Creek soldiers specific duties. Hes-siah-hupt-keh was appointed first sergeant in Co. A, which later turned out to be one of the most active and effective companies in the regiment during the fall campaigns. Joe Barnett and Jim Barnett of Co. C were assigned to duties at the regimental hospital and as interpreters. Other interpreters included John Adams for Co. E, Cully Adams for Co. G, and Ya-fa-la-mart-la for Co. I.[48]

The truncated version of the First Indian participated in the engagement at Maysville, on October 22, located in the far northwestern corner of Arkansas near the border of the Cherokee Nation. According to E. C. Manning, one of the recently appointed white officers assigned to Co. C, the First Indian soldiers were among the first on the field and then actively pursued and harassed the Confederates after their retreat.[49] The victory at Maysville revealed that the African–Indian alliance could provide effective service in the white man's country and helped bolster the morale of the troops. The Creek Confederate troops' morale was affected as well, and some of them began to reconsider their Confederate alliance.[50]

When the defeated Creek rebels came thundering back to the Creek country, they brought with them alarming stories of the imminent arrival of federal Indian home guard troops bent on revenge. Wealthy planters and slaveowners in the Arkansas-Verdigris river valley panicked and hurriedly planned to move their slaves and stock to safety farther south. While the slaveowners were distracted, African Creek slaves in the area began to make arrangements of their own. The men would break for freedom to the north, while most of the women and children would be left in relative safety with the slaveowners packing up to head farther south.[51]

William McIntosh, Jacob Perryman, and Hector Perryman, three brothers who lived in the Choska bottoms area on the north bank of the Arkansas River, huddled together several nights, secretly making plans for a dash to freedom after learning of their owners' intentions. Mary Grayson, Jacob Perryman's daughter, remembered her father and her uncles and another African Creek man holding their secret meetings. She also recalls her mother, Mollie Perryman, crying after her father returned, and she and her siblings overheard their parents arguing later that night. That next day, as Mollie Perryman prepared food and supplies for her husband's exodus, she gave the children but a small portion of what she cooked and told them to stay close to the house and not to play with the other children. The next morning, Mose Perryman, their master, came to the Perryman cabin and angrily ordered Mollie Perryman and the children to the main house. On their way, the children noticed that all the other slave cabins were empty and everything was in shambles. Mollie Perryman then told her children that their father and uncles and the other menfolk "went away" and would be free now and asked the children not to cry or tell Mose Perryman anything about what had gone on in the slave cabins recently. The women and children then helped their master pack up and move farther south, with other families and their slaves, settling near Ft. Washita, on the Red River, for the duration of the war. Other African Creeks, mainly women and children, from the surrounding McIntosh, Perryman, Marshall, Lewis, and Hawkins plantations were also taken south into the Chickasaw and Choctaw nations and across the Red River into Texas.[52]

Meanwhile, the party led by Jacob Perryman and William McIntosh, which included several hundred blacks, most of them armed, headed for the Union lines and freedom. While Perryman would not let his family go on what was sure to be a dangerous journey, others brought their families. William McIntosh brought his, which included twelve children.[53] Along the way through Cherokee country, the party fought several skirmishes with rebel bushwhackers and encountered Stand Watie's Confederate troops. Lt. Col. R. C. Parks, Watie's adjutant, reported "four wagons and a good battalion of Negroes" passing through the area in the first week of November. When the party reached the Union lines at Camp Babcock on the Arkansas–Cherokee Nation line after the second week in November, it was reported that "a good many [of the] Creek contrabands . . . had arms" and had lost seven men in their skirmishes with the rebels.[54]

From this party, many enlisted in the First Indian stationed at Camp Babcock in northwestern Arkansas. Among those enrolled "in the field" were Peter Johnson, who was immediately made a sergeant in Co. C, and Charles Hawkins, enrolled as a private in Co. D. Simon Brown also enlisted at Camp Babcock and joined Co. H, although he had been attached to the First Indian since its inception as a civilian interpreter.[55] A. C. Ellithorpe described others in the party as "in a suffering condition" and "many almost naked." Consequently, those not enlisted at Camp Babcock were sent to Ft. Scott and eventually were recruited at the refugee camps near LeRoy and Burlington, Kansas, in the last week of November. Among them were Book, Tally Lewis, Dennis Marshall, and Jacob Perryman, detailed to Co. C, and Daniel Miller, Isaac Perryman, and Pompey Perryman, assigned to Co. I. Those recruited in Kansas were possibly sent directly back to Arkansas without even so much as a day's training. Gen. Blunt, sorely in need of more troops, reportedly was sent a batch of recruits from Ft. Scott on November 27 whose "only training field was the battlefield."[56]

The role of African Creeks in the First Indian took on an added significance during November and December 1862, as the regiment operated closely with white regiments. As part of Gen. Blunt's Army of the Frontier, they took part in the Union victories at the battles of Cane Hill and Prairie Grove, which kept Confederate Gen. Thomas Hindman from seizing control of northwest Arkansas and possibly being able to strike into Missouri or Kansas.

At the Battle of Cane Hill on November 28, a running fight that stretched four miles through wooded hills and rocky ravines, communicating orders effectively was particularly important. Lt. E. C. Manning, commanding Co. C, later commented that his service with the First Indian was "very irksome" because "[w]ith each company were three or four Negroes who were enlisted men. The Indians either could or would not speak English, so the Negroes were used as translators. If I had no Negro at hand, I could give no orders."[57] Maj. Ellithorpe, on the other hand, praised the soldiers' skirmishing abilities and said his men were "always willing and eager to engage the enemy." The black interpreter-soldiers apparently translated the orders effectively because they kept the men moving and aided in pushing back the Confederate attempt to establish themselves north of the Boston Mountains.[58]

African Creeks in the First Indian also saw service in a skirmish at Reed's Mountain on December 6, the prelude to the Battle of Prairie Grove on December 7. The entire regiment, except Co. B, on detached service guarding Blunt's train at Rhea's Mill, and those holdouts still in Kansas, saw combat at Prairie Grove. At least thirty African Creeks fought, making them the first regularly mustered blacks in the federal army to participate in a major battle.[59]

The First Indian soldiers arrived at the Prairie Grove battlefield, located about twelve miles west of Fayetteville, Arkansas, around 3:00 p.m., where the Confederates under Hindman were dug into a fortified position on a hill overlooking the Illinois River. A detachment of First Indian skirmishers was immediately sent through a wooded area on the left of the Union line to probe the rebel strength; the skirmishers returned with a report, which, no doubt, was translated by African Creek interpreters, saying: "Many men, [m]uch rebel, many secesh up there." Blunt then ordered his left wing to advance up the hill in force. Led by Wattles and Ellithorpe, the Creek and African Creek soldiers began the assault with a chilling war yell, much like the haunting scream the African Creek boy had delivered to the mounted Texans in the days before the Battle at Round Mountain, only amplified by six hundred. One of the rebel defenders on the hill above them described the haunting cry as one of the "most horrible . . . I ever heard." The Union soldiers advanced rapidly through the woods up the foot of the hill; so rapidly, in fact, that as they neared the crest, the farthest advance thus far of any of the Union troops, they were fired on by mistake by comrades in the Twentieth Iowa, who were on their left. They then fell back, regrouped, and reentered the fight, directed by commands interpreted by African Creeks, then fell back again with the rest of the command as the Confederates launched a counterassault down the hill. The Creeks and African Creeks held fast defending the Union batteries at the base of the hill until nightfall ended the fighting. In his report, Wattles praised Ellithorpe and the other white officers, and he also singled out Billy Bowlegs, the Seminole war chief; Joneh, Captain of the Yuchi company; and Tuste nup-chup-ko, of Co. A for their coolness under fire. The African Creek interpreter-soldiers—Joe Barnett, Simon Brown, Peter Johnson, Richard Bruner, Robert Grayson, Alec Minnack, Pompey Perryman—and others who made movements on the battlefield possible were left out of the official reports. Various reports in Southern newspapers, on the other hand, spoke alarmingly of seeing

"Negroes in federal uniforms" at the battle, some even "wearing officers' swords." One Confederate officer reportedly sneered, "the idea of free-born Americans fighting such, is disgusting." The reports were generated, no doubt, to shock white Southerners. Shocking or not, African Creeks were there in uniform, if not wearing officers' swords, in the vanguard of the Black Phalanx that transformed a war to preserve the Union into a war of liberation.[60]

Following the Battle of Prairie Grove, the regiment joined an expedition into the Indian Territory that left the camp at Rhea's Mill, Arkansas, December 23. The soldiers who had remained in LeRoy since September rejoined the command after hearing the First Indian was going into the Indian country. William A. Phillips, promoted to colonel after returning from the Indian Expedition, led the mission. Gen. John M. Schofield, who replaced Blunt as the commander of the Army of the Frontier, gave Phillips the command of the Indian Brigade, consisting of the three Indian regiments plus contingents of the Sixth Kansas Cavalry and Hopkins's Battery. The Indian Brigade did not permanently occupy the Indian country north of the Arkansas, but they did put Ft. Davis to the torch, the rebel stronghold across the river from Ft. Gibson; destroyed an estimated $1 million worth of Confederate property; and provoked another panic among the rebel sympathizers in the area, who once again moved south for protection of their slaves and property.[61]

The expedition brought another wave of African Creek refugees streaming out of the Creek country. Maj. Ellithorpe wrote at the time that "nearly 400 contrabands" from the Indian country followed them into the Union lines. He described them in vivid detail:

> They make their escape in all conceivable ways—some on foot, carrying their children upon their backs and in their arms; in ox teams, mule teams, upon the backs of ponies, donkeys & etc. Old and young —the infirm and crippled, of all shades of color—Creek, Cherokee, Seminole, Chickasaw and Choctaw, male and female. [They] have somehow become impressed with the idea that the war is being waged on their account and the present is the long looked for time when their shackles shall fall and their race shall be free. They seem willing to endure any hardships. They cheerfully undergo hunger and unaccountable fatigue, storms, without shelter, long marches over the

sharp flint roads, without shoes, pressing forward towards a strange land—for what? Simply so that they may say *we are free.* (emphasis in the original)[62]

Recruiting efforts for African American regiments in Kansas reached the African Creek refugees at the Sac Fox Agency in spring 1863. Benjamin Van Horn, a subsistence contractor supplying beef for the refugees, noticed "over one hundred colored men" at the reservation on a trip there in early March. When he told Gen. Blunt and Senator Lane about the situation, they excitedly asked Van Horn to recruit the refugees. Lane and Blunt commissioned Van Horn as a recruiting officer and sent him out to the reservation with a wagon full of rations, uniforms, supplies, and a drill instructor. Twenty-five days later, Van Horn marched into Ft. Scott with eighty men, African Creek former refugees at the Sac Fox Reservation, dressed in new uniforms, and mustered them as Co. I of the First Kansas Colored (later designated the Seventy-Ninth U.S. Colored Troops [New]). Van Horn was also made captain of the company. The unit operated that spring in the Kansas-Missouri border area, seeing some significant action in the first combat operations for the all black regiments in the Civil War. The regiment would be best known for its gallant action on the Indian Territory battlefields during summer 1863 and in Arkansas during 1863–1865.[63]

In April 1863, Col. Phillips led the Indian Brigade back into the Indian Territory and reoccupied Ft. Gibson for the duration of the war. The men in the First Indian—blacks, Indians, and whites—worked shoulder to shoulder with "shovel in one hand and gun in the other," building fortifications and throwing up earth works. Phillips also ordered drill and training exercises in an effort to improve the "military appearance" of his soldiers. Phillips forwarded orders to the new commander of the First Indian, Lt. Col. George Dole, who had (temporarily) replaced Col. Wattles. The new regimen required the African Creeks to be on the training field every step of the way. Apparently, the efforts were successful, because, as Phillips later reported, "the progress of the First gives me great pleasure, for I had despaired."[64]

As the regiment settled into the routine of garrison life at Ft. Gibson, which was renamed Ft. Blunt, the white officers further defined and enlarged duties for African Creeks. These included orderly detail, work at the regimental quartermaster's, and duty as teamsters, assignments in keeping with the white racial stereotyping of blacks as a servile class. The Indians viewed such assignments as beneath the dignity of a warrior, but white observers noted that the African Creeks carried themselves with a self-assurance that was anything but servile. Hospital duty was another assignment that regularly fell to the blacks. From the time when the refugees first came to Kansas, the white doctors found that black interpreters were indispensable in bridging the wide cultural gap between the Indian and white ideas of healing and medicine. Sentry, guard, and picket duties at the fort required the African Creek's bilingual abilities to identify friend or foe. Scouting assignments necessitated the clear transfer of intelligence gathered. The African Creeks' knowledge of the terrain and its inhabitants, coupled with their language abilities, made them valuable scouts. The important role that the African Creeks played in the unit is further underscored in an August 1863 order Lt. Col. Dole issued. Dole posted a list of the soldiers, most of them African Creeks, who had to "hold themselves in readiness to answer to any detail when called for."[65] Thus, the African Creek soldiers did double duty and shouldered double the responsibility. While they had to be "in readiness," they were still accountable for their regular company duties.

One of the African Creeks' most important duties was escorting the subsistence trains that traveled between Ft. Scott and Ft. Gibson. Because of their communication skills and familiarity in handling supply and financial transactions in the prewar days, either as merchants, store interpreters, or go-betweens for Creek slaveowners, the African Creek soldiers were regularly detailed to escort as well as to drive the trains on the long, hazardous trip. While the escort and supply details carried the stigma of unwarriorlike grunt work for the Indians, being directly connected to the supply system had its advantages in a country stripped of subsistence. William McIntosh, after his successful escape to Kansas and enlistment in the First Kansas Colored, used his skills in language, blacksmithing, and horse training to help organize and outfit the subsistence operation that ran between Ft. Scott and Ft. Gibson. Tobe McIntosh also played an important role in the supply operation. As a free African Creek, he had owned and operated a wagon-train service headquartered at the Creek Agency settlement before the war. Tobe was reportedly in charge of the teams and drove a wagon. George Abram, Hackless Corbrey, John Jefferson, Robert Lewis, Isaac Marshall, William Marshall, and Sam Prince were other African Creek teamsters working to bring supplies from Ft. Scott.[66]

African Creek soldiers were also prominent in the extensive combat in the Indian Territory during 1863. Besides the constant skirmishing around Ft. Gibson during the spring and early summer of 1863, the black soldiers fought in the battles at Greenleaf Prairie, First Cabin Creek, and Honey Springs. Pickett Rentie could predict two days in advance when a battle was going to happen because his body would begin to shake nervously, only to calm before the enemy arrived. Jacob Perryman, promoted to sergeant following Peter Johnson's death, prepared for combat in a different way. Reportedly, his captain would get the soldiers "steamed up" on corn whiskey before a battle to make them "mean enough to whip their grannie(s)."[67] However they prepared for battle, the African Creeks' duties as translators and transmitters of orders put them in the front of every fight. They played an essential role in the 1863 summer campaign in the Indian Territory, as they had in previous campaigns.

The African Creeks in company I of the First Kansas Colored also played a key role in the combat operations in the Indian Territory that summer. They joined the First Indian and other Union troops at the first Battle of Cabin Creek on July 2, when the Confederates attempted to capture the supply train that ran between Ft. Scott and Ft. Gibson. Col. Phillips, acting on information supplied in part by African Creek scouts, had alerted Gen. Blunt about Confederate plans for an attack, and Blunt sent along a reinforced escort for the train, which left Ft. Scott in the middle of June. The engagement at Cabin Creek has been cited as the first battle in the Civil War in which white and black troops fought side by side. Actually, Cabin Creek was a tri-racial effort, and the First Indian, with its Indian, African Indian, and white soldiers had joined white troops in combat since the Indian Expedition in 1862. In any case, African Creeks from the First Kansas Colored and the First Indian joined other Indian and white troops on the Union side at Cabin Creek. Confederate troops at the battle, a mixture of Creek and Cherokee Indian regiments and white Texas troops, added to the racial complexity.[68]

Whether any African Creeks faced their former owners in the battle is unknown, but the engagement at Cabin Creek was the first time Loyal and Confederate Creek soldiers had met in battle in appreciable numbers since Chustenahlah eighteen months earlier. But this time, the Confederate Creeks and their Texas allies fled the battlefield after a series of well-coordinated Union attacks dislodged them from their positions in the creek bed.[69]

Two weeks later, the First Kansas Colored soldiers and about thirty-five African Creeks in the First Indian fought at Honey Springs, the largest and most important battle in the Indian Territory. The battle was fought in the Creek country, about thirty miles south and west of Ft. Gibson, along Elk Creek just north of Gen. Cooper's headquarters and a supply depot at Honey Springs. According to Capt. Van Horn, the African Creek soldiers in Co. I stood toe to toe, exchanging fire with the Confederates in the center for twenty minutes. When the men of the First Kansas fixed bayonets for a charge, the Confederate lines disintegrated and fled rather than face the gleaming steel of the black soldiers. All companies from the First Indian were engaged at Honey Springs and led attacks against the Confederate right wing, driving the First and Second Cherokee regiments and Texas troops back across Elk Creek, and then finally into a general retreat after several hours of heavy fighting. According to the battle report of Col. William T. Campbell of the Sixth Kansas Cavalry, the First Indian had made a "gallant charge," turning back an attempted Confederate flanking maneuver that could have proved disastrous for the left wing of the Union line. Following the battle, the Confederates melted away south of the Canadian River and would never gain the advantage north of the river for the duration of the war.[70]

After Honey Springs, the First Indian took part in the federal effort to establish control of their native Creek country. The federal drive into the area in August and September initially drove the rebels out and secured a large amount of corn and forage in the seemingly abandoned countryside.[71] But the combat duties for black soldiers carried an extra danger. Under the "black flag" policy announced by the Confederates, if captured, black soldiers could expect no mercy. In October, William Quantrill's guerilla terrorists massacred eleven First Indian soldiers on scouting detail near the Creek Agency. Several African Creeks were among those murdered, including John Steadham of Co. C. George, an African Creek in Co. D, was captured and then murdered while on picket duty in early 1863. Bob Grayson, also from Co. D, was similarly murdered after being captured while on scouting duty in October 1864. Thirteen men from Co. I were among the 115 First Kansas Colored soldiers slaughtered after they were surrounded and attempted to surrender at Poison Springs, Arkansas, on April 18, 1864. The massacre, one of the most heinous outrages recorded of the entire war, was allegedly instigated by Confederate Choctaws.[72]

The Union troops abandoned the Creek country soon after Quantrill's appearance, but not before enlisting two dozen African Creek and African Seminole recruits, many from around the North Fork settlements. Among those enlisted was Sugar T. George, mustered into Co. H. George would become one of the most visible and active African Creeks in the regiment and would later play a prominent role in postwar Creek politics. Another visible recruit at this time was Robert Johnson. As Confederate Seminole chief John Jumper's body servant, Johnson had been biding his time, waiting for the right opportunity to escape. Confident that Johnson would return, Jumper gave Johnson a furlough to visit his wife, Elizabeth, who was living with the Lilley missionary family in the Seminole country. While at the Lilleys', Robert decided that instead of returning to Jumper, he would strike for freedom. He headed for the Arkansas River and Ft. Gibson, and on the way, in order to avoid suspicion that he was escaping, he stopped at Confederate Creek Timothy Barnet's and acted as if he were going to spend the night there before returning to Jumper's. He spent an anxious evening listening to Confederate boasts of what they had done (or would do) to Yankees when they met them. Finally, after all the boasting rebels were sleeping, he saddled his horse and headed off into the night for the Creek Agency and Sarah Davis's. Davis welcomed him and kept a lookout while Johnson took some rest. As morning came, she awakened him and spurred him on his way saying, "Bob, now is your time, or never." Fearing that Jumper and his men by now were on his trail, Johnson dashed for the Arkansas River, barely a mile away. Astride his horse, he plunged into the river, and while swimming to the other side saw Union soldiers on the bank. When he got there, to get the soldiers' attention, he took off his hat and whirled it around, saying, "Hurrah! Hurrah! Hurrah! I'm in the land of freedom!" The soldiers came over to the exuberant Johnson and said, "You're alright now old man." Later they took him to Ft. Gibson, where he enlisted in Co. F, serving for the duration of the war as an interpreter-soldier.[73]

The First Kansas Colored recruited during their stay at Ft. Gibson in the summer and fall of 1863. The Second Kansas Colored Regiment (later designated the Eighty-Third USCT), organized that summer and fall in

68

Kansas under Samuel J. Crawford, also recruited a company of African Creeks. Lt. J. Tapping, lately with the First Kansas Colored, organized Co. G, primarily comprising African Creek refugees who enlisted after coming into Ft. Gibson following the Battle of Honey Springs. The Second Kansas Colored was active in Arkansas and frequently operated in conjunction with the First Kansas Colored for the duration of the war.[74]

While African Creek soldiers were busy during 1863 establishing their rights to live as free people in the Indian Territory by force of arms, some of their leaders worked to identify and secure their rights by rule of law. Opothleyahola died near the end of March, and although his intractable stand against moving the Creek refugees to the Sac Fox Reservation, and his role in convincing Creek soldiers not to serve outside the Indian Territory, alienated some Creeks, his passing was mourned deeply by African Creek and Creek Indians alike. Oktahasas Hacho (Sands), his chief rival in the controversies, succeeded him as the Loyal Creek chief. A number of African Creeks were close to Sands and his party, among them Harry Island, the former fiddling sinner from North Fork Town and now Sands's chief interpreter. Other African Creek leaders who served as interpreters and advisors for the Loyal Creeks included Monday Durant, Cow Tom, Ketch Barnett, and William McIntosh. The African Creek leaders reminded Sands of Opothleyahola's promise that, if they joined the Loyal Party, "they would be considered as free as their masters."[75]

Sands assured Island and the others that they would not be forgotten in treaty negotiations with the United States, which began after Opothleyahola's death. Island, as Sands's interpreter, was in an advantageous position to put the African Creeks forward. Article II of the treaty ended slavery and accepted "the necessity, justice and humanity" of Lincoln's Emancipation Proclamation. Although the high-flown phrasing implied that the Creeks were compelled by the U.S. Government to abolish slavery, Opothleyahola in fact had issued his proclamation and accepted the African Creeks as comrades in arms in August 1861, fully a year before Lincoln announced his limited emancipation program. Article II further provided that

> the people of African descent in the nation and their descendants, and
> such others of the same race who shall be permitted to settle among
> them, shall have the right to occupy and possess such portions of land

as may be set apart for their use. The laws of said Nation shall be equally binding upon all persons, of whatever race, coming therein.[76]

While the treaty did not specify which portion of the Creek domain would be set aside, "the right to occupy and *possess*" had a ring of finality and promised security for the African Creeks. The Loyal Creeks never wavered from the promise of equality for the emancipated African Creeks, although the treaty process went through many twists and turns during the next three years. Also implied in Article II was the possibility of colonizing freed people from other states on Creek lands. The Creeks, African and Indian, subjected this provision to intense scrutiny, and the idea was alternately rejected and included as the treaty process evolved. Other provisions included an agreement to cede the lands between the Arkansas River and the northeastern boundary of the Creek nation, most of which had been occupied by the wealthy Confederate faction, for relocating the Kansas and other Plains Indians. In exchange, the Creeks would receive a ten-thousand-dollar annual annuity. The treaty was signed by Chief Sands and other Creeks as well as Commissioner Dole and Superintendent Coffin at the Sac Fox Agency on September 3, 1863. Harry Island's name is prominent on the lower left side of the document as the official interpreter. The treaty then went to the U.S. Senate for ratification in spring 1864.[77]

While the Senate considered the treaty, Monday Durant wrote to Commissioner Dole, reminding him of the promises made to the African Creeks:

> Since the death of the Old Chief of the Creek Nation . . . I learn that measures are being taken for making a treaty with said Nation. Now I ask on behalf of the Loyal Africans from the Creek Nation that they have guaranteed to them equal rights with the Indian. . . . All our boys are in the Army and I feel that they should be remembered.[78]

Durant raised an important point. While Article II of the 1863 treaty gave the African Creeks rights to land and made the laws "equally binding," would the Creek laws give them equal protection and allow for equal political participation? The senators kept Article II intact but altered other parts of the treaty to the point that Sands and the Loyal Creeks rejected the final product. Nevertheless, the treaty negotiations signaled an important step in the evolution of the African Creeks' role in Creek society. No longer content with occupying the middle ground, Harry Island and Monday Durant used the negotiations to raise the level of African Creek political participation to near equality. Significantly, when the Creek agent George Cutler took a census of the Creek refugees at the Sac Fox Reservation in December 1863, he grouped his listing of the refugees by towns, in accordance with Creek custom. While some African Creeks were counted in traditional towns such as Coweta, Locha Poka, and Tuckabatchee, among the thirty-six towns listed was a new town—Estu luste. It was a signal that African Creeks—the Estelvste, were indeed a part of the Creek body politic, and it was the beginning of a partnership that would continue through ups and downs until the end of Creek tribal sovereignty in 1906.[79]

As African Creeks were taking the first steps toward securing their legal rights in the Creek nation, the Indian Brigade was securing and fortifying the area around Ft. Gibson. Thousands of refugees, African and Indian, streamed into the fort for protection and subsistence. By all accounts, the Indian country was devastated by the rival armies that had passed through or been stationed there. Roving bands of bushwhackers claiming allegiance to one side or the other left a path of destruction through the countryside. While on scouting or foraging missions, Col. Phillips gathered African Creek families and brought them back to Ft. Gibson for protection. African Creek soldiers from both the First Indian Home Guard and the First Kansas Colored also helped gather African Creek refugees in the area and transport them back to Ft. Gibson. Jim Tomm remembered Tally Lewis, Mose Redman, and other soldiers who rescued him, his sisters, and his mother from the basement of their master's house, which was about to be put to the torch. The soldiers collected three wagonloads of refugee African Creeks and took them back to Ft. Gibson for the duration of the war. Operations in the Creek country that fall, and atrocities committed by Quantrill and other rebel troops, convinced many African Creeks from the North Fork and Canadian River areas, who had led a relatively undisturbed life since Opothleyahola's exodus, to come to Ft. Gibson for protection. The arrival of the additional refugees swelled the number already at the fort and stretched the shrinking supplies available for subsisting refugees and soldiers alike. Although large supplies of corn and wheat were brought in from the countryside that fall, by the end of winter 1863–1864, the refugee families at Ft. Gibson "were reduced to near starvation, so much so that they were glad to hunt the little corn that *fell from the horses and mules of the military*" (emphasis in original).[80]

Even though they were far from the scene of the fighting and were not subjected to the same level of deprivation, African Creeks taken farther west and south by their masters knew hardship as well. The Southern refugees were still slaves, and, as Mary Grayson recalled, "the Chickasaw people didn't treat their slaves like the Creeks did. They was more strict, like the people in Texas and other places." Slaves taken into territory under Confederate control, especially if taken across the Red River into Texas, were also subject to the Confederate impressment laws and could be ordered to work Confederate fortifications or in supply operations. If the work conditions in the Choctaw and Chickasaw country were considered "more strict," then those in Texas were utterly alien to African Creeks. Because most of the able-bodied men "slipped away" to join the Union army, women and children predominated among the African Creek Southern refugees. They were more vulnerable to capture, and many were seized and taken to Texas to be sold.[81]

In February 1864, Col. Phillips commanded an expedition that had both military and diplomatic goals into the western and southern regions of the Indian Territory. Besides hoping to clear the area of remaining rebel forces, he carried with him copies of President Lincoln's Emancipation and Amnesty proclamations. The expedition met little rebel resistance, but few rebel soldiers came in to surrender and accept amnesty. African Indian slaves taken into the far country by fleeing Indian masters earlier in the war, however, flocked to Phillips's party. Thirty African Indians enlisted in the First Indian, among them former slaves from Choctaw and Chickasaw Nations. The regiment now included at least seventy-five blacks from the various Indian Nations in its ranks. Nearly one-third of the men in companies D, E, and I were black.[82]

Even with the increasing enlistment of black recruits, few African Indian soldiers were promoted. Except for Sugar George, promoted to sergeant in May 1864, only a handful of blacks even attained the rank of corporal. George's promotion followed the dismissal of the company commander and the desertion of the second-in-command. Thus, George was the ostensible commander of the unit until September 1864, when George was reported sick in quarters and, rather than have command of the unit devolve to a corporal, 2nd Lt. Co-so-gee from Co. G was attached to George's company as commander. Although George's continuing as de facto commander of his company for five months speaks well for his leadership abilities, that he was not compensated or promoted for his increased responsibilities was only too typical of the army's inability to recognize the contributions of individual African Creeks.[83]

Col. Phillips recognized, in an unofficial way, the important role the blacks played in the unit. Orders issued from the War Department in March 1864 called for the blacks to be mustered out of the Indian regiments and enlisted in the Eleventh U.S. Colored Troops Regiment. Furthermore, Gen. Blunt directed that "all able-bodied male Negroes, within our lines and camps that will pass medical inspection, and are not otherwise employed as servants and laborers, will be required to enter the service as soldiers in Colored regiments.[84]

Phillips realized that most able-bodied African Indians were already enlisted in either the home guards or the First and Second Kansas Colored regiments. He also understood that the African Creeks were "indispensable" to the "good service and discipline" of the First Indian regiment. Consequently, either Phillips ignored the directive or reached some sort of understanding with Gen. Blunt on the issue. Not only did the blacks remain in the First Indian, but their enlistments increased throughout the summer of 1864.[85]

While the federal forces attempted to establish control over more of the Indian Territory, refugees continued to pile into Ft. Gibson for protection. George A. Reynolds, the Seminole agent, said that more than five hundred African Indian refugees, mostly women and children, were camped at the fort or in the immediate area in the early months of 1864. Many of the refugees lived in a camp on the Grand River, opposite the fort; their only shelter were tents made of cowhides from the cattle slaughtered by the government for subsistence. Since the Indian Office disclaimed responsibility for subsisting them and Col. Phillips was without stores for his own troops, the refugees were in a "most pitiable state of distress." Their only subsistence was a small quantity of corn they had with them and beef taken from stray cattle. John T. Cox, a special agent for the Indian Office, reported to Superintendent Coffin that the overcrowded conditions at Ft. Gibson in March 1864 were aggravated by the African Indians who piled into the fort for protection and refused to relocate to refugee camps in Kansas because of "their attachment to the Indian race and the Indian country." Other officials involved with refugees echoed the same opinion, that the refugees, born and raised among the Indians, "had many ties that bind them to this country."[86]

That summer over five thousand refugees returned to the Indian Territory from the camps in Kansas. They joined the ten thousand Indians and blacks who were congregated around Ft. Gibson. The living conditions at Gibson, already frightful, took on truly alarming proportions as disease and hunger grew rampant. A newspaper account described the situation at the fort: "There are thousands of refugees at the Gibson—Texicans, Rackensack Travelers, Indians of various tribes and Negroes, all huddled together around the fortifications and a dirty, lousy, half-starved ragged miserable looking set they were, the sight of which is enough to excite the pity of any human." Under these conditions, it is not surprising that a rash of violence spread through the regiment. There were six murders in the regiment between August and December 1864 and two more in January 1865.[87]

Yet, in what seemed to some to be the low ebb of the Loyal Creek fortunes were glimmers of a brighter future for African Creeks. Through the efforts of African Creeks such as Simon Brown and Monday Durant, and Hannah Worcester Hicks, a white missionary, the American Missionary Society's Freedmen Relief Association provided funds to open Sunday schools for black children at Ft. Gibson in early 1864. Regular Sunday church services were also organized at the fort. Sermons in Cherokee were presented in the morning, in Creek in the afternoon, and services for black refugees were held in the evening. Significantly, unlike during the prewar years in the Creek Nation, the services were segregated into Indian and African congregations, a trend that accelerated after the war. Under the dire circumstances then, the African Creeks were beginning to put their community back together, and, in doing so, they created a different kind of community.[88]

African Creeks from the First Indian were present at the last major engagement of the Civil War in the Indian Territory at Second Cabin Creek on September 18, 1864. In this second battle, the Confederates overwhelmed the Union train escort and captured more than one hundred wagons— subsistence badly needed for the refugees and soldiers congregated at Ft. Gibson. Even though the loss of these critical supplies was quite a blow at the time, this was the only major victory the Confederates would have in the Indian Territory since Union forces had taken control of Ft. Gibson in spring 1863.[89]

Following the disaster at Cabin Creek, most of the soldiering done by the First Indian during the last months of the war involved herding cattle to subsist the soldiers and refugees clustered around Ft. Gibson or chasing the cattle rustlers who plagued the Indian Territory. It was estimated that three hundred thousand cattle, much of the stock belonging to Loyal Indians, were run out of the Indian country to beef contractors in Kansas during the war, decimating the immense herds that were the principal source of wealth in the prewar Creek country. Because many African Creeks were experienced stockmen, they were frequently detailed to round up cattle for subsistence. This brought them into frequent conflict with the rustlers as well as the Loyal Creeks who claimed the cattle. The operations often resembled combat missions. The bands of rustlers were like small armies themselves, allegedly supplied with weapons and ammunition from the Ft. Gibson sutler's shop. The line between official army operations that were intended to subsist the soldiers and civilians and cattle rustling was blurred by conflicting claims to the cattle and the involvement of army officers and Indian Office officials in the illegal trade. Once again, African Creeks found themselves in the middle ground, where their own interests were difficult to define in the clash between white army officers and Creek Indians.[90]

In early 1865, the First Indian returned to the Creek country and this time established permanent camps near the Creek Agency and Tullahassee Mission on the eastern edge of the nation. The soldiers gave some measure of protection for the African Creeks living there and the Creek and African Creek refugees who wanted to return to the area. Many of the African Creeks, among them Simon Brown and Pickett Rentie, resettled in the rich bottomlands of the Arkansas-Verdigris river valley formerly occupied by their rebel masters. Jackson McIntosh and his family continued living on the same farm, the only difference being that it was no longer recognized as part of Roley McIntosh's holdings. Although the First Indian detachments were not specifically ordered to help the blacks to reclaim the land, their presence pacified the area and held rebel bushwhackers at bay while the refugees returned.[91]

As the war neared its end, Phillips asked the War Department to keep the soldiers in service long enough so that they could be detailed to assist in planting spring crops, mending fences, and repairing buildings in the devastated countryside. He also asked the Agriculture Department to send seed and potatoes to help get the planting season started. The African and Indian soldiers worked together beating their swords into plowshares for several weeks before they were mustered out in May 1865. It was a fitting end to a long and brutal conflict.[92]

The African Creek and other black soldiers in the First Indian and the First and Second Kansas Colored played a vital role in the Civil War in the Indian Territory and in Arkansas and Missouri, though their contribution was seldom recognized or rewarded. Nevertheless, they served. During the war, acting as interpreters, scouts, and soldiers, the African Creeks also learned some valuable lessons in politics. The rigors of war tested the African-Indian alliance, but the alliance survived to play an important part in the Creek nation's politics in the postwar era. The blacks sacrificed much for their service in the First Indian and the First and Second Kansas Colored regiments, but they had won their freedom. The testament to that sacrifice and how it was linked to that of the Indians in the Creek Nation can be seen at the Ft. Gibson National Cemetery, where the graves of the African Creeks and Creek Indian soldiers lie side by side.[93]

AFRICAN CREEKS

3

"To Do More Than the Government Has Seen Fit to Do"

Reconstructing Race in the Creek Nation

THE RECONSTRUCTION YEARS WERE FILLED WITH PROMISE for the African Creeks, and chronicle one of the unheralded success stories of reconstructing race relations in the United States in the years following the Civil War. Under the 1866 Creek Treaty, they secured equal political, economic, and social rights in the Creek Nation, which included an equal share in all tribal funds and annuity payments. The treaty also granted African Creeks "full rights to the soil." They quickly established themselves on the lands of their former masters, where Creek laws recognized their rights to share in the Creek commonwealth, and developed as a stable class of yeoman subsistence farmers. Indeed, as Eric Foner has written, alone among the four million emancipated African Americans, the Creek (and Seminole) freedmen in the Indian Territory actually received "forty acres and a mule."[1] African Creeks also participated fully and freely in the fractious political life of the Creek nation during these years, as the Creeks struggled to establish a constitutional government patterned after Euro-American institutions while retaining traditional political organizations.

After the surrender of Confederate forces in the Indian Territory in the early summer of 1865, peace came at last to the Creek country, and the Loyal and Confederate factions searched for a place and time to meet and begin their reunification. On August 4, 1865, showing that Article II of the aborted 1863 treaty was no fluke, Sands and the Loyal Creeks passed a law in their tribal council that gave African Creeks full citizenship rights. African Creeks later designated August 4 as the date for their annual Emancipation Day celebration.[2]

U.S. officials were anxious to revive the treaty-making process that had ground to a halt with the Loyal Creeks in 1864. After a series of discussions with Confederate and Loyal factions over the location of a peace parley, secretary of the Interior James B. Harlan designated Ft. Smith, on the Arkansas–Indian Territory border, as the site. Representatives from all tribes of the Indian Territory who had signed treaties with the Confederacy were summoned to the council, and the parley was set to begin in the first week of September. President Andrew Johnson appointed Commissioner of Indian Affairs Dennis N. Cooley and Southern superintendent Elijah Sells to lead the U.S. peace commissioners. Col. Ely Parker, a Seneca Indian and Gen. Ulysses S. Grant's military secretary, was another member of the U.S. delegation. Oktahasas Hacho (Sands), Micco Hutke, Cowetta Micco, Cotchoche, Locha Hacho, and Sandford Perryman led the Loyal Creek delegation, and Harry Island was the official Creek interpreter. Ketch Barnett, Tobe McIntosh, Scipio Barnett, Jack Brown, and Cow Tom, as citizens of the Creek Nation, represented the African Creeks, and Robert Johnson served as interpreter for the Seminoles. The council began September 9, although the Southern Creek delegates, D. N. McIntosh, James G. Smith, Thomas Adkins, Timothy Barnett, Yah Kinhar Micco, and William Robinson, did not arrive at the meeting until September 16.[3]

Although no Southern delegates were present yet, at the start of the council Commissioner Cooley blasted the delegates for their "perfidious conduct" in joining the Confederacy. He then outlined the seven points that Secretary Harlan wanted to include in new treaties with the Indians. Only the first two propositions had to do with making peace. The various tribes in the Indian Territory were to make a permanent peace with the United States, and each other, and help bring the Plains Indians into peaceful relations with the United States and other tribes. The next two points adjusted relations with free blacks and former slaves in the Indian nations. The tribes must abolish slavery, emancipate their slaves, and give them equal rights in their nations. The fifth point included a proposed land cession for the resettlement of the Indians removed from Kansas "and elsewhere." The sixth point required all tribes to form a "consolidated government" as a prelude to organizing the Indian Territory for entering the Union. The seventh point promised "no white person will be permitted

AFRICAN CREEKS

to reside in the territory, unless formally incorporated with some tribe." Cooley closed saying that the commissioners expected definitive replies to all the points raised.[4]

Cooley's remarks shocked the Loyal delegates. The Commissioner classed them with the treasonous Confederates. They were equally surprised to learn that the United States expected them to make a new treaty, having understood that the Ft. Smith Council was only meant to reunite them with the Southern faction. In his reply to Cooley, Sandford Perryman vigorously defended Opothleyahola, the Loyal Creeks, and the part they had played in defending the Union and disclaimed responsibility for making any treaty with the Confederacy. Indignantly, he informed the commissioners that the Loyal Creeks should not be classed with the rebel party. They had no problems with abolishing slavery, emancipating the African Creeks, or incorporating them into their tribe. In fact, they had already done all these things on their own initiative beginning in 1861. Nor did the Creeks have difficulty with the idea of setting aside a portion of their lands for the Plains Indians. But they and the Seminoles both declined to have their "lands to become colonization grounds for the Negroes of other states and territories," a proposition first put forward during the 1863 treaty negotiations in Kansas. The Loyal Creeks saved their most strenuous objection for the idea of giving up their sovereignty and being incorporated into the United States as a territory.[5]

When D. N. McIntosh and R. G. Smith arrived on the scene, they filed their own response to Cooley's proposals. Although they agreed to emancipate their slaves, they asked to be compensated for it. They objected to giving them equal rights in the tribe, saying, "We agree to emancipation of the Negroes in our Nation but cannot agree to incorporate them upon principles of equality as citizens thereof—and we cannot believe the government desires us to do more than it has seen fit thus far to do." The Southern Creeks agreed with the other propositions but asked that they be given time to consider the territorial proposition and be allowed to form a tribe separate from the Loyal Party.[6]

While it was true that the Creeks were being asked to "reconstruct" racial relations to a greater degree than any of the Southern states, it was to no greater degree than what the Loyal Party had already done. As for the idea of compensated emancipation, it had not been entertained seriously since Lincoln had tried to keep border-state slaveowners loyal to the Union during the early war years. Similarly, the proposition that the Southern Creeks could "secede" from the tribe and be able to share in tribal funds and annuities after they had sided with the Confederacy was not an acceptable alternative. After registering their protests, the Southern and Loyal parties composed their differences, at least outwardly. On September 18, the reconciled parties signed a preliminary agreement of "peace and amity" between themselves and the United States and pledged to negotiate a definitive treaty at a future date in Washington. The Creek delegations returned to their country to begin reuniting their people upon a new foundation in which African Creeks would be considered citizens and participate equally in tribal affairs.[7]

Through the council, the Creeks were introduced to the designs of the government in reconstructing the Indian Territory. The actual document drafted at Ft. Smith was only part of the story. As Annie Heloise Abel has written, the real importance of the Ft. Smith meeting could be discerned only through identifying the "would be railroad magnates," land speculators, and promoters of "Indian progress" who hovered in the wings. Their agenda would be postponed, however, until the definitive treaty was drafted and signed. Also embedded in the subtext of the meeting was how the commissioners treated the delegations. While Cooley upbraided the Loyal Creeks for the rebels' crimes and chided them for their obstinacy in refusing to yield on larger issues, he almost deferred to the former Confederates, promising them protection from any possible reprisals engineered by unionist Indians. The commissioners were a far cry from being the rabid abolitionists as portrayed in later years by Creek "redeemers."[8]

It is not clear whether Cooley and the commissioners solicited the African Creek delegation to attend the council or what part the delegates played in the deliberations, but they were there, and their names were included in the official printed transcript of the proceedings. An African Creek oral tradition suggests that they played a larger role than just names on a transcript:

> The colored delegates were pushed forward to speak for the Indians. They seemed to be able to better express the wishes of the Creek tribe than the Creeks themselves. The Government officials . . . said, "We want to talk to the Indians, what are these colored men doing the talking for?" The Creek Delegates said, "What's the matter? We want

them to talk for us." So the Government saw that the Creeks thought of the Negroes as being equal with themselves.[9]

In later years, some Creek redeemers maintained that the abolitionist commissioners led the Indians by the nose while the wily Harry Island and other willful African Creeks inserted language in the treaty different from the Loyal Indians' true sentiments. But on one of the final days of the council, after both Loyal and Southern factions had signed the agreement, translated by Harry Island, the Loyal Creeks read a statement that would seem to be a straightforward and unequivocal regard for African Creek rights: "We are willing to provide for the abolishing of slavery and settlement of the blacks who were among us at the outbreak of the rebellion, as slaves or otherwise, as citizens entitled to all the rights and privileges that we are."[10] Their position had not changed since a similar statement was made in drafting the unratified 1863 treaty. If the African Creek interpreters were pulling the wool over the Loyal Creeks' eyes, it would have to have been done at least twice. With the Southern Creeks in the room and the ink not dry on the agreement before them, it is not credible that the Loyal Creeks did not understand what the words in the agreement meant.

After the agreement was signed, its outlines were quickly disseminated throughout the Indian Territory. Scattered in refugee camps from Kansas to North Texas, with some still living on farms hidden away in the Creek country, African Creeks got the news that the war was over and freedom was at hand. Yet another great exodus began that fall after the peace council. This migration reversed the movements during the war and created settlement patterns that conformed to the new boundaries of the racial frontier found in the Creek country as a result of the war.

Jackson and Hagar McIntosh and their nine children were an exception —African Creeks who were not refugees. After living out the war on their farm on Gar Creek in the Verdigris River bottoms, Jackson McIntosh received word from former chief Roley McIntosh's family that the Southern Creeks had "done sign up to quit the war" and that he and his family were free. Roley McIntosh had died while in exile near the northeast Texas town of Jefferson in 1863. The McIntosh family told Jackson that he could stay where he was or he could take up some land on his own. Jackson decided to remain on the Gar Creek farm with his family. The chief's family, instead of returning to their holdings in the Verdigris-Arkansas river valley, resettled farther south in the North Fork area after their return from exile in Texas. Although emancipation altered the cultural dynamics of power and obligation that had held sway under the patron-client system, the prewar system had been so loosely jointed that it was but a small step to put African Creeks in control of the land they farmed. In the prewar years, African Creeks could settle anywhere good soil and water could be found on McIntosh's vast holdings; the difference now was that their choice of land was not limited to that land under McIntosh's control.[11]

Emancipation reunited Lucinda Davis with her mother and father, Stephany and Serena Gouge, from whom she had been separated at a young age after being sold to Tuskaya-hiniha. Davis recalled that she must have stayed with her master for some time after the war was over. She said Tuskaya-hiniha did not know where to send her or whether her parents were even still alive. One day, while she and Tuskaya's family were on an abandoned farm in the south Canadian River bottoms that they had occupied during the war, three men rode up and spoke to Tuskaya in English. Davis did not understand the conversation, having heard only Creek spoken since she was a child. Tuskaya told her to go with the men, who were from the Creek Agency, because she was free now and they had come to take her back to her family. He set young Lucinda in front of one of the men on horseback and they took off, without collecting any of Lucinda's things. Eventually Lucinda was reunited with her parents at the Creek Agency, which was used as a repatriation center.[12]

Mollie Perryman and her family also learned about their emancipation from their master. They had spent almost three years at a refugee camp for Southern sympathizers along the Red River in the Chickasaw Nation. Mose Perryman casually and peevishly informed Mollie that the war was over, they were free, and they would have "to root for themselves." He then just rode away without offering any help or advice on what they should do next. Mollie heard from other African Creeks that they were going to get equal rights with the Creeks and that they should go to the Creek Agency for help. So Mollie and her ten children set off on foot for the agency, some two hundred miles away. According to Mary (Perryman) Grayson, Mollie would stop and "find a little something to do" along the way to get food for her children. After three or four days of walking, they met another black family who had a horse, and Mollie paid them to let her children take turns with the other children riding. When they came to a river, they would wait until

AFRICAN CREEKS

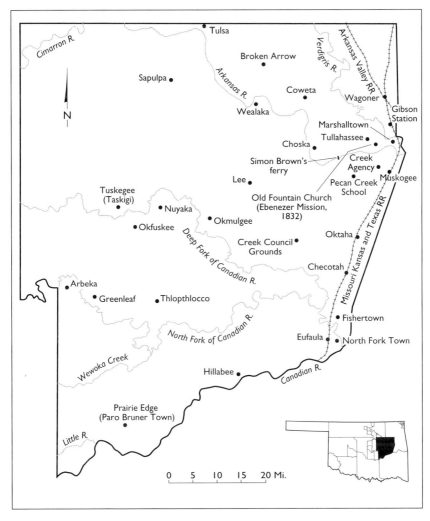

Creek country, 1866–1907.

someone came along with a wagon to cross, and at one stream they had to wait an entire day. When they got to Wealaka on the Arkansas River, they met an African Creek family also on their way to the agency. This family had a wagon, and Mollie paid them to let her family ride the remaining distance. Once they got to the agency, Mollie sent word to her husband, who had been mustered out of the First Indian Home Guard at Ft. Gibson, that they were alive and well. After their reunion, the Perryman family settled just east of where they had lived in the Choska bottoms as slaves, cleared some land, and built up a prosperous farm there. Unlike other former slave-holders from the Arkansas-Verdigris valley, Mose Perryman did not relocate after the war but instead maintained an extensive ranch in the area. Despite his callous treatment of Mollie and her children at the refugee camp, Mose Perryman (and other Creek former slaveowners as well) did not attempt to thwart his former slaves from establishing farms on his plantation lands.[13]

As African Creeks flooded back into the Creek country during fall 1865, the Creek Agency and the surrounding settlement became a beacon for freed people. In November, after returning from the Ft. Smith Council, the new Creek agent, J. W. Dunn, began distributing food and supplies at the agency. Dunn also issued five-dollar stipends so that freedmen refugees and their families could either return to their old homes or resettle elsewhere. Dunn reported that the Creeks "were in advance of all the states, having not only emancipated their slaves, but they have adopted them into the nation with full and equal rights with themselves." Dunn might well have added that African Creeks were given "full rights to the soil," which proved to be the foundation of a stable community life for African Creeks and contrasted sharply with the fate of the virtually landless freed people in the Southern states.[14]

Located about twelve miles west of Ft. Gibson and one mile south of the Arkansas River, the Creek Agency village was a trading center and a thriving community even before the war. After the war, the African Creek population around the agency exploded, in part because the Creek freed people were the first ones to move to the Creek lands from Ft. Gibson in the last months of the war. Their former owners were still in exile in the South. In negotiations for the 1863 treaty and at the Ft. Smith Council, the idea of separate lands set aside for the Creek freed people was aired, but the idea never was incorporated into the final treaty. Perhaps there was an informal arrangement to set aside the rich bottomlands in the Arkansas-Verdigris river valley for the freed people to settle while most of the Creek planters who had allied with the Confederacy relocated in the North Fork area and established the town of Eufaula. More likely, the Confederate Creeks, who knew the Loyal Creeks had ceded the lands north of the Arkansas River to resettle the Kansas Indians in the first version of the 1863 treaty, felt they had nothing to lose by yielding lands that were going to be sold to the United States anyway. Some Creeks arranged transfer of occupancy and sold their improvements to freedmen. Tobe McIntosh bought all of George W. Stidham's cattle, horses, and improvements for nine hundred dollars in gold and settled all his relatives on the former Stidham holdings, and Stidham relocated to North Fork. Cow Tom left his place along the Canadian River and bought the improvements on a new farm and ranch along Cane Creek, near a community known as Blackjack.[15]

Regardless of whether any agreements were reached, formal or informal, African Creeks settled and developed communities throughout the Creek Nation in the coming years, just as they had in the prewar days. Not being confined to a specific geographic district turned out to be a tremendous advantage for the Creek freed people, as subsequent events would reveal.[16]

Freed people, like all tribal members, could settle in any part of the nation not already occupied. Rather than a fee-simple title to a certain section of land, which governed land ownership in Euro-American communities, the Creeks, who held their tribal lands in common, had a use-title arrangement. The fee-simple title to the Creek domain remained in common with the tribe, and whatever part of the Creek lands an individual could cultivate remained under the individual's control. People could sell improvements on that certain piece of land and pass the improvements on to their descendants. In other words, a house, corn cribs, fencing, or even orchards were alienable but not the land itself.[17]

With unlimited access to land and the freedom to use it as they saw fit, African Creeks actually realized the dream of forty acres and a mule that was denied freedmen in the Southern states. In the Creek commonwealth, African Creeks had the opportunity to develop an independent yeomanry that erstwhile Republican reformers in Congress and agrarian Democrats could only dream of but never realize because of the sanctity of private property. While Southern freed people could only begin the process of negotiating for a labor system that gave them more control of their lives, and which dead ended in the sharecropping system, African Creeks came into immediate control of the means to establish an independent livelihood —free and unlimited access to land and the right to develop it as they saw fit.

After the "united" Creeks had returned to their country, a tribal council was held on November 5 to organize the political affairs of the nation. The council was held at African Creek Scipio Barnett's farm, not far from the old council grounds where the Creeks had met in tribal council before the war. Barnett was a prominent free black merchant, pastor, and farmer in the Canadian district before the war, and he would go on to become a major political figure in postwar Creek politics. At the council, Samuel Checote, elected chief by the Southern Creeks in 1864, stepped aside. The unified council accepted Sands as the principal chief and selected him to head the delegation that would negotiate a new treaty in Washington. Sands invited the Southern refugees still living in Texas and in the Chickasaw and Choctaw country to come back and resettle their old homes. The meeting being held at Barnett's farm signaled that the freedmen had arrived as full political participants in Creek affairs.[18]

Following a tenuous concord established between the two factions in November, the United States summoned the Creeks to Washington to conclude the business of negotiating a new treaty. Sands, Cowetta Micco, and Cotchoche, with Harry Island as their interpreter, left Ft. Gibson on December 26. Robert Johnson accompanied the Seminole delegation. The Cherokee delegation, Secretary Harlan, and Seminole agent George A. Reynolds rounded out the rest of the party.[19]

The train trip from the western frontier to the capital covered not only physical distance but racial distance as well. Arriving in St. Louis on January 8, Harlan "fully explained the situation" to the railroad ticket agent, that seven in their party were Indians and two were black. He had no difficulty buying first-class passage from St. Louis to Washington for everyone. The trip went smoothly until they reached the station at Bellaire, on the Ohio–West Virginia line. There the conductor refused to seat the delegates in the first-class section and sent them forward to second-class seats. Harlan confronted the conductor, saying that the Indians were the chiefs and headmen of their tribes, ordered to Washington by the president to negotiate a treaty. The conductor coolly replied, "they are not all Indians." Harlan said, "they are black men, but they are members of the tribe and interpreters to the delegation and all have received first-class tickets and the road has received their fare. And now what do you say, shall they be allowed to take their place or not?" The conductor merely walked away and "insultingly" refused to answer the secretary. Harlan later filed a protest with the railroad company and received an apology from the president of the company, J. W. Garrett. Garrett felt that Harlan and Reynolds were perhaps overreacting because "the party seemed to be comfortable and getting along satisfactorily" in the second-class section and went on to explain: "There is great difficulty in getting conductors and other subordinates to understand the nice questions that arise—especially in this quarter where there has been for so long recognized such a distinction between colors, which circumstances are now rapidly removing."[20]

The incident illustrated the problems people from outside the Creek country had when confronted with the conditions prevailing on the racial frontier. The "nice questions" were ambiguous in the Creek country. But not in the country at large. Perhaps the Indians would have been accorded the same treatment if the freedmen were not with them; but when the Creeks arrived in Washington to make their treaty with the United States, even though the secretary of the Interior tried to intercede for them, they came into the city as second-class citizens because they were accompanied by their African Creek compatriots.

The delegation began negotiations immediately upon their arrival in Washington in early January. D. N. Cooley, Elijah Sells, and Ely Parker acted as treaty commissioners for the United States. Meanwhile, back in the Creek country, the Creeks had been in an almost "continuous council." From one of the councils, led by Samuel Checote, the Southern Party decided that they too should send a delegation to Washington. D. N. McIntosh and James M. C. Smith were selected to represent them. Checote gave the delegates instructions to cooperate fully with the Loyal Party "in a spirit of harmony and friendship and for the best interest of the whole without reference to their former difficulties."[21] They applied to Dunn, who was preparing to leave for Washington, for permission to accompany him. Dunn wired Commissioner Cooley, who authorized the trip with the caveat that furnishing McIntosh and Smith with transportation should not be construed to mean that they were "looked upon as official delegates." The

Southern delegates did not reach the capital until February 22 and were surprised to find that the Loyal Creeks had nearly finished negotiating a treaty and were preparing to sign it.[22]

A draft of the treaty, which the Southern Party had taken no part in negotiating, was ready on March 3. McIntosh and Smith asked to see a copy of the treaty on March 5. Although the Loyal Party signed the document on March 6 and proclaimed themselves satisfied with the results, McIntosh and Smith asked for a meeting between the two parties to discuss making amendments, "provided it could be done with the consent of those who made it." The meeting took place in the Loyal Creeks' rooms at the Union Hotel, where the delegations, according to Creek Agent J. W. Dunn, had a "free and friendly talk in relation to the treaty and their troubles for the past four years." The conference ended, however, when Sands and the Loyal Creeks pronounced that they alone were authorized to make the treaty, reiterated their satisfaction with the results, and declared that McIntosh and Smith had no authority to act for the Creek nation.[23]

After the rebuff by the Loyal Creeks, McIntosh and Smith submitted their objections to the commissioners on March 18. They protested being excluded from the negotiations and argued that the United States offered "inadequate compensation" for the land cession required. Furthermore, they objected to allowing only the Loyal Creeks to be compensated for losses sustained during the war and wanted a guarantee that Indians' rights would be protected if the Indian country was organized into a territory. Their most vigorous protest was reserved for the clauses in the treaty that made African Creeks citizens with full political, economic, and social rights in the Creek Nation on a basis of full equality with the Indians.[24] Their paternalistic remarks could have described the patron-client slave system that had evolved in the Creek country but probably did not represent the conditions prevailing on McIntosh's own plantation, so closely modeled after white Southern plantations: "Our people were proverbially kind to their slaves; indeed their servitude was merely nominal. They possessed plenty and were content and happy." Then, McIntosh's argument took a rhetorical detour and expanded on the opinions already expressed at the Ft. Smith conference:

> We believe it is right, and we are determined to protect the interests of
> the Negroes who were among us before the war; that is, what of them

who are left, and their descendants, care for their welfare and see that they have justice and right *in every respect compatible with their condition* [emphasis added]. But, we believe that our ancient care and kindness ought be a sure guarantee that their interests and welfare will be safe in our own municipal jurisdiction. We never had, and have not now any disposition to injure or tyrannize over them. Still, we cannot recognize them as our equals. . . . It is we conceive, contrary to nature and nature's laws.[25]

McIntosh went on to say that the Southern Creeks were willing to give the African Creeks a "separate locality" in the nation where they could "better work out their own fate."[26]

In a separate letter to President Johnson, McIntosh and Smith composed well-reasoned arguments concerning the land cession, the amounts to be paid the Loyal Creeks, and organizing the Indian country for territorial status. In their argument against incorporating the African Creeks into the tribe, they used the same language that Johnson had used in his recent veto of the Civil Rights Act, saying that forcing the Creeks to give the freedmen full political, social, and economic rights in the Indian nation would only sow discord between the races by requiring the Creeks "to violate our existing laws, usages and customs; to forget in a day the lessons of two hundred years, and to do what thus far, has not been done by any of the states in the union, North or South." They reminded Johnson, "we feel fully assured that the President cannot fail to see that the whole article [Article II] is at war with his own often expressed views and opinions." McIntosh and Smith were on target in pointing out that their beliefs were in accord with Johnson's. However, as far as "forgetting the lessons of two hundred years" is concerned, apparently *they* had forgotten that race consciousness based on skin color was a fairly recent development among the Creeks, and as the Loyal Creeks had shown over the last five years, some Creeks had little use for the idea still.[27]

Nonetheless, McIntosh and Smith hit a responsive cord with the president, who was in the midst of a battle with Congress over the Civil Rights Act and the Freedmen's Bureau bill. Johnson returned the treaty to the Creeks for amendment shortly after receiving the Southern Creek protest. Sands and the Loyal delegates once again rejected any attempts to alter the treaty. They asked Harlan these simple questions: "Who led the brave

Creeks . . . through the snow in the dead of winter, their women and children barefoot, living on horseflesh for weeks, was it McIntosh and Smith? We think not. O-po-the-le-he-yo-ho-lo led us. Who, at Leroy, Kansas, when called upon to fight for our Government entered the Army for the Union, was it McIntosh and Smith? . . . Where were they at the Battles of Honey Springs and Cabin Creek . . . were they in the ranks of the Union Army[?]" Even after this stinging rebuke, Harlan and Cooley tried to convince the Loyal Creeks to compromise, but it was no use. On May 8, Sands, Cotchoche, Cowetta Micco, and Harry Island issued an ultimatum from which they refused to retreat.[28] Cooley reported to Harlan:

> They held out firmly for the freedmen, urging that when the brave Opothleyahola, resisting all the blandishments of the rebel emissaries, and of his Indian friends, stood out for the government . . . they promised their slaves that if they would remain also faithful to the government they should be free as themselves. Under these circumstances the delegates declined to yield, but insisted that the sacred pledge should be fulfilled, declaring that they would sooner go home and fight, and suffer again with their faithful friends than abandon the point.[29]

On May 26 McIntosh and Smith withdrew their protest to Article II, and it remained in the treaty, a testament to the African-Creek alliance that still survived but that the Southern Creeks wanted erased from their history. The article endorsed the Thirteenth Amendment and then went on to state the terms on which the African Creeks would be incorporated into the tribe:

> And inasmuch as there are among the Creeks many persons of African descent, who have no interest in the soil, it is stipulated that hereafter these persons lawfully residing in said Creek country under their laws and usages, or who have been thus residing in said country, and may return within one year from the ratification of this treaty, and their descendants and such others of their race as may be permitted by the laws of said nation to settle within the jurisdiction of the Creek Nation as citizens [thereof], shall have and enjoy all the rights and privileges of native citizens, *including an equal interest in the soil and national funds* [emphasis added], and the laws of the said nation shall be

equally binding upon and give equal protection to all such persons, and all others of whatever race or color, who may be adopted as citizens or members of said tribe.[30]

The Creeks were truly in advance of any of the states, North or South, in extending legal equality to people of African descent. There was, however, one stipulation: African Creeks had to return to the nation within one year of the treaty's signing; otherwise they would not be eligible for citizenship rights and could be expelled from the nation as intruders. At first glance this provision appears reasonable, but many African Creeks, particularly women and children taken south during the war, did not have the means to return, especially if carried to Texas or other former Confederate states.

With full rights to the soil, the dream of "forty acres and a mule" and the development of an independent yeomanry would become a reality in the Creek nation. While the Republican politicians Harlan, Cooley, and Sells were willing to abandon the African Creeks, the Loyal Creeks stood firm and protected their rights. The idea that the radical Republicans in the federal government imposed racial equality on the Creeks, as maintained by some Creek politicians, was a fiction invented to justify disfranchising the Creek freedmen in later years.

The other provisions in the treaty, promoted and endorsed by radical Republican reconstructionists, would have a telling impact on the freedom the African Creeks enjoyed in the Indian nation and, as Angie Debo has written, underscore the Reconstruction treaty's true intent. Under Article III, the Creeks ceded 3.25 million acres of their western lands to the United States for resettling the Plains Indians and freed people. Interestingly, the tract ceded did not include the Arkansas-Verdigris bottomlands as proposed earlier, but did include the less desirable and not as well-watered lands west of 96° 30'. The removal of the Indians from their lands in the West was an integral part of the postwar plans for developing the area. The ambiguous wording in the clause, which made no distinction between Indian freedmen and state freedmen, caused a great deal of confusion and controversy in later years. For the Creeks, the clause referred only to Indian freedmen. For the U.S. government, the term applied to all freedmen from the former slave states. To some government officials and politicians, it seemed an easy solution to the problem of providing for emancipated African Americans short of incorporating them into American society.[31]

The Creeks received a fraction of the actual value of their ceded lands: thirty cents an acre, or $975,168 for the entire tract. The United States then bought the entire Seminole domain for fifteen cents an acre and sold a portion of the Creek cession to them for fifty cents an acre. Although the treaty stated generally that funds were to be distributed among the Creeks, who would receive how much was a source of continued friction in the tribe for many years.[32]

Article V gave rights-of-way for two railroads to run through the Creek country, one east-west line and one north-south line. And, almost immediately, Congress granted franchises to two railroad companies. This provision of the treaty opened the Creek country and the Indian Territory to economic development and to non-Indian intruders from the states. The railroad corporations brought in thousands of nonnative laborers to build the lines, and many remained behind as illegal intruders. Railroad emissaries, with an enormous reservoir of capital and political clout, were the most vocal and active agents for development of the Indian Territory resources and lobbied incessantly in Congress and among tribal leaders for easier access to them.[33]

In Article X, the Creeks agreed to accept the authority of the U.S. Congress to make laws for the Indian Territory. They also agreed to organize a general council of Indian tribes in the Indian Territory as a prelude to establishing true territorial status for the Indian country.[34]

The treaty was finally signed on June 14, 1866, and proclaimed in effect on August 11. Unfortunately for the freed people, the promise of equality contained in Article II, so far in advance of any states in the Union, was compromised by the other provisions in the treaty. The surrender of Creek sovereignty and the railroad grants opened the Indian Territory to economic reconstruction that would offer the lion's share of benefits to nonnative developers. In the process, cultural traditions underpinning the fluidity that characterized race relations in the Creek country were swept aside in the name of progress and civilization.

As the treaty was being negotiated in Washington, back in the Indian Territory, the federal government stepped in briefly to oversee racial reconstruction among the Indians. The Interior Department sent Gen. John B. Sanborn to the Indian Territory as a special agent "to regulate the relations between the freedmen in the Indian Territory and their former masters." Sanborn's appointment was a response to numerous reports concerning freedmen mistreatment sent to the Freedmen's Bureau. Sanborn arrived in Ft. Smith on December 24, 1865, to begin his investigation.[35]

In his first report, Sanborn described the conditions in the Creek country differently from the reports that had drawn him to the Indian Territory. He said that "the Creeks looked upon the freedmen as their equals in rights and are in favor of incorporating them into the tribe," and perhaps more important, the African Creeks themselves felt secure in their rights. The alarming reports that had inspired Sanborn's appointment had principally come from the Choctaw and Chickasaw nations. While he was down along the Red River in the Chickasaw-Choctaw country investigating conditions, he found many Creek and Cherokee freed refugees there and recommended to Commissioner Cooley that the Indian Office provide transportation for them to their homes before the spring planting season began.[36]

In March and April, he issued other directives to ensure that freedmen families had access to enough land to plant their crops. Freed people could remain on the lands they had cultivated or improved before the war or on the plantations where they were held as slaves if the master had abandoned those lands and gone south during the war.[37] He instructed Maj. Pinkney Lugenbel, the commander at Ft. Gibson, to protect freed people who cultivated unused or abandoned fields and to prevent anyone from collecting rents from freed people who put unused lands into production. But, once again, this was more of a problem in Cherokee country than among the Creeks, although J. S. Atkinson, one of the merchants at the Creek Agency settlement, who was filling in for Dunn while he was away in Washington, reported some conflicts between African Creeks themselves over who had preemptive rights to certain fields. Atkinson had to call out the Lighthorse to protect "Aunt Lydia's" rights to a field and even had to "bring one man to the Limerick [jail?]" to settle things. Just when he thought the matter was resolved, another Creek freedman, recently arrived from Kansas, came in and claimed the field "over everybody's head."[38]

Satisfied that matters had been adjusted sufficiently, in April Sanborn handed in his commission and left the Indian Territory. He had found little that needed adjusting. Labor contracts, which consumed so much of the Freedmen's Bureau's time in the Southern states, and elicited so much dissatisfaction from planters and freed people alike, were unnecessary among the Creeks. African Creeks took advantage of the stipulation in the treaty that granted them equal rights to the soil and began establishing farms and homesteads without interference from federal officials or their former slaveholders.[39]

Following the treaty signing in Washington, June 1866, more freed people streamed back to the Creek country. The countryside surrounding the Creek Agency just south of the Arkansas River and the area in the Point on the nation's eastern edge became major settlement areas for African Creeks. From the agency ten miles west along the Arkansas was "a continuous line" of African Creek farms, where an estimated one thousand African Creeks lived and farmed in the bottomlands formerly controlled by wealthy Creek planters. The Creek Agency village became a thriving settlement and trading center almost completely occupied by Creek freed people. Fifty families lived in the settlement, and many freedmen community leaders located there after the war, among them Simon Brown, Joseph P. Davison (also known as Buzz Hawkins), Jesse Franklin, Jonathan Kernel, Harry Island, Tobe McIntosh, Scipio Sango, Pickett Rentie, and Peter Steadham. There were two stores in the settlement before the Civil War, and two more were added as the village grew. After the war, Sarah Davis rebuilt her hotel there as well. Sophia Canard, a Creek freedwoman, opened a cake and sweet shop, which became a favorite hangout for the children. Meanwhile, Canard's husband had a thriving bootleg whiskey business operating in the back of the shop.[40]

Freedmen in the settlement were often employed to carry out routine business for the agency. In addition to providing interpreters, African Creeks helped the agent carry out the government's duties. Jesse Franklin and Sugar George had contracts to provide Agent Dunn with firewood. Tobe McIntosh had the government teamster contract for hauling subsistence and supplies to the agency for distribution. Other freedmen transported noncitizen prisoners to Ft. Gibson and Ft. Smith or served as messengers for Dunn, including posting his important letters. Freedmen became involved in the day-to-day operations of the agency, in fulfilling government contracts, and in forming political connections that linked their interests with those of the federal government.[41]

Education was a primary concern for African Creeks in the years after the war. Even before Creek national funds became available in 1867, they organized schools in communities throughout the nation, using their own resources and hiring their own teachers. A school was located in the center of the Creek Agency village, and Laura Hitchcock, D. D. Hitchcock's daughter, was the first teacher. Ellen Rentie, a Creek freedwoman, also taught there. Schools opened in the Blackjack community, west of the agency village, and at Cannan, to the north. Cow Tom sponsored a school near his Cane Creek ranch in the Canadian district and paid the teacher out of his own pocket.[42]

As the area around the Creek Agency and in the Point, became more populated with freed people, some Creeks complained that the agency "was surrounded by colored people whilst [the] Agency is for the Indians" and felt it should be moved closer to the center of the nation. The Southern faction, who protested the loudest, wanted the agency located farther west and south, on the Deep Fork of the Canadian. Dunn fielded the complaints but reckoned that since freed people were incorporated into the tribe on an equal basis and were not restricted to living in a certain district, "it would seem then that one portion of the country is as legitimate for red as for black and that distinctions of color can not be bounded by distinction of territory." Besides, moving the agency would have meant that Dunn would be a day's ride from established mail routes and supplies at Ft. Gibson.[43]

While a large number of freed people settled near the agency and in the Arkansas-Verdigris bottomlands, African Creeks, as Dunn intimated, settled throughout the nation. An elderly African Creek, interviewed in the 1930s, recalled that after the Civil War, Indians and freed people lived along the Canadian River as next-door neighbors, without racial animosity. A vibrant African Creek community continued in North Fork Town and the surrounding area in the years after the war, even after the planter aristocrat families abandoned their lands in the Arkansas-Verdigris river valley and moved to the area. William Nero operated his store, stagecoach, and blacksmith's shop there until his death in 1872. David Lee, an African Creek who became a Creek tribal lawyer in the years after the war, as well as a leading entrepreneur, established a settlement called Wellington on Cane Creek west of the agency village. The town that sprang up there was later renamed Lee and grew into a thriving settlement, which housed a hotel, store, and stagecoach station after a road was built through the area, linking the agency with the new Creek capital at Okmulgee. Although some neighborhoods were inhabited exclusively by either African Creeks or Indians, as Sigmund Sameth has written, this was largely due to "differences of economic interest rather than racial hostilities." Significant numbers of African Creeks were enrolled as citizens in many Creek towns, and even Coweta, the

Lower Creek town claimed by the McIntosh family, had a substantial African Creek population enrolled there. The Southern Creeks, who had lobbied for a separate district for the freed people, kept African Creeks at a social and residential distance, but they did not sponsor any legislation in the Creek Council to mandate racial segregation, regulate freed people's behavior, restrict their mobility, or impede their access to land.[44]

By summer 1866, some African Creeks were still unable to find transport back to the Creek country. Daniel Miller, a First Indian veteran, led an expedition into Kansas to collect African Creek families and shepherd them back to the agency village. Besides bringing families together and reinforcing African Creek community bonds to correspond to the contours of emancipation, Miller and other Creek freedmen leaders were anxious that refugee African Creeks return to the nation by July 14, 1867—the deadline for taking advantage of citizenship rights outlined in the treaty. Refugees in the South had a much harder time meeting the deadline. Though the physical distance for the Creek freed people taken into the Choctaw and Chickasaw nations and Texas was shorter, the social, cultural, and political separation was much wider. Outrages reported in the Choctaw and Chickasaw nations had prompted Sanborn's special commission. Similar reports came from northeast Texas, where racial violence and murders of freed people were common. Despite the violence and other impediments, some freed people, like Mollie Perryman, managed to make it back to the nation by July 14. But numerous African Creek refugees in Texas, most of them women and children, did not. The cases of these freed people, who for various reasons were unable to return in time, would be a focus of major political conflict in the nation in coming years.[45]

Even though many African Creeks were yet accounted for, the transition to freedom was relatively free of racial tension. At the end of 1866, J. W. Dunn made an optimistic report regarding the African Creek's future: "Several Creeks have predicted that the Negroes will prove the most capable intelligent and industrious citizens, certainly they promise well . . . the freedmen have planted larger crops, have attended them more faithfully and today are farther advanced from want than the former masters."[46]

In early 1867, the Creeks met again in council to begin putting their political nation back together. The old council house at High Springs had been destroyed during the war, so the two sides met at Blackjack Grove, near Rock Creek, six miles southwest of where Okmulgee now stands. At the council sessions and at other meetings during the following months, the Creeks hammered out the outlines of a new government and selected Okmulgee as the new capital. The united Creek council unanimously adopted a constitution in October 1867. The Creeks formed three branches of government roughly resembling the U.S. federal system. The executive branch consisted of a principal and a second Chief elected every four years. The legislative branch, called the national council, comprised two houses—the House of Kings, the upper legislative body, and the House of Warriors, the lower house. Representatives to the national council were chosen by the eligible male voters eighteen or older. Forty-seven tribal towns, which now included three African Creek towns—Arkansas Colored, North Fork Colored, and Canadian Colored—elected representatives to the national council. Each town elected one member to the House of Kings and one to the House of Warriors, with an additional warrior for every two hundred people in the town. The constitution also created a judicial branch, with a supreme court and six judicial districts. The national council elected supreme court and district justices, and the principal chief appointed prosecuting attorneys for each district. The voters in each district elected a Lighthorse Company, which was similar to a sheriff's office, of one captain and four privates to enforce the laws.[47]

The Creek towns served a ceremonial, or cultural, function as well as a political one. It was through the towns that clan and moiety ties were maintained, and local political and social control was established under town chiefs and their assistants. Most Creeks continued to live close to their towns, and even if they moved to another section of the nation, they still participated in the town's cultural and political life. After the constitution of 1867 was adopted, the towns served as electoral districts for tribal elections and remained the most important political and social structures in the nation, despite the federal government's efforts to increase power and respect for the new Creek national government.[48]

The freed people's towns created under the new constitution followed the traditional Creek pattern, though apparently they did not serve ceremonial functions such as providing a location for a poskita ceremony. The Indian towns had a geographic location where the town square ground was located and a kinship network that spread throughout the Creek country. The freed people's towns, on the other hand, had no specific geographic boundaries. Town identification, rather, was based on a family having once lived in one of the areas encompassing either the Arkansas, North Fork, or Canadian River valleys. Identification with a certain town, like in the Indian towns, was based on kinship ties rather than current residency. For example, Simon Brown, Monday Durant, and Tobe McIntosh all lived in or near the Creek Agency settlement. Yet Brown represented North Fork Colored, Durant represented Canadian Colored, and McIntosh represented Arkansas Colored at the Creek Council. Town kings, equivalent to the town chiefs, or miccos of earlier days, kept membership rolls for the towns, and freed people had a much easier time switching their allegiance from town to town since their clan and moiety ties were apparently not a factor in town membership, except when African Creeks were enrolled in the traditional Indian towns. Settlements included in a town were not necessarily geographically contiguous, although they could be. Arkansas Colored corresponded roughly to the freed people who had lived or had kinship ties in the Arkansas-Verdigris valley on the northeastern edge of the nation. North Fork Town originally included the freed people who lived in the North Fork of the Canadian River settlements and those that extended north and west along the Deep Fork of the Canadian River. Canadian Colored was the most amorphous freed people's town. It contained a number of small scattered settlements spread over a wide area that overlapped with North Fork Colored. Originally centered at Wellington (later named Lee), it later shifted south to along the Canadian River, with its headquarters at Paro Bruner's settlement, called Prairie Edge, near the present location of Holdenville. The town of Lee later became the center of North Fork Colored.[49]

Since the majority of freedmen voted in only three towns, their votes were not scattered among the forty-four other tribal towns near which many of them had their farms and businesses. The arrangement, which to the uninformed observer would appear to be an egregious gerrymander, was thoroughly grounded in traditional Creek ideas about community identity and representation and was a significant political advantage for the freed people, especially in the House of Warriors, where the number of representatives allotted a town was determined by population. Arkansas, North Fork, and Canadian Colored, with a combined population of nearly two thousand, sent as many as thirteen representatives to the House of Warriors and three to the House of Kings in the early years of the constitutional government. Although there were more Indian towns, none of them sent more than two or three warriors to the lower house, and most sent only one. Thus, as Angie Debo has written, the freedmen constituted an important faction in the ninety-six-member House of Warriors. Although they voted as a block on issues such as citizenship and equitable division of tribal funds, and they generally could be counted on to support Sands's Loyal Party, on issues of local importance that came before the council, African Creek representatives showed a pronounced independent streak.[50]

Sugar George, Simon Brown, Harry Island, Ned Robbins, and Robert Grayson were some of the earliest African Creek representatives from North Fork Colored. Jesse Franklin, Scipio Sango, and Ben McQueen represented Canadian Colored. Although some of the freedmen in Arkansas Colored apparently sided with the anti-constitutionalist Creeks in boycotting the first sessions of the national council, by 1869 William McIntosh, Tobe McIntosh, Thomas Bruner, and Monday Marshall had taken seats in council representing Arkansas Colored. Sugar George and Simon Brown were some of the most active members. Among the most important of the early laws passed by the council in the freed people's interest was legislation adopting freed people who had returned within the one-year limit specified in the treaty, but who were too late to be counted in the census roll Dunn had compiled in March 1867. One hundred and thirty-nine freed people had their citizenship confirmed under this legislation. Sugar George and Simon Brown sponsored other legislation and actively participated in the debates during the early council sessions. In the process, they gained political reputations in the nation as fixers that transcended the parochial interests of the freed people's community.[51]

African Creek participation also included judicial appointments. The council selected Monday Durant as judge, and Sugar George was elected prosecuting attorney for the Arkansas District. Court sessions were held at the Creek Agency settlement. By 1874, Jesse Franklin, one of the leading African Creek citizens in the agency settlement, was selected by council as one of the five supreme court justices after serving as a judge for the Creek Agency settlement for several terms. Since Creek freedmen formed a sizable majority in the Arkansas District (renamed the Muskogee District in 1877), the Lighthorse officers, elected by popular vote, were typically African Creeks. The Coweta District, which included Marshalltown and other African Creek settlements on the north side of the Arkansas River, also elected African Creek officers from time to time. William Nero and Sugar George earlier had been skilled blacksmiths, so it is not surprising that they were given the public blacksmith contracts issued by the nation for North Fork and Concharty towns, one of the few political patronage jobs given out by the early Creek constitutional government. Judging from the number of Creek freedmen involved in or elected to the Creek government without federal army protection or experiencing violent intimidation, the Creek freedmen's political experience was one of the unheralded freedmen success stories during the early Reconstruction period. What is more, African Creeks not only maintained their level of involvement in Creek politics through the nineteenth and early twentieth centuries but also expanded their role.[52]

There was opposition in the nation to African Creek inclusion, however, and one of the first controversies involving the freed people's status concerned equal distribution of national funds. When Agent Dunn prepared the census roll needed to distribute the two hundred thousand–dollar per capita payment due the Creeks from selling the western portion of the Creek lands to the United States, he counted the freed people, anticipating that they would share equally in the payment. Article II of the 1866 treaty clearly stipulated that African Creeks should share equally in the distribution of tribal funds. Dunn counted 1,774 African Creeks, and the Dunn roll became a talisman conferring legitimate citizenship for African Creeks. While Dunn maintained that he had made every effort to count all Creek freed people then living in the nation, many freed people later testified before Creek citizenship committees or the Dawes Commission that attempts to seek out freed people, except those close to the agency, were dilatory at best. In any case, the census was incomplete, and it was compiled at least six months before the July 14, 1867, deadline for African Creeks to return.[53]

On March 13, 1867, the evening before the per capita payment, a special messenger from Ft. Smith brought a telegram from Commissioner of Indian Affairs Lewis V. Bogy telling superintendent William Byers that freed people were to be excluded from the payment. Apparently, Checote had earlier written to the Indian Commissioner with a legal argument regarding why the treaty should be interpreted to eliminate African Creeks from the payment. Dunn later said that this was the first he had heard that the freed people would not be paid. A letter from William Nero to Freedmen's Bureau commissioner O. O. Howard in February 1867, however, indicated that even before the crucial telegram arrived, the superintendent had decided that freed people were not eligible for the payment. To complicate matters, Byers had earlier distributed a payment to African Seminoles for the sale of the Seminole lands without pause or controversy, even though the 1866 Seminole Treaty contained almost the exact wording found in the Creek Treaty regarding "people of African descent" and their rights to national funds.[54]

The African Creeks immediately sent Harry Island, Cow Tom, and Ketch Barnett to Washington to plead their case. The freedmen brought their complaints to Congress, and with former treaty commissioner and Interior Secretary Harlan sitting as a member of the Senate Subcommittee on Indian Appropriations, they were able to establish that the intent of Article II in the treaty was indeed that freed people should share in the per capita payment. Amid comments from some on the committee that they had never "heard of an Indian of African descent" or that such a person must be a "somewhat singular individual," in July 1868, the subcommittee approved a provision inserted in the 1868 appropriation bill that no moneys appropriated to the Creeks would be paid until the African Creeks received their per capita share of the 1867 payment. Even though ordered to proceed with the payment by Congress, and with freedmen representatives in the national council, the Southern Creeks were able to push a law through council that mandated a $5.34 deduction from the $17.34 payment to cover the nation's "outstanding liabilities." Commissioner Ely Parker, however, disallowed the law, and the full payment finally took place in April 1869.[55]

According to the Loyal Creeks, freedmen participation in the first election for principal chief held in November 1867 was obstructed. Freedmen voters were not directly intimidated, but, according to Sands, Checote's men, knowing that with the freedmen vote the Loyal Party would have the majority, rigged the election, using, as Sands called it, "the white man's law" to ensure that they would come out ahead. Their complaint was that instead of using the traditional Creek voting method in which candidates and their supporters showed up at the council grounds on election day, and the candidate with the most people lined up behind him won, the Checote party insisted that each voter record his choices on paper. Most Creeks at this time were illiterate, and Sands and the Loyal Party objected most vehemently to the process, which gave an advantage to the mission-educated leadership in Checote's party. Sands further charged that the opposing party manipulated the councils leading up to the election to deny Sands the principal chief's post. Despite the protests, the U.S. government affirmed the election results and recognized Checote as principal chief and Micco Hutke as second chief. Checote had invited Micco Hutke of the Loyal Party to run with him in an attempt to form a consensus government, but the gesture was lost on the Loyal Party as Sands and others condemned Micco Hutke as an apostate and refused to accept the results. Following the election, disgruntled Loyal Creeks, in traditional Creek fashion, withdrew from national politics and organized their own government, headquartered at Nuyuka Town on the Deep Fork, northwest of Okmulgee, and sent a delegation to Washington in 1868–1869 to plead their case, to no avail. Aside from their complaints about the fraudulent election, they also objected to what they thought was an unfair distribution of national funds and the Checote government's failure to recognize African Creek rights.[56]

The seething bitterness threatened to spill out of control in August 1869 when Sands sent his Lighthorse to North Fork Town to arrest some of Checote's men, accused of crimes against Loyal and freed people. As Angie Debo and others have written, both sides seemed to have provoked violence, but the U.S. government stood by the so-called progressive Constitutionalist Party because its leadership seemed more willing to assimilate Euro-American political and cultural values. There were also rumors afoot that Sand's men had plans to march on the capital at Okmulgee and overthrow the Checote government. Checote notified the Creek agent, Franklin A. Fields, who immediately sent for U.S. troops at Ft. Gibson. Fields hastened to North Fork and convinced the Loyal Lighthorse to disband. Sands later denied any intention to march on the capital and claimed that Checote had purposively misconstrued the situation in order to enlist the U.S. government's aid in repressing the Loyal Creeks.[57]

Following the 1869 flare-up, both sides aired their complaints at a Creek Council meeting. Political matters appeared to cool. The Constitutionalist Party even offered to amend the constitution, but the intransigents in the Loyal Party were committed to maintaining their separate government and again refused to participate.[58] Most African Creeks supported the Loyal Party during the upheaval, but they were less willing to step completely aside from the operations of the constitutional government. Some African Creek leaders, such as Sugar George and Simon Brown, remained committed to the Creek constitutional government and actively participated in the Creek National Council.

In summer 1870, Harry Island attempted to broaden African Creek participation in tribal affairs. He petitioned Checote to have African Creek delegates appointed to the upcoming First Indian Territory General Council scheduled at Okmulgee that fall. Checote demurred, saying that the decision was up to the national council, which had already selected its representatives, but he did offer to give the matter "his prompt attention" should a vacancy occur. Undeterred, Island next asked Agent Field to take up the matter with the Indian Commissioner. Field asked Acting Commissioner W. F. Cady to give the matter "favorable consideration" because he considered the freedmen equal citizens, and they were "clamoring for their rights." Cady supported the idea but felt the Creeks should work out the details themselves and declined to intervene.[59]

The U.S. government was more willing to intervene in another matter directly related to the freed people's status. In early 1871 several African Creeks were released from custody by the federal circuit court in Ft. Smith on the grounds that they were Creek citizens charged with a crime in the Creek Nation against another Creek citizen; therefore, under the terms of the 1866 treaty and the Indian Intercourse Acts, the federal court had no jurisdiction over them. Agent F. S. Lyon, recently installed as the Creek agent, protested to the Indian Commissioner and urged him to intervene. The men, he said, were desperadoes charged with murder, and he feared they would be acquitted by the lenient Creek courts. Checote sent his own protest to Lyon, saying, "The Colored people are regarded by the Creeks as their citizens having been made so by treaty stipulations. . . . They are to all intents and purposes part and parcel of the Creek nation. We claim full jurisdiction over them subject to be tried in our courts by our laws, which they have helped to make."[60]

Checote's statement was as close as he ever came to admitting that African Creeks were entitled to full citizenship rights in the nation. For Checote, the issue was not race and equality, however, but how to protect Creek sovereignty in the face of federal encroachment, even though by Article X of the 1866 treaty, the Creeks were forced to surrender the ultimate power to make laws to Congress. Acting secretary of the Interior B. R. Cowen weighed the arguments and followed an earlier Interior Department ruling regarding white-adopted Creek citizens and the Indian Intercourse Acts. That ruling held race, not citizenship, as the guiding principle in jurisdiction. According to Cowen, since the accused African Creeks were not "Indians," they were subject to the jurisdiction of the U.S. courts. Lyon's protest and Cowen's decision might have been meant to bring order to the Creek community, but they had the opposite effect. Desperadoes of all types, no matter what their skin color, would welcome freedom from Creek justice. Although Creek courts were considered too lenient by Euro-American standards, particularly regarding property crimes, parties proved guilty of more serious crimes could expect swift and sure punishment.[61]

A new secretary of the Interior, Columbus Delano, reversed the decision in early 1872, saying that the earlier ruling violated the spirit and intent of Article II of the 1866 treaty. He maintained, however, that the African Creeks were still not considered Indians in the government's view. The government's construction of African Creek identity was shared by many of the elite acculturated Creeks, but other Creeks recognized that many African Creeks had stronger Creek kinship ties to "Indianess" than those in leadership positions in the nation, who claimed authority through their Indian heritage. Most African Creeks identified themselves as Indians or natives, followed Creek cultural traditions, but retained their bilingual abilities. African Creek identity would take on fuller meaning during the 1880s and 1890s, but for now the freedmen were busy carving out their place in the political life of the nation.[62]

In spring 1871, the factions began to position themselves for the September election for principal chief. Agent Lyon was also busy, determined to force the Sands party and their African Creek adherents to follow the constitutional forms. Cotchoche, the Loyal Party candidate for chief, told Lyon that the Loyal Party intended to vote "standing on their feet" in the traditional way rather than being counted on paper. Lyon replied that the only method the U.S. government would sanction was the one outlined in the Creek constitution. Sands and the Loyal Creeks persisted and worked out a compromise with the Constitutionalist Party that allowed Sands and his followers to use the traditional Creek method while Checote's votes were recorded on paper. Lyon nonetheless objected to the arrangement and insisted that the U. S government would recognize only officials chosen by the constitutional method. African Creeks stood solidly with the Loyal Party during this voting method controversy, partly because the Loyal Creeks were the ones who held out for retaining Article II in the treaty and had defended African Creek interests on other occasions as well. Also, despite their efforts in establishing schools, most African Creeks at this time were illiterate, and like the uneducated Indian majority of the Loyal Party, they had good reason to be suspicious of measures that required voters to be able to read. Voting on their feet seemed to the Loyal Creeks a much more honest and open way to conduct an election. The Loyal Party instructed their followers to be at the capital, rather than in their separate towns, on the appointed day.[63]

Some days before the election, Martin Vann, a Constitutionalist Party follower, told William McIntosh, the freedman leader from Arkansas Colored, "Whatever you do, stay away from Okmulgee, for Pleasant Porter told me that Col. Checote had issued orders to keep the colored people out of Okmulgee." There was also a report that the Loyal Creeks would impose a fifty-dollar fine on anyone voting in their town rather than on the ground in Okmulgee. Under pressure from both sides, McIntosh confidently led the Arkansas Colored freedmen to Okmulgee anyway. They camped on Cane Creek near Hardy Stidham's farm overnight on September 5. There they got a second warning that Checote's men were armed, picketing on the outskirts of the capital, and ready to use force to keep the Loyal Party from reaching the council house. The next day McIntosh and his followers met Checote's picket guards along the road, about a mile and half from the capital. Pleasant Porter came out to meet McIntosh, and Porter told him, "There is no danger—go in carefully." McIntosh replied, "There is no danger in me. I did not come to fight with my arms—but with my tongue and such little brains as I have." McIntosh and his party then marched into Okmulgee, went through the town, and into camp on the other side with Sands. The next day. the Loyal Party went to the council house, found it empty, and sent a dispatch to Checote, inviting him to council. After waiting some time, the Loyal Party, including African Creeks from the three Colored towns, assembled at the Okmulgee Council Grounds and voted on their feet for Cotchoche as principal chief, Futchalike as second chief, and Sands as speaker. Although there were some irregularities in tabulating the Constitutionalist Party vote, for the most part, Constitutionalists stuck to the mandated procedure and recorded their votes on paper in the towns.[64]

Following the election, both sides laid down their arms and returned home to wait for the council to convene in October and canvass the election results. But again, the opposing parties prepared for armed confrontation in the days before the council meeting. Agent Lyon intervened and convinced both sides to send delegates to a special council to count the votes. Two African Creeks, William McIntosh and Charles Colbert, were among the four delegates representing the Loyal Party. According to Chi Kee, one of the Loyal Party town chiefs, before the special council convened, Checote and the Loyal Party agreed to a plan to allow those "voting on their feet" to be fairly counted, because, as Chi Kee said, "we are one color," and attempts to divide Creeks by color or faction was the cause of the recent trouble. But once the meeting began, Lyon took control, and in the words of Futchalike, the delegates were treated "like a fatherless child," not allowed to speak or to protest the agent's actions as he threw out a majority of the Loyal Party votes. Lyon himself said later that Cotchoche had the majority, but because he was illiterate and wanted to go back to the old ways, he was unfit to be chief. The final "official" count gave Checote 1,129 votes to Cotchoche's 862.[65]

The freedmen towns' votes were among those accepted by the committee, and the freedmen cast their votes in unison for Cotchoche and Futchalike. Their votes counted for over 35 percent of those given to the Loyal candidates. Clearly African Creeks remembered well the pledge that Opothleyahola made to them before their exodus to Kansas and how Sands and the Loyal delegates had stood by them at the Washington treaty negotiations. But abstaining from participating in the Creek constitutional government held no advantages for the freedmen. Except for Arkansas Colored Town, which sent only one representative of the four they were entitled to the House of Warriors (Isom Marshall) and no representative to the House of Kings, freedmen elected two members to the House of Kings, Cow Tom from Canadian Colored and Simon Brown from North Fork Colored. From Canadian Colored, the freedmen sent Jesse Franklin, Benjamin McQueen, and Scipio Sango to the House of Warriors, and North Fork Colored sent Harry Island, Ned Robbins, and Sugar George to the 1871 council.[66]

There was renewed trouble during fall 1872. J. B. G. Dixon, a British citizen, had been employed by the Sands party to represent their complaints to Washington. The Constitutionalist Party vigorously objected to Dixon's activities, portraying him as a foreign intriguer agitating for the overthrow of the constitutional government. Other white men from Kansas, with connections to the railroad interests, including George A. Reynolds, the former Seminole agent, added to the political tensions by working among the Loyal Party and freed people during the year. In early 1872, the north-south railroad provided for in the 1866 treaty established its first terminal in the Creek country, at Gibson Station, and later in the year built a station that would eventually become the town of Muskogee. Railroad boosters from Kansas were anxious to extend their political influence in the nation after Checote and the national council turned aside their requests to develop town sites along the right-of-way. Discord in the nation would work to the advantage of the railroad companies and other speculative interests in their efforts to push territorial bills in Congress, legislation designed to extend federal control over the Indian nations and extinguish tribal title to Indian lands.[67]

Meanwhile, Sands and the Loyal Party's white patrons bombarded Washington with petitions and letters that resulted in an investigation of Agent Lyon's role in the 1871 election. Indian Commissioner Francis A. Walker sent Enoch Hoag, the central Indian superintendent, and Robert Campbell to the Creek country to investigate the matter and to take testimony in summer 1872. After finishing their work, Hoag and Campbell spoke to the assembled parties before leaving and advised them to reject the influence of outside forces and to heal their differences. They suggested that advances in education and industry would be "a more formidable and effective shield to ward off threatened [U.S. citizens'] encroachments than any legislation."[68]

Shortly after Hoag left the Creek country, Checote and the Constitutionalist Party, following Agent Lyon's advice, and ignoring the counsel of the peace commissioners, pushed a body of repressive laws through the national council, intended to rein in subversive activities and impose law and order in the freed people's communities in the Point, where organized gangs of horse thieves allegedly operated in the Loyal Party's district to evade Creek government control. While there was indeed lawlessness, much of the lawbreaking could be attributed to nonnative railroad workers who flooded into the area during this period and were beyond the control of Creek law.[69] Five former First Indian and First Kansas Colored freedmen veterans were charged with stealing horses in the Arkansas District Court in June 1871, but the jury found them not guilty because the horses, lacking brands and ranging freely, "were mistook for wild horses." Checote called out nine hundred Lighthorse in August and early September, ostensibly to pursue horse thieves. But, according to William Graham, a disaffected teacher at Tullahassee Mission and one of the "intriguing white men" whom Checote complained of earlier, "the Lighthorse were patrolling the country in all directions as though they are wanting to provoke a fight" and had captured and punished several men. Graham described the alleged horse thieves as "a set of smart active fellows that had hard masters in the times of slavery, and since the war, consider themselves abused by their government." On one other occasion, the well-armed Lighthorse shot up a freed people's dance party and wounded several people.[70]

By the first week in September, both sides were preparing for battle, and Checote reportedly issued orders saying, "there will be no playing this time." On September 3, Col. B. H. Grierson, commanding a detachment of Ninth U.S. Cavalry, bivouacked at Ft. Gibson and sent Hoag an urgent telegram, saying that the opposing parties were assembled for battle. Checote and five hundred men at Okmulgee were preparing to move against the Loyal Party, now under the leadership of Locha Hacho (Sands had died in 1872, before the troubles in the fall), gathered with three hundred men south of the Creek Agency. Although the freedmen sympathized with the Loyal Party and complained about their treatment at the hands of the Creek government, most stayed home during the confrontation.[71]

Hoag and Lyon again brought the opposing parties together in council in October. Both parties agreed to disband their armies and said they would accept the decision of Hoag's commission, which investigated the 1871 election. The report, finally issued in 1873, criticized the agent's lack of discretion during the election controversy but sustained Checote. It rejected the Loyal Party's calls for a new election and informed the disaffected Creeks that the U.S. government would use force to sustain the Creek constitutional government in the future. Hoag suggested the Creeks hold conferences on election procedures before the next election with the help of "some person" associated with the Indian Office to educate the disaffected Creeks in understanding the proper procedures. While the Loyal Party objected to the report, they abided by the decision and agreed to come under the Creek Constitution.[72]

Following the concord established in 1873, African Creeks and their Loyal Creek allies threw their efforts into preparing for the 1875 elections.[73] African Creek support for Locha Hacho was solid, and they provided able organizers and counselors for his candidacy. One of Locha Hacho's chief advisors was Silas Jefferson from Taskigi Town. Jefferson was known as Tucker in the African Creek community and by his Creek name, Ho-tul-ko-micco. Jefferson was the only African Creek to represent one of the Creek Indian towns in council, serving alternately in the House of Kings and the House of Warriors from Taskigi. He claimed Creek citizenship by blood through his Creek Indian mother Betsey McNac, a member of the influential Wind Clan. Monday Durant, Simon Brown, Sugar George, and William McIntosh also continued their active roles in political affairs. But the African Creeks lost some of their most effective spokesmen during this period; Harry Island, Ketch Barnett, William Nero, and Cow Tom all died in the early 1870s, and new leaders, more amenable to establishing an alliance with the Constitutionalist Party, came forward.[74]

In contrast to the previous elections, that of 1875 went off without controversy. African Creek towns voted unanimously for Locha Hacho and Ward Coachman for principal and second chiefs. The freedmen votes and those from the conservative towns were duly recorded by a clerk, and Hacho and Coachman won the election over Checote and Pahose Emarthla by almost two to one. African Creek towns sent a full complement of representatives to the national council in 1875, three to the House of Kings: Monday Durant from Canadian Colored, Sampson Hawkins from Arkansas Colored, and Simon Brown from North Fork Colored. Eleven African Creeks served in the House of Warriors that council session: Jesse Franklin, Jack McGilbray, Ben Barnett, and Paro Bruner from Canadian Colored; Robert Grayson, Sandy Perryman, and Tom Richards from North Fork; and Thomas Bruner, Jeffrey Smith, Daniel Miller, and Snow Sells from Arkansas. The Creek Council elected Jesse Franklin to the supreme court following Hacho's installation as principal chief and later elected Henry C. Reed as judge in the Arkansas District (which was renamed the Muskogee District). Sugar George was elected prosecuting attorney in the Arkansas District. Most of the Lighthorse elected in the Muskogee District were African Creeks, reflecting the substantial majority the freedmen held there. In the Coweta District, Daniel Miller was elected prosecuting attorney, and he later served there as Lighthorse captain.[75]

But the peaceful transition of power was thrown into jeopardy in late 1876. The council, still controlled by the Constitutionalist Party, impeached Locha Hacho after only a year in office for failing to execute the laws, in particular a law passed by council calling for the removal of the British intriguer Dixon. Hacho had informed the Commissioner of Indian Affairs earlier in the year that Dixon's "services are discontinued," but apparently this did not satisfy the Constitutionalists. All the African Creeks in the House of Kings, except for Monday Durant, who was in Washington, voted against Hacho's impeachment. Even though less than the required two-thirds of both houses voted for impeachment, Hacho was removed and the Indian Office sustained the coup d'etat. Petitions from the African Creek towns on behalf of Hacho flooded the Indian Commissioner's office, but they had little effect beyond identifying the freedmen with the "disgruntled party" and categorizing them as against progress in the eyes of the Indian Office.[76]

Ward Coachman succeeded Hacho as principal chief, and although he was viewed as a usurper by the Loyal Party intransigents, he did work to bring the African Creeks to his side. Coachman endorsed citizenship legislation for freed people who had returned too late to satisfy the requirements of the 1866 treaty. Most of those included in the legislation clearly had ties through kinship to substantial Creek Indian families, and their residency in the Creek Nation predated removal from the East. Monday Durant, Simon Brown, Ned Robbins, Paro Bruner, H. C. Reed, and other freedmen legislators took the occasion to push for more legislation. One item, endorsed by Coachman and passed by the council, included an appropriation to establish a boarding school for freed people's children. The freedmen legislators made a successful case showing that freed people's schools received less than their equal share in tribal education funds. In order to make up the difference, the legislators calculated the shortfall from school appropriations since 1866 and appropriated three thousand dollars to establish a freed people's boarding school.[77]

The boarding school would make secondary education available for young African Creeks for the first time. Since 1868 African Creeks had established eight neighborhood day schools with Creek funds, located in the areas of the nation where freed people had the densest population. Most were located in the Arkansas-Verdigris river valley, but several were built in outlying areas. The leaders in the African Creek communities served as trustees for the various schools, and the rosters of African Creek trustees read like a who's who of important political and religious leaders in the African Creek community. An estimated two hundred African Creek children attended the schools; and, according to Louis Howell, a white teacher in the freed people's schools, African Creek children came to school more regularly and in greater numbers than Indian children because "the Colored parents were more eager for their children to go to school." While the Creek Nation made distinctions between the Colored schools and Indian schools and funded them separately, apparently some Indian children attended the freed people's neighborhood schools and reportedly benefited from being in class with bilingual African Creeks.[78]

Besides increasing political participation and expanding educational opportunities for their children, African Creeks established their own churches during the Reconstruction period. In the prewar years, African Creeks had played a leading role in establishing the first churches and providing the first preachers in the Creek country. Most early churches contained mixed congregations of African Creeks, Indians, and whites. While African Creeks did establish some churches with only black devotees in the prewar years, after the war, the move toward creating separate Indian and freed people's churches accelerated. The separation of Indian and African Creek congregations perhaps indicated a growing racial consciousness among the Indians who followed the Southern Baptist Convention but also pointed to the growing independence of the freed people's community. Anna Eliza Robertson (from Tullahassee Mission) noted in letters to friends that Simon Brown was busy establishing a church "for the Colored people" at the Creek Agency immediately after the war and lamented the fact that they no longer came to services at the Tullahassee Mission. Brown built up the separate freed people's Second Baptist Church, which remained one of the largest and most influential freed people's churches in the Creek country, even after most of the Creek Agency settlement moved west to Muskogee. The estrangement from the Presbyterian mission had less to do with racial identity than sectarian issues. African Creeks at this time generally found the enthusiastic Baptist services and creed more to their liking than the reserved Presbyterian worship and doctrine. The Old Fountain Church, the first Baptist church established in the Creek country, with Ketch Barnett as the pastor, became an African Creek church after the war. Other freed people's Baptist churches included ones at Blackjack, Blue Creek, Cane Creek, Canaan, and Wewoka. Monday Durant, Jesse Franklin, and Jonathan Kernel carried the work forward for freed Baptists. In 1876 and again in 1877, Durant and Kernel went on fund-raising tours in the East and visited congregations in New York, Washington, and Boston, succeeding in gaining "substantial aid" for churches and schools in the Creek country. Freed people took a further step toward independence when they established the Freedmen Baptist Association in 1877, as a separate body from the Indian Territory Baptist Association, to coordinate freed people's missionary and church activities. As in African American communities in the states, African Creek churches became important focal points in the freed people's communities in the Reconstruction years and after. Through the churches, Creek freed people's communities coordinated social, cultural, educational, and political activities, and many African Creek leaders were also preachers, pastors, deacons, or at least involved in church organizations.[79]

The success of African Creeks in developing political, social, and economic independence during the postwar years rested squarely on their "rights to the soil" stipulated in Article II of the 1866 treaty. With unimpeded access to land, most Creek freedmen developed into a class of independent subsistence farmers during the Reconstruction years. Ten acres was considered a good farm, and corn was the principal crop. Most families ground their corn into meal rather than using it as stock feed. Sweet potatoes, peanuts, vegetables, and peach and cherry orchards were also widely cultivated. Rice was raised to a limited extent. Wheat was rarely planted because good seed was expensive and hard to come by. Most farmers also raised cattle, hogs, and horses as well as chickens and turkeys and supplemented their diet with wild game, fish, wild fruits, berries, and nuts. A majority of freedmen maintained a subsistence lifestyle, worked their own land, and had no reason to hire out their labor or work land as tenants or sharecroppers. Their preference was based in part on cultural attitudes toward accumulation and agricultural production they shared with culturally conservative Creeks. As small producers, they also had little incentive to farm for the market beyond the Creek country because of transportation difficulties. Whatever the reason for freedmen's subsistence farming, their choice gave them more control of their lives. They avoided sharecropping and the debt-credit cycle that would draw so many Southern African American farmers into virtual economic slavery.[80]

African Creek cotton production illustrates their lack of engagement in the market economy. Creek freed people raised cotton mainly for home use, cleaned their cotton by hand, and then spun, wove, and dyed their own cloth. The situation changed little after the Creek government issued a permit to John A. Foreman, a white noncitizen, to establish and operate the first gin in Muskogee during the 1870s. Even then, African Creeks maintained their distance from the labor-intensive crop. Foreman tried to entice freed people to plant more cotton by offering free seed to all who promised to raise the crop, but he had little success. According to the Commissioner of Indian Affairs report, there was no cotton production among the Creeks in 1873.[81]

The construction of the railroad through Creek country in 1871–1872 had a major impact on the fate of the African Creeks and Creek society. The laborers used to build the line constituted the first major influx of non-citizen intruders in the postwar period. Also, the railroad interests pressured the Creeks to grant rights-of-way for townsites and further development. The railroad incursion also changed the dynamics of land use as the bulk transportation of agricultural goods from the area became more economical. Creek citizens began to employ noncitizen tenant farmers to raise commercial quantities of staple crops under a permit system drawn up by the Creek Council. Interested citizens could apply to the chief to hire noncitizens to farm their lands. Upon paying a tax, the citizen could then employ a noncitizen for a specified period, usually a year. Many substantial Creeks took advantage of the permit law to restart commercial farming operations that had been in limbo since the war and emancipation. Unlike the situation in the Southern states, where landless freedmen and their families were exploited as an agricultural labor force, the large majority of permit men (as the tenant farmers were known) were landless white farmers from the surrounding Southern states. African Creeks with the means to do so also used the permit system to bring in tenant farmers. Here was a rare situation: black landlords with white tenants. Jesse Franklin, David McQueen, Tobe McIntosh, and Sarah Davis all employed tenants on their lands during the 1870s. Once the permit men and their families were in the Creek country, however, they proved difficult to dislodge. Although the Indian Intercourse laws were supposedly still in effect, and the federal authorities in the Indian Territory supposedly had the authority to remove noncitizen intruders, the authorities rarely took action. Many permit men and their families remained, untouched by any laws and free from paying any taxes.[82]

A dialectic emerged in the workings of the permit system that would have major implications for African Creeks. Because African Creeks worked for themselves, owned their own farms, and for the most part rejected entering into wholesale cotton production on their own lands, progressive Creeks had to look elsewhere for labor to produce cotton and other agricultural commodities for market. Landless white farmers from the neighboring states filled the role that black sharecroppers and tenant farmers did in the South. These newcomers brought their racial attitudes with them and added their voices to the growing clamor in the states to open the Creek lands for settlement and to organize a territorial government for the Indian Territory. The coming of the railroad thus had an impact on the Creek country that went beyond mere economics. Its construction formed the leading edge of a new "reconstruction" of the Creek Nation.

At the end of Reconstruction, African Creeks were in an enviable situation compared with African Americans in the South (and, for that matter, in the North). With unlimited access to land, they established a foundation from which independent political, social, and economic action was possible. From this base, they navigated the tricky political waters and established themselves as a political force in the Creek Nation.

Their alliance with culturally conservative Creeks was a natural one, but combining with that faction perpetually in opposition to the Creek constitutional government held no advantage for the freed people, especially since the constitutional government had the full backing of the United States and the power to distribute national funds (with approval of the national council) as it saw fit. By the time Coachman became principal chief in 1877, an influential majority of freedmen leadership threw in their lot with him, and together they formed the Muskogee Party. The Loyal Party still drew African Creek support, but it was substantially diminished.[83]

While African Creeks developed an independent community life during this period, it was firmly grounded in the Creek cultural milieu. The African Creeks thoroughly identified with the society in which they lived: they ate the same foods, wore the same clothes, spoke the same language, farmed the same lands, and shared blood ties with Creeks. During these years, however, forces were building that would challenge both the freed people's position and the traditional means of living with which they identified. As the Creek country came under increasing assault from forces outside the nation during the 1870s, from the railroads clamoring for land grants to "develop" the Indian Territory, from noncitizen permit men and intruders wanting to claim parts of the vast Creek commonwealth, from cattle drivers wanting access to the miles and miles of "unused" grazing lands, and from reformers wanting to "civilize" Creek society, there was also increasing pressure on Creek society to abandon the fluidity that characterized relations between African and Indian Creeks.

4

"Times Seem to Be Getting Very Ticklish"

African Creeks and the Green Peach War

THE YEARS BETWEEN 1878 AND 1883 were critical for the African Creeks. They saw increasing pressure to open the Indian country to white settlers, economic development, and territorial status with the arrival of David L. Payne and the Oklahoma boomer movement. While African Creeks made continued progress in education, establishing churches, and developing a community life, these years were also filled with racial and political strife, as a racial border war broke out with neighboring Cherokees, and the Creek Nation itself was consumed in its last and most serious constitutional-political crisis of the nineteenth century, the Green Peach War. African Creeks, whether as a key electoral constituency or as a focus for the disaffected, were at the center of events during this critical period.

The pressure to open the Creek lands to development and white settlement took on a new dimension in the late 1870s. Railroad corporations and other development interests led by Elias C. Boudinot, a "progressive" Cherokee, prodded Congress to organize hearings in Washington in early 1878 on territorial status for the Indian Territory and dividing tribal lands in severalty. In November 1878, the Senate Committee on Territories, chaired by South Carolina senator John Patterson, held hearings in Muskogee and Eufaula.[1] It was fitting that the hearings took place in these two towns, because they had been created by the railroads and served as hubs for "progressive" economic development. While Eufaula retained more of an image as a Creek town, both towns, particularly Muskogee, were filled with noncitizen traders and development promoters. But the hearings in the

115

Indian Territory were held not so much to gauge Indian feelings on the subject as to provide a forum for pro-development interests. Boudinot sat next to Patterson during the hearings and questioned witnesses with prosecutorial aggressiveness, all the while extolling the civilizing benefits of railroads through the Indian Territory. The Creeks, despite internal divisions created by Locha Hacho's impeachment, stood together in opposition to the plan for territorial status and allotment. To face this challenge to Creek sovereignty, the Creeks composed their differences (at least temporarily) and presented a united front at the hearings.[2]

To secure African Creek support at the hearings, the Creek National Council approved an appropriation of three thousand dollars to open the freed people's boarding school that had been promised since 1876. Chief Coachman had earlier in the year turned down an African Creek request for the money, pleading lack of funds. But given the importance of cooperation at the scheduled hearings, the council approved the measure in fall 1878. The council also acted in another area of concern to African Creeks by granting citizenship to sixty-eight African Creek Graysons, who had returned too late to be adopted under the 1866 treaty. The same legislation gave other African Creeks the opportunity to come forward and "prove" themselves through a petition to the Council. Simon Brown and other African Creek leaders let it be known that as long as the parties had a legitimate claim to citizenship, their adoption would be a simple matter.[3]

At the hearings in Muskogee, African Creeks stood shoulder to shoulder with other Creeks in their opposition to territorial status and severalty. In the face of sharp questioning by the committee, six of the seven African Creek witnesses, including Sugar George, Simon Brown, Jesse Franklin, Monday Marshall, Joe Howard, and Ned Robbins identified themselves as Indians and told the committee they enjoyed full political rights and had access to as much land as they cared to cultivate. George Dann, the seventh African Creek interviewed, did not claim to be an Indian but made the point that he was treated equally. The committee learned there were sixteen African Creek representatives in the ninety-six member House of Warriors and three members in the forty-four member House of Kings. Jesse Franklin, the African Creek leader elected to the Creek Supreme Court, explained how the court operated and affirmed that African Creeks were treated equally before the law and had full and equal access to the Creek legal system. Senator Patterson, fresh from his experience with violent racist intimidation of freed people in South Carolina, closely questioned Monday Marshall, the African Creek leader from Arkansas Colored, after Marshall told him that he farmed fifteen acres for himself, made a "tolerable" living from his acreage, and did not want the lands allotted.[4]

PATTERSON: Do you know what I mean by allotting the lands?
MARSHALL: Yes sir; I understand you. I would rather hold the lands in common.
PATTERSON: Are there any [freedmen] in favor of a change of government?
MARSHALL: None that I have seen. None with whom I have talked.

At this point, Patterson refused to believe that African Creeks could possibly object to becoming private landholders and suspected that Marshall was holding something back.

PATTERSON: Why do they keep it a secret; are they in fear of intimidation?
MARSHALL: I do not know. I never heard any speak in favor of sectionalizing the lands.
PATTERSON: Suppose a man should be in favor of it and should undertake to talk about it, would anybody interfere with him?
MARSHALL: I do not know that they would. Our people have their own opinions.
PATTERSON: You allow men to vote their own views and opinions?
MARSHALL: Of course; in all cases.[5]

Marshall gave a generally positive assessment, but he did not hesitate to express his opinion regarding African Creeks who were "shut out" or denied their rights because they did not return in the time stipulated in the 1866 treaty. Marshall's comment drew a pointed response from G. W. Stidham, a leading Constitutionalist Party member, who reminded Marshall that the council had just adopted sixty-eight of those "shut out" and made provisions for others who wanted to bring their cases before council. Marshall also commented on African Creeks not getting their share of school funds, and Stidham once again flared up, stressing that African Creeks received their portion of school monies and were opening their first boarding school that week. After he conceded that he did not know whether African Creeks received the correct dollar amount of school funds, Marshall would not retreat from his point, saying: "If they [African Creek children] were treated the same as the Indians I do not see why we are behind; but what we are lacking I do not know."[6]

If the committee members came looking to record racial animosity in the Creek country, Stidham's sharp questioning and Marshall's tempered responses were as close as they came. Patterson and the other Republicans on the committee may have marveled at how the Indian nation had succeeded so admirably at racial reconstruction. While questioning the African Creeks, the senator had continually tried to place them on par with freed people from the South, and he was continually frustrated. Clearly, African Creeks enjoyed opportunities in the Indian nation not available anywhere else in the country. But in attempting to cast African Creeks in the same light as African Americans from the Southern states, the senator and his colleagues, as most other federal officials would do throughout the tribal period, missed an essential point that governed African Creek identity. All but one of the African Creek witnesses identified themselves as Indians, statements that went unquestioned by the other Creek delegates and witnesses. While Stidham and other leading figures in the Constitutionalist Party recoiled at the idea of African Creeks being classed with themselves, for the moment there was harmony as the Creeks faced the twin threats of territorial status and allotment.[7]

One of the last Creek witnesses at the hearing was not so opposed to identifying with the African Creeks. Robert Leslie, an expatriate from the Creek country since before the Civil War, had just recently returned to supervise the new freed people's boarding school scheduled to open that fall. Leslie wore a dark Episcopalian preacher's coat buttoned to the chin, a curious costume for a Baptist preacher, but an image that was consistent with Leslie's personality and his own upbringing in the Presbyterian Church. Leslie had attended Tullahassee Mission before the war with other children of prominent Creek families, including two principal chiefs in the postwar era—Legus C. Perryman and Pleasant Porter. Before taking the job at the boarding school, he had taught in freed people's schools in Louisiana and Mississippi and was involved in the fractious and violent Reconstruction politics in Louisiana. Senator Patterson knew Leslie's reputation and asked him to compare the status of African Creeks with Louisiana freed people. Leslie unhesitatingly stated that African Creeks were "able to take care of themselves, and I know they can take care of themselves better than they do in Louisiana," an understatement that was not lost on the Creek audience, but that apparently glided easily past Patterson's Southern freedmen fixation. Leslie did not hesitate to speak for the African Creek community as well, saying, "I think we can get along without mixing up with the white man or their business and attend to our own business without a military government over us." What white man's business African Creeks should avoid is not clear; perhaps Leslie was referring to allotment, but clearly the Creeks did not need federal interference to enforce racial reconstruction.[8]

Whatever his intent with the committee, Leslie intended a larger role for himself in the African Creek community than just boarding school principal. Soon after Leslie's arrival in summer 1878, the Freedmen Baptist Association adopted him as a member. He was selected as the association's missionary, and he soon organized an African Creek Baptist church in Muskogee that had fifty members.[9]

Leslie staked such a claim on the African Creek community in part because his wife Nellie Ann was African American. But she was not just any African American. The former Nellie Ann Colles was a highly educated free black woman born in Virginia, who had graduated from Oberlin College in Ohio before going South at the war's end to teach in the freed people's schools in New Orleans. Nellie Ann had taught Greek and Latin in the New Orleans schools, where she and Robert first met.[10]

The Leslies were also a highly ambitious couple, and their ambitions extended beyond the schoolhouse and church door. Robert took up politics soon after his arrival and joined Coachman's Muskogee Party. He helped Coachman forge a coalition of freedmen, conservative Creeks, and disenchanted progressives that hopefully would lead to Coachman's election as chief in his own right in the upcoming 1879 elections. Leslie attempted to forge a leadership role for himself in the African Creek community, using the school and the church as his base of support. But the African Creeks were not easily led, and they showed Leslie in no uncertain terms that they had their own ideas about community life, identity, and politics.[11]

After many delays, including Coachman's plea of Creek financial distress, the concord established in anticipation of the Senate committee's arrival finally broke the logjam, and the freed people's boarding school project went forward in spring 1878. Congress had ordered the Union Agency, the combined agency that served the Five Tribes, closed as a cost-cutting measure, and African Creek leaders convinced the Indian Office to let them use the vacated building as a school. The Baptist Home Mission Society also supported the project and agreed to pay the teacher's salary.[12]

In late summer 1878, when Leslie arrived to begin organizing the school, he immediately encountered an intruder problem. He wanted to use the agency grounds as a demonstration farm to teach male students agriculture but found the acreage already occupied by a white permit man, John Shaneyfeld. Shaneyfeld obstinately refused to leave and dared anyone to remove him. It took the combined persuasive power of Leslie, Chief Coachman, the Indian agent, the Indian Commissioner, and the Home Mission Society over three months to remove Shaneyfeld, who finally vacated the grounds on September 30, taking "his" crop with him. The whole episode illustrated not only the Creeks' impotence in dealing with the problem, but also the flaws in the permit system drawn up to benefit large landholders involved in commercial agriculture. When combined with the federal government's failure to live up to its 1866 treaty responsibility to keep non-citizens from intruding on Creek lands, the effects of the permit system would prove disastrous. In most cases, no action was taken at all, and though the intruder problem in 1878 was still a relatively small one—only fifty whites and a handful of state freedmen, some with their wives and families—the intruder population had been growing, and it would soon reach menacing proportions.[13]

The way finally cleared of intruders, Leslie began the school November 1. During the first term, he boarded forty students between the ages of eight and eighteen, twenty girls and twenty boys. He offered "various branches of instruction as taught in the primary and high schools of the United States." Besides teaching advanced reading, writing, and arithmetic, Leslie developed a classic liberal arts curriculum he was familiar with from his days as a student at Tullahassee. He taught courses in geography, natural philosophy, and U.S. history. Bowing to the current trend toward vocational education for people of color, he also taught the male students agriculture, although it is likely his students knew a good deal more about agriculture and farming techniques adaptable to the Creek country than he did. Female students received instruction in "household arts," provided by Nellie Ann Leslie, who ran the Leslie home as a first-class boarding house and hotel with exacting standards. According to Leslie's school report for the year, the students "progressed well," and they all passed their examinations at the term's end. The students' progress boded well for the school's future.[14]

Despite its promising beginning, the school operation at the agency building did not last past its first term. Congress restored the Union Agency in spring 1879 and notified the Creeks and the Baptist Missionary Society that the building had to be turned back to the government in June. Leslie offered to continue the school next term at his home in Muskogee until a suitable building could be found. He arranged with the school trustees, Scipio Sango, Snow Sells, and Monday Durant, to provide him with the lumber and labor needed to build an addition to his house to quarter the students, and he operated the school there during 1879–1880. But Leslie did not continue the school beyond the 1880 term due, in part, to his loss of influence in the African Creek community and the 1879 election outcome, which shuttled the patronage for the school to another faction within the African Creek community. But the precedent for a tribally funded boarding school was established, and funding for African Creek schools and education would not only continue but expand throughout the duration of Creek tribal government.[15]

In early 1879, the intruder problem took on a new dimension after Elias Boudinot published a story in the national press declaring that the so-called Unassigned Lands were open for homesteading. The lands were the Creek domain's western acres, conditionally set aside in the 1866 treaty for settlement by western Indian tribes or for the Five Tribes freed people. The land, however, remained unsettled and was used illegally by cattlemen to graze herds during cattle drives from Texas to Kansas. The boomer movement, led by David L. Payne, began in earnest in April and May 1880 as white settlers from Kansas formed companies and invaded the Unassigned Lands. They set up tent towns and squatter's shacks and dared the U.S. government to remove them. President Rutherford B. Hayes sent in federal troops to remove the boomers, but they returned again and again to what they called Oklahoma during the 1880s, until the federal government grew weary of its treaty obligations and pressured the Creeks to sell their residual rights to the Unassigned Lands. For the moment, the Creeks were separated from a boomer frontal assault by the fifty-mile-wide barrier of "resettled" Indian reservations (Sac Fox, Iowa, Kickapoo, etc.). But the barrier proved as thin as the federal government's promise to protect the Creeks from intruders, as thousands of Shaneyfelds streamed into the Creek country over the next decade.[16]

Leslie had problems with another intruder during his first year back in the Creek country. His trouble with Turner Duncan revealed just how tenuous Leslie's influence in the African Creek community actually was. In spring 1879, Duncan, a freedman from Texas, showed up in Muskogee. Duncan was a Baptist preacher, and he had been traveling through the Indian Territory from Texas to Kansas on the Exoduster migration when he had met Rev. John Kernel. Apparently, Kernel thought enough of Duncan to present him to the congregation at the Muskogee Baptist Church and let him preach. Duncan's preaching style electrified the congregation. Many glowing testimonials described the moral impact of Duncan's sermons; the Texas preacher ignited a revival among the Muskogee freed people, and soon the Muskogee Baptist Church became the place where dozens of "unregenerate" freed people renounced drinking, gambling, racing, fiddling, and dancing and pledged themselves to the straight and narrow. They also turned their backs on Leslie, their Episcopalian-coated pastor. Leslie's reserved style was much better suited to his wife's African Methodist Episcopalian roots and his own background in the Presbyterian Church than to African Creek Baptist singing and shouting. Leslie accused Duncan of taking over "his" church and intimated that Duncan was leading the congregation astray through preaching the "Campbellite heresy." Duncan offered to step aside after Leslie's objection, but the congregation insisted on a vote and voted overwhelmingly to keep Duncan in the pulpit.[17]

After the vote, Leslie turned to intimidation. He wrote to Coachman and asked to have Duncan removed as an intruder, saying, "[Duncan] is endeavoring to do all the harm he can against my influence with the colored element, politically as well as religiously. He has turned John Kernel against our interest [and] teaches them that they ought to have colored teachers, not Indians." With the 1879 election just months away, and Coachman depending on the African Creek vote to carry him through, any erosion in African Creek support was a cause for concern. Leslie also dug up scurrilous charges of whiskey smuggling, horse thievery, wife abandonment, and church wreaking against Duncan, charges that were later proved false and that only further discredited Leslie within the African Creek community. Although the Commissioner of Indian Affairs issued an order that Duncan could continue his good work in the Indian Territory, Duncan moved on to Kansas, much to Leslie's relief.[18]

Duncan had struck a chord that resonated in the African Creek community. His campaign against immorality coincided with the view of many that something needed to be done to clean up Muskogee and other settlements in the vicinity. Chief Coachman, other leading Creeks, and former agent Sylvester W. Marston endorsed campaigns against gambling, liquor, and lawlessness, but their efforts were stymied by the continual influx of intruders of all types into Muskogee, which was quickly becoming the commercial development center for the Indian Territory and losing whatever claim it ever had to being a Creek settlement. Ever since the Missouri-Kansas-Texas Railroad had established its station at Muskogee in 1871, the community's identity was influenced more by the intruders on Creek soil than by the native inhabitants, the majority of whom were African Creeks. Geography and railroad engineering put Muskogee in the center of one of the areas of the nation most densely populated by African Creeks, and for many years, at least until the last decade of the nineteenth century, most of the town's native residents were African Creek. Indeed, Muskogee would come to host one of the most vibrant enclaves of black commercial and cultural activity in the West, but, unfortunately, African Creek involvement in the development of this "foreign" enclave would also serve to estrange them from defenders of Creek tribal identity and sovereignty.[19]

Conflict and confusion over who had jurisdiction over the intruders, and their activities, was a major barrier to any effort to remove the whiskey traders from Muskogee and to clean up the town. Although liquor was supposedly illegal in the Indian Territory, whiskey peddlers openly sold "the devil's dew" in the streets of Muskogee. According to Marston and others, liquor was responsible for much of the violence that gave Muskogee its reputation as a dangerous place where decent citizens were not safe. But illegal liquor was only part of the problem. Nearly everyone carried a gun in the Indian Territory. It was fashionable, and some would say prudent, to wear a six-shooter when tending to business, making a social call, or even going to church. Shootings and murders were commonplace, not just in Muskogee but throughout the Indian Territory towns experiencing rapid commercial development.[20]

A malignant dose of racism was mixed into this complex brew of emerging commercial development, noncitizen intrusion, Creek nationalism, liquor, guns, confused jurisdiction, and lack of law enforcement. The result was a race war between African Creeks and Cherokees that broke out along the Creek Cherokee boundary in 1878–1881. The conflict would contribute significantly in breaking down the concord that had been established between the African Creeks and the Creek government during the congressional hearings.

Race relations in the Cherokee nation during the postwar period did not exhibit the fluidity and flexibility found in the Creek country. The 1866 Cherokee treaty limited Cherokee freedmen's political and land rights to those African Cherokees who returned to the nation within six months after the treaty's ratification, and many felt the provisions were unfairly and arbitrarily enforced. Additionally, African Cherokees were barred from social activities by racial barriers like those found in Southern states. While African Cherokees were not subjected to a systematic and widespread campaign of racial terrorism, several high-profile incidents of racist violence and murder in the early 1870s highlighted the potential for such a contagion to spread. In their 1870 report, speaking specifically about several egregious incidents of Cherokee racist violence, the Board of Indian Commissioners observed, "There seems still to exist a leaven of Southern chivalry among some hot-blooded natives [Cherokees] which impels them, under a false notion of revenge, to take the law into their own hands." Some aristocratic Cherokees and intermarried white Cherokee families that lived along the Creek-Cherokee boundary held this type of virulent racist attitude. Further friction developed when Cherokee cattle ignored the boundary and ranged into Creek territory, and African Creeks took advantage of what they claimed were unmarked cattle and either butchered them or sold them on the hoof to the livestock markets in Muskogee. But African Creeks were not the only ones rustling cattle on the range between the two Indian nations. Cherokee cattlemen were also charged with stealing African Creek stock, and, though warrants were issued by the Creek courts for the arrest of those involved, Cherokee authorities refused to act.[21]

A nearby African Creek settlement, Marshalltown, had an unsavory reputation as a rough place, infested with outlaws and cattle thieves who sought refuge there and were, as Angie Debo speculated, "protected by the close-knit racial consciousness" of the African Creeks. Even the Creek Lighthorse, many of whom were African Creeks, were reluctant to enter the settlement alone. But Marshalltown, despite its reputation for sheltering the lawless, also contributed significantly to the African Creek's civil and cultural life. The Old Fountain Church, the first Baptist church in the Creek Nation, served as the settlement's principal house of worship. Ketch Barnett, a leading figure in the African Creek community, ministered there for many years until his death in 1873. Although the congregation, like the area's population, was principally African Creek after the war, at the summer camp meetings, both Indians and African Creeks worshiped together, with African Creek interpreters translating the sermons as in earlier days. Other leaders, active in African Creek community political and social life, as well as in the nation, came from the Marshalltown settlement, among them Snow Sells, Ben Barnett, Scipio Sango, Kellop Murrell, Robert Marshall, Daniel Miller, and Gabriel Jamison. Jamison built his home near the Old Fountain Church, using the logs from the old building when a new church was built in the 1870s. The Marshalltown neighborhood school, one of the first African Creek schools established in the postwar years, also served the community well. Forty students regularly enrolled, and at the 1877 public examination exercises, the students answered questions in natural philosophy for which they "earned well-merited praise, having stood a thorough examination most admirably. This . . . is the first and only class of colored boys and girls [in the Creek country] that have received instructions in this heretofore neglected branch of education." So, while Marshalltown may well have earned a "reputation" in the minds of some observers, and later historians, there was another side to the community that escaped notoriety but did contribute to African Creek community identity in a positive way.[22]

Tensions between African Creeks and "hot-blooded" Cherokees came to a head on Christmas Day, 1878. The Creek government was attempting to rein in the violence in Muskogee during the holiday season by deputizing more Lighthorse to patrol the streets and disarm those who had no legitimate reason for carrying a gun. Despite extra Lighthorse patrols, there were incidents, similar to those described by the Indian commissioners in 1870, in which armed Cherokees opened fire on "every Colored man they saw" in the streets of Muskogee. Since the Lighthorse and their deputies were, for the most part, African Creek in Muskogee, the stage was set for more violence. On Christmas Day, John and Dick Vann, two young Cherokees from a prominent family, came through Muskogee on their way to Brushy Mountain. They were confronted by an African Creek Lighthorse posse under George McIntosh and forced to surrender their weapons. According to a later witness, the posse "rudely" disarmed the Cherokees and "abused them" afterwards. A certain "lawless Texas intruder" observed the deputies' "impertinence" and convinced the Cherokees to confront the deputies and demand the return of the pistols. Following the confrontation, a gun battle broke out between the posse and the Cherokees in which George McIntosh was killed and two deputies were wounded. The Vanns escaped and were never charged in the shooting.[23]

Violence against African Creeks continued, but no steps were taken to arrest the Cherokees involved, though their identities were known to all. In May 1879, the leading voices in the African Creek community sent a petition to Coachman asking for protection and redress: "Repeated outrages have been committed against our race by Cherokees most grossly; therefore, we deem it necessary to lay the matter before you for protection. As it is now we cannot go to the town of Muskogee on business in pursuance of our civil occupation without being shot at for no other reason than our color." The petition went on to pledge obedience to the Creek laws and called for the three African Creek towns to organize mass meetings to bring the issue to wider attention.[24]

The tensions escalated that summer when another gun battle broke out in Muskogee. Once again, a group of Cherokee men confronted African Creek Lighthorse. The battle took place in the middle of Muskogee's commercial district during a busy Saturday market day. Apparently, William Peters, an African Creek Lighthorseman, was observed talking amicably with some Cherokees, John Vann, Ed Cobb, Bob Steele, and Simpson Bennett, at the Muskogee fairgrounds on the outskirts of town earlier in the day. It is unclear whether the Cherokees provoked the fight or not, but apparently they accused Lighthorsemen Joe and Ben Barnett of cattle rustling. It seems unlikely, however, that Peters and his posse would have purposefully instigated a shoot-out in the crowded market area. In the gun battle that followed, which took place in front of Muskogee's meat market, the men blazed away with shotguns and revolvers. John Vann was killed, William Peters was seriously wounded, Joe Barnett was slightly wounded, and bystander James Carter, who was clerking at a store in the market, was killed by a stray bullet.[25]

The Cherokees immediately called for the arrest of Peters and his posse and made ominous threats. The African Creek community was literally up in arms and vowed to defend themselves. The shootings also sparked a wave of indignation from the white developers over the endemic violence in Muskogee, and they peppered Coachman with petitions calling for immediate action in preventing further outbreaks. After consulting with other Creek leaders, Coachman called on Richard Berryhill, a Creek Indian Lighthorseman from the Okmulgee District, to take up a special assignment in cleaning up Muskogee. Berryhill, unlike the lawmen heroes of the mythic West, politely refused to swagger into Muskogee, saying, "If . . . Muskogee was really an Indian town I would not wait a moment. . . . I don't see how I am to risk my life for non-citizens." One condition that Berryhill asked for, but which Coachman could not agree to, was to "leave the Colored Lighthorse out" and allow Berryhill to deputize his own men. Because the 1879 election was only weeks away, and Coachman was counting on African Creek support to carry him through, nullifying African Creek participation in protecting their own community would have been political suicide.[26]

As it was, Coachman had other matters to weigh as well. The developers, railroad promoters, and the "territorial men" used the incident to agitate both in the African Creek community and among the Cherokees. They spread rumors about preparations being made for revenge by one side against the other in hopes that an all-out race war might lead Congress to impose federal control. To lessen the possibility that the Cherokees might be provoked, Coachman ordered Peters, Joe Barnett, Ben Barnett, and Mose Redmouth bound over for trial in the Creek courts for killing John Vann. Although it was unlikely that a jury from the predominantly African Creek Muskogee District would convict the accused, nevertheless, the trial was called and delayed many times until the charges were finally dropped. But the idea that Peters and the others were held at all galled African Creeks. Peters was later compensated by the council for wounds he suffered and his legal expenses. For his part, Joe Barnett left the area altogether and was later elected to the Lighthorse in the Wewoka District, where he would play a principal role in sparking the incident that began the Green Peach War. Still, Cherokee vigilante activity continued unabated along the border for the next eighteen months, and Ben Barnett and other African Creeks would feel the sting of racial violence again. But before the Vann trial fiasco began, the 1879 election and its results added to the bitterness felt in the African Creek community over their rights in the nation.[27]

As the angling for support of the African Creek community before the

1878 Senate committee hearings revealed, all political factions in the nation recognized that African Creeks were a key constituency in any successful Creek political equation. But the African Creek community was not simply a monolithic collection of votes that could be manipulated at will. As the Turner Duncan affair and the various wranglings over the direction of schools, churches, and other African Creek social institutions showed, African Creeks had a multiplicity of interests that were not governed strictly by racial identification. As the African Creek community matured, individuals and particular settlements ceased to be governed by the same social, political, and economic needs and pursued divergent interests.

Coachman and his Muskogee Party had been reaching out to African Creeks for some time. He employed John Island, an educated African Creek, as his private secretary as part of his effort to establish credibility in the African Creek community. He also tailored his 1878 annual message to appeal to African Creek voters: "the intent of [Article II] was so plain that no one can mistake or misunderstand it"—African Creeks were entitled to full and equal rights in the Creek Nation. Furthermore, he recommended civil rights legislation, similar to that passed by Congress in 1875, that would further protect African Creek rights. Coachman was no doubt sincere, but political calculation also guided his efforts.[28]

The two other parties, the Constitutionalists (now the National Constitutionalists) and the Loyal Creeks, also angled for African Creek support. After the death of Locha Hacho in 1878, the Loyal Creeks were led by Isparhecher (Spahecha), a conservative traditionalist from Cusseta Town. African Creek loyalties to the old Sands coalition, formed during the Civil War, were still strong in some settlements, particularly in the outlying areas of Canadian Colored Town. But around Muskogee and other areas close to the railroad towns, which were undergoing development pressures and the lure of marketplace gains, the attraction to the conservative social and political agenda had less appeal. One attraction the Loyal ticket did have for African Creeks was Silas Jefferson, the African Creek from Taskigi Town, who ran as the Loyal candidate for second chief. As election day drew near, however, the Loyal Party abandoned the race and refused once again to participate in the official political life of the nation.[29]

The other two parties continued to campaign, and African Creek rights and racial identity were issues that remained in the spotlight. Checote's National Constitutionalist Party platform pledged equal protection and equal rights for all, and the Muskogee Party published its slate of African Creek candidates for council positions. The race issue also appeared in campaign broadsides in a negative way. Pleasant Porter's African ancestry, a scarcely mentioned but widely known personal detail of one of the most visible and effective Constitutionalist leaders, was featured in a story in the *Indian Journal* on "race mixing" in the Indian Territory. What the Muskogee Party (or any political faction) had to gain from publicly airing the other party's racial laundry is a matter that defies logic because many prominent Creek leaders in the postwar era had African blood to some degree (Checote was an exception). In 1879, W. O. Tuggle's optimistic assessment of the future of a multiracial society developing in the Creek country could still be entertained, but as the racist implications in the campaign propaganda indicate, it would take some work.[30]

African Creeks and their influence in Creek politics can clearly be seen in the 1879 principal chief election. The winner would be decided on whether or not the votes in the African Creek towns were counted fairly, but due to "irregularities" in tabulating votes and sealing the ballot boxes, the Arkansas and Canadian Colored towns' votes were thrown out. Whether the boxes were tampered with to add votes for Coachman or the irregularities were part of a conspiracy engineered by Constitutionalists to make sure the votes were thrown out is open to question. Snow Sells, the Constitutionalist town chief of Arkansas Colored, supervised the Arkansas Colored election and was responsible for the ballot box, which lends credence to later reports of a Constitutionalist plot. But the vote was still extraordinarily close, even with the two African Creek towns thrown out. Constitutionalist Party leaders like Pleasant Porter, Thomas Adams, and F. B. Severs were deeply involved in the hard-ball politics during the campaign and election. William Fischer, a Muskogee Party member, said there was outright fraud in Thomas Adams's Hillabee town count. According to Fischer, none of the Grayson African Creeks who were enrolled in the town voted "on the ground" for Checote, but their votes were tabulated in the Checote column nonetheless. This number of votes, if counted correctly, could have tipped the election in Coachman's favor. Severs reportedly used bribery and intimidation to influence the election outcome and was overheard saying to Porter, "there will be no compromise or backing away from the position we are taking." Charles Foster, the North Fork Colored Town chief, said that Severs offered him twenty dollars to use his bilingual ability to influence voters for Checote. Foster turned him down, saying his town was already pledged to Coachman. But Severs possibly found more pliant officials in Arkansas and Canadian Colored towns. In the final report of the Council's election committee, Checote bested Coachman by only eleven votes. The reports on Constitutionalist vote tampering and bribery apparently made no impact, however, because Indian Office officials recognized Checote as the legitimately elected chief. The impeachment of Locha Hacho and the 1879 election frauds confirmed for many African Creeks that neither the Constitutionalists nor the U.S. government was interested in giving them a fair shake. Disgruntled African Creeks once again showered Washington with protest petitions, but the petitioners were not even accorded the dignity of a reply, further estranging them from the political process.[31]

Following the election, the border race war with the Cherokees flared up again. In revenge for John Vann's killing, Dick Vann led Cherokee vigilantes in raids on African Creek settlements along the border in early 1880, terrorizing African Creek citizens. One of their targets was Ben Barnett, one of the Lighthorse deputies accused and released in the Vann shooting. Vann and four other Cherokees attacked Barnett's home on the night of February 20. Surprised in his sleep, Barnett escaped his burning house through a window while his niece was wounded twice by gunfire blasting through the walls and door of his house. The terrorists chased the unarmed Barnett into the night, firing away at him, and "might have ended his life had it not been for the timely arrival of some . . . neighbors" who drove them away and rescued his injured niece from the flames. Vann and the others also made a similar assault on Cyrus Herrod's home near Muskogee. Following the attacks, African Creek citizens petitioned Checote for protection:

> This state of Affairs has been pending for several months. As law abiding citizens we have chosen to be termed cowards rather than return like for like. Four have been killed already and six wounded. *Nothing Done*. "Tis Niggers." We cry for justice in one accord. Please exert influence with Chief of the Cherokees to turn over the above named men to be dealt with justly under our law. Or else we need to seek the aid of some other authority.[32]

The "other" authority they referred to was, no doubt, the U.S. government, though by this time federal authorities had developed a well-recognized disinterest in protecting Southern freed people. Certain congressmen, however, interested in developing the Indian Territory, could be persuaded to aid African Creeks if it would advance the territorial and allotment plans. Another veiled meaning in the petition is that African Creeks would aid themselves in fending off the attacks; as they had demonstrated in the past, they were perfectly capable of doing just that. Whatever the subtext implied in the petition, it is less important than the very real and urgent plea to protect African Creek lives.

Another petition was sent to Checote in May, asking him to remove H. C. Reed as Muskogee district judge for his refusal to hear complaints regarding "high crimes committed by Cherokees." Reed, like Snow Sells, was a Constitutionalist supporter. At the time, Reed was preparing to try the Vann case; and, whether or not he was influenced by the petition, Reed made an important ruling in the case just a week later that determined its final outcome. He ruled that the four key prosecution witnesses could not lawfully testify because they were all Cherokees who had sided with Vann in the shoot-out. Without their testimony, the case, as thin as it was, stood no chance. Judge Reed eventually dropped the case entirely and released the defendants.[33]

The Creek government finally did take some steps to protect African Creeks from Cherokee lawlessness. The Creek courts charged Cherokee cattlemen with stealing African Creek cattle; and though warrants were issued, and Checote sent requests to Cherokee chief Bushyhead to surrender the accused for trial, the requests were ignored, and the lawlessness continued. For their part, the Cherokees never sought a legal remedy to the rustling accusations they claimed were at the heart of the trouble. That summer, as the days grew hotter, the border war grew more intense and deadly. On the night of July 26, a party of nine Cherokees claiming to be U.S. deputy marshals came to Marshalltown and demanded the surrender of two African Creek citizens, Monday Roberts and Robert Jones, for cattle rustling. The men willingly gave themselves up, thinking the men were U.S. officers. They were bound, taken a short distance from the settlement, and hanged. Seventeen shots were fired into Jones's body. An African Creek who lived nearby heard the shooting and went out the next morning to investigate. He found Jones's bullet-riddled body and rushed to Marshalltown to report the murder. A group of ten African Creeks then rode out to retrieve the body and to find what had become of Roberts. The group then split into two parties to cover more ground. The exact sequence of what happened next is obscured by conflicting testimony, but another gun battle broke out between two young Cherokees, William Cobb and Alexander Cowan, and four African Creeks, Dick Glass, Ben Doaks, James Sampson, and Abe Marshall. Cobb and Cowan were shot, and several African Creeks were wounded. After pistols on both sides were emptied, the Cherokees fled to their homes nearby, and Cobb died from his wounds several hours later.[34] The news of Cobb's death drew an immediate and angry reaction from the Cherokee community gathered at nearby Ft. Gibson for an annuity payment. Soon the road to the Grand River ferry was clogged with hundreds of enraged, armed men bent on revenge. The ferry was busy all that day and into the evening, shuttling vigilantes across the river and depositing them on the Cherokee-Creek border, where Cherokee ranchers provided them with food and ammunition. But before the mob went into action, Chief Bushyhead arrived and convinced them to break up, return home, and wait for the law to take its course.[35]

Bushyhead's decisive intervention probably prevented a bloodbath, but allowing the law to take its course in this case still resulted in injustice for the African Creek community. The case went badly for the African Creeks from the start. The first issue addressed was not who was responsible for the lynchings but whether the Creeks or Cherokees had jurisdiction in charging those African Creeks involved in the gun battle. A combined commission from both tribes investigated but could not agree on whether the shootings took place on Creek or Cherokee soil. The Union Indian agent, John Q. Tufts, was called in to referee and decided the shooting took place in Cherokee territory. The Creeks on the commission, African and Indian, all signed a vigorous protest. Following the ruling, the Cherokees demanded the Creeks hand over all ten men who were out searching for the lynching victims, not just the four involved in the shoot-out. Seeking to placate the Cherokees, Chief Checote ordered Coweta district judge R. C. Childers to turn the accused men over, but Childers refused. The Creek Council then asked the judge to investigate and turn over only those who had participated in the shooting. After corroborating Cobb's dying testimony that at least five of the accused were not present at the shooting, Childers sensed (correctly as it turned out) that no African Creek would receive justice in the Cherokee courts and once again ignored Checote's order. Goaded by the Cherokees to do something, Checote dismissed Childers "for neglect of duty" and replaced him with James McHenry in December 1880.[36]

AFRICAN CREEKS

McHenry, along with Daniel Miller, the African Creek Constitutionalist elected prosecuting attorney in the Coweta District, worked together to clean up the lawlessness in the Point throughout 1881. They arrested, convicted, and sentenced several African Creek rustlers implicated in stealing Cherokee cattle, including Douglas Murrell and another of those accused in the Cobb case. Murrell was let off with a light sentence, and the other was pardoned, but still no African Creeks were surrendered to the Cherokees. Creek jurors, judges, and the chief, using his pardoning power, invariably showed a lenient attitude toward property crimes, very different from the attitudes of Cherokee ranchers. The idea that the alleged thieves were black added a racist leavening to the violence.[37]

The case took a new turn when Cherokee officers, emboldened by a two hundred–dollar reward offered by the Cherokee Nation, slipped into the African Creek settlement and seized one of the accused, Daniel Luckey, and brought him to trial in the Cherokee courts. During the raid, the officers killed another of the accused, James Sampson, allegedly while he tried to escape. The Cherokees did not bother to give Luckey even rudimentary legal safeguards, and the trial, held in April 1882, was a travesty of Cherokee justice. The judge, R. C. Parks, was William Cobb's uncle, and Luckey was not allowed to call any witnesses in his defense, nor was his court-appointed attorney allowed any time to prepare for trial. Not surprisingly, he was found guilty and sentenced to hang. Although Alex Cowan testified at the trial that Luckey was in the gunfight, other witnesses, who were not allowed to testify, were willing to say that he was not. Daniel Tucker, an African Creek leader from Marshalltown, told Chief Checote that the reason the Cherokees condemned Luckey to death was that they wanted him silenced. Luckey apparently knew the identities of the nine-member Cherokee lynch gang who had murdered Robert Jones and Monday Roberts and could testify against them.[38]

While the farce of a trial continued, some Cherokees questioned the proceedings. The Cherokee second chief declared the trial unfair, and four hundred Cherokees were prepared to sign a petition for clemency. In response to the pressure, Chief Bushyhead issued a reprieve for Luckey, which was periodically extended until finally he was pardoned in late 1883. Douglas Murrell, another of the accused, was also seized by the Cherokees and put through a similar ordeal until he too was given an "indefinite respite," and, though not officially pardoned, he was finally set free. Ben Doaks, a third member of the party in the gunfight, was killed in a shoot-out with Creek Lighthorse attempting to arrest him. Dick Glass was involved in this fray as well but escaped. Glass earned his reputation as a notorious outlaw based on his arrest record and consistent lawbreaking, but he preferred to be classed as a misunderstood target of Cherokee (and Creek) racism. Glass later told his side of the story in a letter to Indian Commissioner J. C. Atkins, penned in 1885:

> I feel that we did nothing but what men might do who were attacked by others. We did not seek the fight and only defended ourselves. I do not know that I killed Billy Cobb. No one could tell when so many shots were fired. I do know that he shot my horse and shot me. The weapons we used were six-shot revolvers and each party emptied theirs. Had I been an Indian and my companions the same nothing would have been said, but because I am a Negro I am blamed as much as I was the aggressor. I know that I could not get a fair trial in the Cherokee Nation.[39]

Glass went on to take a significant role on the insurgents' side during the Green Peach War, which the Constitutionalists pointed to as an example of Isparhecher's illegitimate claim to power. After the Green Peach War, Glass returned to rustling and whiskey smuggling and was killed in a gun battle with Sam Sixkiller and the U.S. Indian police in 1885.[40]

The Cherokees never attempted to investigate, much less charge anyone in, the lynching of Jones and Roberts nor any of the other vigilante crimes. And although the Creek government bound over for trial the African Creeks present at the Cobb shooting, it also issued warrants for Billy Clinging and Charly Haynes, two Cherokees identified as members of the lynching party, and charged them with the murders of Jones and Roberts. Chief Bushyhead refused to surrender the accused, however, even after Checote repeated the requests for over two years.[41]

Just as they had done in times past, the African Creeks defended themselves, an action tolerated within the Creek racial milieu but that would have provoked further racist violence in any Southern state at this time. In the end, the lack of protection given African Creeks during the border race war further estranged them from the Creek constitutional government and set the stage for African Creek participation in the Green Peach War.

The threat posed by the border war pulled the African Creek community together in many ways but also served to conceal factionalism that had developed as the community matured in the years after the Civil War. Factionalism emerged, however, in discussions over where to locate the African Creek boarding school after Leslie's school closed in spring 1880. The discussions on the topic were inconclusive until several events pushed the issue forward. In December 1880, the venerated Tullahassee Mission was partially destroyed in a fire. The Creek Council took advantage of the tragedy to push for relocating the Indian boarding school in an Indian neighborhood because the school was located in the middle of one of the most heavily populated African Creek neighborhoods in the nation. Simon Brown came forward to urge the council to act. They passed a resolution in April 1881 for the Tullahassee trustees to turn over the mission remains, including houses, farms, orchards, and other improvements "to the Colored People of the Nation" for use as a boarding school. A concurrent resolution called for building a new Indian school at Wealaka, fifty miles southwest of the old mission, on the south side of the Arkansas.[42]

African Creeks did not greet the "gift" of the burned-out mission with universal enthusiasm. A convention held at Simon Brown's ferry on the Arkansas in July resolved not to accept the site. Petitions and letters presented by leading African Creeks, Monday Durant, Jonathan Kernel, Paro Bruner, and others from communities south of the Arkansas said "a wide majority" of African Creeks objected to the Tullahassee site and wanted the school closer to their own communities. The new Union agent, John Q. Tufts, who was moving the agency into Muskogee, suggested the agency building where Leslie's school was held would again be available. Simon Brown, who had reconsidered his earlier endorsement of the Tullahassee site, argued that not only was the agency location more healthful but the building was in better condition and could be used immediately. Tullahassee, on the other hand, still needed to be rebuilt, and Indian students would be attending classes there until fall of 1882. The logic of these arguments could not withstand the pull of politics and political patronage, however. Apparently, the plans to hand over the mission ruins to the African Creeks were hatched before the embers from the fire cooled and had some powerful backers. Snow Sells and H. C. Reed, two leading Constitutionalist African Creeks, sat on the first building committee for the school, and both were eventually elected trustees. Pleasant Porter, a Tullahassee alum, pushed the plan forward in council and soothed the Robertson family, who objected to the transfer of the mission property to the African Creeks. The family's opposition was primarily sectarian and not racial, for nearly all African Creeks, even the ever-faithful Simon Brown, had gone "under water," as the Presbyterians called it, and joined the Baptist church. Despite the objections, the council designated Tullahassee as the official location in late 1882, and the school opened there with fifty African Creek students in fall 1883. Rev. J. P. Lawton served as the first superintendent for the school, and Tullahassee would continue as an African Creek boarding school for the rest of the tribal period.[43]

The drive to open an African Creek boarding school south of the Arkansas did not die out with the council's funding of Tullahassee. Monday Durant, Jonathan Kernel, Samuel Soloman, and Simon Brown kept the movement alive, and with funds raised through private subscription and the cooperation of the Baptist Home Mission Society and the Indian Office, they reopened the agency school in fall 1883 as Evangel School, with Rev. Ira A. Cain as director. The Creek Nation also provided further educational opportunities by funding African Creek students' higher education in the states. Five students were funded in 1882, and the numbers would increase steadily in following years. Most students attended either the Nashville Institute in Tennessee, Hampton Institute in Virginia, or Bishop College in Marshall, Texas. Warrior Rentie and James Coody Johnson were two early beneficiaries of the program.[44]

Factionalism, as long as it was kept within civil bounds, benefited the African Creek community in opening educational opportunities for African Creek children. But gains on the education front could not mask the strains that were pulling the Creeks inexorably toward the Green Peach War. The threat posed by the boomer movement and the clamor of developers and railroad corporations to open the Indian Territory to outside market forces added to the internal political friction ignited by Locha Hacho's impeachment and the 1879 election frauds. Added to this equation were the bitter feelings arising from the border war with the Cherokees, and the factionalism within the African Creek community itself.

The conservative Creeks, now led by Isparhecher and his chief lieutenant, Silas Jefferson, withdrew from constitutional politics after the 1879 election and established a rival government at Nuyuka, west of Okmulgee. While Isparhecher's faction fancied the label Loyal Creeks, and one of their grievances was government inaction on the Loyal Creek claim, the term had

AFRICAN CREEKS

lost much of its meaning in the years since the war's end. Like Sands's party, at its core the faction was guided by a brand of nativism that was culturally conservative, embracing the more traditional and relaxed Creek racial attitude. But in the intervening years, the Loyal Party had also become a haven for various political and social discontents. Indeed, Isparhecher's enemies categorized him as nothing more than a "disgruntled office-seeker" and made an issue of the insurgent party harboring outlaws such as Dick Glass.[45]

Soon after setting up headquarters in the Deep Fork District, Isparhecher and Silas Jefferson asserted the Loyal Party position. In September 1880, they sent Checote a message, insisting the government take swift action against the murderer of one of their young supporters. In a sense, they were challenging the government to extend the same consideration to Loyal Creek citizens that was so willingly given to Cherokee citizens in the Vann and Cobb cases. As the border war intensified, Loyal Party emissaries reached out to disgruntled African Creeks and the old Loyal Party–African Creek alliance was born anew. When the Creek government began cleaning up the Point, arresting and punishing stock thieves, Isparhecher and Silas Jefferson thought their supporters in the Coweta District were unfairly targeted, and they warned Checote "not to step too quick" in the prosecution of African Creeks. In his reply, Checote quoted Article II of the treaty, assured the opposing party that all Creeks, regardless of color, were entitled to equal rights, and noted that in the 1867 councils, all parties had agreed to come under the constitution and be led by one government. Checote closed his message with a warning of his own, saying that the insurgent party should themselves weigh matters carefully and not step too quickly. The tensions between the two factions heightened after Isparhecher and his party recruited their own Lighthorse to enforce their laws and rejected the constitutional government's authority, setting them on an unavoidable collision course with the Creek government.[46]

That summer there were several skirmishes around African Creek settlements near Pecan and Sugar creeks, west of Muskogee, between Constitutionalist forces and armed groups claiming allegiance to the Loyal Party. The major collision came on July 26, 1882. Following the advice of Agent Tufts, Loyal Party members were meeting at Isparhecher's homestead to draw up a petition protesting treatment at the hands of government Lighthorse and the sale of a disputed strip of Creek land to the Seminoles. Jim Kannard, a Lighthorse officer from the Deep Fork District, and two other

Lighthorsemen from the Wewoka District, Capt. Sam Scott and Pvt. Joe Barnett, broke up the insurgent meeting, disarmed the participants, and arrested one of the party, Heneha Chupco, for resisting arrest. Chupco was turned over to Scott and Barnett for safekeeping, pending trial. A group of armed insurgents, claiming that Heneha had committed no crime, followed shortly thereafter. Arriving at Scott's home, they demanded the prisoner's release and, when fired upon by Scott, shot and killed Scott and Barnett and released Chupco.[47]

The incident that sparked the Green Peach War illustrated several salient features of that conflict, features that were distorted by the opposing parties for their own political reasons. For one, the conflict was not a rehash of the Civil War, pitting Confederate supporters against Union supporters. As the Board of Indian Commissioners' investigation and report on the war pointed out, veterans from both sides were in leadership positions in both parties, although the Constitutionalist Party leadership was top-heavy with former Confederates. Both the Constitutionalist Lighthorse officers killed were First Indian Home Guard veterans who had fought for the Union as Loyal Creeks. What is more, both had claims pending under the Loyal Creek claims being pushed as a cause celebre by Isparhecher's party, and both were Constitutionalist party supporters.[48]

The breakdown was more between the progressive development-minded Creeks, who wanted to centralize and modernize the Creek government and extend educational opportunities as a way to protect Creek sovereignty from intruders, and the conservative traditionalists, who wanted to maintain local control and political patronage through the town chiefs and to protect against the further erosion of Creek traditions through sustaining the power of the town chiefs and representatives in council. Both factions wanted to protect and preserve the Creek nation and society; on that point, there was no dispute. Where the parties differed was on who should wield power and how that power should be employed against encroachment on Creek sovereignty.[49]

Another feature of the conflict distorted in many contemporary (and subsequent historical) accounts was the role of African Creeks. G. W. Stidham put the blame for the conflict squarely on the African Creeks and their agitation for equal rights in the nation. While it is true that African Creeks were an important part of the insurgent militia and that leading African Creeks lent support to Isparhecher, one sign that the African Creek com-

AFRICAN CREEKS

munity had matured was the lack of universal sympathy for the insurgent cause. Some prominent African Creeks supported the Constitutionalists, and many others served in the Creek government militia. With the maturing of the African Creek community, individuals and particular settlements had divergent interests. There were entrepreneurial African Creeks, such as Sugar George and Simon Brown, who supported the government because they approved of its progressive policies regarding development and access to markets, though even the most accommodating Creek progressives wanted the benefits for Creeks only, not for intruders. Also, the African Creek politicians Snow Sells, H. C. Reed, Sugar George, Simon Brown, Monday Durant, Hardy Stidham, and Ned Robbins, all early supporters of Sands's party and the Loyal Creeks in the years immediately after the war, were solidly ensconced in the political patronage system, and by 1882–1883, had little sympathy for the insurgent cause, giving strong support to the government. Robert Marshall, one of the principals accused in the Cobb case, led a Coweta District Lighthorse contingent for the Constitutionalists, and Ben Barnett, lately charged (and released) in the John Vann shooting, served as a private in the same outfit. So the most aggrieved African Creeks had reasons for backing the government, even if it was only for the daily stipend paid for militia service. At the center of the incident that sparked the war stood Joe Barnett, an African Creek and First Indian Home Guard veteran.[50]

If anyone had cause for alienation from the constitutional government, it was Joe Barnett. As a target of Cherokee vigilantes, he was given no protection by the Creek government and was charged with murder in the Vann case, yet he gave the government his allegiance. While his being held for the "trial" was more an attempt to mollify the Cherokees than a serious move to get a conviction, being held in limbo for nearly two years and watching the continuing vigilante activity could hardly have instilled much loyalty. After his case was dismissed in July 1881, he moved to the western Creek country to put some distance between himself and Cherokee vigilantes. Barnett's loyalty to the Constitutionalists paid off at this point because he stood for, and was elected to, the Lighthorse in the Wewoka District in September, shortly after his arrival there. Whether by mere circumstance or by choice, in July 1882 Barnett found himself on the front line in the government's efforts to impose authority on the insurgents and, indeed, he paid the ultimate price for his alliance with the government.[51]

Checote, with the assistance of African Creek politicians, moved swiftly to contain the insurgent outbreak and called up additional Lighthorse and militia forces. To the surprise of many, Silas Jefferson abandoned the Loyal Party after he learned of Isparhecher's armed opposition to the government. After the outbreaks that summer, he worked diligently to bring the warring factions together. Snow Sells, as the town chief, enlisted a contingent of African Creeks from Arkansas Colored to serve in the Constitutionalist militia, with its full complement of African Creeks. Following Checote's instructions, H. C. Reed indicted fourteen African Creeks for treason in the Muskogee District Court. Two of them gave evidence against the others and were set free, and a cooperative jury, headed by Monday Durant, convicted twelve of the accused. After Checote denied their petition for clemency, Robert Grayson, Manuel Warrior, and ten others received fifty lashes. They were the only ones so punished for political crimes arising from the insurgency that summer, and it confirmed their earlier protests that they were unfairly targeted for punishment by the government. At the same time, an African Creek jury in the Coweta District acquitted Jacob Perryman, Isom Marshall, and Gabriel Marshall of treason charges. Others convicted in Coweta and other district courts received pardons after taking a loyalty oath to the government.[52]

There were scattered skirmishes over the next several weeks, but the government militia appeared to have no trouble restoring order. In fact, the militia men spent more idle time than was good for them. Unoccupied rounding up insurgents, they spent their time foraging, which perhaps gave the conflict its name, as government soldiers helped themselves to unripe peaches in an insurgent orchard and suffered from the ill effects. Isparhecher, with a number of African Creek followers, fled into the western Cherokee country, and another band of insurgents under Tuckabatchee Hacho and David McQueen slipped across the border in the other direction into Seminole country. The rebellion's first phase dissipated rather quickly, and the insurgency appeared to be over by the middle of August. Those involved in the shooting of Scott and Barnett eventually stood trial, and though Checote pardoned eight of the eleven convicted and sentenced to death, two men were finally executed. Checote issued, and the council endorsed, a blanket amnesty that fall, and matters appeared to settle down except that Isparhecher and his followers were still at large.[53]

The conflict's next phase began in December 1882. In the first week of

December, H. C. Reed told Checote that rumors were afoot in the African Creek communities along Pecan and Sugar creeks that a renewed round of troubles were in the cards: "the old women seem to be in a great deal of secret excitement of another trouble going to be very soon . . . I want to call the boys together at once and tell them to be on the watch. Times seem to be getting very ticklish." Checote called up the militia once again and tried to convince Agent Tufts that the situation was serious.[54]

The predicted troubles broke out again December 22, after 150 of Checote's men, led by James Larney and H. C. Reed, attacked an African Creek homestead (Hunter Grayson's) on Pecan Creek in the predawn hours, allegedly looking for horse thieves. They captured and disarmed one African Creek, Jim Easy, and then shot and killed him "while escaping." Easy's brother Sam and several others did escape, however, and spread the word of the killing. Soon Isparhecher's followers, joined by Dick Glass and other African Creeks mustered from various settlements, were on the move, reportedly on their way to Okmulgee to confront Checote's forces, bedecked in war paint, with corn shucks tucked in their hats to signify their allegiance. The "secret excitements" the old African Creek women were whispering about earlier had come to pass. At the same time, insurgents under Tuckabatchee Hacho crossed back into the Creek country from their refuge in the Seminole Nation, and they met Checote's militia on Christmas Eve, about twenty miles southwest of Okmulgee, in the largest pitched battle of the rebellion. Seven Constitutionalist militia were killed along with an unknown number of insurgents.[55]

When the news of the battle reached Tufts, he finally called for a detachment of federal soldiers from Ft. Gibson to help quell the disturbance and issued a call for each side to appoint a five-member negotiating committee to begin discussions on how to compose their differences. For the next several months, there were negotiations, many promised surrenders, feints and near attacks, withdrawals, and pursuits until finally Isparhecher and Tuckabatchee Hacho were captured by U.S. troops in April on the Wichita lands west of the Sac Fox Reservation. An African Creek oral tradition, in Greek tragedy form, recounts how Loyal Creek women, whose concern for the nation's welfare eclipsed partisan concerns, convinced Isparhecher's men to surrender. On learning that heavily armed federal soldiers were being dispatched to round up and destroy the insurgent army, Hagar Myers, wife of John Myers, Isparhecher's African Creek private secretary, interpreter, and advisor, volunteered to take a plea to surrender from the African Creek women to Isparhecher and his men. She bravely navigated through Constitutionalist lines using cunning, wile, and her knowledge of the countryside to bring the news that the soldiers were coming and that the insurgents should surrender peaceably. When Hagar's message was read to the assembled five hundred men, enough of them accepted the wisdom of surrender to make the insurgent stand untenable. Black federal troopers from the Ninth and Tenth cavalries easily captured the insurgent leaders and confined them, along with sixty-five die-hard supporters, at the nearby Sac Fox Reservation at the beginning of May 1883, before transporting them to Ft. Gibson in July.[56]

Island Smith, an African Creek interviewed in the 1930s, recalled seeing the soldiers at their camp outside Okmulgee while they were on their way to capture Isparhecher and his men. Their encounter illustrates the cultural distance between African Creeks and African Americans from the states. Smith, who had two uncles with Isparhecher, one Indian and one African Creek, observed that the soldiers were small black men, not much taller than he and his Indian friends (Smith was about six years old at the time). They were dressed in blue uniforms with bright brass buttons and rode small ponies. When Smith and his friends tried to talk to the soldiers, they got no reply. The soldiers, fresh from duty rounding up white boomers who resented black soldiers lording over them, must have truly felt like strangers in a strange land, trying to ignore the black youth dressed like his Indian companions in a long shirt made of homespun, belted at the waist, as he talked to them in heavily accented English and then reported to his companions in Creek.[57]

Just as in 1872, the Board of Indian Commissioners came to the Creek country in August to arbitrate the dispute. African Creeks attended the peace conference as delegates on both sides of the table. Silas Jefferson and H. C. Reed played key roles on the Constitutionalist side; and David McQueen, Daniel Childers, Gabriel Jamison, Isom Jamison, William McIntosh, John Myers, Robert Grayson, and Manuel Warrior all played a part in presenting the Loyal Party's case. Under the agreement signed on August 10, 1883, the Creek government granted a full and unconditional pardon for offenses arising from the rebellion. The insurgents agreed to recognize the present laws and constitution of the Creek Nation. Both parties acknowledged the need to reorganize and reform the Lighthorse and "use every

AFRICAN CREEKS

effort to secure a free and fair count" in the approaching 1883 election, and abide by its results. Other provisions outlined a fair processing of claims for damages arising from the conflict and the terms under which U.S. troops would be temporarily stationed in the Creek country to oversee and enforce the terms of the agreement.[58]

The Green Peach War was the most serious Creek intratribal cultural and political conflict in the postwar era, but it was not the last. The cultural, political, and economic tensions that provoked the conflict remained prominent features in Creek national life and even increased as noncitizen intrusion escalated many times in comparison to previous levels. Yet the Creek political system and society had matured and was seasoned by the conflict, preparing it to withstand conflicts to come. Although a handful of African Creek insurgents were targeted for corporal punishment for their political crimes while Creek Indian insurgents received pardons or clemency in the first stage of the rebellion, some of those punished went on to raise arms against the government and were pardoned once again, indicating that race relations retained a fluidity in the Creek Nation unequaled in any of the states at the time.

As soon as the Green Peach War political crisis was settled, the Creeks faced yet another test of the nation's viability. The 1883 election, held barely one month after the peace agreement was signed, brought unresolved tensions to the surface. Three parties fielded candidates in the election, held in the first week in September. Checote and Coweta Micco ran as first and second chief on the Pin Party ticket, which most of the Constitutionalists backed. Some progressive Creeks, however, recoiled at the government's use of excessive force in the run-up to the rebellion and during the war itself, and they backed the Muskogee Party, which was now headed by Joseph M. Perryman, a progressive Coweta Mission School alum, Eufaula rancher, and a Confederate Creek Regiment veteran. Under Perryman's leadership, the party took a more progressive stance toward development, losing some of its traditionalist sheen in the process, and attracted a number of influential African Creeks as well as a sizable portion of the rank and file in Arkansas and North Fork Colored towns. The Loyal Party of course, nominated Isparhecher, and even those African Creeks who had not supported his insurgency backed his legitimate bid for power wholeheartedly. All three parties published platforms in the *Indian Journal*, the Muskogee newspaper, and promised equal treatment for all citizens, a commitment to education, and the promotion of friendly relations with the United States. The Loyal Party platform stood out because it endorsed granting citizenship to people who married Creek citizens "irrespective of race or color." The provision was drafted to appeal to African Creeks married to freed people from the states or to African Creeks who had returned too late to qualify for citizenship, but it would also apply to whites who married into the tribe.[59]

Despite the conciliatory words and gestures exchanged at the peace conference, the agreement to hold a free and fair election broke down once the voting began. Once again, there were irregularities in counting the votes, which threatened to plunge the nation back into civil war. As in previous elections, the controversy centered on counting the votes in Arkansas Colored, the largest town in the nation. The voting at Simon Brown's ferry had just started when Clinch Barnwell, an Isparhecher supporter, and Dan Tucker, a Constitutionalist man, began arguing. Apparently, Barnwell started the fuss, saying to Tucker (in reference to his Constitutionalist Party affiliation), "you all does nothing but dress [fine] and steal money." Tucker replied, "If I stole anything from you, prove it and let the law handle me for it." At this point another Isparhecher man, Jesse Hawkins, came forward, removed his coat, and said, "step aside, I'll fight Tucker." Tucker's friends then hustled him away to safety. Barnwell later apologized, but after Tucker did not reciprocate, Barnwell started in again. Daniel Miller, the Coweta Lighthorse captain, tried to order Barnwell to desist, but Barnwell swung around and shouted, "get away from here," and batted Miller's hat away. A general melee erupted, guns were drawn, but fortunately no one opened fire. Snow Sells, the town chief, immediately called the election off. Many suspected that the disturbance was engineered, like the 1879 election fraud in the Colored towns, to keep the African Creek votes from influencing the outcome. But the Barnwell-Tucker feud seemed to be a spontaneous political and personal affair, possibly fueled by liquor. However, Miller's strong-arm tactics and Sells's quick action in shutting down the election had a distinctly partisan tone. Two other towns had votes thrown out as well. In Taskigi, Silas Jefferson's town, the town chief, a Constitutionalist supporter, instructed his people to vote in Okmulgee instead of in Taskigi itself. Okmulgee was not a great distance away, less than ten miles, but the town chief also ordered the election on a different day than the one specified by Checote. At Quassarty, the Muskogee Party fraud was so heavy handed that not even Perryman's supporters in council would defend the returns.[60]

Checote ordered new elections in the towns, but for council positions only, not for chief. In Arkansas Colored, there were further complaints of the new election being a "one-sided game," and this time Checote's party protested after the council seats from Arkansas Colored were filled with Isparhecher supporters. Under these circumstances, it is surprising that there was no renewal of the civil war. But rather than instigating another war, the Checote and Isparhecher parties came together to oppose seating Perryman as chief. This sudden redrawing of political boundaries and the coming together of disgruntled office seekers was perplexing for some but probably saved the Creek Nation from further bloodshed. Even though the Indian Office recognized Perryman as the official winner, the newly elected council, seated in December, was dominated by Checote- Isparhecher supporters, and they proceeded to declare Isparhecher chief. At this point, the secretary of the Interior, Henry M. Teller, began yet another investigation and concluded what the *Indian Journal* had maintained all along: however the vote was calculated, with or without the votes disallowed by the October council, Perryman had won by a squeaker. Furthermore, by any reckoning, African Creek votes counted in the other two African Creek towns provided the margin of victory for Perryman and the progressives.[61]

The five years between 1878 and 1883 had been tumultuous ones for African Creeks and the Creek Nation as a whole, and African Creeks had played leading roles in the most significant events of the period. At the Senate hearings, the elections, the border war, and the Green Peach War, African Creeks were at the very center of events that determined the course that the Indian nation would take for the next twenty-three years. Whether acting as central agents of political and social change or in the familiar role occupying the middle ground between contending forces, African Creek identity had shown its remarkable ability to adapt to conditions and adopt roles to fit the circumstances. At the same time, the African Creek community was also busy creating its own communal identity within the Creek Indian cultural milieu with the establishment of schools and churches that were tailored to the needs of the African Creeks and yet still served the wider Creek community, especially for those Creeks who still spoke no English and wanted no connection with commercial development, which was increasingly weaving its way into the Creek country.

Silas Jefferson (1835–1913), also known as Ho-tul-ko-micco (Wind Clan chief), was a leading figure in the African Creek community. He was the only African Creek elected to represent a traditional Indian town and was eventually enrolled by the Dawes Commission on the by-blood roll rather than the freedmen roll (ca. 1877).
Smithsonian Institution, National Anthropological Archives, negative no. 1117.

Silas Jefferson with Creek chief Locha Hacho. This photo was probably taken in Washington, D.C., when the Loyal Creek delegation went to the capital to protest Locha Hacho's impeachment in 1877. Left to right: John McGillivray, unidentified (probably J. B. G. Dixon), Locha Hacho, Silas Jefferson.
Smithsonian Institution, National Anthropological Archives, negative no. 1164-B.

Study of Creek freedman boy (ca. 1900).
University of Tulsa, McFarlin Library Special Collections,
Alice Robertson Collection, photograph 1:7E.

African Creek woman and child at their homestead
in the Creek Nation (1898–1899).
*National Archives, RG 48, Photographs Accompanying Reports to the
Secretary of the Interior, 1887–1930, identification NWDNS-48-rst-5b-2.*

"Cotton Picking Time" in the Creek Nation (1898–1899).
*National Archives, RG 48, Photographs Accompanying Reports to the
Secretary of the Interior, 1887–1930, Identification NWDNS-48-rst-5b-4.*

Old Creek Agency School and Baptist Church (ca. 1900). Located at the former site of the Creek Agency outside Muskogee, the agency school and church were among the first established by African Creeks after the Civil War.
University of Tulsa, McFarlin Library Special Collections, Alice Robertson Collection, photo 2:1B.

Little River Colored Baptist School children
(ca. 1900). Perhaps these African Creek children
were similar to those from "an outlying district"
whose parents petitioned Creek School
superintendent Alice Robertson to send them
an "Indian teacher who spoke Creek."
*University of Tulsa, McFarlin Library Special
Collections, Alice Robertson Collection, photo 4:2J₃.*

Tullahassee Mission ruins after December 1880 fire. It's little wonder
that some African Creeks rejected the offer of the "burned out hulk"
seen in this picture as the location of the "new" boarding school for
African Creek children. What we can't see in the photograph are the
hundreds of acres of improved farmland and orchards that
accompanied the mission and that, no doubt, played a part in the
decision to accept the site.
*University of Tulsa, McFarlin Library Special Collections, Alice
Robertson Collection. Photo 7:6A5.*

Eleven years after the fire, the Tullahassee Manual Labor School (April 1891) stood as the premier institution for educating African Creek children. The photo was taken during Nellie Ann Leslie's brief tenure as superintendent in 1891, after all Creek schools were taken away from supervision by church missionary societies and supervised instead by Creek citizens.
Oklahoma Historical Society, Alice Robertson Collection, photo 1553.

James Coody Johnson (left) with Seminole chief Halputta Micco (seated) and Okcha Hacho (right) in Washington on official business for the Seminole Nation (1901–1905). Johnson was the official interpreter for the Seminoles as well as an advisor to Chief Halputta Micco at the time. He was also active in the Creek National Council. As Creek chief Pleasant Porter said at the time, "he carries the responsibilities of two nations on his shoulders and he carries them lightly."
Oklahoma Historical Society, James Coody Johnson Collection, 1141.

Black family in the Creek Nation.
Oklahoma Historical Society, Heye Foundation, photograph 398-12632.

African Creek school at Pleasant Grove (ca. 1900). Formerly known as Sodom,
the community changed its name to Pleasant Grove to attract African
American settlers from the states after restrictions on the sale of
allotments were removed in 1904.
Oklahoma Historical Society, Heye Foundation, photograph 14707B.

Island Smith in his role as a native healer (ca. 1935). Anthropologist Sigmund Sameth photographed Smith at his desk "writing" a prescription. Smith thought it was a great joke because he was a native doctor only and was illiterate.

Paro Bruner, long-time African Creek leader and Canadian Colored Town chief (ca. 1900). Bruner founded the settlement of Prairie's Edge on the southwestern edge of the Creek Nation, just north of the Canadian River and southwest of present-day Holdenville. Although he aided the Dawes Commission in getting African Creeks properly enrolled for allotment, he had warned the assembled Creeks at Okmulgee in 1894, when the Dawes commissioners first arrived in the Creek country, that "nothing good could come of allotment," and he predicted that the Creeks would be robbed of their homes and driven from their land.
Oklahoma Historical Society, Aylesworth Collection, 1922-41.

Emanciption Day ✗ ✗ ✗

Will be Celebrated with a Grand Street Parade in which all the Colored Citizens will Participate, with

John Porter

As General of the Day, and

Miss Emma Brown

as the Queen.

FREE BARBECUE

in the afternoon. Everbody invited. Speaking by celebrated orators. Dancing day and night.

WILEY McINTOSH,
President,
LOUIS SANGER,
Clerk.

Times Job Print, Muscogee, I. T.

Emancipation Day flyer. African Creeks designated August 4 as Emancipation Day because the Loyal Creek Council had proclaimed African Creeks citizens with full equal rights in the Creek Nation on August 4, 1865, more than a month before the Loyal Creeks and the former Confederates signed the preliminary agreement with the United States at the Ft. Smith Peace Conference, which outlined the rights of the African Creeks.
Oklahoma Historical Society, Alice Robertson Collection, box 1, file 6.

5

"The Strong Vein of Negro Blood"
Creek Racial Politics and Citizenship

Following the end of the Green Peach War and the settlement of the 1883 election controversy, the Creek country settled into a period of relative calm. Seen in terms of increasing political influence, educational opportunity, and formation of community identity, the next ten years were golden years for African Creeks. Unfortunately, this tranquility did not last. In the years following the collapse of Indian resistance in the West, with the "wild tribes" confined to reservations in areas deemed unsuitable for farming or ranching, white settlers and ranchers poured into the newly opened lands. Gilded Age entrepreneurs created bonanza wheat farms and cattle factories in the northern plains. By the late 1880s, the last significant portion of arable undeveloped land in the West was in the Indian Territory. Settlers, developers, and entrepreneurs increasingly directed their attention toward the Unassigned Lands and those of the Indian republics. Although African Creeks were in a relatively strong position at the end of the Green Peach War and used the opportunity to increase their influence, pressure from a new onslaught of intruders, who had little use for the traditional fluidity that governed race relations in the Creek country, constantly undermined the African Creek position. Factionalism developed within the Creek Nation and the African Creek community itself on how to deal with the threat to Creek sovereignty as the issues of identity, citizenship, and who was entitled to share in the Creek commonwealth became major issues. The African Creek position was also affected by the racial attitude in the nation at large, as clear racial lines were drawn in the post-Reconstruction South, and blacks were being legally excluded from social and political life. Politicians and reformers alike viewed the multiracial society evolving on the

161

racial frontier as an impediment to "progress" and "civilization" in the Indian Territory.

In response to this pressure, Congress dispatched yet another investigating committee to the Indian Territory in 1885. Led by Henry L. Dawes, the Senate Indian Appropriations Committee chairman and a leading advocate for allotting Indian lands in severlty, the committee questioned Creek citizens closely in meetings held at Muskogee. Committee members, including Dawes, appeared transfixed on African Creek citizenship rights. Some Creeks suspected that the federal government intended to use the issue to break the Creek land title. Accordingly, George Washington Grayson, George W. Stidham, Pleasant Porter, L. C. Perryman, and others affirmed the justice of African Creek rights in one degree or another in their testimony.[1]

Grayson told the committee that while being put on an equal footing with African Creeks was "distasteful," the Creeks had accepted the situation and had gone to work to make the best of it. Grayson reckoned there was "a good feeling and harmony" between African Creeks and other Creeks, although some African Creeks might have seen the matter differently. He told the committee of going to Ft. Smith on behalf of one of his family's former slaves, who had been jailed in a case of mistaken identity and then robbed of his horse by an unscrupulous lawyer. Grayson's paternalistic motives were mixed with his desire to protect Creek sovereignty. He said that while the wronged man "was a Negro, [he was] nevertheless a Muscogee" and thus worthy of protection from the white man's legal system. For many Creeks like Grayson, who believed that blacks were inferior, protecting tribal sovereignty was more important than racial considerations.[2]

G. W. Stidham, G. W. Grayson's father-in-law, also testified at the hearing. Stidham begrudgingly acknowledged African Creek citizenship rights but decried their undue political influence. He blamed the African Creeks for the Green Peach War, saying that their insistent demands about their rights not being respected were at the center of the controversy. He went on to say Africans Creeks held the balance of power in the nation, and within ten years they would control political affairs because of their increasing population. Stidham claimed that the African Creek natural increase far outstripped the Creek Indian population and was further reinforced by African Indian intruders from the neighboring Indian nations. Increasing numbers of freed people coming from the South complicated the picture, making it difficult to determine just who was entitled to citizenship rights. Stidham also declared that African Creeks with "Creek blood" were considered Indians.[3]

John H. Harris, a member of the House of Warriors from Arkansas Colored, was the sole African Creek to appear before the committee. Harris identified himself as a Creek and nothing more. Apparently, Dawes wanted some clarification because Harris was clearly of African descent. But when asked if he had been a slave, Harris simply replied, "No," and when asked if the majority of people living in his district were "colored," he replied, "we have both Colored and Indians up there [in the Coweta District north of the Arkansas River]." After assuring the committee that African Creeks participated freely in politics and were given equal educational opportunities, he went on to say that he opposed allotment and territorial status and supposed that most African Creeks felt the same. Harris mentioned the chief complaint voiced by many African Creeks in his part of the country: intruders and the Indian agent's failure to do anything about the problem. Harris was particularly concerned about white adopted or intermarried Cherokee cattlemen who continued to run their herds on Creek lands in defiance of Creek law and despite the violence during the border race war. As far as African American intruders were concerned, Harris admitted that freed people from the states came among them, but he added that the Creek people "treated them very well when they complied with the law." (Apparently Harris was speaking of permit holders, not actual intruders.) When asked if state freedmen tried to pass themselves off as African Creeks and thereby gain rights to land and other advantages, one of G. W. Stidham's chief complaints, Harris replied that this was not a problem in his part of the country.[4] After the hearings, even though Dawes was committed to the allotment policy and a proponent of putting an end to Indian sovereignty, he promised the Creeks that he would seek no changes in their position unless they approved.[5]

Perhaps freedmen intruders from the states were not a problem for Harris and did not interfere with his cattle operation in the way the white Cherokee intruders did, but what to do about the freedmen intruders was a problem for other Creeks that quickened during the late 1880s. While the white boomer movement led by David Payne held the Creek's attention, African American intruders were also a source of concern. They trickled into the Creek country from different avenues. Some came as railroad workers constructing the lines across the Indian Territory in the 1870s and 1880s; they reveled in the unfettered atmosphere and stayed on. Others came as permit men, working the farms of Creek Indians and freed people. Still others came as spouses who had married African Creek refugees during their Civil War exile. In 1881, two years after David Payne organized the white boomers in Kansas, a black boomer movement emerged in Missouri. Two enterprising African American Missourians, James Milton Turner and Hannibal Carter, began the Freedmen's Oklahoma Immigration Association. Interpreting the 1866 treaty provisions broadly (and erroneously), Turner and Carter issued a circular in April 1881 that promised all freedmen one hundred and sixty acres of public lands in Oklahoma. Although Turner managed to raise the hopes of many African Americans with his announcement, he had far less luck raising resources or getting official sanction for a concerted migration. Lack of resources and adverse rulings against freed people's settlement on the Unassigned Lands by federal courts and government officials stemmed the African American immigration tide. Enough state freed people did come into the Creek country in the early 1880s, however, to cause concern among all Creeks, no matter what their skin color.[6]

Faced with an influx of intruders and a mounting number of questionable citizens, the Creek National Council created a Committee on Citizenship in 1883. Town chiefs traditionally handled citizenship questions and kept the town rolls of those eligible for per capita payments and voting rights. As the cases of disputed citizenship increased after 1867, district courts and judges took on some of these responsibilities. Town chiefs still kept the rolls, but now the final decision-making power in citizenship cases was left up to the committee. It acted as a tribunal; people whose rights were questioned could come before the committee, call witnesses, and introduce evidence. The committee then weighed the evidence and, after consultation, rendered a decision. G. W. Stidham, a leading critic of the "Negro influence" in the nation was the first chairman, and African Creeks Simon Brown and William McIntosh served as members.[7]

In its first years, the committee was mainly concerned with African Creek cases. A majority of these revolved around whether the person had established residency within the time specified in the treaty. At first, the committee returned favorable verdicts if the applicants could prove that they had either belonged to a Creek Indian or had Indian kinship ties and through hardship or other exigencies had simply failed to return within the time required. Politics also played a part in the decision process. Simon Brown claimed that as the 1883 election drew near, a certain party (probably the Constitutionalists) told him that, if he used his influence for their ticket, at the next council the people he sponsored would be adopted. Brown refused to go along, saying that his town (North Fork) was already pledged to Isparhecher. Other African Creek families, however, took advantage of the offer. A group of African Creek McIntoshes and some African Creek Graysons circumvented the committee process and were adopted at the next council meeting after the election. But playing politics with citizenship rights cut both ways—as in the case of the African Creek McGilvray family claim. Apparently the McGilvray adoption was held up because Lipscomb McGilvray, their former owner, attempted to go over the council's head and appealed directly to the Indian Office for his former slaves' adoption. According to Simon Brown, the council so resented the interference that they postponed the adoption to show McGilvray (and presumably other applicants) who was "running the government [and] who adopted people here."[8]

But as the intruder problem increased, the committee's standards changed. They questioned applicants more closely regarding which Indian nation they resided in and whether they had spent any appreciable time outside the Creek country or had kinship ties to noncitizens. The committee began to adhere more strictly to the one-year standard stipulated in the treaty and to reject claims made by African Creeks based on Creek Indian kinship ties. Instead of using the traditional Creek standard that conferred legitimacy through the matrilineal line, any taint of African blood, either on the mother's or father's side, classified the applicant as African and therefore eligible for citizenship only as an adopted citizen under Article II. Ironically, if these same standards were applied to many leading men in the Creek government, they would have their citizenship credentials questioned as well. African Creek women refugees and their children, particularly those who had married noncitizens during their exile, were vulnerable under the new guidelines. Many of these rejected applicants cited kinship ties to Creek Indians, and although the facts were known by all in the community, they still were rejected. Indian agent John Q. Tufts speculated that if the citizenship applicants had been half white, instead of half black, citizenship would have been freely granted.[9]

Not all decisions on citizenship, identity, and the right to live in the

Creek commonwealth were handled through the committee or council or were based on interpreted legalities; some decisions were informal arrangements based on human needs. Monday Durant's petition on behalf of his three daughters and his grandchildren in many ways goes to the heart of the identity and citizenship question as well as the tragedy of slavery. Durant, who was born in the Creek Nation before the Red Stick War, told of his lifelong residence in the Creek country, his memories of the Red Stick War, the Creek removal, the exodus to Kansas, and other pivotal events in Creek history. He also detailed his many years of service to the nation and his role in helping establish Christianity in the Creek country. He pointed out that he had always been considered an Indian and was accorded the same privileges. When burdened with taxes imposed on all free blacks in the years before the war, he paid the tax in full without complaint. Although Durant was a free black, his first wife was a slave, and according to the slave code, his three daughters from that marriage were also slaves. His wife's master and mistress both died before the war, and their daughter, who had inherited Durant's family, married a white man and moved to Texas. After the war, Durant's daughters all married state freedmen from Texas, had children, and moved back to the Creek country. Now their rights to live there were questioned. Durant's petition never went before the Citizenship Committee because he knew that even the most liberal interpretation of the treaty provisions would not admit his family. Adoption was not an option because the blanket adoptions enacted by council covered those families who lived in the Creek nation at the outbreak of the war. Instead, Durant appealed to Chief Checote's sense of humanity as a "God-faring man" who would do what is right and allow an old man to live out the rest of his life in company of the family that slavery had torn from him. He closed his letter with this appeal, "I write these things to you knowing . . . you are a man with a family and knowing how dear a child is to you." Though Checote and Durant had been on opposite sides in many a battle, Checote, in an act of compassion, wrote a letter allowing Durant's children to live on their father's place, plant crops, and build houses without being molested by Creek authorities. But other African Creeks and state freed people married to them were not fortunate enough to have such a well-regarded and politically powerful figure as Monday Durant in their corner and were cut off from citizenship by the more stringent guidelines.[10]

Black intruders also came from the adjoining Indian nations. This development further complicated identity and citizenship issues. Conditions for African Indians in other Indian nations steadily deteriorated during the 1870s and 1880s. In the Choctaw, Chickasaw, and Cherokee nations, African Indians had limited access to land and were virtually shut out from politics. Many African Indians from the other tribes responded, as G. W. Stidham put it, by trying to "fasten themselves onto the Creek Nation," where the racial climate was more favorable. As the number of Choctaw and Cherokee freed people coming into the Creek country increased, African Creek families with family ties in other nations faced difficulties convincing the Citizenship Committee that they had legitimate claims to citizenship.[11]

For many years, open boundaries between the Indian nations, as well as fluid citizenship standards and kinship ties, were an accepted fact in the Indian Territory, especially along the border areas. Some Indians and their slaves had dual residency. In the case of the McGilvray African Creeks, Lipscomb McGilvray had farming and livestock operations in both the Creek and Chickasaw nations and regularly sent his slaves back forth between the two in the years before the Civil War. Although the McGilvrays were eventually adopted, the Reconstruction treaties erected barriers to cross-cultural citizenship for adopted freed people, and a number of African Creeks were shut out as a result. Stidham, as one of the Creek delegates in Washington during the mid-1880s, actively campaigned to have the federal money returned to the Creeks, money he claimed was wrongly distributed as annuity payments to freed people he said were ineligible because they had come from the other Indian nations. In some cases, Cherokee freed people were clearly attempting to "fasten themselves on to the Creek Nation"; in others, Stidham claimed that dual citizenship or kinship ties to other Indian nations disqualified people of African descent from claiming rights with the Creeks even though such connections were no impediment to bona fide citizenship for many prominent cross-cultural Creeks with mixed Indian ancestry.[12]

Another problem affecting African Creek status and identity was the stridency with which J. Milton Turner pushed for Cherokee and Choctaw freed people's citizenship rights while advocating the opening of Indian lands for settlement by state freed people. Turner won a favorable ruling regarding African Cherokee rights to tribal annuities in the late 1880s and won several high-profile cases involving Choctaw and Chickasaw freed people's rights in the following years. Progressive Creeks were galled by Turner's rhetoric justifying Indian freed people's citizenship claims and opening Indian lands to settlement by state freed people:

> It is a fact that the principal industry and tendency to civilize themselves is in many parts of the Territory among the Negroes. Whatever else may be said upon the subject, it is true that the Negro is in no sense advanced or improved by contact with the Indians. While the Indian goes down showing no longevity to withstand Saxon civilization, the Negro there [in the Indian Territory], as elsewhere, shows a desire for the textbooks and takes to the ways of civilized life.[13]

African Creeks, besides opposing opening land to state freed people, resented Turner's sweeping identification of Indian Africans with African Americans. African Creeks identified themselves as natives and related culturally with Creek Indians, not African Americans. While it is true that African Creeks had established a separate community identity within the Creek cultural milieu, most of them still shared language, customs, and worldview with Creek Indians. As they showed in the 1878 and 1885 hearings, they were also resoundingly committed to Creek sovereignty and communal land tenure and realized that noncitizen intruders, whatever their skin color, threatened their existence.

As was seen in the friction that developed between African Creeks and African American "contraband" refugees in Kansas during the Civil War, there was a wide cultural gap between African Creeks and African Americans from the states. Henry Clay, an African American who came as a slave into the Creek country from Louisiana before the war, felt more comfortable with his white owner who had married a Creek woman. He recalled in an interview in the 1930s: "I never did get along good with these Creek slaves out here and I always stayed around the white folks. In fact I was afraid of these Creeks and always got off the road when I seen Creek Negroes coming along. They would have red strings tied in their hats or something wild looking."[14] Speaking about his reluctance to court an African Creek girl in his neighborhood, he said, "them Creek Negroes was so funny to talk to anyways." Another state freedman also commented on how African Creek bilingual abilities set them apart from African Americans from the states: "those freedmen are smart as a whip. They talk around a feller. It's a handy thing to know Creek. . . . They just jabber jabber and a feller can't get a word of it." Despite his initial reluctance, Clay eventually did get a conversation going, married an African Creek woman, and settled down to raise a family in the Creek country.[15]

As the number of black intruders and permit holders increased during the 1880s, they were met with growing hostility from African Creeks. Cultural differences were exaggerated by the presence of an increasing number of Southern white intruders and permit men. Early white traders who came into the Creek country in Georgia and Alabama, as we have seen, not only established kinship ties with Creek Indians but also with African Creeks. Thus, some of the leading Creek families were from a blended ancestry that contained Euro-American, Indian, and African elements: the Graysons, the McIntoshes, the Perrymans, the Durants, the Steadhams, the Hawkinses, the Barnetts, and others. It is no accident that the leading African Creek families carried names of the white Indian traders who came into the Creek country. While it is true that some African Creeks used the surnames of their former owners, in many cases the names signified kinship ties. After the removal to the West and up through the immediate post–Civil War period, the white traders continued the pattern of intermingling with both Creek Indians and African Creeks. The traders also relied on African Creek translators to help them conduct their businesses. At the very least, they accepted the racial fluidity in the Creek country and showed little compunction to draw racial lines in their economic and social interactions. The more recent Gilded Age developers, tradesmen, and homesteaders, however, brought a different attitude to the racial frontier. Reflecting the prevailing racial ideology in the country at large that solidified in the years after Reconstruction, the new entrepreneurs and settlers who flooded into the Indian Territory viewed people of African descent as unsuitable candidates for the social and economic benefits generated by the Gilded Age.[16]

Most African Creeks maintained a subsistence lifestyle like that of most culturally conservative Creeks throughout the tribal period, and they posed little economic threat to the entrepreneurs and developers seeking to establish a commercial market economy in the Indian Territory. There was, however, a notable class of enterprising African Creeks who wanted to take advantage of the burgeoning commercial network that was emerging in the Indian Territory. This class of enterprising African Creeks had more in common with other development-minded Creeks who wanted access to the white man's commercial network yet were also keen on protecting Creek sovereignty and nationality. Many of these "go-ahead" African

Creeks were also involved in the political and religious life of the nation, had a solid foundation as landholders or business operators, and were protected by Creek law and presumably by U.S. treaty obligations. This group was viewed as a threat by the new white arrivals and indeed was perceived as an obstacle to establishing white hegemony because of these African Creeks' independent assertiveness.

Simon Brown, for example, a noted politician and founder of the African Creek Second Baptist Church in Muskogee, operated a lucrative ferry on the Arkansas River northwest of Muskogee. After the Civil War, Brown was a clerk and interpreter at F. H. Nash's store in Ft. Gibson. He also interpreted and acted as a go-between for Judge John W. Wright in paying bounties, back pay, and pensions to the Indian and freedmen veterans. Wright and his ring allegedly defrauded the veterans of over five hundred thousand dollars in pensions and back pay. It is not clear how involved Brown was in the frauds—he later gave damning testimony against Wright in the case—but it is clear that Brown emerged as "a man of means" in the years after the war. He bought his ferry and its improvements in a questionable deal from a recently orphaned boy, John Davis, for ten dollars. Davis, still a minor at the time, had inherited the ferry from his mother shortly after the war and promptly sold it and the improvements to Brown. At the time of the sale, it appeared that the Creek Agency, located nearby and the major source of the ferry's business, would be moved to Okmulgee. But, as it turned out, the agency was reestablished just two miles south to Fern Mountain before moving to Muskogee in 1878, where it was rechristened the Union Agency. Brown turned the ferry into a going enterprise that benefited from its proximity to Muskogee, the major commercial center in the Indian Territory in the postwar years. Brown was also involved in other commercial activities as well and left a considerable estate after he died in 1888.[17]

Sugar George, H. C. Reed, and other prominent African Creek politicians also did quite well for themselves in the postwar years due in no small part to their political connections. George practiced law in the tribal courts and was involved in building and renting property around Muskogee, enterprises that required deft maneuvering between (and outright violation of) the conflicting Creek laws and Interior Department regulations. He was reported to be one of the wealthiest African Creeks and built "a fine mansion" on his ranch north of Lee. H. C. Reed, in addition to his many years as judge in the Muskogee District, ran a hotel at Lee, practiced law in the tribal courts, and dealt in real estate around Muskogee. But his most lucrative enterprise was an immense cattle operation that enclosed 31,160 acres along the western border of the Creek nation, an operation that would later cause much controversy and resentment.[18]

Another prominent African Creek active in the development of the Creek country and its politics was Joseph P. Davison. Davison was born in 1840, the son of Julia Gibson, Sarah Davis's daughter, and D. N. McIntosh, Chief William McIntosh's son. Having kinship ties to the McIntosh family was certainly an advantage for Davison. Also, being the grandson of Sarah Davis, one of the wealthiest and most respected African Creeks, aided his rise to prominence. Davison combined these advantages with a headstrong and willful personality that would frequently land him in the center of controversies that erupted in the Indian nation over identity, citizenship, and land during the coming decades.[19]

Growing to maturity under the watchful eye of his grandmother, he was raised in the Creek Agency village in the years before the Civil War; he helped his grandmother and mother establish a prosperous farming and cattle operation in the area, which included several hundred head of cattle, fenced fields, and thriving apple, peach, and cherry orchards. During the war, Davison was a government teamster employed by Tobe McIntosh to carry supplies between Ft. Scott, Kansas, and Ft. Gibson. After the war, he remained in the Creek Agency settlement, helped his grandmother rebuild her hotel, and restored the family farm and cattle operation. He also became very active in Creek politics and was elected to the House of Warriors from Arkansas Colored in 1887. He was particularly concerned with expanding African Creek educational opportunities. It was mainly through his efforts that the Creek government agreed to establish the Pecan Creek Boarding School west of Muskogee for African Creek students in 1892. He also ran a sizable cattle ranch of his own west of Muskogee, building his herd and ranch from cattle and improvements inherited from his grandmother and mother. He and his wife, Sarah, who was reputed to be one of the best cooks in the Creek country, also ran a catering service that served barbeque and all the trimmings at fairs, picnics, and celebrations.[20]

Warrior (W. A.) Rentie, an African Creek politician and tribal attorney, was also involved in commercial and political activities in the postwar years, and, like J. P. Davison, took a leading role in expanding African Creek educational opportunities. Rentie, born in January 1862, also came from a privileged background. His parents, Caroline and Rentie McIntosh, had been household slaves of Creek chief Roley McIntosh and as such were accorded a special status. His uncle, the African Creek William McIntosh, was one of the leaders of the dramatic exodus through the Confederate-controlled Indian Territory to freedom inside the Union lines in Arkansas in November 1862. Rentie, who was ten months old at the time, was carried by his parents on the dangerous journey and spent the next three years in refugee camps in Kansas. As a young man, Rentie was fortunate enough to have his college education at Nashville Institute sponsored by the Creek Nation. After his graduation, he enjoyed a brief sojourn in the states and returned to the Creek country in 1886, taking a job in 1888 as a teacher in the newly opened African Creek day school in the Paro Bruner settlement at Prairie Edge. Determined to make his mark in the nation, Rentie stayed on and became active in politics, being elected to the House of Warriors from Arkansas Colored in 1891. Rentie also became well versed in Creek tribal law and was a much sought-after tribal lawyer, having compiled, translated, and published a Muskogee English compilation of the laws, acts, and resolutions of the Creek Council.[21]

Yet another up-and-coming figure in the African Creek community during this time was James Coody Johnson. Johnson also came from a privileged family background. He was the son of Robert Johnson, the interpreter for the Seminole Nation, and Elizabeth Davis (Johnson), another daughter of Sarah Davis. Since he was Sarah Davis's grandson, he was also a cousin to Joseph P. Davison. Johnson was born in 1864 at Ft. Gibson, where his mother had gone for protection after James McHenry, acting under orders from Confederate Cherokee General Stand Watie, burned Sarah Davis's home and hotel at the Creek Agency village. As a boy, Johnson lived with his family four miles from Wewoka, barely inside the Creek boundary line. He received his early education at the Presbyterian mission north of Wewoka, which his father helped Rev. James Ross Ramsey locate and build. Later, the Seminole Nation sent him to Lincoln University in Chester, Pennsylvania. He returned to the Indian Territory in 1884, after his graduation, and hired on as a cowboy with a cattle company, and for the next year and a half, he rode the range in New Mexico, Arizona, and Texas as one of the many black cowboys in the West. At the death of his father in 1886, James Coody returned to the Creek country. Growing tired of the roving life, he decided to stay on and parleyed his bilingual abilities, education, and, no doubt, his family connections, into a job as interpreter for judge Isaac Parker, the hanging judge who presided over the federal district court for western Arkansas, which at the time had jurisdiction over the Indian Territory. Johnson's language skills and knowledge of the geography as well as the social and cultural contours of the Indian Territory proved invaluable to Parker and to the operation of the court. Johnson earned the respect of Indians and freed people alike as a knowledgeable and ardent defender of native rights during his tenure at Parker's court. After studying law under Judge Parker and being admitted to practice in the federal courts, Johnson became involved in Creek politics. Although his father, Robert, was considered a Seminole citizen, he had belonged to a Creek citizen and lived in the Creek nation before the war. James Coody also retained his ties to the Creek Nation through his grandmother and mother and was one of the few freed people accorded dual citizenship in both the Creek and Seminole nations. Johnson would later become a leading figure in Creek politics and earned a reputation as a savvy entrepreneur as well.[22]

Both James Coody Johnson and Warrior Rentie stood out because of their education and their privileged backgrounds, but other characteristics set them apart from the older generation of African Creek leaders. Rentie and Johnson were too young to remember the dislocations and devastation of the Civil War or slave life, and although both were involved in the lay leadership of their churches, they were not pastors and they conducted their affairs with a secular outlook. These characteristics prepared them for the role they would play as brokers in later years, as the Creek country was transformed by the land allotment process and the dissolution of tribal sovereignty.

African Creeks owned and operated scores of shops, hostelries, and other businesses in Muskogee, Okmulgee, and in settlements scattered throughout the Creek Nation, such as Lee and Prairie Edge. They continued in their role as cultural brokers, acting as go-betweens for culturally conservative Creeks in commercial activities, but they also made significant contributions to the growing market forces developing in their own right. While development-minded African Creeks were still a bare minority of the total African Creek population, their influence went beyond their numbers.[23]

Development-minded African Creeks concentrated their energies in and around Muskogee, which during the 1880s and 1890s experienced phenomenal growth and was the commercial center of the Creek Nation and the Indian Territory. Since its inception in the early 1870s, Muskogee was considered an alien enclave in the Indian nation, and most of the feverish commercial energy that characterized the town was generated by non-citizens—traders, merchants, railroad men, and others intent on developing the Indian Territory. Most of the commercial activity was conducted despite Creek legislation and federal law that limited and regulated the rights of noncitizens. Creek citizens were involved in the development around Muskogee, however, and in many cases were in partnership with noncitizens, using their citizenship to shield various commercial enterprises from interference by Creek and federal authorities. Business-minded African Creeks such as Sugar George, Sarah Davis, H. C. Reed, J. P. Davison, W. A. Rentie, and others were intent on getting both their share of the wealth being generated and in claiming their rights to the Creek commonwealth guaranteed them under the 1866 treaty. These African Creek entrepreneurs frequently went to the tribal courts to legitimize their claims to valuable property around Muskogee. Angie Debo noted that most cases of disputed rights to use the Creek commonwealth were between African Creeks rather than Creek Indians. But this was not necessarily because African Creeks were more contentious; it was because they constituted the majority of the native population around Muskogee, where the most feverish development occurred. Because Creek sovereignty was still intact at this early stage of development, and protected by treaty obligations, white intruders and developers were compelled to tread lightly and work out mutually beneficial arrangements with Creek citizens.[24]

While African Creeks' identity and their relationship to the emerging commercial development was in flux, their political life stabilized. The 1887 election marked a turning point for African Creek influence in the political process. For the first time since the 1875 election, African Creek votes in Arkansas, Canadian, and North Fork Colored towns were freely and fairly counted, and that vote was critical in determining the outcome in the principal chief election.

There were four tickets in the 1887 contest. Legus C. Perryman and Holtuke Emarthla ran for principal chief and second chief on the Union Party ticket, a new party alliance formed as the Checote and Isparhecher supporters came together. Their platform called for a retrenchment of Creek finances, opposition to the sale of the Unassigned Lands to the federal government, and improved educational opportunities in the nation. Their platform also insisted that the federal government faithfully carry out the provisions of the 1866 treaty in protecting the Creeks from intruders. The Union Party originally asked Isparhecher to head the ticket, but the cagey leader objected to parts of the party platform. Then he withdrew his candidacy, called his own convention, and formed a Loyal Party ticket with Tulwa Fixico, the Wewoka District judge, running as second chief. A new party, the Independent Party, also entered a slate of candidates in the 1887 election. The Independents were a group of educated, reform-minded young men alarmed by the growing Creek debt generated by the national council through free-wheeling payment of claims arising from the Green Peach War. They were also disturbed by lax enforcement of tribal law, particularly in Muskogee, where whiskey peddlers and "hops shops" were allowed to proliferate, and noncitizens dominated most of the commercial activity. They nominated John R. Moore for principal chief and James Fife for second chief. The thrust of the Independents' platform was reducing Creek government expenses through shrinking the size of the national council and paring down the number of Lighthorsemen. They also opposed selling the Unassigned Lands. Because the Independents drew few established political faces into their ranks, they earned the nickname "the Poor Man's Party." The fourth ticket in the crowded field, the Muskogee Party, put Joseph Perryman forward for reelection along with Hotulke Fixico as second chief.[25]

Legus C. Perryman rolled up substantial majorities in all three African Creek towns, which helped put him over the top. Although African Creek votes indeed helped engineer Legus Perryman's victory, they were not unanimous in their support. In Arkansas Colored, 30 percent of the voters stayed with Joseph Perryman, three voted for John Moore, and, surprisingly, only five cast their ballots for Isparhecher. Clinch Barnwell and Jesse Hawkins, the two Isparhecher supporters who sparked the fracas that scuttled the 1883 election in Arkansas Colored, both voted for Legus Perryman in 1887. Dan Tucker, the Constitutionalist stalwart and the target of Barnwell's wrath, supported Joseph Perryman in his losing bid for a second term. Tucker, however, was elected to the House of Warriors from Arkansas Colored. In North Fork Colored and Canadian Colored, Legus Perryman also did well, gaining 70 and 65 percent of the vote, respectively. Joseph Perryman and John Moore gained only a handful of votes in these towns, but the real story regarding the African Creek vote in the 1887 election lies in Isparhecher's failure to draw support from these two towns where he had won huge majorities in 1883.[26]

African Creeks as a constituency were moving away from the conservative, localist position embraced by Isparhecher and his supporters and aligning themselves with the more progressive agenda espoused by Legus Perryman and the Union Party. While the traditional Creek attitude toward fluidity in race relations still prevailed in the culturally conservative settlements where Isparhecher drew most of his support, Legus Perryman's alleged African heritage, a symbol of the racial fluidity of earlier years, may have attracted some African Creek voters. But tangible benefits, not racial identity, probably influenced most African Creeks to support Perryman. Perryman's many years as Creek delegate to Washington, his years on the national council, lately as speaker of the House of Warriors, meant his political influence, already established within the Indian nation, extended beyond the Creek country's borders. Also, Perryman's Civil War service in the First Indian Home Guard, where he frequently worked on details with African Creeks, probably influenced African Creek veterans to support him. So, whether African Creeks wanted more funding for schools, access to markets, action on the Loyal Creek claim, or help with Civil War pension claims, Legus Perryman's experience offered a positive viable alternative.[27]

After the election, African Creeks parleyed their political influence into expanding educational opportunities. During these years, African Creek education, like African Creeks' role in politics, seemed to bode especially well for the future. Legus Perryman and the Union Party made good on their promise to expand educational opportunities; in particular, they rewarded their African Creek supporters. In 1888, the Creek Council established two new day schools for African Creeks, one at Coal Creek in the Coweta District, in the northeast corner of the nation, and one at Paro Bruner's settlement along the Canadian River, on the southwestern border. These two schools brought the total number of African Creek day schools to ten. These neighborhood schools, although under the overall supervision of the Creek Board of Education, were run by trustees in individual African Creek communities and by and large had African Creek teachers. While the quality of the instruction varied according to the teachers' skills and the community resources available, it was generally agreed that African Creek schools were on par, if not above, the standards of any schools for African Americans in neighboring states.[28]

The schools, like the churches, were focal points of community identity, and African Creeks pointed with pride to students' (and teachers') accomplishments in numerous articles submitted to the *Indian Journal* and the *Muskogee Phoenix*. Indeed, African Creek children were the most schooled African Indian population in the Indian Territory and attended more school hours than African American students in any of the neighboring Southern states. In addition to the neighborhood day schools, there was also the Tullahassee Mission School, which boarded fifty students, and three privately operated schools for African Creeks—the Evangel Mission, a school run by the Methodists at Eufaula, and a private school at Okmulgee.[29] Despite the controversy that erupted over turning the Tullahassee Mission over to African Creeks, Tullahassee stood as the premier educational institution for African Creek students in the nation, and for many years it was the only school with advanced grades for freed people's children in the Indian Territory. While the control of the school rested ultimately with the Creek Board of Education and the Tullahassee trustees (African Creeks Sugar George, Snow Sells, and Jonathan Kernel), the Baptist Home Missionary Society was contracted to provide a superintendent and teachers who oversaw the day-to-day operations. The Baptist missionaries also determined the curriculum and the scope of the educational program. The Baptists replaced the liberal education provided by the Leslies at the original African Creek boarding school with an industrial and manual training program structured similarly to those used at freed people's schools throughout the South. The program took shape under the first superintendent, Rev. J. P. Lawton, who took charge of the school in November 1883.[30]

When Lawton first came to the school, he had high hopes. Although H. C. Reed, in charge of the building committee that oversaw the rebuilding of Tullahassee, had declared the school ready for operation in spring 1883, when Lawton arrived to take charge in the fall, he found that the roof leaked, there were no beds or bedding, and there was very little furniture for the children. Neither were there livestock or tools for the school farm, which covered some eighty acres. If industry and manual labor were the focal points of the instructional program, then the boys and girls would need something to be industrious with. By the time an inspection committee from the Missionary Society had visited the site some six months later, however, they found things to be in order: "we were greatly pleased with the order, neatness, the decorum, and the progress of the pupils. The Bible is the textbook, and the formation of Christian character is the constant aim."[31]

Lawton spent one year at Tullahassee and was succeeded in 1884 by Truman Johnson and his wife, Jennie Bixby Johnson. The Johnsons continued the industrial and manual labor program and encountered many of the same problems, among them lack of supplies and tools for teaching mechanical arts. Nevertheless, the boys raised staple crops on the farm and planted and cultivated vegetable gardens and fruit orchards, much the same as they would do at home. They were also instructed in shoemaking, and with money and supplies provided by the Creek Council, helped build an additional boys' dormitory building. The girls, under the supervision of Jennie Johnson and the matron, Mrs. E. A. Wooster, were taught in "all the branches of housewifery," sewed their own clothes, and were responsible for all the cooking, and like the boys, they were instructed in occupations not much different than what most of them experienced at home.[32]

For the Johnsons, the most gratifying part of their experience at Tullahassee were their successes in converting the children to Christianity. When they first arrived at the mission, they found that most students selected by the trustees were "unredeemed." According to Jennie Johnson, the pinnacle of their conversion efforts occurred in January 1885, when Snow Sells accepted Christ after hearing a student sing the hymn that his late wife had sung on her deathbed some years before.[33]

The next year the Johnsons left Tullahassee and were replaced by G. E. Burdick. Apparently, the transition was a contentious one because most of the staff, including the matron, and most of the teachers who had served at the institution from its beginning, resigned. Burdick voiced the perennial complaint about the lack of tools and equipment but nonetheless stressed the manual labor training program. In his 1887 report to the Missionary Society, he attributed the program's success to teaching the students the "dignity of labor" as well as Christian principles.[34]

The last superintendent sponsored by the Missionary Society was E. H. Rishell, who supervised Tullahassee from fall 1887 until January 1891, when the Creek Nation turned the school over to African Creek supervision. Rishell, with the longest tenure of any missionary superintendent, left the clearest record concerning the school's operation. Under his supervision, the school expanded to take on fifty more students in 1889 and allowed other children not sponsored by the nation to attend for seven dollars per month. In 1890 yet another wing was built to accommodate the additional students. Regarding his students' cultural background, Rishell wrote that the children could speak Creek much better than English when they first arrived. About two-thirds of the students became church members during their stay there, but apparently most children, as in earlier years, arrived at school "unredeemed." Concerning matters of religion, Rishell wrote, "there is much prejudice and superstition to overcome," which he addressed by regularly holding services and prayer meetings in both Creek and English at the nearby Fountain Church for mixed congregations.[35]

According to Rishell, the children were generally well behaved, and he experienced few discipline problems, which was fortunate because he wanted to avoid having the school serve as a reform school, which so many African American manual labor schools indeed became.[36] The instructional program, as before, stressed farm work, carpentry, and woodwork for the boys and domestic work for the girls. During Rishell's tenure, the farm was expanded to include over two hundred acres. The boys raised sweet potatoes and turnips and banked them for later use. They also raised and cured their own meat and supplemented their meat supply with wild turkeys and venison bought from local Indians as well as with fish caught at the Point. The girls tended bountiful vegetable gardens and dried and canned the produce from the gardens and the school orchards, which included apple, peach, and cherry trees. Visitors were delighted and amazed at the progress at the farm and commented favorably regarding its orderly and industrious regimen.[37]

Rishell also noted progress in academics during his term at the school. Although the students arrived with a better command of Creek than English, Rishell found them to be apt pupils, and they quickly learned to speak read, write, and sing well in English. Their lessons included rhetorical drills, object lessons, drawing, algebra, natural philosophy, physiology and hygiene, botany, and, most particularly, the principles and practice of teaching, because most students were expected to become teachers. While the boys received more academic training than the girls, more Tullahassee female graduates actually went on to teach in African Creek schools. In 1889 Rishell noted with pride the number of Tullahassee graduates who went on to "higher pursuits," either as teachers, preachers, missionaries, or to school in the states, but apparently most students used the skills learned at the school to return to farming or to set up households in the Creek country.[38]

Rishell and the other missionary superintendents followed the prescribed program used at freed people's schools throughout the South and identified with the manual vocational training pioneered at Hampton Institute in Virginia by Samuel Chapman Armstrong and later carried out by Booker T. Washington at the Tuskegee Institute. Washington and other manual training advocates believed that slavery had instilled in freed people a disdain for manual labor, which they maintained was a barrier to productive citizenship in the socioeconomic structure evolving in the New South. This barrier they believed could be overcome through teaching "the dignity of labor." Washington's program was geared to prepare freed people for a place in that structure. African Americans were counseled to avoid political agitation and instead concentrate on economic achievements and "moral uplift" of their communities.[39]

Interestingly, the same manual labor approach to education was used in the Indian boarding schools run by missionary groups, where the students were also taught the "dignity of labor" and other values treasured by white reformers. The focus of the program for the Indian students was to abandon their tribal identity and ready themselves for assimilation into Euro-American culture. Most of the Indian students in the Creek Indian boarding schools were from so-called progressive families and embraced many of the attributes that white reformers valued, but still they harbored an intense Creek nationalism. Development-minded Creek nationalists accepted industrial education at the Indian boarding schools, but they insisted that the schools also maintain a liberal, classical curriculum in order to train the next generation of Creek leaders.[40]

How well suited an industrial education program was for African Creeks is open to interpretation. Washington and a host of reformers tailored the manual labor approach to what they perceived to be the needs of, and opportunities available to, freed people in the South. While the program received widespread acceptance and was used widely throughout the South in the coming decades, there was criticism that manual labor training did not address the higher needs of African Americans, and the education they received at the schools would only ensure that they would remain the mudsills of the Southern socioeconomic structure. But the socioeconomic and political conditions in the Creek country were vastly different from those found in the South. Nearly all African Creeks owned their own farms as part of the Creek commonwealth, and a number of the leading men were involved deeply in the emerging commercial network in the Indian Territory. African Creeks played a pivotal role in Creek politics and had little to fear, and much to gain, from increasing rather than diminishing their political involvement. It appears that the instructional program at Tullahassee had a dual purpose. Just like the civilization agenda practiced at the Indian boarding schools, Rishell and the other missionaries attempted to de-Indianize the cultural outlook of the African Creek students. The program's emphasis on production agriculture, which stressed abandoning the subsistence farming practiced by most African Creeks (and culturally conservative Indians), had a definite cultural purpose as well as an economic one. Also, the stress put on learning and speaking English rather than Creek had a cultural purpose. Rather than preparing the students for assimilation into Euro-American culture and society as done in the Indian schools, they attempted to recast their students' identity toward that of Southern African Americans and to prepare them for second-class citizenship rather than assimilation.[41]

African Creek churches played a key role in the development of schools as well as African Creek community identity. In the postwar years, African Creeks and Creek Indians began establishing separate churches. By 1876–1877, a full-blown schism had developed within the Creek Baptist community over race. It is not clear who among the Indian Baptists objected to African Creeks being members of the Creek Indian Baptist Association, but the association stymied the efforts toward separation at their annual meeting in 1877 and passed a resolution saying that no Baptist would be denied a place in the association because of race. Nevertheless, African Creeks formed the Creek Freedmen Baptist Association as a separate organization that year, and while there was communication between the two groups, and the freedmen association created a corresponding secretary as a liaison with the Indian Baptists, the two groups pursued different agendas.[42]

The Freedmen Baptist Association held regular meetings and coordinated communication and activities among the various African Creek churches. In 1886 there were ten congregations represented at the annual meeting from all sections of the Creek country, ranging from Tullahassee in the northeast to the Canadian River on the southwestern border. Jonathan

Kernel remained the principal spokesman for the African Creek Baptists until his death in 1897. Monday Durant was also active until declining health and age sapped his vitality in the late 1880s. His death in 1889 robbed the African Creek community of one its most respected and longest-serving spokesmen. A rising star among the African Creek Baptists during the 1880s was the Rev. Samuel Soloman. Soloman first came to prominence during the controversy between Robert Leslie and Turner Duncan over control of the Second Baptist Church in Muskogee. Soloman became one of the most popular and effective African Creek preachers and was also active in establishing schools for African Creek children.[43]

While the churches served to cement community identity and cohesion, they also served as conduits for Euro-American cultural values. The pastors attempted to wean their flocks from "heathen" practices such as stomp dances (bangas), poskita ceremonies, and traditional Creek ball games. They also encouraged their faithful to solemnize common-law unions in the church and tried to discourage plural marriages, a traditional Creek custom still practiced in some outlying communities. In these efforts the churches were only partly successful because both African Creeks and Creek Indians continued to attend the busks, dances, and ball games despite their pastors' injunctions. African Creek Baptists such as Monday Durant, Scipio Sango, Jonathan Kernel, and Samuel Soloman felt that the key to overcoming these "heathen practices" was education, and they all worked to this end through their churches, the Creek Council, and their trusteeships for established schools.[44]

Although African Creek Baptist churches and their pastors worked to eliminate vestiges of "heathenism," they retained a native outlook. Services, particularly in the outlying districts, were conducted in Creek, accompanied by English translation if necessary. And while evidence is lacking that African Creek Baptists adapted Creek cultural elements to the degree that Creek Indian Baptist churches did—constructing church buildings oriented to the four cardinal directions and in patterns conforming to the ceremonial square grounds—African Creek Baptists did develop a unique musical style that incorporated Creek elements with African American spirituals, and that would play a key role in launching renewed interest in African American spirituals during the 1930s. African Creek historic involvement in forming churches and providing ministers who understood the unique cultural conditions in the Creek country also reinforced African

Creek identity. Like other Baptist congregations in the states, they enjoyed a considerable degree of local control. This control, as well as the knowledge of their historic role in bringing Christianity into the Creek country, solidified the native outlook of African Creek Baptists. Additionally, nearly all prominent African Creek Baptists were involved in Creek politics and were committed to Creek nationalism, and they used the pulpit to oppose allotment and territorial status.[45]

Then, in the late 1880s, three events forced Creeks to consider more carefully the issues of identity and citizenship and who was entitled to share in the Creek commonwealth: the passage of the General Allotment Act, better known as the Dawes Act, in 1887; the cession of the Unassigned Lands to the United States in 1889, which paved the way for the Oklahoma land run of 1889; and the establishment of U.S. district courts for the Indian Territory in 1889.

The Dawes Act, fittingly named for Senator Henry L. Dawes, was the capstone of nearly twenty years of work done by white Indian-reform groups. The reformers were ministers, missionaries, and educators who called themselves "the Friends of the Indian" and who were dedicated to the idea that Indians, to advance in "civilization," must abandon tribal identity to be assimilated into American society. They believed the quickest route to assimilation was to abolish Indian reservations as well as the Indian republics in the Indian Territory and transform the communally held lands into individual allotments that the Indians would hold in fee-simple title. The Dawes Act, besides embodying this most cherished principle of the Indian reformers, also would open more land for settlement by white homesteaders. Passed by Congress and reluctantly signed into law by Grover Cleveland, the Dawes Act initially excluded the Five Tribes from allotment. It was clear, however, that it was only a matter of time before they too would be included in the forced march toward "free enterprise" and "civilization."[46]

Reformers' ideas about the future prospects for African Americans and Indians as part of American society in fact wove together in interesting ways, as illustrated at the annual gathering of the Friends of the Indian at the Lake Mohonk Conference in upstate New York. As the movement to disfranchise African Americans and enact de jure segregation took form in the South during the late 1880s and early 1890s, the so-called Negro question became a topic of concern for reformers. In 1890 and 1891, the reform groups at the Mohonk conference decided to look into the matter and organized the

Mohonk conferences on the Negro question. Significantly, no African Americans were invited to the conference, because as conference member Lyman Abbott, one of the leading white clergyman of the day, said, "a patient is not invited to the consultation of the doctors on his case." Timothy Thomas Fortune, the militant African American journalist, on the other hand, observed that there were over twenty thousand black professionals more qualified to deal with the "patient" at Mohonk, and if they were not allowed to consult, "the scalpel will be constantly gliding into the wrong portion of the patient's anatomy." Nevertheless, former president Rutherford B. Hayes, one of the first to suggest such an approach, chaired the conferences. His opening remarks to the 1890 conference set the stage for the discussions. Posing the question, "What are the true condition and prospects of the Negroes in the South?" Hayes went on to say that in addition to widespread illiteracy, African Americans were in a condition "compounded of ignorance, shiftlessness, superstition, vulgarity and vice," and unfortunately the majority did not yet possess the necessary qualities for full citizenship. Samuel Chapman Armstrong told the conference members that the great problem for African Americans "was not ignorance, but deficiency of character," which could be solved only through teaching the "dignity of labor." Yet, some of the speakers at the Mohonk conferences were more judicious in their appraisal of African American prospects, and Hayes himself felt that the "problem" was not insurmountable. With enough instruction in right religion and educated in the proper way, "in good time" the efforts would prove "adequate to lift the African up to the full stature of American manhood." For the reformers at Mohonk, inclusion of African Americans in the fabric of the nation still lay in the future. The conference members seemed to be saying that African Americans were themselves to blame for the racism that permeated American society and were on probation until they proved themselves worthy of a nation that refused to obey its own laws.[47]

Reformers were more optimistic regarding Indian inclusion, especially of the Five Tribes, who were considered much more advanced in the "arts of civilization," once, that is, they were shorn of tribal identity and communal land tenure and blessed with individual allotments and white homesteaders as neighbors. The reformers' relative attitude toward African Americans and Indians, however, left African Creeks with a double burden; their cultural outlook embraced Indian identity, which was the target for the Friends of the Indian, and their skin color marked them as part of the "Negro problem," which the reformers at Mohonk had deemed unsuitable for inclusion until such "good time" had passed. The question of future possibilities for African Indians was never addressed at the conference, although it would have been interesting to note if the reformers thought that African Indians could also "benefit" the development of their character by becoming private landholders.[48]

The second event, cession of the Unassigned Lands, made certain that Creeks would soon have many more intruders and homesteaders as neighbors. All promises given during the 1887 Creek election campaign regarding the disposition of Oklahoma lands were put aside in fall 1888 because chief Legus Perryman and other development-minded Creeks convinced the council to approve selling Creek residual rights to the Unassigned Lands to the federal government. Indeed, as part of the delegation in Washington in 1885, stationed there to keep an eye on developments regarding Oklahoma, Perryman played a key role in hiring Samuel Crawford, the former governor of Kansas, and an influential political figure and lobbyist, to begin negotiations regarding the sale of the Oklahoma lands. Reasoning that the Creeks should move quickly to gain some financial compensation for the Oklahoma lands, which the federal government was clearly intent on seizing anyway, no matter what the 1866 treaty said, Perryman, Pleasant Porter, and other progressive Creeks began negotiations with the federal government in hopes that the money from the sale would stave off looming financial disaster for the Creek treasury. In the final agreement signed by Creek delegates in Washington, and approved by council on January 31, 1889, the Creek Nation received $2,280,857 for the Oklahoma lands. In April president Benjamin Harrison opened the lands for homesteading, and a year later, filled with one hundred thousand new settlers (twice the number needed to apply for territorial status), the area was organized into the Oklahoma Territory. In the next three years, the former Indian lands on the Creek western and northern boundaries (the Sac Fox Reservation, the Pawnee Reserve, and the Cherokee Outlet) were also opened to homesteading and added to the Oklahoma Territory.[49]

The Oklahoma sale and the land openings that followed had both short-term and far-reaching effects on African Creek status and identity in the Creek Nation. On the political side of the equation, Chief Perryman brought the African Creek leadership in council around to his way of thinking through promises of funding additional African Creek schools with the money from the Oklahoma land sale. Perryman's alignment with the boomer interest in council was seen as a betrayal of Creek sovereignty by Creek conservatives and set the stage for political conflict between the former allies during the 1890s. Some progressive nationalists were also uneasy with the alliance between African Creeks and Perryman and would take steps to try to limit African Creek political influence, but the most significant result was the onslaught of intruders that the land openings brought into the Creek country itself. In 1873, the Creek agent estimated the number of intruders in the Creek Nation to be fewer than two hundred. In 1888–1889, Union agent Leo Bennett reckoned that there were more than thirty-five thousand intruders in the Indian Territory. Then, in the year following the Oklahoma land run, the number tripled and continued its explosive growth in the years thereafter. By 1900 white and black intruders vastly outnumbered Creek citizens. Under these circumstances, questions of identity, citizenship, and rights to the Creek commonwealth became more crucial than ever.[50]

The third event, creation of federal courts in the Indian Territory in 1889, reopened the old debates about whether the Creeks or the United States should have jurisdiction over Creek freed people and whether African Creeks were considered Indians or U.S. citizens who were merely adopted by the tribe. The law defining the new federal court's jurisdiction seemed to imply that only Indian citizens "by blood" (according to the U.S. government's construction) were residents in the Indian nation under the jurisdiction of the tribal courts. All others, "mixed-bloods" and adopted citizens (which would cover the entire African Creek population), were under federal authority. Congress may have excluded freed people, "mixed bloods," and adopted citizens from tribal jurisdiction out of ignorance of the racial mix in the Creek country, but some Creeks believed Congress's intent was to use the freed people and others as a wedge to attack Creek sovereignty and divide the Creek community. Articles addressing the issue, entitled, "Negroes as Lawmakers," appeared in both the *Indian Journal* and the *Muskogee Phoenix*. Probably written by George Washington Grayson, a leading Creek nationalist writing as Iste Maskoke (loosely translated as Creek patriot), Grayson argued:

> We believe it a step unwise and detrimental to the Negroes' interest in
> this country for them, of their own accord, to seek to evade the

AFRICAN CREEKS

jurisdiction of our Indian courts. The best thing for these . . . citizens to do is to hold tenaciously to, and contend to the last, for all rights guaranteed to them by treaty stipulations. The *Journal* [the *Indian Journal*] censures the Negro—and justly too—for his unwillingness to submit to the laws he aids in making."[51]

Grayson also addressed another issue having to do with political fallout from the Oklahoma lands sale, the "ten percent frauds." Some African Creek council members (among them, Sugar George) joined a faction calling for federal authorities to investigate and prosecute the Creek delegates (Legus Perryman, Efa Emarthla, and Pleasant Porter) involved in arranging, and allegedly profiting from, an unauthorized contract made with lobbyists and political fixers in 1885 to negotiate the Oklahoma land cession from which the fixers would receive a 10 percent commission ($228,000). Apparently, many council members, and Indian Office officials who approved the contracts, received bribes to authorize paying the contract fee. What bothered Grayson was that African Creek politicians had joined the faction led by D. N. McIntosh, G. W. Stidham, and others who called for federal intervention and investigation of the alleged financial misdeeds. Grayson considered the matter a purely Creek affair and questioned the motives of those African Creeks who sided with the leading advocates of limiting African Creek rights in calling for a federal investigation. Grayson chided the African Creeks involved: "Apparently the Negroes in question have simply followed the example given them by that majority in our National Council who represents that 'enlightened constituency' whose verdict would place them in the back seat."[52] Grayson summed up the nefarious effect of factionalism in this way:

> Every step we take in this direction is indicative of our inability to manage our own affairs and conformable to our enemies['] wishes. While we should not stand in opposition to progress, we ought, at least, to perpetuate that unity of spirit and action that will make us stronger and better able to meet successfully its variable phases of life and competition. Each estrangement weakens the bond and if continued, only a few years will suffice to eradicate our honored title of a Nation. Let a spirit of patriotism pervade each breast and awaken resolution to stand firm to what is in the best interests of our country.[53]

Grayson's call for Creek unity in the face of an assault on Creek sovereignty had been sounded in the past but never had the threat been more ominous nor the choices available to the Creeks so limited. Issues of race, identity, citizenship, and land ownership became more divisive than ever as African Creeks found themselves in the very epicenter of controversies that erupted in the 1890s.[54]

As the 1891 elections drew near, L. C. Perryman and the Union Party began campaigning for Perryman's reelection. The promise to use the money from the sale of the Oklahoma lands to support more schools was a key element in solidifying African Creek support for Perryman. In the months before the election, Perryman supporters in council approved the establishment of two more African Creek boarding schools, one at Pecan Creek and a Colored Orphan's school at the agency building west of Muskogee that had been the site of Ira Cain's Evangel School. Supervision of the nation's boarding schools, African Creek and Indian, were also taken away from missionary societies and put under control of Creek citizens. While there was some protest over this action, the loudest being from James R. Gregory, a prominent and combative nationalist, who warned of the dangers of the schools being put in the hands of "political vampires," the appropriations for the boarding schools were a major portion of the nation's annual budget and as such represented particularly ripe patronage plums. J. P. Davison, who championed the establishment of the Pecan Creek school, was appointed its superintendent in 1892, and George H. Taylor was put in charge of the Colored Orphan's Asylum. Although technically a noncitizen, Nellie Ann Leslie, who had returned to the Creek country in 1889, was appointed the new superintendent of Tullahassee beginning in January 1891.[55]

Leslie's tenure at Tullahassee was brief. She replaced the erstwhile Rishell in January 1891 and then resigned in October, reportedly to return to Texas to look after the education of her recently widowed brother's daughters. While this explanation may well have been true, she probably breathed a sigh of relief when she got her brother's call. Beginning when the council turned over the operation of the venerated school to the "political vampires," the school had become embroiled in controversy over control of patronage. Rishell later revealed that he was offered a chance to stay on as superintendent if he paid a fifty-dollar bribe to "a prominent" African Creek politician. Leslie's successor was greeted with a fire set at the school, which fortunately was put out before any major damage was done. Most likely, the fire was a warning to the new superintendent to toe the political line with regard to teaching appointments. George H. Taylor, the first superintendent at the Colored Orphan's school, was accused of gross misconduct, drunkenness, and immorality and was suspended after J. P. Davison conducted a successful petition campaign against him. Affairs at the other Creek Indian boarding schools followed a similar pattern during this uneasy period in Creek history, enmeshed in the quagmire of political patronage and personal and political rivalries at the expense of African Creek and Creek Indian children alike.[56]

Responding, in part, to the Union Party's efforts in establishing more educational opportunities, African Creek voters supplied Perryman with solid backing in the 1891 election. Sixty percent of Perryman's winning vote totals came from the Colored towns. In contrast, other Creek towns split their votes between Isparhecher, John Reed, and Wesley Smith. Once again, Isparhecher captured only a handful of African Creek votes, most of them from the outlying settlements in Canadian and Arkansas Colored. As Angie Debo has written, "the power of the Negro towns was strikingly shown in this election." But the triumph had repercussions, especially for Creeks concerned with the growth of the African Creek population being buttressed with the arrival of more state freed people. The African Creek role as arbiters in elections for principal chief was particularly troubling for some. In response, a group of Creek politicians launched an effort to disfranchise African Creeks, just as African Americans were being excluded from politics in the South.[57]

Feeding the effort to exclude African Creeks was the increasing number of intruders. Caravans of state freed people from Arkansas, Texas, and other Southern states, as well as an increasing number of Southern whites, passed through the Creek country on their way to land openings, and many of them stayed despite federal laws barring them from the Creek lands. The land-hungry settlers, fleeing the inequities of crop liens, sharecropping, and tenant farming as well as the deteriorating political situation in the South, looked on the vast "uncultivated lands" in the Creek and Cherokee nations and began "booming" the agricultural lands there in much the same way as developers and promoters had fastened themselves on Muskogee, with little interference from federal authority. *The Afro-American Advocate*, a Coffeyville, Kansas, newspaper established in 1891, was entirely devoted to developing the agricultural lands in "the Beautiful Indian Territory," giving tips on where the best lands could be found and how to evade tribal and federal regulations regarding occupancy. Some of the "reporters" dubiously claimed to be Creek or Cherokee citizens and loudly proclaimed the "B.I.T" (acronym for Beautiful Indian Territory) to be the best country for freed people seeking a better life, indeed far superior to, and more familiar than, Liberia.[58]

Embedded in this challenge to African Creek citizenship rights was the African Creek attitude toward African American intruders. African Creeks harbored considerable prejudice against state freed people, and those feelings grew as the number of black intruders increased. African Creeks themselves drew race and identity lines and separated themselves from the new arrivals. They labeled the state freed people "Watchina," a pejorative term roughly translated as "white man's Negro."[59] Many African Creeks blamed the state freed people for "turning the Indian's heart away from the natives [freed people]" through the subservient behavior they showed when encountering white intruders, so much at variance with African Creek independent assertiveness. An African Creek interviewed in the 1930s explained hostility toward the state freed people in this way:

> State People come into the country before statehood, pulling they hats off and kneeling and scurrying down to the white folks. They ruined the country and made a lot of natives [i.e., African Creeks] leave for the North. Natives won't go to the back door if they has to see a white man. They won't go at all rather than that. If the Southern Negro didn't Uncle Tom so much they never would have drawed the line between the races.

Another African Creek explained the racial dynamics that were evolving as a result of the increasing presence of both white and black intruders: "What do I need to mix with those state folks for . . . I was eating out of the same pot with the Indians, going anywhere in this country I wanted to, while they were still licking their master's boots in Texas."[60] African Creeks socially ostracized state freed people, would not allow their children to marry them, refused them admission to their churches or even to be buried in their graveyards. But still the state freed people came, because "Goin' to the Territory" was preferable to conditions in the South.[61]

The problem was further aggravated by an influx of landless white Southerners competing for Indian lands. Unlike the white traders and merchants who had come into the Creek country before the Civil War, many of these new white intruders held white supremacist notions that the lands should belong to white men, and all other people, whether they were Indian or black, should show subservience. Creek Indians, many who had previously held relaxed racial attitudes, began to adopt the white outlook lest they be classed with those with black skin in the racial hierarchy demanded by the intruders in the Indian Territory. The prevailing national attitude at the time regarding race relations, tellingly revealed at the Mohonk Conference, added to the imperative to redraw racial boundaries.

Not all state freed people were met with hostility, however. Some African Creek politicians solicited bribes to put black intruders on the tribal rolls. Responding to the outcry that too many African Creeks were included on the 1891 payment rolls, some African Creek politicians "scratched off" legitimate citizens to temper the storm and to make room for intruders willing to pay a fee to be included. William McIntosh, the Arkansas Colored Town chief, earned the nickname Bill Bacon for padding his town rolls, and his successor, Gabriel Jamison, was tried for treason in the Coweta District Tribal Court for accepting bribes from noncitizens. Many African Creeks shared in the outrage over the sale of tribal citizenship, and although Jamison was actually acquitted by a sympathetic jury, the scandals brought a vigorous response.[62]

In this atmosphere, Roley McIntosh, G. W. Stidham, G. W. Grayson, and other Creeks initiated a series of discussions on the "Negro question" in the national council and in Indian Territory newspapers. They called for altering the 1866 treaty, disfranchising African Creeks, or at least putting a "check on the ascendancy of the Negro race in the [Creek] Nation." The council debated the question and passed a toothless resolution asking the U.S. Supreme Court to rule on whether Article II of the 1866 treaty extended to African Creek slaves who were "sold or removed beyond the limits of the Creek Nation" prior to the Civil War. Pleasant Porter, in his role as Creek delegate in Washington, asked Indian Affairs Commissioner T. J. Morgan to bring the matter before the Supreme Court, but the Court refused the case, saying it was a matter for the Creek courts to decide.[63]

These attempts at disfranchisement fizzled in council, and African Creek representation on the national council actually increased over the next several years; but the damage had been done, and many Creek Indians, both conservative and progressive, who had counted African Creeks as allies in the struggle to maintain Creek sovereignty now considered African Creeks, at the worst, a Trojan horse within the citadel of the Creek nation, and at the least, expendable.[64]

A blunt African Creek response to the proposed exclusion appeared in the *Muskogee Phoenix* in November 1892, and Warrior Rentie was most likely the author. His remarks went to the heart of the complexities of race, identity, citizenship, and land in the years leading up to allotment and the end of Creek sovereignty:

> Have the Indians been living here with Negroes marrying and inter-marrying with them . . . and have just now found that they are the Negro's superior? If so, I am sorry for them. There are no Negro citizens if the stipulations of the Treaty be true, but all are Indians. Those Indians, or rather, would be Indians, are the very ones that have the strong vein of Negro blood in them. I am sure that the full-blood Indian wants no change, but it is the man who hardly knows whether he is black, red or white. Of course such a man is lost and is trying to find himself. Whenever the Treaty of '66 be changed the Indians them-selves shall have the reward of damnation as much so as the Negroes. The Negroes are ready to stand any change the Indians can, so let it come. Take away all men who are now holding positions of trust and honor who have Negro blood in them and see how many of those positions can be rightly and readily filled. The Negro certainly can fill any position as honorably as any Indian.

Rentie concluded his response not with soothing words intended to evoke the long history of racial fluidity and common interest that typified relations between African Creeks and Creek Indians, but with a challenge—a challenge that roused the memory of slavery and warned that "the present generation" would never tolerate a retreat from equality promised in the 1866 treaty: "You have used our forefathers as you do now your horses and mules, but the time shall never come when the present generation shall be treated thus. It is true that you once had him as property, but now he is on equality with you."[65]

No one would have dared issue such a challenge, much less call for it being printed in a newspaper, in the poisonous racial atmosphere in the South during the early 1890s. But the Creek Nation, Indian Territory, was not part of the South, at least not yet. Here, in 1892, on the eve of the congressional decision to include the Five Tribes in the land allotment policy, African Creeks drew on what fluidity remained on the racial frontier to turn back the challenge that would "place them in the back seat" and asserted their rights in the Indian nation. But in the coming years, as the Creek people scrambled to save what they could in the face of allotment, tribal dissolution, and eventual statehood, immutable race and identity standards imposed from without eliminated the luxury of "hardly" knowing whether a man is "black, red, or white" as the racial frontier collapsed in the onslaught of development, "progress," and "civilization."

6

"If I Ain't One, You Won't Find Another One Here"

African Creek Identity, Allotment, and the Dawes Commission

DURING THE YEARS BETWEEN 1893 AND 1903, the racial frontier collapsed under the weight of intruders flooding into the Creek Nation through various openings of Indian lands between 1889 and 1895. The arrival of the Dawes Commission in 1893 was the beginning of a process in which the Creeks, African and Indian, contended with the federal government and among themselves over race, identity, citizenship, and land issues. In 1898, Congress, under the Curtis Act, forced the terms by which the Creek Nation divided its communally held tribal lands into private holdings and extinguished tribal sovereignty. Although subsequent agreements made with the Dawes Commission softened the blow somewhat, the division of the tribal estate that began in 1899 not only divided Creek lands but also divided the Creek communities, African and Indian. In the process, the African Creek position was undermined by the prevailing attitude in late nineteenth- and early twentieth-century America that deemed Indians suitable for assimilation but left African Americans outside the charmed circle that defined first-class citizenship. For the African Creeks, the question of what constituted their identity loomed large as they struggled to define themselves and their place in the cultural equation emerging in the Creek Nation as well as their place in the American nation at large.

Congress passed legislation in spring 1893 that created a commission whose responsibility was to negotiate land allotment agreements with the Five Tribes. The voluntary agreements (as opposed to treaties) would outline the terms under which the Indian nations would divide their common-wealths into private land holdings and extinguish tribal sovereignty, prepar-ing them for territorial status and eventual statehood. President Grover Cleveland appointed the commission and selected the aging ex-senator Dawes as the chair. Many considered Dawes the logical choice, considering his experience on the Senate Committee for Indian Affairs and his role in shaping the allotment policy legislation generally known as the Dawes Act. Immediately after his appointment in November 1893, Dawes announced that the commission would visit the Indian Territory and begin negotia-tions in early 1894.[1]

At an outdoor meeting held in Okmulgee in April, the commissioners tried to explain the benefits of partitioning the Creek commonwealth into individual allotments, terminating the Creek government, and preparing the Indian Territory for eventual statehood. They warned the two thousand Creeks, both Indian and African, that resistance was futile and admonished the assembled crowd to cooperate before Congress imposed a solution.[2] Chief Perryman then asked all those who supported the commissioner's proposals to step to the left and those who opposed to move to the right. The commissioners were no doubt dismayed when the entire assemblage shifted together to the right. White promoters and developers had misled the commissioners into believing that culturally conservative Indians and African Creeks (the principal audience at Okmulgee) would welcome allot-ment and statehood because they were being oppressed by corrupt aristo-crats who monopolized the land, resources, and politics. Not satisfied with the plan's overwhelmingly popular rejection, which was seconded in the Creek National Council (where the oppressed African Creeks had 24 repre-sentatives in the 166-member body, and the culturally conservative Creeks were disproportionately represented), a Senate committee and the Dawes commissioners made their own inspections of conditions in the Indian Territory. After collecting more misleading evidence, mainly from white intruders, developers, and booster groups, the government reports painted a dismal portrait of corrupt and oppressive tribal regimes lording over their helpless citizens and of white settlers living without protection of federal law, out of the reach of the tribal courts, and without access to schools for their children. The last three charges were true insofar as the people were there willingly and in violation of treaty promises made to the Indians.[3]

But it was neither the conservative Indians nor African Creeks who came out in support of allotment after the commissioners' visit, rather it was leading development-minded nationalists such as G. W. Grayson, Pleasant Porter, and James R. Gregory. All three endorsed allotment under certain conditions and reckoned that allotment would provide an opportunity to purge the Creek country of unwanted black intruders. Grayson voiced his tempered support for the policy in the *Indian Journal*, and as Mary Jane Warde has written, he only reluctantly supported allotment as a way to "save what we may from the approaching wreak." He and other nationalists, who included some of the African Creek leadership, were confident they could manage their own affairs as they had done for many years. But they also maintained that splitting the Creek commonwealth into individual allotments could only benefit the Creeks if they were allowed to keep their tribal government intact and to divide their entire tribal estate among themselves, leaving no surplus for sale to U.S. settlers—conditions that were in direct conflict with the intentions of the Dawes commissioners.[4]

While the Creek policy toward adopting freed people with questionable ties to the nation had tightened in the 1880s, many could still get on the tribal rolls if they could afford the necessary bribe. Although citizenship matters were supposed to be handled by the Citizenship Committee, politics in the Creek legislature made it possible for people (and families) with influential sponsors to become citizens through acts of council. African Creek representatives formed an important voting bloc in deciding citizenship cases, and adoption cases served as currency in political horse trading. Another reason behind the rise in the number of adopted freed people was a change in the tenor of the Citizenship Committee's decisions. After G. W. Stidham stepped down from the Citizenship Committee in 1890 (Stidham died in 1891), freed people's cases were decided by less-stringent standards. For example, Alec McIntosh, the Muskogee District judge who decided many of the cases in 1893–1894, approved Henry Loudon's application, and "in spite of weak evidence *for* [emphasis added] citizenship," he judged that the evidence *against* Loudon was not beyond a reasonable doubt. Interestingly, Gabriel Jamison and William McIntosh, two African Creek leaders implicated in taking bribes to get noncitizens on the tribal rolls, provided favorable testimony in Loudon's case. Politics and less-stringent standards aside, many Creeks attributed the burgeoning citizenship rolls in the Colored towns to bribery and corruption. It was clear to some that African Creek politicians had taken fees to present spurious citizenship petitions to council and that Colored town kings had shamelessly padded their town rolls.[5]

Whether or not charges of collusion and corruption were true, the perception of corruption alienated a key constituency from African Creeks —those Creek Indians who were agreeable toward including them in tribal affairs or at least had come to accept it as an accomplished fact. Memories of the hardships of "the road to Kansas" had faded, as had the common support shown toward equal rights for the freedmen at the 1866 treaty negotiations. The Dawes Commission's arrival focused attention on an uncertain future. In this future, the Creeks would be forced to confront issues of race and identity and the question of who was entitled to share in the tribal estate.

Island Smith, the African Creek youth who had tried to talk to the African American soldiers camped outside of Okmulgee during the Green Peach War, viewed the Dawes Commission's arrival from a different perspective. The teenager had grown up on the family homestead southwest of Okmulgee, immersed in a life of subsistence farming, hunting, gathering, and communal land tenure increasingly threatened with extinction. Out in these hinterlands, peopled mainly by culturally conservative Indians and African Creeks, racial boundaries were still fluid. African Creek and Indian children went to school together, and their parents lived and worked together in everyday life. The African Creeks living there pursued a traditional subsistence lifestyle indistinguishable from their Indian neighbors. An African Creek woman interviewed in the 1930s recalled the postwar years in the Canadian settlements: "We live right in amongst them, sometimes a nigger in one side of the house and an Indian in the other . . . we was next door neighbors . . . no Jim Crow then . . . we raise rice, peas, peanuts, potato then and live good . . . not all the time chop, chop, choppin' cotton like the fool niggers do now."[6]

Island Smith recalled that the family cultivated about an acre of corn for home use and raised cattle, hogs, and horses, which, like their neighbor's livestock, were allowed to roam free. They never had chickens when he was young because wild fowl, mainly turkeys and prairie chickens, were abundant. They gathered wild grapes and berries as well as pecans, walnuts, and hickory nuts as important additions to their food supply, and they supplemented their diet with deer, rabbit, squirrel, possum, and raccoon, keeping some as pets. Smith and his companions also hunted and trapped for furs and pelts and abided by the traditional Creek custom never to kill rattlesnakes. With this lifestyle, Smith recalled that they "seldom had use for money in the early days [the 1880s and 1890s] and spent it as soon as we got it." When the family needed flour, coffee, sugar, or other household items, they simply rounded up some hogs and sold them in Okmulgee.[7]

Smith described other practices that bound his family to the traditional Creek subsistence culture. With the corn they raised they made *sofka*, the traditional Creek corn dish. Smith learned to identify and prepare roots and herbs and to administer them as medicines in the traditional Creek way, and after he was older he became known for his abilities as a native healer. African Creek children in the Canadian backcountry wore long shirts or dresses spun from homespun cloth, just like their Indian companions, with the boys belting their shirts at the waist until age twelve, when they graduated to wearing pants. Smith also recalled attending Indian ball games and the Creek Indian Compsah Dinah Baptist Church; and when he was older and had learned to play the fiddle, he performed at local dances and celebrations.[8]

Other memories suggest the cultural distance separating native African Creeks from the concepts and promises of the allotment program. Smith's mother, who was half Indian and half African, was born in Alabama in the old Creek country. She calculated her age using the night "when the stars fell" as a marker, referring to the Leonid meteor storm that turned a November night into day in 1833 when she was twelve. Smith also recalled that when he was a boy, they did not always have a calendar in their house. Traveling peddlers sold almanacs for fifty cents to every third or fourth house in his neighborhood, so all he had to do was "go see a neighbor to find out the day of the month." When the Dawes Commission arrived in Okmulgee to explain the allotment program, with their the talk of deeds, conveyances, surveys, filing deadlines, and property values, their words must have sounded strange indeed to people who counted their ages in the stars and for whom knowing the date was less a necessity than an excuse to visit a neighbor.[9]

The day the Dawes Commission came to Okmulgee, Smith recalled a large crowd "listening to a couple of representatives of the U.S. government . . . in long tailed black suits . . . trying to get the people to agree to allotment of the Creek Nation." He remembered Jim Parkinson, the long-

AFRICAN CREEKS

time white merchant and trader in the Creek country, toting ten thousand dollars in a wooden candy bucket weighted with two flatirons. He was working the crowd, trying to get them to sign up for allotment and telling them about all the nice things they could buy for their families with the money. But Paro Bruner, the town chief of Canadian Colored, had a different message for the people, one that gave a clearer prediction about the ramifications of the allotment policy.

[He] told the people that if we were allotted land it would be taken from us. He said he could see people with packs and bundles on their backs having to leave their homes. He reminded them of the treaty with the government which stated that this would be their home as long as the water ran and the grass grew and nothing good would come from a division of common property.[10]

Over the years, Bruner and other African Creeks had consistently told congressional committees that they would rather hold the Creek lands in common. They understood that their freedom to settle anywhere in the Creek Nation and develop a farm or business depended just as much on the traditional Creek practice of holding tribal lands in common as it did on the 1866 treaty provisions. The advantage of the traditional way seemed clear in light of the thousands of landless African Americans who were streaming into the Indian Territory from neighboring states, trying to escape share-cropping and tenancy rates as high as 90 percent.

In 1893–1894, a group of progressive Creeks in council engineered a response to the Dawes Commission's criticisms. They drafted a new Creek constitution. Ostensibly, the move was an attempt to reduce the size and cost of the Creek government, to show a degree of financial responsibility, and to prove themselves more democratic by making more tribal offices elective. They also wanted to show Creek solidarity on the allotment issue by inserting a clause forbidding the Creek government to make any treaty or law that would divide the tribal estate into individual land holdings. African Creeks approved of all these things, but they saw the proposal to reduce the size of council as nothing more than an attempt to curb African Creek political influence. Under the plan, representation in the House of Warriors would be reduced to one member per town rather than one seat for each two hundred town members. This would have cut the number of African Creek Warriors from twenty to three. When the referendum election was held in summer 1894, the Colored towns voted 429 to 2 against the plan. Their lopsided opposition defeated the reforms. Some Creeks read the returns as an overwhelming African Creek approval for allotment and as a refusal to aid the nation in blunting the Dawes Commission's criticism. Most, however, understood the vote was more about being "placed in the back seat" than a measure of Creek patriotism. And though African Creeks were again successful in turning back the attempt to exclude them from Creek politics, the vote revealed a disturbing trend—the Indian towns had voted overwhelmingly for the measure.[11]

Coinciding with the referendum election, the Creek Supreme Court defined African Creek rights under the 1866 treaty more narrowly. The Court was acting on the initiative introduced in the 1892 council seeking to limit freed people's access to citizenship. After the U.S. Supreme Court refused jurisdiction in the case, the Creek Court acted. Chief justice William F. McIntosh ruled that African Creeks taken beyond the limits of the nation before the Civil War were ineligible for citizenship rights. The five-member court was attempting to do what a minority in council had so far been unable to accomplish—purge the rolls of unwanted citizens. In this, the court was setting an ominous precedent that it would attempt to expand over the next two years. But the pull of local interests was still a strong current in Creek politics. Because the power to enforce the decisions lay beyond the grasp of the court, McIntosh's ruling had little impact beyond arousing those Creeks who wanted to rein in the "Negro influence" in Creek politics. In any case, the decision would soon become irrelevant. Congress and the Dawes Commission were poised to take control of citizenship and identity questions and decide who was entitled to share in the Creek estate.[12]

The Creek National Council also addressed the citizenship issue once again in summer 1895. The move was prompted by an increasingly complex political situation in the nation that included such issues as an upcoming per capita payment due the Creeks from the sale of the Oklahoma lands, the impeachment of Chief Legus Perryman, and the approaching 1895 Creek elections. Because the federal treasury was nearly bankrupt from the disastrous effects of the 1893 depression, the U.S. government had only reluctantly approved the payment. Corruption and mismanagement had also left Creek finances teetering on the brink of insolvency. In fact, the House of Warriors impeached Legus Perryman and Creek treasurer Samuel Grayson in May 1895 on charges of improper use of tribal funds, with Warrior Rentie acting as the chief prosecutor. Perryman and Grayson refused to surrender their offices, however, and a constitutional crisis ensued as second chief Edward Bullet, backed by a majority in the council, began to exercise the powers of the chief's office, which included the power to decide how to distribute national funds. Besides the charges of financial mismanagement, one of the issues dividing the Creeks during the crisis was how to handle the per capita payment. Perryman and Grayson wanted the money to go directly to the merchants and traders who had extended $150,000 in credit to Creek citizens in anticipation of the payment. Bullet and Napoleon M. Moore, whom Bullet had appointed treasurer following Grayson's impeachment, wanted the "bread money" paid to individuals. African Creeks in council, including H. C. Reed and Sugar George, had been solidly behind Perryman until the distribution issue was raised.[13]

In this atmosphere, the council also created a special Committee of Eighteen, with responsibility to examine the census taken by the Town kings to guide the per capita payment and to remove noncitizens from the existing tribal rolls. African Creeks H. C. Reed, Abe Kernels, William McIntosh, and Gabriel Jamison served on the committee. The tenor of the times was revealed in the wording of the resolution passed by council that accompanied the legislation, that noncitizens had obtained recognition through "the undue use of money and other fraudulent means."[14]

Perhaps it was a case of appointing wolves to guard the henhouse, but the committee's supposedly meticulous inspection of the rolls revealed 13,841 Creek citizens, eliminated 619 "doubtful" citizens, and added over two hundred African Creeks to the rolls. The new count entitled 4,393 African Creeks to participate in the payment and increased African Creek representation in the House of Warriors—Arkansas Colored Town gained two additional seats and Canadian Colored, one. According to the 1895 census, African Creeks constituted 32 percent of the population.[15]

The act also created a new Citizenship Commission of Five that became known as the Colbert Commission after its chairman James Colbert. The council gave the Colbert Commission expanded power to decide disputed citizenship claims and required that a tribal attorney be present at all hearings to guard the nation's interest. Abe Kernels, William McIntosh, and other influential African Creeks served on the commission from time to time, and African Creek tribal attorneys were employed to represent the Creek Nation in cases that came before the commission. While the legislation creating the commission implied that strict legal standards should guide the committee's decisions, the decisions were guided more by "the facts known by the Old Settlers" rather than written records of any kind.[16]

The commission heard many cases of people claiming African Creek citizenship by virtue of Indian descent. But, as before, such cases were routinely denied unless the people were adopted by council or could prove that they had been owned by a Creek citizen and returned in the time stipulated in the 1866 treaty. Nonetheless, these cases opened some lively discussion regarding identity, race, and citizenship. When the commission denied Nancy Wallace's claim because she was taken South during the war and had not returned until many years later, Wallace asserted her rights on the basis that she was the illegitimate daughter of Robert Johnson, the well-known interpreter for the Seminole Nation, whom she claimed was part Creek Indian. Testimony revealed that the "old folks" knew that Johnson's father was half Indian and that Wallace's half sister Jane Grayson had an Indian father as well. The Creek tribal attorney then called Silas Jefferson to give adverse testimony. But Jefferson's testimony turned out to be more ambiguous than damaging. While Jefferson had never heard Johnson mention that he had "Indian blood," he noted that it was impossible to tell in the Creek country whether someone was Indian, black, or white by merely looking at them. And furthermore, Jefferson testified, "it was more than he could swear to" that Johnson was not part Indian. When asked if he knew any former slaves who were descendants of Indians, he simply replied, "I have seen many a one."[17]

Paro Bruner, the Canadian Colored Town chief, gave testimony that questioned the veracity of the Dunn roll, the census Creek agent J. W. Dunn had taken in 1867. Bruner said that a great many "good citizens" were left off the roll because Dunn had made no effort to collect the names himself and then had sent the roll to Washington before the town chiefs had the time to collect all the names. The question of the Dunn roll would also bedevil the Dawes commissioners, who early on declared that because Dunn's erratic census was the earliest written freed people's citizenship record, it was the standard by which African Creeks needed to prove their citizenship. The citizenship commissioners, on the other hand, had more faith in the history provided by the "old ones." Though the elders' memories were shaky at times, they understood the importance that Creeks attached to descent and knew who belonged to whom, whether as slave to master or kinfolk to kinfolk. And if people had trouble recalling the year and month, they cataloged important events from their world in a way understood by most Creeks—how high the corn was, whether the river was low, and when the peaches ripened.[18]

The 1895 election was held in September, amid the swirl of events of the past two years. Complex and divisive issues animated different constituencies. In addition to the questions regarding race and citizenship, other issues divided the stereotyped groups. On the surface, at least, nearly all agreed on how to deal with the Dawes Commission—which was not at all. But Perryman's impeachment, the per capita payment, opposition to both the permit law and the pasture law, which allowed wealthy Creeks to enclose thousands of acres for their own use, all found different champions. In this situation, the various parties and factions formed six tickets in the contest for principal chief. The old Union Party coalition, splintered over Perryman's impeachment, divided into three factions and split their votes. A majority in the Colored towns supported Ellis Childers, the Union Party's official candidate, but they generously split the other 45 percent of their votes among three other candidates. Isparhecher, running for the third time, drew huge majorities from most of the Indian towns and won the election. Once again, his support among African Creeks was negligible; he drew only 35 out of the 640 freedmen votes cast. But Isparhecher's election did not spark a new civil war as many had feared. After the election was certified, the supporters of Childers and Isparhecher held meetings in both houses and pledged support for each other in electing presiding officers and putting through a program that included voiding the pasture law, repealing the permit law, resisting land monopoly, removing intruders, encouraging education, and opposing allotment.[19]

The election brought a new face into Creek politics. Phillip Lewis, an African Creek from Arkansas Colored, was elected to the House of Warriors on a platform of opposition to the pasture law. Lewis was born near Tullahassee in 1869, on a portion of the old Kendell Lewis plantation settled by his parents Abram and Mary Ann after the war. When Phillip was one year old, his father died and he went to live with his grandmother, Rachel Kernel, who lived nearby and ran one of the largest plantation farming operations in the area. His grandmother was also the community humanitarian, and Lewis remembers sharing his grandmother's home with as many as twenty widows and orphans, both Indian and African. Lewis and the other children went to grade school at the Old Fountain Church school, an old log building that was steeped in the history of African-Indian cooperation. His teacher there was Mattie Birdoff (Birdie), who later married Pleasant Porter. After his grandmother died in 1885, Lewis went to live with his mother and stepfather, Denis Marshall, who lived on a farm west of where the town of Wagoner was built. In 1887 he left to study and serve as assistant teacher at Tullahassee. When Lewis entered Creek politics at age twenty-six, he brought skills to the job that would serve the nation and the African Creek community well in the troubled years to come. Educated and resolute, he was a man of principle who had learned the value of shared community responsibility from his grandmother and was unafraid to tackle difficult issues that required him to take unpopular positions for the greater good of the community.[20]

With the help of leaders like Phillip Lewis, the Creek Council passed a series of laws in their 1896 session meant to protect what remained of Creek sovereignty. The council had been unsuccessful in passing a law prohibiting leasing of tribal lands to cattle companies, and the federal courts refused to back the chief in his efforts to enforce existing laws that allowed him to order the Lighthorse companies to take down illegal fences. H. C. Reed, the African Creek judge in the Muskogee District, was a key figure in the controversy. Reed had enclosed thousands of acres under the pasture law and then leased the acreage to noncitizen cattlemen. Isparhecher's office was besieged with petitions from outraged citizens after Reed refused to carry out the chief's orders to take down his illegal fences. Among those leading the petition drive were Phillip Lewis and Warrior Rentie. Reed was suspended from office, pending an investigation into the charges, and then was reinstated after he took the fences down. The council also passed measures that voided the permit system and prohibited signing long-term labor contracts with noncitizens. Creeks who depended on noncitizen labor to operate their farms, businesses, and ranches objected strenuously, but they could have saved their breath. Acting Commissioner of Indian Affairs Thomas Smith considered the legislation detrimental to "progress" and development in the Indian Territory and had no intention of allowing the law to be enforced. Other measures provided funds so tribal attorneys could take concerted legal action in the federal courts against intruders. But all these efforts were in vain against the onslaught of intruders whose violations of treaty obligations and Indian Intercourse laws were ignored by federal courts and Indian Office officials waiting anxiously for the allotment process to begin. By this time, an estimated one hundred thousand non-citizen permit holders and intruders in the Indian Territory were clamoring for access to land and the protection of federal laws.[21]

They would not have long to wait. The process began in 1895, as Congress mandated the survey of Creek lands into individual allotments. Coinciding with the survey, a federal court ruled that white boomer towns springing up in the Indian Territory could incorporate and establish municipal governments. Convinced that the Creeks had no intention of voluntarily cooperating with allotment, Dawes asked Congress to give the commission power to enroll Creek citizens and to determine their eligibility for allotment. In June 1896, Congress gave the commission the power to "hear and determine the application of all persons who may apply to them for citizenship" and "determine the right of such applicant to be admitted and enrolled."[22] In a notice sent to the Creek government (addressed "to whom it may concern"), the commission tried to take the sting out of coopting the power to determine citizenship: "Said Commission shall respect all laws of the several nations or tribes not inconsistent with the laws of the United States, and all treaties with either of said nations or tribes, and shall give [due respect] to the usages and customs of said tribes." The congressional legislation also gave persons denied citizenship by either the tribe or the commission the right to appeal their cases in the federal courts. The commission began taking applications for enrollment at various locations in the Creek country in July 1896 and asked Isparhecher to provide them with copies of the tribal rolls to assist them in the process. The Creeks resisted turning over the rolls for two more years, which not only prolonged and complicated the entire process but also compromised their ability to challenge the commission's decisions. Additional blows to Creek sovereignty came the following year, when Congress gave the president veto power over most important acts of the Creek legislature and made the tribal courts subject to federal court jurisdiction.[23]

Underlying all this was the firm belief of Congress, and the Dawes commissioners, that people of African descent in the Creek Nation were entitled to share equally in the tribal estate. Many Creeks felt that the government's obsession with freed people's rights was merely an excuse to break the Creek land title. After all, the federal government had only grudgingly accepted that the Creek government should have jurisdiction over Creek freed people in the first place. But Congress's main concern was not racial equality, or even a regard for African Creek rights to the soil under Article II, but to transform the Indian commonwealth into individual allotments and eventually to have allotted lands opened for sale and development. Still, some Creeks thought it peculiar that the government insisted that the Creeks stay faithful to treaty obligations regarding African Creeks' rights while the government itself ignored other treaty provisions protecting all Creeks from intruders.

In response to the Dawes Commission's requests, Isparhecher asked the council to pass legislation that would "be most effective in securing a correct census of our citizens." He then went on to say that while he "does not insist upon any legislation that would indicate a discrimination touching the rights of any citizen," the biggest problem was with the Colored towns rolls and therefore, "a special census should be made of all our colored citizens."[24]

The Creek Council gave the responsibility to the Colbert Commission, and the commissioners went to work, without the help of the Colored town chiefs, and over the next two months created the Colbert roll, which struck 123 names from the Colored town rolls. But the Colbert Commission's actions amounted to little when compared with a ruling made by the Creek Supreme Court that August.[25]

The court ruled that the national council had no right to adopt noncitizens because, as chief justice Thomas J. Adams wrote, "The act of adoption cannot vest the adoptee with property rights nor make such person an heir to the common estate of the tribe." According to Adams, the council would then be seizing the property of lawful citizens and transferring it to noncitizens without their consent. Adams went on to maintain that, while the council had the right to recognize citizenship of bona fide Creeks, it had no power to grant citizenship to people without ties to the nation. While the decision made no mention of race and confined its reasoning to the issues of citizenship and land, the implications were clear. If enforced, the court's ruling would have stricken 1,781 African Creeks and their descendants adopted by council since 1867 from the tribal rolls. When coupled with earlier decisions that eliminated former slaves taken out of the Creek country and that denied citizenship rights to free African Creeks who lived in the nation before the Civil War over three thousand African Creeks would have been eliminated from the rolls. But if the rulings were strictly carried out, Chief Justice Adams, along with other substantial leaders who "carried the strong vein of Negro blood" in them, would have been eliminated from the rolls unless they could "prove" their citizenship under Article II of the 1866 treaty. As with the Creek court's other adverse rulings on African Creek citizenship, there was no concerted attempt to enforce the ruling. In any case, Adams's decision became moot after federal courts later ruled that the Creek Council, acting as representatives of the Creek people, did indeed have the power to grant citizenship rights.[26]

As the controversy over citizenship rights escalated, the Dawes Commission, without access to the tribal rolls or the cooperation of the Creek government, continued to enroll citizens. Despite its noncooperation, the Creek Nation still had the right under the Dawes Commission regulations to challenge persons admitted by the commission. The Creek Council hired Benjamin T. Duval, an attorney from Ft. Smith, Arkansas, to represent the nation in hearings before the commission and to challenge cases heard before the federal courts.[27]

Duval had more than just a superficial knowledge of affairs in the Indian Territory. His uncle, Marcellus Duval, was the controversial and rabidly proslavery Seminole agent in the Indian Territory from 1845–1851. His father, William Duval, had represented Cherokee, Creek, and Seminole clients before the war. Benjamin Duval followed in his father's footsteps, taking up a legal career and representing Indian clients in the years after the war. Duval was also among the Confederate prisoners captured at Locust Grove by the First Indian soldiers. While there is no indication that he pursued cases against First Indian veterans or their families out of spite, most of the major cases that Duval handled for the Creeks did involve freed people claiming ties to the nation. Since the standards applied were higher in these cases, applicants had to prove they complied with the 1866 treaty stipulations, and the cases involved some very large families. *Creek Nation v. Mary Escoe et al.* included more than fifty individuals claiming descent from Escoe. Duval used the nation's scant resources where he had the greatest chance of success in protecting the tribal rolls. In the process, Duval introduced mountains of evidence that implicated African Creeks in bribery and corruption in getting state freed people on the rolls. The evidence alienated Creek Indians from African Creeks and divided the African Creek community as African Creeks were called to counter one another's testimony.[28]

The African Creek community was further divided as political patronage was distributed following the 1895 election. While harmony seemed to prevail in council as the friends of Childers and Isparhecher came together, an uproar occurred among African Creeks when the coalition decided to replace nearly all African Creek school officials. The situation was aggravated when the condition of Creek finances forced some schools to close temporarily in late 1895. The changing of the guard at Pecan Creek Mission School sparked a particularly bitter political feud. J. P. Davison, the powerful (and some would say, ruthless) Arkansas Colored leader, was the leading force behind establishing the school and had served as superintendent there since its founding in 1891. He did not take his involuntary retirement lightly.[29]

The new council seated in October 1895 chose Warrior Rentie as Davison's successor. Rentie had political aspirations of his own, having been elected to the House of Warriors from Arkansas Colored in 1891, and had served on the Committee of Eighteen selected to revise the citizenship rolls for the 1895 per capita payment. He was also becoming a well-known tribal lawyer, having edited, translated, and published the acts and resolutions of the Creek Council, and he had taken a leading role in the impeachment cases against Legus Perryman and Samuel Grayson. Rentie posted a bond with the nation in December 1895, with Sugar George signing as surety, and began his duties immediately. He found the school "was nearly destitute of supplies" and in poor repair. He reviewed the school accounts and charged Davison and members of the Creek School Board with making unspecified withdrawals from the schools' account and failing to deliver purchased supplies. In July 1896 Rentie was representing a client before the Creek Citizenship Commission when the commissioners informed him that he was debarred from practicing in the tribal courts because his own rights to citizenship were questioned under the recent Creek Supreme Court decision. H. C. Reed, whom Rentie had antagonized over the fencing controversy, was one of the commissioners. Although this decision was not generally enforced, it was applied selectively, as in Rentie's case, to punish political opponents. Rentie took his own case before the citizenship commission and introduced documentary evidence that proved his citizenship, but he was summarily denied and stricken from the rolls.[30]

After Rentie was stricken from the rolls, Davison mounted a petition drive to have him suspended as superintendent at Pecan Creek for misconduct and incompetence. Davison solicited signatures from Creeks from all parts of the nation. Davison prevailed, Rentie was suspended, and Roley McIntosh, as acting chief (Isparhecher was recovering from the effects of a stroke), reappointed J. P. Davison as superintendent.[31]

Rentie had reason to be cautious. Davison had only recently taken "extreme measures" in avenging those who crossed him. When a friend sent word to Davison that John Island was loading some cattle claimed by Davison at the railroad depot at Oktaha, Davison rushed off to confront him; and when he found Island loading the cattle, he drew his revolver and told him he was under arrest. After Island drew his gun, Davison shot him dead. Davison was brought before the Creek court, but the case was dismissed as justifiable homicide. John Island was no desperado; he had served as Ward Coachman's secretary during Coachman's tenure as chief and had represented North Fork Colored in the House of Warriors since 1891. To further prove his point, Davison ran for, and won, Island's vacated seat in the House of Warriors in a special election held to fill the position in 1897, even though Davison had previously been a member of Arkansas Colored Town and had already served several terms as a Warrior from there.[32]

True to his name, however, Warrior Rentie fought on. Finding no justice with the Creek commission, he turned to the federal government and took his case before the Dawes Commission. He complained to the commissioners that not only was he unfairly stripped of his citizenship, but Davison had also come to the school to try to throw him, his wife, and his infant son out of the superintendent's quarters. Failing that, Davison had sent the Muskogee District Lighthorse to accomplish the task a week later. Rentie also accused Davison "of living a polygamous life, with two of his wives living in the same house, and [he] is known to be a confessed murderer and libertine." While the first two charges were true, and the third a matter of opinion, Davison remained a powerful figure in tribal politics and the superintendent at Pecan Creek until the end of the tribal period (with a short hiatus from 1899–1900). Even though Rentie's citizenship remained in limbo until 1899, when he was reinstated by the Dawes Commission, he went on to play a crucial role in tribal politics and was a central figure among black Republicans in the Indian Territory during the rush toward statehood.[33]

It was unfortunate that politics and personal rivalries took such a toll on the African Creek schools at this time in particular. The timing could not have been worse. The troubles seemed to confirm the Dawes Commission's charges of Creek corruption and inability to handle their own affairs. While Creeks chased each other with pistols and squandered their educational resources (Indian as well as African Creek superintendents were charged with corruption and incompetence), the commissioners pointed to the tens of thousands of white and black noncitizen children in the Indian Territory without access to education. Consequently, Congress mandated federal control over the tribal schools, appointed John D. Benedict as superintendent of education for the Indian Territory, and appointed supervisors for each of the Five Tribes tribal schools to oversee their operations. Despite all the political turmoil and criticism leveled at the Creek schools by Superintendent Benedict, it was a fact that the Creek nation spent more money per capita on educating black children than any state in the Union, and that African Creek children went to school in greater numbers, for longer periods, and had higher literacy rates than in any neighboring states. The comparison is even more remarkable considering that for most African Creek children, English was their second language.[34]

While Isparhecher and a majority in the national council evaded cooperating with the Dawes Commission throughout 1896–1897, influential progressives in council led by Pleasant Porter in the House of Kings and Phillip Lewis in the House of Warriors were able to muster the votes necessary to create a special committee to begin negotiations. Lewis later said the Creeks should at least listen to what the commissioners had to say "out of courtesy to the government." Porter felt that obstructing the work of the commissioners only jeopardized the chances of negotiating a favorable settlement. To some Creeks, however, a favorable settlement meant excluding the freed people. The committee proposed to reinterpret Article II of the 1866 treaty as well as the history of its negotiation:

> By the Treaty of 1866 we were induced to adopt a large number of freedmen, not expecting that they would demand part of our funds and lands and we think that the Indian owners of the title should be indemnified for this charge on our property made as it was, on the demand of and for the accommodation of the government.[35]

Just as the government had refused to indemnify Creek slaveowners in 1866, the Dawes Commission now refused to curry to Creek "redeemers." The commissioners curtly replied, "We think there is no power in this commission, or the Creek government, by agreement or otherwise, to curtail the rights of the freedmen as granted under the treaty of 1866."[36]

After the Creeks rejected the agreement, Dawes wrote to fellow commissioner Tams Bixby, who was acting head of the commission while the aging Dawes remained at home in Pittsfield, Massachusetts: "What would be the view of the Commission as to the next step advisable?" Still clinging to the belief that opposition to allotment was a conspiracy engineered by corrupt wealthy Creek land monopolists, he asked, "Were members of the Creek Council who rejected the Agreement among those who hold the great leases of Creek Lands?" As a matter of fact, Pleasant Porter, one the wealthiest and largest landholders, was the head of the committee that drafted the ill-fated agreement, and many substantial African and Indian Creek "monopolists" were among the strongest supporters of negotiation with the commission. The Creek people rejected an amended version of the agreement in 1898 and then approved yet another version in early 1899. Henry Dawes vetoed the 1899 version his commission colleagues had accepted because it denied Creek freed people any equalization payments. A Creek agreement with the Dawes Commission was not finalized until 1901.[37]

Meanwhile the allotment program went ahead under the Curtis Act. Faced with overwhelming intransigence and obstruction, the Dawes Commission advised Congress to impose a solution. In June 1898, Congress passed legislation euphemistically titled "An Act for the Protection of the People of the Indian Territory," known as the Curtis Act, after its sponsor Kansas representative Charles Curtis, who was himself part Kaw Indian. The law gave the Dawes Commission the power to use "whatever means necessary" to carry out the allotment policy, even if it meant going forward without the consent of the tribes. The message was clear: either the Creeks must forge a negotiated agreement with the Dawes Commission or accept the will of the commission without recourse to appeal. Under the terms of the act, each Creek enrolled as a bona fide citizen would receive one quarter section of land (160 acres). Forty acres would be classified as a homestead and would be inalienable for twenty-one years. The remaining 120 acres, classified as the surplus, would have restrictions on its leasing or sale for a period, but eventually the surplus lands could be either sold or leased, and it was implicitly understood, at least by government policymakers, that the surplus lands would wind up in the hands of homesteaders and developers. Creek finances, which included administration of the schools, were placed under the control of the secretary of the Interior, and all acts of the Creek government were subject to the will of the federal government. Once allotment was complete, the Creek government would be dissolved, and any remaining resources, such as proceeds from the sale of mineral rights and town sites that were segregated from allotment and sold under a special bidding system, would be used for equalization payments to citizens whose allotment selections were assessed at a lower value than the average for the nation as a whole. The Dawes Commission was also given the right to decide all questions of citizenship, subject to appeal to the federal courts. The Curtis Act established the Dunn roll as the talisman on which African Creeks were to prove their citizenship, but given the problems associated with the roll, the commission left the door to allotment open if African Creeks could show that their names were legitimately on any of the authenticated tribal rolls or that they had been adopted by council.[38]

African Creeks participated in allotment as free and equal citizens of the Creek Nation as specified under Article II of the 1866 treaty. But this was not a belated proffer of forty acres and a mule by the federal government. African Creeks had developed as a class of subsistence and commercial farmers, landlords, tradespeople, businesspeople, professionals—and exploitive land monopolists with unparalleled access to education and to the political system under Creek communal land ownership and under a cultural belief system that had a history of racial tolerance. What allotment, U.S. citizenship, and statehood offered was much less than forty acres and a mule. Under these circumstances, the offer of an allotted quarter section was not an opportunity but a threat. Allotment was only the first step in imposing Euro-American cultural hegemony on the racial frontier. With allotment came homesteaders, speculators, and developers leading the forces of progress and cultural consolidation that animated late nineteenth- and early twentieth-century America. Flushed with pride over the victory over Spain, and with the economy at full steam after the depression of the early 1890s, those who led the charge into the Indian Territory had no doubt about the superiority of Euro-American culture. They equated economic development with progress and civilization and considered the subsistence farming practiced by the wide majority of African Creeks a sign of backwardness and inferiority. If that was still not enough to place African Creeks on the lowest rung of the cultural hierarchy, there was the matter of their

African descent, which during this period in American history automatically qualified them for second-class citizenship.

Immediately after Congress passed the Curtis Act, the Dawes Commission finally obtained the 1896 tribal rolls. Those of 1890 and 1891 (the omitted roll) soon followed, and armed with citizenship evidence and a bevy of hired clerks, the commissioners began a concerted enrollment campaign. They began by opening an enrollment office for Creek freed people in Muskogee on August 1, 1898. During the next month, at Okmulgee, Wellington, and other locations throughout the Creek country, they registered African Creek applicants and completed most of the work by the beginning of September. The enrollment avalanche alarmed some Creeks who saw collusion between federal officials and African Creeks in allowing the freed people to enroll first.[39]

Other questions regarding race, identity, and citizenship surfaced during the enrollment process. Robert Grayson, a Creek Indian from Coweta, had married Jacob and Mollie Perryman's daughter, Mary. He was told by the enrollment clerks that he did not have to enroll at that time since he was Indian "by blood." But because his wife and three children were African Creeks and enrolled in Arkansas Colored on the separate freed people's roll, Grayson was told that he would have to come back with his wife, children, and his wife's parents as witnesses. James Grayson (Robert's brother) was in a similar situation and asked if his deceased wife's mother could enroll his children. If the Graysons had come before a Creek citizenship commission, the matter would have been disposed of in an instant. Everyone in the nation knew of Jacob Perryman and his family and that some of the Graysons were Indians of African descent married to African Creek women. In fact, more than 10 percent of the people on the Coweta and Hillabee town rolls were African Creeks. The clerks had orders to place freed people and Indians "by blood" on separate rolls, and they were supposed to follow the "one drop rule"—children descended from either a black father or mother had to prove themselves under the 1866 treaty and show their names (or their descendant's) on either the Dunn roll or the Colored town rolls to be admitted. But what about those African Creeks enrolled in Indian Towns? What about those who were recognized by the tribe as Indian citizens but to the Dawes commissioners and clerks were clearly of African descent? Did the one drop rule have a chronological limit? For those accustomed to drawing rigid race and color lines, the racial ambiguities in the Creek country and the cultural and political customs that further blurred the lines were perplexing in the extreme.[40]

Andrew Sullivan, an African Creek in his eighties, testified on his own behalf and for the admission of his daughter, Sarah, at an application hearing before the commission. At the time, Sullivan was nearly blind and was supported by the Creek government as an indigent or infirm citizen with monthly payments, which would seem to confirm his bona fide status. But the commissioners still had difficulty understanding life in the Creek country and how African Creeks contributed to the development of the Indian Territory:

Commissioner: Do you consider yourself a citizen of the Creek Nation?
Sullivan: If I ain't one, you won't find another one here.
Commissioner: Have you lived here all your life?
Sullivan: Yes, backwards and forwards all my life.

At this point the commissioner turned testy.

Commissioner: I ask you, how long have you lived in the Creek Nation?!
Sullivan: That's what I'm trying to tell you. I've been living here forty years or more [actually more than sixty] ever since I came to this country. I came here when I was twenty years old [1838].
Commissioner: Then you wasn't born in the Creek Nation?
Sullivan: Yes, in Alabama, in the Creek Nation with the Injuns. I came here with them.
Commissioner: How long did you live in Alabama?
Sullivan: About twenty years, I left Alabama and come here.
Commissioner: When did you come to the Indian Territory?
Sullivan: I can't tell you that. I can't read; but I can tell you who carried me here. Captain Runnels; he brought me out with the Injuns [perhaps the late 1838 emigration of the Upper Creeks].

Everyone in the room, except the commissioners, knew Sullivan. He was born in the Creek Nation and had driven a wagon from Alabama to the Indian Territory during the Creek removal. Before the Civil War, Sullivan had worked as a teamster for James A. Patterson, the merchant trader at the Creek Agency, hauling freight between the Creek Agency (and later Muskogee and Okmulgee), Ft. Gibson, Ft. Smith, and Texas for many years. The commissioners understood his answers to questions about his comings and goings to mean that he was "a transient man" rather than a key contributor to the economic development of the Indian Territory—an issue so dear to the hearts of the commissioners and white boomers alike. But Sullivan's application was ultimately approved. By the time the Dawes rolls were closed in March 1907, having wound through a maze of appeals, challenges, and court decisions, adding newborn children and lopping off deceased citizens, they contained some 6,800 African and 11,890 "by-blood" Creeks. No one will ever know how many bona fide citizens were left out by the commission and the courts based on arbitrary notions of race and citizenship or how many intruders made it on to the rolls through chicanery and falsehood, but the commission forged ahead, oblivious to racial complexities, satisfied that their mission was to allot the lands, not to ensure the survival of a multiracial society.[41]

The business of dividing the tribal estate into individual land holdings began in earnest on April 1, 1899, when the commission opened a land office in Muskogee. It was later said that African Creeks were the first to come forward and to make their selections, claiming much of the rich agricultural lands in the Arkansas River bottoms. The reports intimated that Creek freedmen, with the help of white speculators, pushed other allottees aside in order to grab the most valuable land. In fact, African Creeks made up the majority of native Creek citizens around Muskogee, so it was no hardship for them to show up at the land office. Additionally, they were already in possession of most of these lands anyway and had been farming and improving them in some cases even before the Civil War. They were simply claiming land that was already under their control under the conditional use title recognized by the Creeks.[42]

To keep a hand in the process, the Creek Council appointed a committee to aid the commission and oversee the land selection policy. James Gregory and Abe Kernels, two of the committee members, sent reports to Isparhecher with observations on what transpired at the land office. Gregory was appalled at the scene of "corrupt politicians, parading as patriots . . . selling citizenship certificates to Louisiana and Texas mulattos." He was convinced that these same politicians, in league with white boomers, persuaded freedmen to petition Congress in support of the Curtis Act in order to break the Creek land title. Although Gregory mentioned no one by name, he was most likely writing about William McIntosh, Gabriel Jamison, and H. C. Reed. But he reserved his special venom for the "foul monster . . . Legus Perryman" and the architect of accommodation with the Dawes Commission, Pleasant Porter, both of whom he classified as Negroes. Gregory also observed white men attempting to pose as freedmen jamming the halls of the land office, a phenomenon that would become increasingly common as the allotment process unfolded. Gregory continued to serve as a Creek advisor to the commission and aided Duval in purging the rolls of some 250 questionable applicants. His increasingly hysterical charges against Creek freedmen, however, limited his effectiveness. Gregory later claimed African Creeks were conspiring with state freedmen to take control of tribal lands and resources, sell out to white boomers, and then use the proceeds to emigrate to Africa after engaging in a final spate of pillage and plunder through the countryside.[43]

Abe Kernel's less strident report illuminated problems Creeks had experienced for many years in deciding citizenship questions. Such questions now took on increasing importance with the final division of the tribal estate. Among those initial five thousand who thronged into Muskogee to select allotments that spring and summer, Kernel noted numerous freedmen from the other tribes as well as state freedmen at the land office. Kernel was over sixty years old at the time and had lived in the Creek country all his life. He had traveled the many miles "on the road to Kansas" during the Civil War, leaving his farm in the southwestern corner of the nation on the Little River in August 1862 and later enlisting in the First Kansas Colored. After the war, he was active in Creek politics and civic life and was well known and respected throughout the nation as an intelligent and fair-minded person who was often called to duty during difficulties that required the ability to see both sides of a question. Kernel was a walking repository of African Creek citizenship information. After being mustered out, Kernel had helped agent Dunn distribute rations and bread money at the Creek Agency and had made several trips to Kansas to bring back refugees. He also assisted in compiling the Dunn Roll, registering the Loyal Creek claims, and keeping town rolls. Having been raised on the border between the Creek, Chickasaw, and Choctaw nations, he also knew the comings and goings of the people there. From his experience in gathering and seeking out members of the African Creek community, Kernel drew a fine line when it came to citizenship qualifications. He objected to Chickasaw, Choctaw, and Cherokee freed people who married African Creeks and then tried to put their children on the Creek rolls, because he felt that many of these applicants had long since severed ties with the Creek Nation and were merely trying to take advantage of the more generous Creek allotment policy. The Dawes Commission and the courts would later admit some of these applicants if they could prove they were actually born in the Creek Nation. Warrior Rentie, for example, succeeded in getting his children admitted under these guidelines. Kernel's work won the appreciation of many Creeks and the enmity of others, and it probably saved the nation tens of thousands of acres and perhaps hundreds of thousands of dollars that would have been lost to fraudulent claims. Phillip Lewis, Paro Bruner, and other African Creeks also worked in a positive way with the Dawes Commission, seeking out bona fide citizens and making sure they were properly enrolled.[44]

While there were many complaints about bogus additions to the Creek freed people's roll, there is also evidence that many bona fide citizens were left out of the enrollment of more than six thousand. In 1904, as the enrollment work neared completion, the Dawes Commission published a list of thirty-five hundred names found on authenticated tribal rolls who were not enrolled for allotment. After duplicate names and those of the deceased were eliminated, more than one thousand "lost Creeks" were still on the list. The overwhelming majority were African Creeks. While it is clear that many ineligible state freed people fattened the rolls, their numbers only served to fill slots left vacant by lost Creeks. Amid complaints that the Creek freed people's roll was inflated, there is an explanation of how African Creeks came to compose 33 percent of the Creek citizens enrolled by the commission. In the first place, the African Creek natural population increase had far outstripped that of Creek Indians since the Civil War. Additionally, there is every reason to believe that Dunn roll count of 1,774 African Creeks was nowhere near accurate. Agent Dunn called for the census in January and accepted rolls through February, a full five months before the July 1867 deadline for freed people to return. Weather during this season was typically cold and wet, which turned the few roads in the Creek country into impassable quagmires, making travel and communication difficult. The planting season did not begin until April, so African Creeks, the majority being farmers, felt little need to return to claim homesteads in late winter, when the land could not be worked. Dunn, furthermore, did not take the count in person but stayed at the Creek Agency (most likely in front of the fire at Sarah Davis's rebuilt hotel) and sent African Creek enumerators from the Creek Agency village out to collect the names. In many cases, the people (apparently Abe Kernel was an exception) sent to take the count were unfamiliar with the settlements, farms, and families outside the Arkansas River valley area. Dan Tucker testified, "the old man . . . sent out to take the census . . . couldn't talk good English, so he got a lot of the names wrong." According to Paro Bruner, the census takers missed whole communities located in the hinterlands and then "failed to get the names right" of those they did count. Testifying at an enrollment hearing for Louisa Olden, whose name did not appear on the Dunn roll, Bruner compared the Dawes Commission's efforts with those of Agent Dunn; "Dunn was ruling just like how you men are ruling today; the person would have to come up themselves to be enrolled or not at all." Bruner also said that Dunn missed the majority of names brought in from the outlying areas of Canadian Colored Town because he had already sent the roll to Washington and refused to send an amended list. Given these conditions, the number of African Creeks was quite possibly closer to two thousand.[45]

It is also possible that the African Creek population more than doubled in the two generations that separated the underreported Dunn roll and the Dawes Commission final rolls. Many African Creeks had large families, even by the standards of the day. Plural marriage, a part of Creek traditional culture, was still practiced in outlying settlements in the years after the war, and it accounted for the size of some families. And, as Lucinda Davis related in a Work Projects Administration interview in the 1930s, "Dem Upper Creek took de marryin' kind of light anyways." Davis's observation is born out as African Creeks testified before the Dawes Commission and federal judges. And while adultery was still considered a serious social breach in the Creek community, in their testimony some described courting, coupling, and separating with bewildering regularity that must have shocked Victorian sensibilities—what modern sociologists might term "serial marriages." Social mechanics and morality aside, doing the math on some leading African Creek families can illustrate the potential population growth. For example, William McIntosh and his wife Rhody had thirteen children, nine of whom survived to be enrolled by the Dawes Commission, along with more than forty grandchildren and great-grandchildren. Monday Durant, who died six years before the Dawes Commission began enrolling Creek freed people, left behind seventeen children and over one hundred grandchildren and great grandchildren who enrolled, even though two of Durant's three wives had been state freed people and the children and grandchildren from those unions were ineligible for allotment. Pickett Rentie had ten children enrolled, and his brother Morris, seventeen. Paro Bruner, the Canadian Colored leader, enrolled fourteen children and more than sixty grandchildren. The all-time patriarch among the African Creeks, however, was Robert Grayson, a well-known North Fork Colored leader who had alternately represented the town in both the House of Kings and House of Warriors since 1867. When Grayson enrolled for allotment, he was probably in his nineties; twenty-one of his surviving children also enrolled, along with an untold number of descendants who no doubt numbered in the hundreds.[46]

The principal effect of the Dawes Commission taking control of citizenship and identity questions, then, was not to enroll more Creek freed people than was justified but to eliminate the luxury of racial ambiguity. The systematic recording and cataloging of people's identity and descent according to standards demanded by the dominant white society quantified racial abstractions with an air of finality that was in sharp contrast with the lackadaisical, informal, and at times corrupt methods employed by the Creeks themselves, as the Dawes Commission judged Creek citizenship practices. And while the kinship-based social structure of Creek society had undergone severe disruptions attended by removal, the alarming mortality and dislocations of the Civil War, and the onslaught of intruders in the postwar years, kinship relations were still the governing principle that governed legitimate citizenship for the Creeks. The Creeks' loss of control of race and identity questions to the federal government under pressure from the hundreds of thousands of white and black settlers pouring into the Indian Territory began the process that ended with the Oklahoma legislature imposing Jim Crow and disfranchisement after statehood. Although the Creeks had imposed a form of segregation of their own in establishing separate Colored towns and listing citizens on separate rolls, the Colored towns were *Creek* towns and their citizens were *Creeks* with legitimate claims to citizenship by virtue of their kinship ties, grounded in their towns. African Creeks still held title to the Creek lands in common with other Creeks, participated equally in tribal politics, and had an equitable share in tribal educational funds. By separating Creeks into freedmen and by-blood categories, however, the Dawes Commission set the stage for application of racial distinctions to land ownership as well.

At the same time that African Creeks were being outfitted with a new identity, the Dawes Commission was also redefining the African Creeks' relationship to the land. As Danny Goble has written, the transition from communal land ownership to private ownership was a wrenching process. The claiming of land squared off in metes and bounds—land that had been defined by custom and natural features for generations—bewildered most African Creeks. For others, this was a golden opportunity. James Coody Johnson established quite an estate in the western reaches of the Creek country through consolidating his family's allotments and using his considerable legal and financial skills. Reportedly, he employed between thirty-five and forty sharecroppers after the turn of the century to work his lands, and by statehood he was a major player in the Oklahoma real estate and financial marketplace. Warrior Rentie and J. P. Davison attempted the same thing in the lands outside Muskogee but at some cost to the social stability of the African Creek community. But for each Warrior Rentie or James Coody Johnson who knew the ins and outs of the white man's land system, there were twenty Island Smiths who "had little use for money" and no familiarity with surveys or deeds and who were left at the margins as a result of allotment.[47]

One of the first controversies to surface as the allotment process got under way involved renting or leasing prospective allotments. Under the regulations governing allotment, any Creek citizen had the right to select any section of land in the Creek domain as long as someone else had not filed on it or could prove that he or she had occupied or improved it. The commission did not consider mere fencing of pasture lands improvements, however. In theory, this was to prevent land monopolists from claiming title to the lands they leased to large cattle companies but had no actual control over, or interest in, other than a strand of fence. The cattle companies got around the commission's regulation by bribing incredulous Creek freedmen to file for allotments in sections designated by the companies and then inducing them to sign leases that stipulated they would sell the land to the company once it became alienable. As news leaked out that freedmen were being used by the cattle companies to "sell out the Nation's birthright," Creek nationalists such as James Gregory were enraged. Even though Creek elites had been involved in what amounted to the same practice for years, it was just more proof for people like Gregory that the freed people were a serious liability when it came to protecting Creek lands.[48]

The new system was also an opportunity to reopen old land disputes. Just weeks after the land office in Muskogee opened in April 1899, Joseph P. Davison initiated an allotment contest against his stepfather, Edward (Ned) Gibson, trying to prevent him from claiming Julia Gibson's (Davison's deceased mother and Gibson's former wife) homestead as his allotment. It was a rehash of a campaign Davison had waged earlier through the Creek courts. In those cases, he had won control of the property, but Gibson had remained at the homestead nonetheless. The contest case was presided over by Tams Bixby, the acting chairman of the commission and later Chairman, who was a controversial figure himself. Bixby was quite solicitous toward Gibson during the hearing, patronizingly calling him Uncle Ned and offering him every opportunity to show that he only wanted to claim his home acreage and was not grasping for any more than his due. Bixby, on the other hand, was quite dismissive toward Davison. He accused Davison of trying to dominate the allotment process around the old Creek Agency, saying, "they tell me you have been attempting to control that entire country up there." Davison coolly replied, "They told you a little something wrong." Davison further testified that the land in question had first been claimed by his grandmother, Sarah Davis, as far back as 1853–1854, and that he had built up the acreage and improvements there, which included apple and peach orchards as well as improved pastures, cultivated grounds, beehives, and a home for his mother. "With these hands I built that farm," he said, "and plenty of people knows that's our home." Davison reiterated that the Creek Supreme Court recognized his claim, not Gibson's, to which Bixby replied, "I haven't any great respect for the judgement of the Creek Court, you know." Neither, apparently, did Bixby respect the commission's regulations because he ruled in favor of Gibson, despite Gibson's own testimony that he had not belonged to any Creek Indian before the war, had come from Missouri in 1865, and had not been adopted by the Creek Council. Perhaps Bixby saw Gibson as a victim of Davison's well-known wrath and took the opportunity to reward Gibson at Davison's expense. More likely, however, Bixby calculated that by placing Gibson in control of the valuable property, it would pass more quickly into the hands of the developers and speculators with whom the commissioner was closely connected.[49]

A number of other allotment contest cases that worked to divide the

African Creek community arose over control of acreage outside Muskogee in the old Creek Agency area. Warrior Rentie, his mother, Caroline, and his brother, Island Rentie, were parties in a number of these contests. Contrary to the initial intent of the allotment policy, which implicitly urged enrollees to select their 40-acre homestead and 120-acre surplus allotments in separate tracts some distance from each other, the Rentie family, like James Coody Johnson and J. P. Davison, tried to consolidate their holdings. There was no question that the Renties had occupied and improved land in the area for many years, and little doubt that they sought control of the most valuable acreage.[50]

The Creek courts settled one long-standing feud between the Renties and Dave Roberts over control of some pasture land in 1890, but only after Roberts accused the Renties of trying to enforce their claim "with winchesters" (Roberts "might have" had a shotgun). After their dispute cooled down, Island Rentie told Roberts he could use the pasture because his neighbor needed it to graze livestock. Rentie was not using it at the time, did not want to fence it, and sharing pasture land was a common practice. He also testified that at the time they had no idea the land was going to be divided into individual allotments and said he did it to be "friendly" to his neighbor. As Roberts used the pasture, Rentie cultivated a small portion connected to his improved acreage. After the allotment policy was announced, the two neighbors agreed that the arrangement should continue until the general allotment. It appeared for a time that the dispute was settled. Island Rentie agreed to let Roberts use part of the contested pasture, and in exchange, Roberts let Rentie, who was a Baptist preacher, build a church for state freed people on Roberts's part of the claim. Then the Dawes Commission survey reignited the argument. For generations, land use and occupancy had been governed by natural features. The survey lines broke the land into sections that took no account of the flow and ebb of seasonal need and use priority. The land in dispute was eighty acres, described as "the northeast corner of the southwest quarter of section 15, township north, Range 18 east of the Indian meridian," and took in improvements claimed by Roberts, Island, and Warrior Rentie.[51]

Island and Roberts initially agreed to split eighty acres between them. Roberts would take the north forty, which included some of Island's improvements, the church house, and some cultivated acreage, and Island would take the south forty, which included mostly pasture land, which the

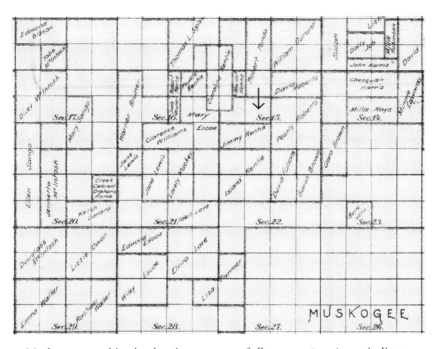

Muskogee township plat showing progress of allotment, 1899. Arrow indicates
acreage contested by the Renties and Dave Roberts.

Creek Court had previously decided that Island Rentie could claim. The agreement broke down when Warrior Rentie objected to the arrangement because Roberts's tentative north forty would take in part of his claim as well. The three arranged to meet at the land office in Muskogee, but Island was held up officiating at a funeral at the old agency church and did not arrive until after the office closed. Meanwhile, Warrior had pressured Roberts into splitting the north forty with him and then left on other business while Roberts waited for Island. In the interim, Roberts began to regret the deal he made with Warrior and felt the Renties had tricked him into settling for a mere twenty acres. When Island arrived, Roberts wanted to renege on the deal, but Island pulled him up short and said, "if a fellow give you a horse and you let somebody take it away from you [is it the fellow's fault]?" Roberts was incensed that a preacher might be party to a bait-and-switch scheme. But, instead of pulling out the Winchesters and shotguns, Roberts and Rentie filed a contest with the Dawes Commission.[52]

Two themes emerge from the hearings. Neither Island Rentie nor Dave Roberts accepted or understood the language of the commission's survey lines, and neither the commissioners nor the white lawyers in the case could fathom the flow and ebb that governed communal land tenure. The dialogue at the hearing was conducted at two levels. That between Rentie and Roberts described the land and the history of its use. Boundaries fluctuated with the seasons and were adapted to priority of need. The dialogue between the white lawyers and the commissioners focused on fixed lines with no history and on how the contestants should conform to the new reality contained in the plats and surveys. Early on in the hearing, Rentie corrected Roberts's lawyer, Edward Hastain, when the attorney stated that the Creek Court "gave" the contested acreage to Rentie, saying, "Gave me the *claim*, yes sir. You could not own the land at that time." Rentie's own lawyer, Richard Martin, then asked him about his claim to the pasture:

> Martin: When you permitted Dave Roberts to fence this pasture on the west of his cultivated land (did) you intend to claim it again?
> Rentie: We didn't know anything, you know, about the allotment coming up, and a man a going to get 160 acres of land, but we never had any more land in cultivation, you know, and we didn't care.

Hastain then seized on the idea that Rentie "gave" the pasture to Roberts.

Hastain: Why did you let Dave have it?

Rentie: Because I wanted to act friendly with him.

Hastain: You just let him come over and take your land, any part he wanted, and you let him do it, did you?

Rentie: He wanted it and I done it for friends' sake. Just to be friends; to be at peace, because I didn't want to fence right then.

At one point, an exasperated Rentie broke down, having failed to make the commissioners or the lawyers understand that use title in the Creek country was not considered absolute.

The Commission: At the time when you told Dave that he could fence that pasture did you reserve any right to the land inside of that pasture at that time?

Rentie: No! no!! no!!!—???!!!

The Commission: You gave it over to Roberts, absolutely, did you not?

Rentie: Yes sir, *as far as I could.*

The commission found in the Renties' favor because they had the superior claim, having made more permanent improvements on the surveyed land (the church house, cultivated fields) than Roberts, who had merely enclosed some pasture land with a fence, which the commission did not consider a permanent improvement.[53]

While Rentie had the superior claim to the land by virtue of earlier improvements, no matter who was using the pasture, the land remained public domain, which allowed some give and take. Roberts could graze cattle, and Rentie could build a church. Then the Dawes survey lines bisected the pasture. Boundary lines now became distinct, like the racial lines that separated the freedmen's rolls from the Indian by-blood rolls.[54]

Warrior Rentie was less successful in establishing a landed estate around the old Creek Agency. He tried to consolidate his children's acreage but ran into citizenship problems. Roy Bismark, his oldest son, was enrolled as a Creek citizen, so he was no problem. Warrior did, however, run into problems with his three younger children, Ina Victoria, Leopold Augustus, and George Washington Lubiture (a rendering of Toussaint L'Ouverture, the Haitian liberator). The commission initially considered his three youngest children Chickasaw freed people, so Rentie was prevented from filing immediately on choice lands for them. The commissioners followed the traditional Creek form of charting descent through the matrilineal line, because Rentie's wife, Aurelia, was born and raised in the Chickasaw Nation. This strict rendering of the commission's power to decide citizenship qualifications was rarely used and was probably residual fallout from Rentie's earlier citizenship and political problems. If the commission applied the same logic to Pleasant Porter (who was Creek chief at the time), for instance, he would have been placed on the Creek freedmen's rolls. The commission finally approved the transfer of Rentie's children to the Creek freed people's rolls in 1902, most likely in exchange for Rentie's support for the Creek Supplemental Agreement of 1902. In the meantime, Rentie kept considerable acreage tied up in one contest case after another, most of the challenges based on technicalities—missed filing deadlines or allotments being used for the benefit of noncitizens.[55]

The commission's survey of the lands and the allotment process, then, did more than draw lines on a map. It divided orchards, pastures, fields, homes, families, and communities. It also divided the Creeks politically and limited their ability to protect themselves from the predatory practices of white developers and land speculators or to channel the transformation of the Indian Territory in ways that would most benefit their community.

After the Curtis Act became law in summer 1898, internal Creek politics, elections, and legislation became a mere sideshow. The Creeks could still negotiate an agreement with the U.S. government that could soften the blow of the Curtis Act, but they could no longer dodge the punch altogether. Whatever any future agreement might say, Creeks could no longer exercise tribal sovereignty or hold title to their tribal lands. Consequently, the 1899 Creek election turned on the issue of which candidate could most competently oversee the final settlement of the Creek Nation's affairs. Pleasant Porter was elected by a substantial margin, with Moty Tiger as second chief, on the National Party ticket, which called for accommodation with the Dawes Commission. Porter and Tiger received 72 percent of African Creek votes, while 35 percent backed Legus Perryman and William McCombs, who were trying to rehabilitate the old Union Party coalition. The third ticket in the race, Roley McIntosh and G. W. Grayson, garnered most of their votes from the conservative Creek towns that had previously supported Isparhecher, who had retired from politics because of ill health. McIntosh and Grayson received only two African Creek votes. That the freedmen and the conservative Creek factions backed different candidates

again does not necessarily imply that the two groups were estranged. Mc-
Intosh and Grayson were the only candidates to endorse continued resistance (albeit limited) to the Dawes Commission, an issue that still resonated in the conservative Creek community. However, even if freedmen
were opposed to accommodating the government (and some were), giving
their support to McIntosh and Grayson, the principal leaders of the disfranchisement movement that had fizzled in the Creek Council during the
1890s, had less appeal.[56]

Porter's widespread support among African Creeks is more difficult to
reconcile. Although he and Tiger promised to do their utmost to protect all
Creeks, regardless of color, in negotiations with the Dawes Commission,
Porter's words did not come close to matching his deeds. Porter had played
his part in trying to limit African Creek influence in the Indian nation over
the years. First of all, he was a Confederate veteran and former slaveowner,
and, as the general of the Constitutionalist forces during the Green Peach
War, he had turned captured African Creek insurgents over for trial on
treason charges, while most of the Indians he captured were simply paroled.
As Creek delegate to Washington in the early 1890s, he had asked the U.S.
attorney general for a legal opinion on whether the Creeks could void
Article II of the 1866 Treaty. He was also head of the House of Warriors
committee that began negotiations with the Dawes Commission in 1895–
1896, the same committee that asked the commissioners to indemnify the
Creeks for adopting the freed people and to modify Article II of the 1866
treaty. And just prior to his election as chief, Porter was the guiding force
behind the 1899 agreement that Dawes himself had rejected because African
Creeks were not included in equalization payments.[57]

African Creek support for Porter might have been tied to Porter's well
known African ancestry, but there is no indication Porter ever tried to
generate political capital from his mother's lineage, which in any case would
have been political suicide. Porter could, however, (and did) bargain for
support on an issue that was always important to African Creeks: education. Porter had served as superintendent of the Creek schools in the 1870s,
later was an influential member of the Creek Joint Committee on Education, and was involved in establishing the first boarding schools for African
Creek children. His wife, Birdie, was one of the first teachers at the Creek
Agency school in the years after the war, and many of her former students
remembered her fondly. Under the Curtis Act, the Creeks had to surrender

control of their financial affairs and the direction of their schools to the secretary of the Interior. Porter promised to return some measure of school control and patronage to the Creeks under any negotiated agreement with the Dawes Commission.[58]

Leading African Creek politicians did support Porter in getting both the Creek Agreement of 1901 and the Creek Supplemental Agreement of 1902 through council. The chief needed the support to present at least the appearance of a united front to the commissioners and Congress if a favorable agreement were to be had. Yet even though Porter and Tiger had carried the 1899 election with a large majority, their accommodation program was being assailed on two fronts. From one direction, the die-hard opponents of allotment, mainly conservative traditionalists from the outlying Deep Fork District settlements, had organized a movement under the leadership of Chitto Hacho. In traditional Creek insurgent fashion, Hacho and his followers withdrew from participation in the constitutional Creek government and set up a rival government based at Hickory Ground, a traditional square ground six miles south of the railroad town of Henryetta. Chitto Hacho was nicknamed "Crazy Snake" by noncitizen opponents, which was a fanciful English rendering of his Creek name. The Snake Indians repudiated the constituted Creek government and set up their own regime with an elected assembly, principal chief, and second chief. The Snakes also appointed their own Lighthorsemen to enforce the "old laws." They called for a return to the "old treaties," refused to enroll or to accept allotments, and commissioned their Lighthorsemen to mete out punishment to Creeks who did. Support among African Creeks for the insurgents was negligible, but the white boomer newspapers made it appear that a race war pitting Indian and black malcontents against the white "civilizing influence" was imminent.[59]

In early 1901 rumors ran rampant that the Snake Indians, their numbers swelled by newspaper reports, were making plans to join with bands of lawless state freedmen for a general uprising against the Creek government. After a series of incidents in which Snake Lighthorsemen whipped several Creeks and intimidated white developers, white residents of nearby Henryetta asked for protection, and U.S. marshals were sent to arrest those responsible for the trouble. In the tense atmosphere, a gun battle broke out in which a federal officer was killed. Chief U.S. marshal Leo Bennett responded immediately and called in the Eighth Cavalry from Ft. Reno to round up the insurgents. One hundred insurgents, including Chitto Hacho and a handful of African Creeks, gave up willingly to deputy marshal Grant Johnson and were taken to the federal lock-up in Muskogee. A sympathetic federal judge, John R. Thomas, who saw more danger to the public from inflated newspaper stories than from the Snake insurgents themselves, handed out suspended sentences after they promised to make no more trouble. The Crazy Snake Rebellion was over for the time being, "crushed like an eggshell by the federal marshals" in the words of African Creek Jim Tomm. But Chitto Hacho and his followers continued to refuse allotments and agitate for a return to the old ways. Ultimately, however, they could not prevent the Creek agreement from getting through Congress and the Creek Council by May 1901.[60]

To get the agreement passed in council, Porter still had to negotiate a supplemental agreement that would take care of some of the defects in the original. Specifically, the agreement provided additional time to enroll newborns and lost creeks and gave additional protection for selling or leasing allotments. This time the accommodation program was attacked by booster groups and cattle companies, which found the new regulations too restrictive. Under the supplemental agreement, all leases would require the secretary of the Interior's approval, and there could be no agricultural leases for longer than one year. Also, surplus allotments would be inalienable for five years after the allottee received his or her deed. Allottees, however, could petition the secretary to sell their surplus lands earlier—if the secretary found the allottee competent to handle the property and needed the income to improve his or her forty-acre homestead. The Indian Affairs Office would then advertise and sell the lands by sealed bid if the bidders could at least match the appraised price. Homestead allotments would still remain inalienable for twenty-one years.[61]

As the date approached for council to consider the supplemental agreement (July 17), approval appeared unlikely. Cattle companies and land speculators, attempting to scuttle the agreement, poured whiskey, money, and other "nefarious resources" freely into Okmulgee. The federal government sent numerous agents to the Creek country to back up the U.S. marshals on duty there and raided gambling dens and seized and spilled hundreds of barrels of liquor. Meanwhile Pleasant Porter, Phillip Lewis, and other supporters of the agreement rallied support in council. While all seemed hopeless in the first weeks of July, the government's efforts bolstered the agreement's supporters in council, which approved the supplemental agreement July 26.[62]

By the agreements of 1901 and 1902, the Creeks gave their official approval for the final division of the tribal estate and the dissolution of their tribal government. All tribal government functions would officially cease March 4, 1906. In voluntarily agreeing to their own demise, the Creeks obtained some government protection for their allotted lands and were allowed some measure of control over their schools and tribal finances. As a consequence of concluding what many felt was a favorable agreement, Porter and Tiger easily won the elections of 1903, with 58 percent of the African Creek vote, concentrated mainly in Arkansas Colored. Legus Perryman, running again as the Union Party candidate, polled a respectable 42 percent of the freedmen vote and actually bested Porter in both Canadian and North Fork Colored towns. Many people were surprised at Chitto Hacho's showing; he captured 20 percent of the vote with only 3 of his 464 votes coming from African Creeks. With the 1903 elections, Creek tribal politics as a main attraction came to an end, and, as Mary Jane Warde has written, very few Creek Indians became involved in politics beyond the tribal level. And though some tribal political wrangling was still to be done over the composition of the final rolls, land appraisement, equalization payments, Creek schools, and other issues, African Creeks increasingly turned their attention to territorial politics and the politics of eventual statehood, which by 1903 had taken on an alarming racial tone.[63]

7

"A Measure So Insulting as This"
Jim Crow in the Indian Country

By 1903 THE MORE THAN 350,000 white and black intruders in the Indian Territory vastly outnumbered the members of the Five Tribes. The intruders were led by a corps of land speculators, developers, industrialists, and commercial interests who believed the commercial development of the Indian Territory was to be the next great chapter in America's march of progress and cultural consolidation. All clamored for access to land and for statehood. While the Creek agreements provided that restrictions on the sale of the 120-acre surplus allotments could be removed under Interior Department guidelines, and that all restrictions would be taken off in 1907, it was not soon enough for booster elements, who led the push for statehood. One real-estate broker complained that it would take 120 years to sell the surplus lands under the bid system initiated by the Interior Department. It was during this battle over access to allotted lands that African Creek identification with tribal lands became even more racially polarized. Coinciding with the push for statehood and the campaign to open allotted lands for sale, African Creeks, attempting to salvage a place at the table in the new state, also became increasingly active in racial politics.[1]

Most developers and boosters grudgingly conceded that Indians, especially the cultural conservatives unfamiliar with the white man's system, should have at least some restrictions on selling their allotments. African Creeks, however, were a different matter. To the white newcomers, particularly those from the South, they were simply Negroes and had no rights that white men were bound to respect. To the Indian Territory boosters, African Creeks represented an impediment to progress; and, echoing the feelings of some Creeks, boosters generally agreed that Creek freedmen had no right to the land anyway—the 1866 treaty was a mistake radical Republicans had made more than three generations ago. African American immigrants and boosters regarded African Creeks with a mixture of envy, jealousy, and exasperation. They envied the position African Creeks had carved out of the racial frontier and were jealous of the place that prominent African Creeks had made for themselves. They were also exasperated with African Creek reluctance to share racial solidarity with them and puzzled by the outright hostility some African Creeks showed toward state freed people. The black boosters viewed African Creek subsistence farmers in much the same way as their white counterparts did—an obstacle to development. But some African American entrepreneurs, guided by B. T. Washington's Tuskegee spirit, saw an opportunity to put Washington's "racial uplift" philosophy to work on a grand scale. All these groups shared the idea that the sooner restrictions were removed on the sale of Creek freedmen's surplus allotments, the better. Under this avalanche of propaganda, the voices of African Creeks themselves were barely heard. They were recorded in a lone petition forwarded by the Creek Council, which strongly opposed lifting restrictions, and by numerous letters from freedmen to federal officials pleading for protection from "land gobblers."[2]

As the debate over restrictions grew, removal supporters received an unexpected boost for their cause in August 1903. S. M. Brosius of the Indian Rights Association, after investigating how the Dawes Commission was carrying out the allotment policy, found that members of the commission and other government officers were all involved in buying, selling, leasing, and speculating on the Indian lands they were supposed to protect. The scandal drew national headlines, and President Theodore Roosevelt was obliged to appoint Charles Bonaparte, a Republican stalwart and a member of the Board of Indian Commissioners, to investigate. While reformers in the East clicked their tongues and called for even tighter controls, the boosters in the Indian Territory failed to see what the fuss was about. One exasperated developer exclaimed, "My god, a work unparalleled in the history of civilization is threatened by fanatical reports and questionable journalism!" Bonaparte's investigation found that, far from being dubious muckraking, Brosius's charges had only scratched the surface concerning federal officials and their investment and speculation in allotted lands.[3]

While Roosevelt scrambled to contain the scandal, the opponents of restrictions seized the occasion. They charged that the complicated regulations not only stifled development but were also the root cause of the scandal. Bonaparte's investigation and report became the launching pad for an all-out campaign to get Congress to lift restrictions on selling allotted lands. As Bonaparte took testimony in the Indian Territory in late 1903 and early 1904, his primary mission, uncovering involvement of federal government officials in land transactions, was buried under an avalanche of testimony that favored removing restrictions. The boosters' special targets were African Creeks.[4]

Judge John R. Thomas, writing as a representative of the Muskogee Chamber of Commerce, told the investigators:

> The Indian Territory is now being held by the grasp of the throat which is literally killing it and stifling all business, it is killing all improvement, it is killing every business enterprise. If the restrictions on the sale of [freedmen's] land were removed this country would blossom like a rose and the material condition of the people would be vastly improved. These Negroes won't work if they can avoid it and as long as they have 160 acres of land, they won't.[5]

Robert L. Owen, the former Union Indian agent, who would go on to become Oklahoma's first senator, called loudly for removing restrictions on freedmen's land, saying such protection was unnecessary because "no statute can protect an improvident man from himself." Furthermore, Owen charged that freedmen filed many complaints against land developers without just cause, and some had taken money for five or six leases on the same allotment, knowing the leases were invalid. But Bonaparte gave a different account of Owen's charges in his report, politely saying the land men had been "overreached" while attempting to "overreach" the freedmen. Nonetheless, Owen hammered away at the freedmen, who were, in his opinion, "unscrupulous, engaged in craft and guile, and willing to defraud. . . . He is more intelligent than the white man and ten times as shrewd as his brother [the Indian]." Pleasant Porter and other Creek Indians took exception to Owen's overheated remarks, which were circulated widely in the Indian Territory booster newspapers. Although the chief believed that most Creek freedmen did not have the necessary experience with private property to protect themselves from the sharpers and grafters that were swarming the Creek country, he endorsed removing restrictions on the freedmen's lands, saying that it was time for African Creeks "to take their chances with the white man." In fact, that was one of the recommendations in Bonaparte's report: "The freedmen, who constitute, on the whole, an uninteresting and unpromising class of the population, seem to need the care of the government no more than the other people of their race throughout the Union." Bonaparte's remarks were particularly chilling given that lynching rates and racist violence as well as campaigns to disfranchise African Americans and impose racial segregation were at high tide during these years, while the federal government blithely ignored its responsibilities in protecting the rights of African American citizens.[6]

In March 1904, representative John Sebastian Little, a Democrat from Arkansas, introduced an amendment to the Indian appropriations bill calling for the removal of restrictions from the surplus allotments of adult Creek freedmen and adult intermarried white Creek citizens. Restrictions would remain, however, on their forty-acre homestead allotments. During the debate over the amendment, Little presented the Creek freed people in a different light than had most Indian Territory boosters.[7]

> I can say for the Negroes of the [Creek Nation] Indian Territory that as a body of people they are in advance of any body of colored people that I know of in any of the States. They have had the benefit of free schools and colleges for more than half a century. They are educated, they are self assertive, they are aggressive and it is folly for the government to require the Secretary of the Interior . . . to hold and maintain the present restrictions against these people.[8]

If Little wanted to show African Creeks competent to handle their own business affairs, he had to point no further than to W. A. Rentie, J. P. Davison, J. C. Johnson, and others. While these African Creeks and many like them had business experience and had taken advantage of opportunities available to them in the Creek country, the large majority of African Creeks, though educated in the Creek schools, were subsistence farmers with no practical experience with private property, much less dealing with grafters and their methods of acquiring land. But as Little told his fellow representatives, the real benefits of restriction removal did not accrue to the freed people but to those who would settle the lands offered for sale: "When you do this [remove restrictions] you will build up in this country 10,000 homes in twelve months." And as the Indian Territory booster press added, "the land that will be sold without restrictions will be the cream of the

AFRICAN CREEKS

Creek Nation. It will place a great deal of rich land in the hands of white farmers who will soon develop it into a high state of cultivation." It did not matter that white boosters inconsistently classified Creek freedmen as both incompetent to develop their own lands and yet competent enough to sell them; what mattered was to get the lands developed and speed the road to statehood.[9]

Congress passed the amendment, and President Roosevelt signed the appropriation bill April 21, 1904. The *Muskogee Phoenix* put out an extra edition that afternoon, proclaiming that over eight hundred thousand acres of surplus allotments were open for sale. What followed was what historian Danney Goble described as "a public orgy of greed as ignorant freedmen were quickly divested of most of their land." J. C. Johnson estimated that two-thirds of the freedmen's surplus lands were gone within the week, and 90 percent of the land was sold for "grossly inadequate compensation." Arkansas River bottomlands appraised at forty dollars an acre were sold for less than one dollar an acre. One developer bragged of "bagging" between fifteen and twenty surplus allotments on the first morning lands were open for sale and paying less than one thousand dollars for the entire acreage. According to Alice Robertson, such "deals" were possible only because most Creek freedmen were "as simple and credulous as full-blooded Indians" when it came to managing property. Indeed, as M. L. Mott, the Creek Nation attorney, later testified, the methods grafters used to get the land preyed on freedmen's ignorance. Mott said that the land sales were accomplished through "all disreputable methods, unjustified and unwarranted, that could be imagined. Every species of trickery, every device of fraud were resorted to get land from these people." One method involved presenting conveyance instruments as agricultural leases to unsuspecting freedmen who believed they were selling their hay crop when in fact they had sold their entire surplus allotment for twenty-five dollars. Some grafters invited freedmen to a "party" some distance away and then refused to take them home until they signed over their land. Other grafters specialized in under-age allottees, who under the new legislation were still restricted from selling their land. The grafter would convince minor freedmen to lie about their age in order to sell their allotments and then would threaten them with arrest and jail for perjury if they exposed the swindle. But perhaps the most appalling aspect of the 1904 land sales was that Indian Territory boosters, developers, and federal officials applauded the grafters' methods, seeing them as necessary to get the land settled with the right kind of people so the Indian Territory could "blossom like a rose."[10]

Instead of stories about the scope and depth of the land swindles in the Creek country, the booster newspapers carried racist stories lampooning improvident and ignorant freed people who squandered what everyone was sure would be their temporary wealth. "There was a swell turnout on the streets of Muskogee yesterday, consisting of Tallaho coach, four white horses gaily caparisoned, silver trimmed harness and six freedmen. The outfit represented probably six allotments sold since the removal of restrictions." In one story, a Creek freedwoman reportedly traded her entire surplus allotment for two watermelons. Other stories told of allotments traded for whiskey, "a few baubles," or less. The *Daily Oklahoman* claimed that the money Creek freed people acquired from the land sales caused friction because "[a] Negro with money is insolent." The Creek writer Alexander Posey, no great friend of the freed people, described the scene contemporaneously through the eyes of his character Fus Fixico, a progressive full-blood Creek Indian sage known for his wry commentary and twisted irony: "the newspapers could find lots of stuff to fill up on, like the removal of restrictions so the niggers could squander their land for a blue suit of clothes and a rubber tired buggy and make room for progress, while the Injun he look on and learn a good object lesson." The object lesson came through loud and clear on the pages of the *Phoenix*, which said, "The removal of restrictions will bring more white farmers to the Indian Territory and begin a process that makes this area a white man's country."[11]

Just how rapidly the Creek country would become a white man's country was made clear by the ease and swiftness with which 75 percent of the lands allotted African Creeks fell into the hands of white developers and speculators. Less than two years had passed since the Creek Supplemental Agreement had put African Creeks in official possession of their allotments and the Secretary of the Interior had begun delivering their deeds. Restrictions still remained on African Creek forty-acre homesteads, but agitation for removing them as well began after the bulk of surplus lands were snatched up. African Creek access to land in the Indian Nation had been the foundation of their independence and the key to their advantageous economic, political, and social position. The removal of restrictions eroded that base of support; and as the push toward statehood quickened, the politics of race threatened African Creeks with exclusion from the political process as well.

The politics of making the Indian Territory into a white man's country first had to confront the racial complexities in the Creek country. The very presence of educated, independent, assertive, and successful business and professional people such as J. C. Johnson, W. A. Rentie, Phillip Lewis, and J. P. Davison, who were experienced in politics from the tribal regime, seemed to confirm the wisdom of including people of African descent in the organizing and leading of the new state. These African Creeks, along with other new faces such as Alexander G. W. Sango, son of Scipio Sango, the long-time African Creek leader, and George Davison, son of J. P. Davison and Amy Island, would lead the charge for a seat at the table.[12]

J. C. Johnson and W. A. Rentie paved the way for involvement in territorial politics through organizing groups like the Afro-American League and the Suffrage League, which worked within the Republican Party in the late 1890s and early 1900s to bring potential voters together and keep them informed of the latest political developments. Through these political organizations, African Creeks put aside their cultural differences with immigrant African Americans, who had been pouring into the Muskogee and Arkansas River valley area, and joined their common political interests. After 1900, the African American immigration had accelerated considerably, drawn by reports that the so-called black belt of the Creek country was a sort of Promised Land, where African Americans had opportunities not available in other parts of the country. African Creek leader Paro Bruner said as much in 1904 when he was quoted in the Muskogee *Cimeter*, describing the Creek country as "an island surrounded by land" where African Creeks participated on an equal footing in politics and public affairs, unlike in neighboring states.[13]

Bruner might well have lauded the economic opportunities as well. By 1905, African Americans in Muskogee could boast two black-owned banks; one, the Creek Citizens Bank, was founded by African Creeks A. G. W. Sango, W. A. Rentie, J. C. Johnson, J. P. Davison, and George Davison. Three African American newspapers served Muskogee, the most prominent being the *Cimeter*, owned and operated by William H. Twine, a lawyer who came to Oklahoma from Texas in the 1890s and later moved to Muskogee to open his newspaper. Twine became very involved in politics and was an uncompromising defender of African American rights. Numerous other black businesses owned and operated by African Americans included two millinery establishments; twenty-seven grocery stores; one wholesale grocery; one gentlemen's clothing and furnishing store; a jewelry store; a furniture store; two dry goods stores; one steam laundry; several dress-making establishments; two drug stores; seven good hotels; and numerous barber shops, cafes, and ice cream parlors. Among African American professionals were several real estate agents, including a cooperative venture—Afro-American Investment and Realty of Muskogee—nine doctors, five dentists, more than a dozen lawyers, teachers, stenographers, numerous other professions, and the Muskogee Businessmen's League headed by A. G. W. Sango.[14]

In addition to business and professional opportunities, Muskogee offered educational opportunities for African Americans. By 1905 three business schools operating there taught typing, stenography, and other business skills. In 1904, A. G. W. Sango was the leading force behind opening Sango Baptist College and Industrial Institute in Muskogee. The Creek Council endorsed the enterprise and even earmarked funds for the school. Booker T. Washington sent a hearty endorsement but declined an invitation to speak at the school's opening ceremonies, citing previous commitments. Sango Baptist's president, J. C. Leftwich, addressed the Oklahoma territorial legislature and received a donation for the college from governor Thompson B. Ferguson's wife, Elva.[15]

Outside Muskogee, in the Creek countryside, another development seemed at first glance to bode well for African American opportunity in the Indian Territory—the establishment of all-black towns. By statehood, there were thirty-two in Oklahoma, and all but a handful were located in the Creek country, most of them in the Arkansas-Verdigris river valley black belt. Rentiesville, Taft, Redbird, Wildcat, Grayson, Porter, Summit, Tullahassee, Lima, and Wybark were all-black towns that grew up from African Creek settlements, some that predated the Civil War, while Boley, Bookertee, and Clearview were primarily state freed people's towns established on African Creek allotments. It was no accident that so many of these "experimental" communities sprang up where they did. African Creeks had been fashioning an independent lifestyle on the racial frontier for generations. African Americans, particularly from the South, were attracted to the area because they would have some measure of control over their lives. Boley drew the most attention because of its size and the notoriety it received when Booker T. Washington visited in 1905 and heaped praise on the experiment in African American self-determination. The brief success of the all-black communities was made possible by concerted African American effort and in part from their isolation from white cultural and economic domination. But even as the all-black towns were being established, a more ominous development was taking place in the predominantly white towns established in the Creek country. Blacks were forcefully excluded from such towns as Sapulpa, Claremore, and Holdenville. As white immigration into the area increased in the years leading up to statehood, there was a concerted effort among developers to make the area into a white man's country. Along with exclusion of blacks from the white towns, the all-black communities' isolation decreased and the towns declined as white hegemony was imposed. There was also friction between the residents of the towns who were state freed people and the native African Creeks. Although the two groups had established a concord in Muskogee, and some of the all-black towns had mixed populations of state and native freed people, the alliance apparently did not extend to some parts of the countryside. And while Boley's leaders tried to reach out to their African Creek and Creek Indian neighbors through sponsoring activities and entertainments in the town, friction continued, punctuated on several occasions by gunfights on the town's streets between the Creek freed people and Boley's residents.[16]

Despite such friction and heightened racial antipathy shown by white immigrants, black immigrants continued to come to the BEAUTIFUL INDIAN TERRITORY because of the opportunities available and the very real advantages still open for African Americans there. But as the politics of statehood switched into high gear between 1904 and 1907, Democrats and Republicans both played the race card and manufactured a fear of "Negro domination" in the struggle to win political control of the new state. The dream of a Promised Land on the racial frontier faded as the future state of Oklahoma developed into yet another Jim Crow state.[17]

All seemed well, however, as a special Pullman sleeping car filled with Indian Territory black Republicans sped off triumphantly to Theodore Roosevelt's inauguration in March 1905. The party included leading African Creeks A. G. W. Sango, W. A. Rentie, J. P. Davison, George Davison, and Steven Grayson, as well as William H. Twine and other Indian Territory African American businessmen. They detrained in Fayetteville, Arkansas, and took dinner at a private dining hall in nearby Rogers before continuing across the state. Twine described the journey as "uneventful except for the looks on the faces of the 'crackers' of Arkansas [who] were very much surprised and chagrined to see a special car of 'Colored men' pass through their state on a car not known as 'Jim Crow.'" Twine's other special dispatches from the trip, which appeared in the *Cimeter*, were filled with the same boastful confidence in the future possibilities for the BEAUTIFUL INDIAN TERRITORY. Roosevelt's Republican triumph in the 1904 election buoyed that confidence because he was still seen as a friend of African Americans who would provide them with a "square deal." Twine and the African Creeks marched proudly in Roosevelt's inaugural parade that spring, optimistically aware of the black contribution to Roosevelt's election.[18]

The jaunty confidence was shaken, however, after their return from Washington. The Republicans suffered a humiliating defeat in the Muskogee municipal elections that spring, sideswiped by an unanticipated racist campaign that manufactured a fear of Negro domination. The Democrats used the same race-baiting tactics that had proved so effective for Southern politicians like Tom Watson in Georgia and James K. Vardaman in Mississippi. Democratic newspapers in Muskogee had hammered away relentlessly that Republicans were running five black candidates for city offices on the ballot, and that black men such as A. G. W. Sango, T. W. Twine, J. C. Johnson, and W. A. Rentie held leadership positions in the party. Democratic papers also drove home the assumption that Republicans favored mixed schools and race mixing because black Republicans opposed segregation laws as a general principle. While Republicans strenuously denied they favored mixed schools and presented their black candidates' credentials in terms as nonthreatening as possible, the Democrats swept the municipal contests and were ready to use the same tactics in the upcoming constitutional convention elections. Amid the political wreckage, Twine and other black Republicans blamed white Republicans for bolting the party on the race issue. Twine might point his pen, but he could not undo the damage done to the Republicans. As a result, the party split into three factions. A lily-white faction emerged, ironically calling itself the Roosevelt Club, and pledged to rid the party of "Negro influence." The Lincoln Club, or "ivory blacks," were mostly state freedmen, who insisted on full participation in party affairs, including African American candidates and patronage jobs for blacks. A third group, led by W. H. Twine, A. G. W. Sango, W. A. Rentie, and other leading African Creeks, styled themselves the Muskogee Club, or the "stand patters." The Muskogee Republicans' main goal was to defeat the Democrats. While they were uncompromising in opposing segregation and disfranchisement, they criticized the Lincoln Club for agitating for candidates and jobs and even accused them of being tools of the lily-whites in playing into the hands of the race-baiters.[19]

In April, President Roosevelt briefly visited Muskogee, Guthrie, and Oklahoma City, and rallied Republicans long enough for an appearance of harmony. His visit also ignited the statehood movement, because in his remarks he gave his offhand approval for the plan to merge the Indian and Oklahoma territories and have them admitted as a single state. In response, the single-staters began organizational meetings in July. African Americans were barred from most of the local single-state meetings, and their prospects dimmed further at the organizational meeting in Oklahoma City, when the convention refused to seat J. C. Johnson and his delegation.[20]

The political situation was further complicated by the emergence of a movement to have the Indian Territory and Oklahoma admitted as separate states. Under this plan, the Indian Territory would enter the Union as the Indian state of Sequoyah. After the rebuff at the single-state convention, African Americans gathered in a meeting of their own at Muskogee to map out a strategy for the upcoming Sequoyah Convention in August. It first appeared that African Americans might have a voice at the Sequoyah Convention. Morris Rentie, J. P. Davison, J. C. Johnson, and other Indian Territory blacks were at least seated at the convention. But as the proceedings continued into the fall, the Sequoyah Movement shed whatever Indian character it had (besides the name) and became a forum for populist and progressive reform issues and a vehicle to launch the ambitions of the white Democratic politicians William F. "Alfalfa Bill" Murray and Charles Haskell. The convention also brought Robert Owen and W. W. Hastings, both of whom claimed to be one-sixteenth Cherokee, to public attention. All were pledged to white supremacy and claimed to have the Indians' best interests in mind. The framers put together a model progressive reform document that regulated corporations, mandated safety standards in the workplace, prohibited harmful food additives, and called for initiative and referendum measures. The Sequoyah Constitution also contained some not-so-progressive features: it imposed restrictions on voting through a poll tax and literacy requirements, mandated segregated schools, and called for separate railway cars and waiting rooms.[21] After the Sequoyah Convention adjourned and submitted their finished work to the Indian Territory voters, W. A. Rentie published an open letter to the Sequoyah leaders that was also a call to both Indians and Indian freed people in the Indian Territory to unite:

> It is very obvious that the spirit of antagonism toward the Colored population of this country exists in the minds of the framers of the constitution of the state of Sequoyah, . . . In the face of the facts it cannot be expected that the Colored people of this country should lend their aid to a measure so insulting, so detrimental to their progress as a people, as this is. While we do not now urge matters which will take care of themselves eventually, we know that whatever will be beneficial to the Indian in the matter of lifting him up to [a] higher plane of civilization will be beneficial to us and any attempt on the part of the white man who comes to this country to separate us from the Indian whose status is identical with ours will be detrimental to both the black and red man. It is the one aim of the Territorial Suffrage League to promote that fellowship between the black and red man of this country which will tend to promote the welfare of both.[22]

On November 7, 1905, 86 percent of the Indian Territory voters approved the Sequoyah Constitution, but that is as far as the idea of an Indian state went. It was understood by most of the major players in the Sequoyah Movement that neither Congress nor the president would approve separate statehood for the Indian Territory, and it was no surprise when the matter never even came to a vote in Congress. One result of the whole political shadow play, and perhaps its purpose all along, was the creation of an organized white Democratic statehood machine that claimed the racial high ground and magnanimously offered to share it with the Indian. As the focus became a single state of Oklahoma, buttons began to appear reading:

Democracy = White Man and Indian
Against Negro and Carpetbagger[23]

And as it became clear that white supremacy advocates controlled the politics of statehood, African Americans looked to other ways to protect their position on the racial frontier. One place they looked was Congress, where statehood mixed with racial politics on a different level. Shortly before he died in May 1904, senator Matthew Quay of Pennsylvania offered the Quay amendment, which would prohibit any Oklahoma law or section in the new state constitution that would restrict African American suffrage. Although the amendment was delaying tactic with other political objectives, not an attempt to impose racial justice, it appeared that Senate Republicans had an opportunity to pass the amendment after Quay's death as a high-minded memorial to one of the Senate's most adroit machine politicians. The efforts were stymied, however, by the 1904 election campaign season. Still, African Americans lobbied hard for the amendment.[24]

Following the Sequoyah debacle, Twin Territory African Americans got a much needed morale boost when Booker T. Washington began an eagerly anticipated tour of the Indian Territory and Oklahoma in the third week of November. Washington was at the peak of his career at the time, and few people would argue with the caption that accompanied his portrait in the special edition of the *Cimeter:* "Booker T. Washington, the Greatest Living American Negro." More than ten thousand black, Indian and white people packed into downtown Muskogee to greet Washington and listen intently to his address, delivered from a special stage and podium built for the occasion. He gave another address that evening at the Hinton Opera House and remarked at the unusual assortment of the crowd. In the North, he usually addressed all-white audiences, and in the South, all African American. But on the racial frontier, it was "a melange," much as W. O. Tuggle had described thirty years earlier.[25]

While in the Creek country, Washington was naturally curious about the native Creeks. His Tuskegee Institute was located on their ancestral lands, and indeed the name was a Creek word that meant "warrior"; Taskigi was one of the Creek tribal towns associated with old Creek Nation and was currently represented in the Creek Council. When he was a teacher at Hampton Institute, he was in charge of the Indian students there, including several Creeks. When he sought out what he called "the genuine native Indian," however, he ran into the ambiguity of the racial frontier.[26]

When I inquired, as I frequently did, for the "natives" it almost invariably happened that I was introduced, not to an Indian, but a Negro. During my visit to the city of Muskogee I stopped at the home of one of the prominent "natives" of the Creek Nation, the Hon. C. [*sic*] W. Sango, Superintendent of the Tullahassee Mission. But he is a Negro. . . . I was introduced later to one or two other "natives" who were not Negroes, but neither were they, as far as my observation went, Indians. They were, on the contrary, white men.[27]

Washington, though puzzled by the racial frontier, had high praise for African American efforts already made in the Indian Territory and Oklahoma. And as he made the rounds with influential African Americans in the area, he was prodded to make a declaration endorsing the Quay amendment. Many African Americans felt that if only the "greatest living American Negro" would make a public statement, it would provide the momentum needed to make the amendment part of any statehood bill. There were even rumors that he intended to do just that, having witnessed in the territory enough evidence of African American advancement and enterprise to justify the political consummation of black aspirations. But as he prepared to leave the racial frontier, he disappointed many territorial blacks when he followed his own advice to steer clear of political matters and refused to comment.[28]

The Hamilton statehood bill, which enabled Oklahoma and the Indian Territory to organize itself as a single state and hold elections for its constitutional convention, and the Five Tribes Act, which legislated the tribes out of existence, were passed in the same Congressional session. Under the Five Tribes legislation, the Creek tribal government would cease operations March 6, 1906. But Pleasant Porter received Roosevelt's approval for extending tribal government functions until October 18, 1906, and made arrangements to keep the tribal schools in operation and under Interior Department supervision for an unspecified time. At the same time, developers and booster groups besieged Congress to remove the remaining restrictions on the sale of freedmen's homestead lands. Amid the clamor for statehood and the removal of restrictions, the passing of the Creek Nation elicited barely a murmur in the territorial press. For African Creeks, however, the passing was loaded with significance, especially in the racially and politically charged atmosphere of the final dash to statehood.[29]

As it became increasingly clear that Oklahoma would enter the Union as a Jim Crow state with African American voting rights abridged, the contrast between the past and present positions of African Creeks stood out in stark relief. While citizens of the Creek Nation, African Creeks had enjoyed equal rights and had wielded real political power, holding high positions in every branch of Creek government. James Coody Johnson was a leading figure in the House of Warriors in its last sessions and seemed to be in Washington on business for both the Creek and Seminole nations more often than he was at home. Chief Porter gave a laudatory speech to the council praising Johnson's efforts on behalf of the nation: "This man carries the affairs, and I might add, the destiny of two nations on his shoulders and he carries them lightly." Johnson was just one of a number of African Creek politicians who had influence. Their citizenship also gave them equal access to land, which was the foundation of their independence and of opportunity that made them among the wealthiest group of black people in the United States. With the removal of restrictions on the sale of their lands, however, the U.S. government had reckoned that they were no more in need of protection than any other African Americans. Indian Office and Interior Department officials stood aside as the Creek freedmen were divested of their surplus allotments through all manner of chicanery and fraud. Neal Trotter, a Creek freedman, even wrote a letter to President Roosevelt asking for help and received this reply from an Indian Office official: "In as much as you are a freedmen and your restrictions have been removed, if you have sold your surplus allotment and have made a bad bargain, the department can give you no relief."[30] Violet Crain, an African Seminole, wrote a plaintive appeal to the secretary of the Interior that could just as well have described the grafting activities in the Creek Nation:

> It is a burning shame in the sight of God the way these people are being treated in this land buying business. This country is made of a class of cold hearted land gobblers who have left all thoughts of fair dealing behind and are here for no other purpose than to rob and cheat these ignorant people out of their homes for a few baubles, barely enough to cover notary fees and the paper which the so-called deeds are written upon. Can nothing be done to stop this?[31]

Apparently not, as Charles Bonaparte, who had earlier said that Creek freedmen did not need the protection of the government, was now the attorney general and the United States' chief law enforcement official. But even though the Creek Nation was short of funds and sputtering ever more closely toward its own demise, Pleasant Porter gave the following instructions to M. L. Mott, the Creek Nation attorney: "Negro citizens or freedmen are still citizens of the Creek Nation, even after restrictions are removed from their lands. If called upon, you, as attorney for the Nation, should render services respecting allotments." Mott not only provided services for many defrauded freedmen but also would go on to be a major force in calling for reform, appearing before congressional investigating committees numerous times and defending Indian and freedmen's land rights well into the 1920s. Furthermore, after witnessing the results of removing restrictions on the freedmen's lands, Porter and the Creek Council also came out in support of measures to protect African Creeks and other citizens in their allotments and to keep the remaining restrictions on homesteads in place. Yet their protests were barely heard in the stampede to statehood and considered of little consequence in light of tribal dissolution.[32]

As the end of tribal government and the financial system that supported the Creek schools approached, Creeks were greatly concerned for the fate of their schools. As it turned out, having the schools under the control of the secretary of the Interior once the Curtis Act went into effect was not nearly the disaster that they had imagined. Superintendent Benedict wrote menacing reports that threatened the independence of the Creek schools but in actual practice, he did little more than bluster. Among his chief complaints were that the Creeks were too "lavish" in their educational spending and that the liberal arts curriculum prepared Creek students for college or for the professions rather than training them to be farmers and housewives.[33]

Despite the criticism and the unsettled conditions, the schools actually went through a brief renaissance between 1899 and 1905, until the system was swamped with white and black immigrants. The first Creek schools supervisor, Calvin Ballard, served out the 1899–1900 year and generally praised the schools, which contrasted with Benedict's hostile assessments. The next appointee, Alice Mary Robertson, the youngest daughter in the Robertson missionary family, served between 1900 and 1905 and could take a great deal of the credit for the improvements made during the school system's last years. Robertson had spent nearly her entire life either living in, teaching, building, or supervising Indian schools, most of the time in the Creek country. Most important, she understood the people, the politics, and the great pride that Creeks took in their school system.[34]

From the beginning, Robertson showed special concern for African Creek schools. Her detailed reports as well as her observations of African Creek life provide a candid picture of the last years of the racial frontier. Realizing that she could never take politics completely out of the operation of the schools, Robertson did the next best thing. She appointed responsible politicians who valued education to head up the boarding schools. She drafted Phillip Lewis as superintendent for the troubled Colored Orphan's school and asked A. G. W. Sango to take over at Tullahassee. After Sango left Tullahassee to open Sango Baptist College in Muskogee, she moved Lewis to the position and appointed another young forward-looking African Creek, Alexander Mike, to superintend the Colored Orphan's school. She also organized Summer normal (teacher) training programs for African Creek teachers and instituted an exam system, through which teachers would be hired according to merit rather than political influence. This greatly improved the caliber of teachers in the African Creek schools.[35]

Robertson was constantly looking for ways to improve the schools. Early in her tenure, she drafted a letter to Booker T. Washington, asking to attend an upcoming conference at Tuskegee, where she hoped to absorb some of Washington's ideas. She asked Washington to recommend some teachers trained in Tuskegee principles and freely gave her opinion on the African Creek situation:

> I suppose there is no place on the face of the globe where the Negro has so good an opportunity as here and he is letting it slip. In property rights, in political power, the Negro is placed on par with the Indian. Land, school privileges, even books are absolutely free. With all this the large majority live in hovels and eke out a hand to mouth living. What are we going to do about it? I think we need men imbued with your spirit.[36]

While Washington had a higher opinion of African Creek accomplishments after his own brief visit to the Creek country, Robertson was probably more familiar with the African Creeks who lived in the countryside. There is little doubt that the Wizard of Tuskegee would have also equated their traditional subsistence lifestyle with backwardness and seen most African Creeks as needing a stern dose of "racial uplift."

Robertson recorded in her reports the fluidity that still existed on the racial frontier. In the outlying districts were "several instances where trustees allowed Negroes to attend Indian schools if there was no Negro school within a reasonable distance" and two African Creek schools where Indians attended. At one remote school, a group of citizens sent a request through their Indian town chief for a "full-blood Indian teacher." After sending a suitable teacher, Robertson decided to check on the progress of the school and drove all day in her buggy to reach there. She was surprised to find a "Negro school instead of an Indian school," where the students spoke only Creek and were obviously satisfied with her selection.[37]

But apparently the fluidity did not apply to state freed people. According to school regulations, noncitizen children could attend the neighborhood day schools (but not boarding schools) for one dollar per month. As more noncitizen immigrants poured into the Creek country, and schools became overcrowded, a movement began in the African Creek rural communities to exclude state freed people's children. In 1904, the Creek Council passed a resolution to that effect, but it was quickly disallowed by the secretary of the Interior. Robertson's opinion regarding the state freed people's influence on African Creek life also changed during her tenure. At first she thought young African Creeks were being led astray by the state freed people's "showy attire, jewelry, and smattering of piano playing." But, by the end of her term, she believed that "their presence has not so harmful effect on our Negro population as that of the renter whites on the Indians." She said that because many Southern African Americans saw the Indian Territory as a sort of Promised Land, and this encouraged "a better class" of black immigrants, including many professional people as well as trained teachers. If statistics can indicate the presence of an educational Promised Land," then the African Creek schools were indeed such a place. The Creek Nation spent more money per capita on African Creek students in the boarding schools than on Indian students—$127.00 as opposed to $116.00—and the teacher's salaries were higher at African Creek schools. The amount spent per capita was far higher than in the neighboring states of Arkansas and Texas. African American high schools in Arkansas spent an average of only $48.00, and Texas, $70.00. Also, African Creek school terms were held for a full nine months in stark contrast to Arkansas and Texas, where African American students spent only between five and six months at school.[38]

But the flood of immigrants finally undid the Creek school system. Throughout Robertson's tenure, the number of state freed people in the Creek schools had steadily increased. But it was not until her successor, Walter Falwell, took over in 1905–1906 that a demographic Rubicon was crossed. That year the number of state freed people's children in the Creek schools outnumbered African Creeks for the first time and continued to climb in the remaining years of the tribal schools (white noncitizen students outnumbered Indians earlier, in 1903–1904). Falwell recorded a scholastic population explosion as the number of neighborhood day schools more than doubled and the noncitizen students more than tripled. And although Congress appropriated one hundred thousand dollars to help defray expenses, the per capita amounts spent schooling African Creeks plummeted as the noncitizen scholastic population skyrocketed. While the Creek schools were being inundated with noncitizen students, Chief Porter and the Creek Council were making agreements with the federal government in early 1906 to keep the tribal schools operating under federal control after tribal dissolution, until such time as the Oklahoma state and local school system was in operation. The outline of what kind of schools those would be became clearer over the next eighteen months, as the new state of Oklahoma took shape.[39]

The Republicans began the 1906 political season in a harmonious and upbeat mood. The various factions had come together and swept to victory in the Muskogee municipal elections in April. There were no black candidates on the ballot this time, but Muskogee *Cimeter* editor Twine ran stories urging African Americans to vote the Republican ticket nonetheless. He also gave detailed instructions on how to vote, what to do if challenged, and how to foil obstructionists' tactics. Politics shifted into high gear after Roosevelt finally signed and proclaimed the Oklahoma Enabling Act in June, which did indeed incorporate the Quay amendment, but it also allowed for the establishment of segregated schools. Elections for delegates to the Oklahoma Constitutional Convention were scheduled for November, and the various factions and parties began to take positions on the race issue. The Democrats came out loudly and strongly against "Negro domination," hammering home the message that had been so effective earlier. Indian Territory African Americans watched warily as the Republican party stammered, hemmed, hawed, and then failed to offer any black candidates for the convention. Blacks also reacted angrily when J. C. Johnson, A. G. W. Sango, and other prominent blacks were not offered places in the party apparatus. In reaction, Indian Territory African Americans called a territorial Suffrage League Convention in Muskogee in September and blasted the lily-white Republicans' political maneuvering. Meanwhile, white Republicans tried their best to imitate the Democratic message. The bloom was off the rose, and the well-orchestrated harmony that had won the day in the spring municipal elections vanished as the election for the constitutional convention neared.[40]

The Democrats, sporting "Democracy = White Man and Indian Against Negro and Carpetbagger" buttons, won an overwhelmingly lopsided victory in those elections; 99 of the 112 delegates to the constitutional convention would be Democrats. As Goble has written, the Democratic sweep "was only partly attributable" to the white supremacy message, yet it was clear that the new state would be governed by its tenets. Indeed, as a Democratic paper proclaimed: "the election of delegates has settled the negro question. This is a white man's country." The Democratic platform carried into the convention called for "laws providing for separate schools, separate coaches and separate waiting rooms for the negro race."[41]

As the convention began its first session, which lasted from November 1906 through the end of January 1907, one of the first orders of business was classifying race. Article XXIII, Section 11, of the Oklahoma Constitution states:

> wherever in this Constitution and laws of this state, the word or words, "colored," or "colored race," "negro," or "negro race" are used, the same shall be construed to mean or apply to all persons of African descent. The term "white persons" shall include all other persons.[42]

According to Oklahoma law, Indians would be considered "white," but only those Indians without African blood. Democrats and lily-white Republicans feared that Roosevelt would reject a document that contained provisions mandating segregation or voting restrictions. Accordingly, over the protests of die-hard segregationists, the convention produced a constitution that mandated separate schools but did not apply Jim Crow to public accommodations or restrict voting. However, the Democratic leadership promised to make the issue the first order of business at the new legislature. For his part, W. H. Twine, who had predicted that "Jim Crow would never fly in the B.I.T. [Beautiful Indian Territory]," now dared the legislators to try, saying that he had a "double barreled injunction gun" loaded and waiting for them.[43]

African Creeks and other concerned African Americans organized a spirited but ineffective opposition campaign when the constitution came up for ratification in September 1907. After the constitution was overwhelmingly ratified, J. C. Johnson, A. G. W. Sango, J. P. Davison, W. A. Rentie, H. C. Reed, Phillip Lewis, W. H. Twine, and over one hundred other delegates organized the Negro Convention of the Creek Nation, which met in Muskogee at the end of September to protest "the unholy document." They deputized J. C. Johnson, H. C. Reed, Morris Sango, and W. A. Rentie as spokesmen and raised the funds necessary to send the delegation to Washington to arrange a conference with Roosevelt and entreat him not to sign the constitution. The delegation did get a conference with the president, who advised them to take their objections to the Justice Department, but as they continued to implore him, Roosevelt cut them off, saying, "please don't ask me not to sign it." Even though he had his own objections to the document, Roosevelt signed and proclaimed the constitution, and Oklahoma became the forty-sixth state on November 16, 1907.[44]

True to their word, the segregationists in control of the Oklahoma legislature passed Senate bill 1, in December 1907, as their first order of business. The bill mandated separate railway cars and separate seating rooms at railway depots. And, true to his word, Twine unpacked his "injunction gun." He and other Oklahoma African Americans raised money, retained William Harrison Hart, a prominent African American lawyer from Howard University, and mounted an unsuccessful legal challenge to the legislation. The law also sparked violent protests at the railroad depots at Taft and Redbird, two all-black African Creek towns outside of Muskogee. At Taft, protesters set fire to the Jim Crow waiting room being built there. The ashes from the fire were not even cold, however, before the citizens of Taft, anxious to distance themselves from the "mob action," had raised fifteen thousand dollars to rebuild the depot. At Redbird, angry African Creeks released "a fusillade" of coal and stones at a trainload of Oklahoma state legislators, who were on their way to Muskogee to attend a Democratic convention. Opposition to the Jim Crow measures in Oklahoma in the form of both organized legal challenges and sporadic individual resistance continued for many years, but eventually Jim Crow became a way of life in Oklahoma, as the racial frontier evaporated under the pressure of legal sanctions.[45]

The Oklahoma legislature had to move more cautiously in disenfranchising African American voters. Republicans, after a brief resurgence in the 1908 elections, stymied Democratic efforts to push a voting restriction measure through. By the 1910 session, however, the legislature had drafted a constitutional amendment that called for a stringent literacy test and a "grandfather clause" that would qualify illiterate voters. To preserve the white-Indian political equation, Democrats engineered the Oklahoma grandfather clause so it allowed Indians of the Five Tribes to vote. It specified that no person (or their lineal descendent) entitled to vote on or before January 1, 1866, *under any form of government or who at the time resided in some foreign nation* would be denied the vote because they could not read and write. The legislators decided (and later court rulings agreed) that the Five Tribes Indians did indeed have such rights on or before January 1, 1866, and in any case, their status as Indian "nations" qualified them on the second count. However, members of the so-called wild tribes removed to the Indian Territory after 1866 did not qualify, nor did the Indian freed people, who missed the cutoff date by six months because the 1866 treaties were not signed and proclaimed until June and July 1866. The amendment was approved by 60 percent of Oklahoma voters, but there were enough reports of "bulldozing" at the polls, the destruction of African American ballots, and other electoral fraud to cast doubt on the results. Twine once again pulled out his injunction gun, but until the U.S. Supreme Court ruled the grandfather clause unconstitutional in the landmark *Guinn v. United States* decision in 1915, African Americans were effectively disenfranchised in Oklahoma.[46]

As the Creek Nation was being dissolved and the new state of Oklahoma was being created, booster groups and developers began a new campaign to remove the remaining restrictions on the sale of allotted lands. Restrictions on the sale of the forty-acre homestead allotments were still in place, and restrictions on Indian surplus lands were due to expire in summer 1907; with the new state of Oklahoma in the offing, a Senate select committee visited the Indian Territory to assess the situation. Hearings were held at Muskogee and other Indian Territory towns from the end of November 1906 through January 1907. The senators heard testimony from witnesses ranging from Chitto Hacho (Crazy Snake) to C. M. Bradley (the acknowledged "king of the grafters"). It was clear the senators had little sympathy for conservative Indians like Chitto Hacho or for freed people robbed of their lands by grafters like Bradley. Their sympathies were with those who wanted the Indian Territory settled by white farmers and its resources developed by white entrepreneurs.[47]

Many issues were brought up at the hearing, including mineral leasing, probate protection for minor allottees, Indian, white, and black education and taxes, but the committee was not deterred. The whole exercise became a forum to promote removing restrictions on the remaining homestead allotments. Boosters told the senators that the new state would need tax income from tax-exempt restricted lands to build schools, roads, and infrastructure. One popular argument maintained that removing restrictions would drive down the price of land and deny grafters and speculators the monopoly they enjoyed under the restriction system. One booster even claimed that his constitutional right to the "pursuit of happiness" was being violated because he was not allowed to buy restricted allotments. J. C. Johnson, M. L. Mott, and a delegation from the Creek Council came out strongly against removing restrictions, especially on freedmen homestead allotments. They recounted in detail the methods used by grafters to get control of freedmen's lands in 1904. Johnson said that if the freedmen's homesteads were released from restriction, the senators would be "making paupers of a once industrious people." Senator Henry M. Teller of Colorado, the chairmen of the committee, took offense at such remarks because he was convinced by the booster element that the abuses were only a temporary result of the evils of the restriction system. Once the forces of progress were unfettered and put under local control, all would be made right. When J. S. Murrow, a lifelong resident Baptist missionary in the Choctaw country, warned the senator that turning the matter over to the people who would be running the state of Oklahoma would be a disaster. Teller shot back, "I don't believe it. It is a slander on the State of Oklahoma to make such a statement!" Murrow replied, "I believe it as firmly as I believe I am standing here before you that the State of Oklahoma will rob these people of every foot of land they own if the opportunity is given it to do so."[48]

At further hearings held in Washington the next year (1908), Johnson, Mott, and Ellis Childers, the former speaker of the Creek House of Warriors, gave more testimony against removing restrictions, presented a memorial from the Creek Council that decried the fraud and outright robbery that accompanied the "sale" of surplus allotments and pleaded to retain the restrictions:

> Freedmen restrictions should stay in place. Freedmen regard the land
> quite the same as they do the other cardinal elements of water, air and
> light—something spontaneous and ever existing which has been bene-
> ficially provided by the Great Spirit for the free use and support of his

children and not a thing on which a money value may be placed. A large percentage of freedmen therefore possess no more adequate idea of the true value of an acre of land than many of our most inexperienced Full-Blood Indians. Therefore, removing restrictions will pauperize this class of citizen.

signed,
Moty Tiger, Principal Chief; G.W. Grayson, Creek Delegate; Samuel J. Haynes, House of Kings; and Johnson Tiger, House of Warriors.[49]

After Mott testified in favor of the restriction system, presenting reasons why the freedmen needed protection from the "itchy palms" of developers, representative Bird S. McGuire, the Republican from Oklahoma, said that is was simply time for the freed people to "root hog, or die." Mott replied that African Creeks were not "begging for anything"; they were asking the government only to live up to their promises and allow them to hold what they have. Otherwise, Mott warned, the state of Oklahoma will be the ones begging for federal money to take care of landless paupers.[50]

Despite the protests, the 1908 Indian Appropriations Act removed all restrictions from the property of freedmen, intermarried whites, and Indians of less than one-half Indian blood, and the lands became taxable. Much to the annoyance of developers and speculators, however, the legislation kept restrictions on homesteads of Indians of between one-half and three-quarters blood, and the entire allotments of full-blood Indians. The legislation later earned the nickname "the Crime of 1908" because it also gave the responsibility for overseeing the estates of minor allottees to Oklahoma probate courts, which were ill-equipped, both temperamentally and functionally, to handle the responsibility. The act provided guidelines for discontinuing Indian neighborhood schools and directed the Interior Department to make arrangements to sell the buildings and improvements. State and local governments were given first preference, and the money was supposed to go into the tribal equalization funds. The department was also instructed to maintain a limited number of boarding schools, principally for the use of "restricted" (designated as "full-bloods" by the Dawes Commission) Indian students.[51]

The regulations became effective July 27, 1908. In Muskogee, merchants, real-estate companies, banks, and civic boosters planned an entire week of festivities to mark the event. There were parades complete with floats and

AFRICAN CREEKS

bands. Out in the countryside, grafters established tent camps filled with food, whiskey, and other enticements for freedmen allottees who shunned the noise and crowds in town. In Muskogee, freedmen were corralled in hotels, lodge rooms, business stalls, and even stables and plied with victuals and intoxicants. Guards were stationed at the exits to ensure that the "clients" did not leave until a deed was secured. One scheme involved "inviting" freedmen allottees to a craps game, notifying the police, and then having the grafter on hand at the jail to negotiate for deeds. A similar ploy had people pick fights with selected freedmen. The grafter would then bail the fighter out and negotiate with the freedmen for his allotment. There were many instances of kidnapping similar to what happened in 1904. Allottees were taken to St. Louis, Kansas City, or Denver, wined and dined in regal fashion, and then charged the price of the deed to their homestead for their revelries. Grafters also took advantage of the new taxable status of unrestricted lands, convincing credulous freedmen to take out exorbitant mortgages to pay their tax bills and then seizing the land when mortgage payments were delinquent. There were many stories of forgery, outright robbery, and even murder, especially after one of the richest oil fields ever discovered in the United States, the Glenn Pool, was found under Creek freedmen allotments.[52]

Perhaps the most sordid aspect of the whole episode is the treatment received by African Creek orphans and minor allottees placed under guardianships by the Oklahoma Courts. The abuse and neglect experienced by these children, who had the misfortune to hold title to some of the most valuable oil lands in the country, gave new meaning to McGuire's "root hog, or die" philosophy. M. L. Mott made an extensive investigation into the handling of the children's estates, some of which were extremely valuable. Mott's inquiry eventually paved the way for reforming the system, but the immediate impact on the lives of the minor allottees was quite the opposite of allowing the country to "bloom like a rose."[53]

The pace of the land sales was actually much slower than in 1904, but because the sales involved homestead allotments, the impact was more debilitating. One investigator found that out of the thirty African Creeks visited in the Arkansas River bottomlands outside Muskogee, only two retained their allotments. The rest were tenant farmers, some of them farming their former allotments for white owners. Census figures also show a precipitous decline in black farm ownership in the lands of the former Creek Nation. In 1900, the figure stood at 75 percent. The number dropped to 44 percent in 1910, and by 1930, only 22 percent owned their farms, the reverse of the number at the turn of the century. The drop in farm ownership was accompanied by a migration to town. Alice Robertson mentions in her last report in 1905 that young African Creeks were "giving up the farm" following the 1904 restriction removal and moving into town, and the process no doubt accelerated after the 1908 sales deprived African Creeks of their homesteads.[54]

Coinciding with the 1908 restriction removal, African Creeks began to feel the effects of the separate school laws in Oklahoma. For several years after tribal dissolution and statehood, the Interior Department continued to operate the neighborhood and boarding schools, but by the 1908–1909 school year, the Indian Office began closing neighborhood schools not taken up by the state or counties. Falwell wrote in one of his final reports that the situation "works hardship on the Negroes" because of inadequate funds made available by county commissioners for black schools. In some cases, the Indian Office continued funding for former African Creek schools because local governments refused to provide for black schools at all. The mixing of Indian and white children at the schools went ahead as provided for in Oklahoma law, except when an Indian student was suspected of "having any degree of Negro blood." Then, according to Oscar Lipps, Benedict's successor, "there is an immediate and violent objection to his admission to public schools for whites." In 1906–1907 the Colored Orphan's school was the first Creek boarding school to be closed. The students were moved to Tullahassee, and the building and forty acres of prime real estate were sold to Muskogee County for forty-five hundred dollars and later converted into the Muskogee Veteran's Home. In October 1909 the Muskogee County commissioners asked Five Tribes commissioner J. G. Wright to let them buy the Pecan Creek School to be used as a county poor farm. Wright put them in contact with chief Moty Tiger, who was reluctant to let the school go. Tiger dragged his feet long enough to give the African Creeks a chance to find an alternative. Finally, the Oklahoma Colored Baptists made a bid to rent the building and property, which was accepted, and the school operated for a brief time as Davison Baptist University, named for J. P. Davison. The venerable Tullahassee Mission School was the only African Indian school of the eight among the Five Tribes to remain open. It was operated by the Interior Department until 1914, when it was taken over by Wagoner County and continued as a school until 1924. By 1910 most

African Creek children attended segregated schools run by local school boards that, if they provided funds for African American schools at all, vastly reduced funding for black schools.[55]

By 1910, as the new state of Oklahoma redrew the boundaries on the racial frontier, African Creeks had been disenfranchised, excluded by Jim Crow laws, displaced from their lands in the Beautiful Indian Territory, and crowded into segregated schools. In 1908 the *Oklahoma City Times* published an article, "The Creek Negro, a Study in Criminology," that illustrates the white attitude that eroded the African Creek position. "The Indian is naturally an inoffensive person. . . . It is only when the negro blood became mixed with that of the Indian that the barbarity of both races showed up in its true colors." The article goes on to say that the Creek Negro is "the most dangerous man on the American continent today . . . a combination of aborginal [*sic*] cruelty and ferocity [that] can be found perhaps nowhere on earth except in the new state of Oklahoma."[56]

But despite this brand of racist rhetoric that accompanied the imposition of white hegemony, there were still African Creeks who not only retained their native identity but also celebrated the results of such a "judicious crossing." Island Smith held onto his allotment in the Deep Fork District, outside Henryetta in Okfuskee County, and was able to continue in his role as a celebrated native healer. While he was disdainful of state freed people and resented the Indian collusion with the white man, he credited his healing powers to his mixed blood:

> Cross blood means extra knowledge. I can take my cane (a hollow reed that channels a native healer's energy and is used to administer herbal medicines) and blow it twice and do the same as a full-blood Creek doctor does in four times. Two bloods means two talents. Two bloods has more swifter solid good sense and I is one of them.[57]

African Creeks had entered the twentieth century holding full political, legal, and economic rights as citizens of the Creek Nation. As the first decade of the new century passed, the foundation of those rights—Creek citizenship and the right to hold and improve any part of the Creek domain —was kicked out from underneath them in the guise of reform and progress. The racial frontier's fluidity had always depended on its ambiguity, as W. O. Tuggle's rhapsodic celebration of the "judicious crossing" illustrated so well. Out in the Creek country, the luxury of not having to know whether a person was white, Indian, or black was possible as long as the dominant Creek culture, with its history of tolerance, held sway. At key points in Creek history, African Creeks had demonstrated their contributions as cultural brokers, as warriors, as slave laborers, as messengers for Christianity, and as political leaders. But with allotment and statehood, the tradition of Creek tolerance was eliminated, and any acknowledgment that Creeks had benefited from African Creek contributions stood in the way of Creek Indians being admitted to first-class citizenship in the new state of Oklahoma. As the Dawes Commission imposed property boundaries on the Creek commonwealth, racial boundaries were defined and fixed as well, first by the Dawes Commission, then by the Oklahoma State Legislature. W. O. Tuggle's "judicious mixing" became the crime of miscegenation. The decline of the African Creek position coincided with the imposition of Euro-American cultural hegemony in the Indian Territory. For nearly four hundred years, African Creeks had held a unique position that had withstood the shocks of war, relocation, and slavery to find a place of equal standing within Creek society. And while pockets of African Creek identity survived and are today making a resurgence, the forces of progress, racism, reform, and cultural consolidation that animated late nineteenth- and early twentieth-century America all but eliminated African Creeks as an identifiable and unique part of America's historical tapestry.

Abbreviations

ABFMS	American Baptist Foreign Mission Society Records
AGO	Adjutant General's Office
AIMA	Proceedings of the Annual Meetings of the American Indian Missionary Association
ARCOHS	Alice Robertson Collection, Oklahoma Historical Society
ARCUT	Alice Robertson Collection, University of Tulsa
BHMM	*Baptist Home Mission Monthly*
BTWP	Booker T. Washington Papers
CIMA	Creek Indian Memorial Association Archives (roll number)
COIA	Commissioner of Indian Affairs reports (U.S. Congress)
CRN	Creek Nation Records (roll number), Oklahoma Historical Society
DC	Dawes Commission Records
FCTR	Five Civilized Tribes Agency Records
FWP	Federal Works Project Administration Papers
GIAAH	Gilcrease Institute of American Art and History
IJ	*Indian Journal*
IPH	Indian Pioneer History Papers, Oklahoma Historical Society
KSHS	Kansas State Historical Society
LCC	Records Relating to the Loyal Creek Claims
LS	Letters Sent
LR	Letters Received
LT	Daniel F. Littlefield, Jr., Transcripts, Littlefield Research Files
MP	*Muskogee Phoenix*
NA	National Archives, Washington, D.C.
NAFW	National Archives, Fort Worth
OIA	Office of Indian Affairs
OHS	Oklahoma Historical Society
OR	United States War Department, *War of the Rebellion: A Compilation of the Official Records of the Union and Confederate Armies*
RCFCT	Records of the Commissioner to the Five Civilized Tribes
RACC	Records of the U.S. Army Continental Commands
WHC	Western History Collections, University of Oklahoma Libraries

Notes

Introduction

1. Current-Garcia, *Shem, Ham, and Japheth*, 80.

2. Krauthamer, "Kinship and Freedom"; Miles, *Ties That Bind*; Mulroy, *Freedom on the Border*; Naylor-Ojurongbe, "Born and Raised Among These People"; in addition to *Black, White, and Indian*, see Saunt, *New Order*, especially chap. 5; Sturm, *Blood Politics*; Wickett, *Contested Territory*. See J. F. Brooks, *Confounding the Color Line*, for additional essays dealing with the African Indian experience.

3. Debo, *Waters* and *Disappearance*. Although Debo's work is not specifically about African Indians, she does mention the significant role that African Indians played in tribal histories, particularly among the Creeks. Porter, *Black Seminoles* and *Negro on the American Frontier*. Porter also published dozens of articles, beginning in the 1930s, many of which are cited in the bibliography. D. F. Littlefield, *Africans and Creeks*, *Africans and Seminoles*, *The Cherokee Freedmen*, and *The Chickasaw Freedmen*; Perdue, *Slavery and the Evolution*. See Perdue's *"Mixed Blood" Indians* for insight into how Euro-American racial classifications had little meaning in Indian communities, which runs counter to the reading of the situation Saunt presents in *New Order*.

Chapter 1

1. Hall-Pennant Document (1775), GIAAH; Forbes, *Africans and Native Americans*, 14–18; Forbes scrutinizes the evidence for an Africa-to-America transit predating Columbus, finds "intriguing possibilities, but no hard evidence" for a human migration, but allows that the presence of African plant species (banana varieties, yams, cotton) in pre-Columbian America may indicate a human migration. J. L. Wright, *The Only Land They Knew*, 257; Van Sertima, *They Came Before Columbus*, 45. Van Sertima's controversial thesis that African arrivals influenced the ancient advanced cultures in central Mexico is dismissed by most academics but has currency among some Afrocentrists and even some contemporary African Creeks.

2. M. T. Smith, *Coosa*, 118–19, 14–17; Scarry, *Political Structure and Change*, 248–50; Gallay, *Indian Slave Trade*, 23–25; Hudson, *Knights*, 12, 215–17; Halley, Smith, and Langford, "Archaeological Reality," 126–27.

3. Scarry, *Political Structure and Change*, 13–14; Hudson, *Knights*, 13–14; Gallay, *Indian Slave Trade*, 23–25.

4. M. T. Smith, *Coosa*, 13–17; Hudson, *Knights*, 13–15; Robertson, "Gentleman of Elvas," *De Soto Chronicles*, 1:92–93, 198–199 n. 131; de Biedma, "Relation of the Island," *De Soto Chronicles*, 1:232; Rangel, "Account of the Northern Conquest," *De Soto Chronicles*, 1:284; and Lyon, "Cañete Fragment," *De Soto Chronicles*, 1:308–309; Ethridge, *Creek Country*, 22, 60; Waselkov and Smith, "Upper Creek Archaeology," 242–43.

5. M. T. Smith, *Coosa*, 55; Perdue, *Slavery and the Evolution*, 4–18; Gallay, *Indian Slave Trade*, 29, 34–35, 345–47, 424–25 n. 9; de la Vega, "Florida of the Inca," *De Soto Chronicles*, 2:315, 326; Ethridge, *Creek Country*, 115; Perdue, *"Mixed Blood" Indians*, 7, 10–11; Sameth, "Creek Negroes," 70; Pierson, *From Africa to America*, 16–18; Klein, *Atlantic Slave Trade*, 11, 13; Hudson, *Knights*, 9–10.

6. D. F. Littlefield, *Africans and Creeks*, 8; de la Vega, "Florida of the Inca," *The De Soto Chronicles*, 2:315, 326; de Biedma, "Relation of the Island," *De Soto Chronicles* 1:230, Robertson, "Gentleman of Elvas," *De Soto Chronicles* 1:87, Rangel, "Account of the Northern Conquest," *De Soto Chronicles* 1:285.

7. Ethridge, *Creek Country*, 22–23; M. T. Smith, *Coosa*, 118–19; Gallay, *Indian Slave Trade*, 26–28; Saunt, *New Order*, 18–19; Hudson, *Knights*, 422–24.

8. Gallay, *Indian Slave Trade*, 29–30; Ethridge, *Creek Country*, 27–28; Waselkov and Smith, "Upper Creek Archaeology," 242–58.

9. Gallay, *Indian Slave Trade*, 29–30; Ethridge, *Creek Country*, 230–32.

10. Saunt, *New Order*, 50–51; Hudson, *Knights*, 422–24; Gallay, *Indian Slave Trade*, 29–33; Ethridge, *Creek Country*, 22–25; Hahn, *The Invention*, 52–53.

11. Porter, "Negroes on the Southern Frontier," 58–59, 63; Searcy, "Introduction of African Slavery," 23–24; Littlefield, *Africans and Creeks*, 17–18, 21–22; Landers, "Spanish Sanctuary," 297–301.

12. J. L. Wright, *The Only Land They Knew*, 272; Daniel Pepper to Governor Lyttleton, Mar. 30, 1757, and June 28, 1757, in McDowell, *Documents Relating to Indian Affairs*, 357, 388; Gallay, *Indian Slave Trade*, 424–25 n. 9; Chaudhuri and Chaudhuri, *A Sacred Path*, 60–62; Willis, "Anthropology and Negroes," 47. Towns in the Creek Confederacy were divided into "white," or "peace," towns and "red," or "war," towns, reflecting the Creek bipolar worldview. The chiefs of the white towns played important roles in diplomacy and trade, and the white towns traditionally offered sanctuary to those accused of crimes until justice could be meted out.

13. Saunt, *New Order*, 30–31; J. L. Wright, *Creeks and Seminoles*, 28–29, 83–85; Braund, "Indians, Blacks and Slavery," 624; Martin, *Sacred Revolt*, 204–205 n. 8; Krauthamer, "Kinship and Freedom."

14. Saunt, *New Order*, 26–37.

15. Martin, *Sacred Revolt*, 73–74, 203–204 n.3; Porter, *Negro on the American*

Frontier, 47; J. L. Wright, *The Only Land They Knew*, 269, and *Creeks and Seminoles*, 35, 97; Searcy, "Introduction of African Slavery," 25.

16. D. C. Littlefield, *Rice and Slaves*, 108–114; Ohadike, *Anioma*, 98–101, 92, 72; Pierson, *From Africa to America*, 12–16; Dundes, "African Tales"; Vest, "From Bobtail to Brer Rabbit"; J. L. Wright, *Creeks and Seminoles*, 94–96; Herzog, "African Influences"; Krauthamer, "Kinship and Freedom," 151–55. Krauthamer's article offers a clear critique of how kinship and the affinities between African and Creek cultural attitudes influenced the reception that runaway slaves, particularly black women, received in the Creek country. My purpose here is merely to point out that the *affinities* between Creek and African cultures may have made the acceptance of African peoples more likely among the Creeks. It is not my intention to get into the debate about the African *origins* of folktale archetypes like the trickster rabbit, which seems to have been settled in favor of Native American origins with the publication of Vest's article. I am following Alan Gallay's critique of the southeastern Indians' worldview found in *Indian Slave Trade*, 28–30.

17. Littlefield, *Africans and Creeks*, 18–19; J. L. Wright, *Creeks and Seminoles*, 83.

18. Braund, "Indians, Blacks and Slavery," 609–11; Saunt, " 'The English Has Now a Mind, 163–64; Piker, *Okfuskee*, 123–24; Braund, *Deerskins and Duffels*, 153.

19. Krauthamer, "Kinship and Freedom," 157–59; Wood, *Black Majority*, 115–16, 260–61; Saunt, *New Order*, 121–23.

20. Martin, *Sacred Revolt*, 71–72; T. S. Woodward, *Woodward's Reminiscences*, 105–106; Braund, "Indians, Blacks and Slavery," 607.

21. W. H. Brooks, *Silver Bluff Church*; George, *An Account*. After the Revolution, David George left with the British to Nova Scotia, later journeyed to England, and finally led a mission to Sierra Leone before returning to England, where he published his *Account* in 1793.

22. D. F. Littlefield, *Africans and Creeks*, 10, 16–19, 26–27.

23. Braund, *Deerskins and Duffels*, 181.

24. J. L. Wright, *Creeks and Seminoles*, 84–85; Martin, *Sacred Revolt*, 76–78; Braund, *Deerskins and Duffels*, 169–73; Littlefield, *Africans and Creeks*, 28–29; Saunt, *New Order*, 50–63, 67–89. One of the principal themes of Saunt's important work is how this new class of propertied "mixed bloods" took control of tribal politics after the American Revolution, much to the detriment of most Creeks, including those with black skin. Theda Perdue disputes Saunt's read of the situation in her "*Mixed Bloods*," in which she shows that the term "mixed blood" had little meaning in Creek society.

25. J. L. Wright, *Creeks and Seminoles*, 94–99; Woodward, *Woodward's Reminiscences*, 108; Hawkins, *Letters*, 43, 48–49; Braund, "Indians, Blacks and Slavery," 624–25.

26. J. L. Wright, *Creeks and Seminoles*, 98–99; Littlefield, *Africans and Creeks*, 87–88.

27. J. L. Wright, *Creeks and Seminoles*, 93–98; Martin, *Sacred Revolt*, 87–88, 93–96.

28. Peterson and Karsten, *Partners*, 9–10.

29. Ibid., 22–23, 30, 42–45, 53 (Alexander Colonels quote); Pope, *A Tour*, 54.

30. Peterson and Karsten, *Partners*, 52–53, 55; Martin, *Sacred Revolt*, 76.

31. Peterson and Karsten, *Partners*, 52–53, 55, 59.

32. W. H. Brooks, *The Silver Bluff Church*, 17–23; Martin, *Sacred Revolt*, 73.

33. Peterson and Karsten, *Partners*, 9–10.

34. Martin, *Sacred Revolt*, 156–57; Stiggins, *Creek Indian History*, 104, 108, 112, 116–17, 119–20, 124; D. F. Littlefield, *Africans and Creeks*, 45; J. L. Wright, *Creeks and Seminoles*, 164–66; Martin, *Sacred Revolt*, 157; T. S. Woodward, 36. When Israel R. Vore, an adopted Creek, who also served as a clerk for the Creek agent, was taking the 1860 Slave Census in the Creek country he noted on the schedule that one of Susie Herrod's slaves, a man claiming to be 105, aided some of the whites in making their escape from Ft Mims in 1813.

35. J. L. Wright, *Creeks and Seminoles*, 190–91, 197–98; Porter, *Black Seminoles*, 14, 17–24.

36. J. L. Wright, *Creeks and Seminoles*, 223–24; *The Latter Day Luminary* 1, no. 2 (May 1818): 91–92; *American Baptist and Missionary Intelligencer* 1, no. 7 (July 1818): 374.

37. Martin, *Sacred Revolt*, 166.

38. Braund, *Deerskins and Duffels*, 6; Littlefield, *Africans and Creeks*, 85, 90–91.

39. Waring, *Laws of the Creek Nation*, 20. If Law 20 had been strictly enforced, a generation of future leaders would likely have been destitute of the means to put themselves forward in Creek affairs or to mask their African heritage.

40. Champagne, *Social Order*, 120–21; Waring, *Laws of the Creek Nation*, 17–18, 21–25; Berlin, *Slaves Without Masters*, 138–41.

41. Littlefield, *Africans and Creeks*, 40, 46, 87–88, 101; Sameth, "Creek Negroes," 16–17; "Licenses and Emancipation Papers," John Crowell journal; "Creek Claims for Property," frs. 259–78, 337–87, and 538–44, roll 61, M574, special file 207, RG 75, OIA, NA (transcribed by Lance Hall, Creek Indian Researcher, http:///freepages .genealogy.rootsweb.com/texlance/main.htm).

42. J. L. Wright, *Creeks and Seminoles*, 223–25; Capers, "Report Before the Bishops," 21–29; The Christian Index, *History of the Baptist*, 93–98; Capers, "Second Annual Report," 14–15; William Capers to John C. Calhoun, May 17, 1824, and John Crowell to John C. Calhoun, Mar. 18, 1824, frs. 35–43, 55–70, roll 219, M234, LR, OIA, NA; Lee Compere to Lucius Bolles, Sept. 21, 1826, 2–5; Compere journal, Jan. 13, 1828; and Compere to Bolles, May 19, 1828, roll FM98, ABFMS.

43. Compere to Bolles, Sept. 21, 1826, 2–5; Compere journal, Jan. 13, 1828; Compere to Bolles, May 19, 1828, roll FM98, ABFMS. Thomas L. McKenney to Capers, May 24, 1824, and McKenney to Capers, July 9, 1824, frs. 44–45, 50, roll 219, M234, LR OIA, RG75, NA.

44. Green, *The Politics of Indian Removal*, 64–66.

45. Debo, *Disappearance*, 88–90; Green, *The Politics of Indian Removal*, 67; J. L. Wright, *Creeks and Seminoles*, 238–40; W. L. Jones, "A Lettered Portrait," 89.

46. Littlefield, *Africans and Creeks*, 110–12.

47. Debo, *Disappearance*, 99; W. L. Jones, "A Lettered Portrait," 73–98; J. L. Wright, *Creeks and Seminoles*, 246–48, 270–73; Index of Creek Land Transactions, frs. 4, 12, 16, CIMA 1.

48. Littlefield, *Africans and Creeks*, 112.

49. Creek Agent (James Logan) Report, 1845, fr. 842, roll 923, M234, LR OIA, RG75, NA; Sameth, "Creek Negroes," 16.

50. Creek Agent (James Logan) Report, 1845, frs. 839–42, roll 923, M234, LR OIA, RG75, NA; Charles Kellum to Lucius Bolles, June 13, 1839, June 28, 1839, roll FM99, ABFMS; Baker and Baker, *WPA Oklahoma*, 109: Louis Rentie interview, IPH 70:475–76; C. T. Foreman, "North Fork Town," 83.

51. Debo, *Disappearance*, 110–11.

52. Ibid., 124.

53. McCoy, *Periodical Account*, 39–40; *Missionary Herald* 26 (Sept. 1830): 287; Debo, *Disappearance*, 116.

54. Lewis to Bolles, Oct. 29, 1832, July 9, 1833, May 12, 1834, and July 14, 1834, roll FM99, ABFMS. Isaac McCoy told Lucius Bolles, the corresponding secretary of the Baptist Board of Foreign Missions, that the schoolhouse and cabin Lewis had contracted to be built, rather than "economical," was exorbitantly expensive because, though the cabin was humble in appearance, Lewis had been charged an outrageous sum by the contractors. McCoy, *Periodical Account*, 39–40.

55. Lewis to Bolles, July 9, 1833, May 12, 1834, and July 14, 1834; Kellum to Bolles, Apr. 17, 1837, roll FM99, ABFMS; James Buchanan, "Fountain Church," IPH 89:299–303. J. Leitch Wright also comments on the possible parallels between Creek traditional religious practices and the fervor displayed at frontier camp meetings; see *Creeks and Seminoles*, 225–26.

56. Kellum to Bolles, Jan. 5, 1837, Dec. 31, 1837, Apr. 4, 1837, Jan. 22, 1839, June 6, 1839, Aug. 7, 1839, Aug. 13, 1839 (Chief McIntosh quote), Sept. 15, 1839, Nov. 30, 1839 (Blacksmith Jack quotation), Jan. 26, 1840, Aug. 1, 1842, roll FM99, ABFMS; Henry Buckner, a Baptist missionary and preacher who was later very active in the Creek country for the Southern Baptists, noted that many of the African Creek preachers had Indian ancestry. Rough, "Henry Frieland Buckner," 459–60.

57. Kellum to Bolles, Aug. 1, 1842, roll FM99, ABFMS; Rough, "Henry Frieland Buckner," 458–59; Creek Agent (James Logan) Report, 1845, fr. 842, Roll 923, M234, LR OIA, RG75, NA; Sameth, "Creek Negroes," 16, 25; Current-Garcia, *Shem, Ham, and Japheth*, 156; Mary Ann Lilley, "Autobiography of Mary Ann Lilley," 17–18, WHC.

58. AIMA (1844), 29–31, and (1845), 32–34.

59. AIMA (1844), 19–20; Billy Hawkins, claim 228, LCC, OIA, RG75, NA.

60. Creek Agent (James Logan) Report, Sept. 26, 1845, frs. 831–36, roll 923, M234, LR, OIA, RG75, NA; AIMA (1848), 10–17; AIMA (1849), 11, 17–21; Ethan Allan Hitchcock, Diary 26, Feb. 1, 1842, GIAAH.

61. Mary Ann Lilley autobiography 17–18, WHC.

62. Baker and Baker, *WPA Oklahoma*, 83.

63. Littlefield, *Africans and Creeks*, 138–39; Debo, *Disappearance*, 115.

64. Littlefield, *Africans and Creeks*, 138–39; Baker and Baker, *WPA Oklahoma*, 31, 109, 172, 224, 226; John Harrison interview, 4:403–406; Jim Tomm interview, IPH 112:277.

65. Ned Thompson interview, IPH 112:179–80; Baker and Baker, *WPA Oklahoma*, 226.

66. Alfred Barnett interview, IPH 12:128; Baker and Baker, *WPA Oklahoma*, 172–73, 109, 224–26; G. Foreman, *The Five Civilized Tribes*, 174; Sameth, "Creek Negroes," 23.

67. G. Foreman, *The Five Civilized Tribes*, 174; Baker and Baker, *WPA Oklahoma*, 108–109

68. Littlefield, *Africans and Creeks*, 139; Baker and Baker, *WPA Oklahoma*, 172–73, 226–27.

69. Doran, "Negro Slaves," 341–42, and "Antebellum Cattle," 48–58; Jim Tomm interview, IPH 112:278–80; Graebner, "Pioneer Indian Agriculture," 233–34; Littlefield, *Africans and Creeks*, 138; Baker and Baker, *WPA Oklahoma*, 30, 109–10, 172–73, 226–27; John Harrison interview, IPH 4:404–406; George McIntosh interview, IPH 7:73–74; G. Foreman, *The Five Civilized Tribes*, 148–49, 170–71, 188; Jacob Perryman, claim 91; Troy Steadham, claim 98; Toby Drew, claim 102, LCC, OIA, RG75, NA.

70. Littlefield, *Africans and Creeks*, 151; George McIntosh interview, IPH 7:73, David Barnwell, claim 519; Thomas Bruner, claim 143; Joseph Cooney, claim 55, LCC, OIA, RG75, NA.

71. Sameth, "Creek Negroes," 20–23; Siegal McIntosh interview, IPH 35:236–37.

72. C. T. Foreman, "North Fork Town," 81–83, 95. Sameth, "Creek Negroes," 38; Hitchcock, *A Traveler*, 95 n. 56; Littlefield, *Africans and Creeks*, 139–40; Baker and Baker, *WPA Oklahoma*, 111–12; Alex Blackston interview, IPH 90:371–72.

73. Littlefield, *Africans and Creeks*, 154; Creek Nation, *Laws of the Creek Nation*, Laws 110–111, Foreman Collection, OHS; COIA (1857): 200, 202; "Non-Citizens," roll 52, M653, U.S. Census Bureau, RG29, NA.

74. Council Minutes of the Creek Nation West, 1831–1835, frs. 228–30, 232–35, CIMA 2; "Non-Citizens," roll 52, M653, U.S. Census Bureau, RG29, NA; Monday Durant, claim 177, LCC, OIA, RG75, NA; Gaskin, *Black Baptists*, 94–95.

75. Elizabeth Johnson jacket 74, Creek Enrollment Jackets, and *J. P. Davison v. Edmund Gibson*, case 20, Creek Allotment Contest Cases, FCTR, OIA, RG75, NAFW; "Non-Citizens," , M653, U.S. Census Bureau, RG29, NA; Sarah Davis, claim 113, LCC, OIA, RG75, NA. Joseph P. Davison (also known as Buzz Hawkins) was the son of D. N. McIntosh and Sarah Davis's daughter Julia. Interestingly, Davison's birth coincided with the time that Sarah Davis was able to buy her freedom as well as that of her two daughters.

76. Monday Durant, claim 177; William Nero, claim 1229; Scipio Barnett, claim 966, LCC, OIA, RG75, NA; Gaskin, *Black Baptists*, 94–95; George McIntosh interview, IPH 7:74; Debo, *Disappearance*, 115–16; G. Foreman, *The Five Civilized Tribes*, 195.

77. Ned Thompson interview, IPH 112:178–79; Cow Tom, claim 160, LCC, OIA, RG75, NA; R.L. Littlejohn, "Notes on Cow Tom," OHS.

78. "Non-Citizens," , M653, U.S. Census Bureau, RG29, NA; Berlin, *Slaves Without Masters*, 217–49.

79. Baker and Baker, *WPA Oklahoma*, 108, 218–19. It should be noted, however, that most Euro-American slave traders and owners considered slaves raised among the Creeks and Seminoles unreliable and scarcely worth buying. Consequently, before Creek slaves were offered for sale, the slave traders frequently took them to neighboring states or manufactured titles showing that the slave was from the states rather than the Indian nations.

80. Littlefield, *Africans and Creeks*, 208–12, 224–26, 228; Daniel F. Littlefield, Jr., gives the sordid tale of the slave-hunting activities a thorough treatment in chapters 7–9 in his *Africans and Creeks*; Baker and Baker, *WPA Oklahoma*, 108, 218–19; Richard Atkins interview, IPH 12:128; Ned Thompson interview, IPH 112:180. Daniel F. and Mary Ann Littlefield explore one of the more notorious cases of the era in "The Beams Family." Ironically, Douglas Cooper, the Choctaw agent, came forward to defend vigorously the Beams' claim to freedom. Cooper would later command the Confederate Indian troops in the Civil War and would detail the troops to round up free blacks and runaway slaves.

81. Littlefield, *Africans and Seminoles*, 179–99. D. F. Littlefield, treats the African Seminole saga and the flight to Mexico in his *Africans and Seminoles*. Also see Mulroy, *Freedom on the Border*, and Porter's seminal study, recently revised and edited with painstaking devotion by Alcione M. Amos and Thomas P. Senter, *Black Seminoles*.

82. Abel, *American Indian as Slaveholder*, 21–23, 30–31; Littlefield, *Africans and Creeks*, 228, 233–35, 144–45; William S. Robertson to Mrs. Samuel Robertson, Nov. 28, 1855, folder 1 box 19, series II; William S. and Anna Eliza W. Robertson to Mrs. Samuel Robertson, Oct. 24, 1856, folder 1, box 19, series II, ARCUT; Creek Laws, Foreman Collection, OHS, 55, 73–74, 110, 111; Tax List of Free Negroes and Their Property for 1859, file 4, box 2, Moore Collection; Monday Durant affidavit, doc. 24956, Citizenship, CRN 3.

Chapter 2

1. Taylor, *In Search of*, 95–96; Cornish, *The Sable Arm*.

2. "Non-Citizens," roll 52, M653, U.S. Census Bureau, RG29, NA; Berlin, *Slaves Without Masters*, 136–39.

3. *Van Buren Press*, Mar. 8, 1861, 2:1; Mar. 27, 1861, 2:2; Apr. 3, 1861, 2:1–3; D. F. Littlefield, *Africans and Creeks*, 234–36; Abel, *American Indian as Slaveholder*, 58–62, 70–72, 80–84, 84 n. 123.

4. Creek Laws, 124–33, Foreman Collection, OHS; Bass, *Story of Tullahassee*, 90;

William Robertson to Nancy Thompson, Mar. 1, 1861, folder 5, box 19, series II, ARCUT; Debo, *Disappearance,* 142–46.

5. Debo, *Disappearance,* 146–47; Abel, *The American Indian as Slaveholder,* 82–83; Clark, "Opothleyohola and the Creeks."

6. D. F. Littlefield, *Africans and Creeks,* 235–36; White and White, *Now the Wolf,* 9–10; Debo, *Disappearance,* 142–47.

7. Porter, "Billy Bowlegs II," 391; "Slave Schedules," roll 52, M653, U.S. Census Bureau, RG29, NA; Alfred Barnett interview, IPH 12:128; Baker and Baker, *WPA Oklahoma,* 172–73, 109, 224–26. The term "Loyal Creeks" was not used until Opothleyahola's party reached Kansas. After they repudiated the Confederate treaty during the summer of 1861, they were called "the disloyal party" by the Confederate Creeks. But, in the interest of clarity, I will use the term Loyal Creeks to describe those Creeks who opposed the Confederate treaty.

8. *Van Buren Press,* Nov. 7, 1861, 2:2.

9. Doran, "Negro Slaves," 348; Clark, "Opothleyohola and the Creeks," 49–64; Meserve, "Chief Opothle Yahola," 446–50; "Slave Schedules," roll 52, M653, U.S. Census Bureau, RG29, NA. Although I have found no accounts of what slavery was like on Opothleyahola's plantation, the 1860 slave schedules reveal the demographics of the slaves living there. Of Opothleyahola's twenty-five slaves, eight were fifty years old or older, three were in their forties, only four were at the "prime age"—in their twenties—and ten were sixteen or younger.

10. Warde, *George Washington Grayson,* 57; *Van Buren Press,* Nov. 7, 1861, 2:2.

11. Abel, *American Indian as Slaveholder,* 245–46 n. 491.

12. *New York Times,* Feb. 9, 1862, 2; Baker and Baker, *WPA Oklahoma,* 31, 173; Littlefield, *Africans and Creeks,* 236.

13. OR, series 1, 8:5; McReynolds, 292–94; Baker and Baker, *WPA Oklahoma,* 112; Charles Renty [Rentie], claim 154, Lilas Marshall, claim 17, Kizzie Sells, claim 43, Hardy Steadham, claim 50, Joe Sambo, claim 215, Billy Hawkins, claim 228, and Scipio Barnett, claim 966, LCC, OIA, RG75, NA.

14. Simon Brown, card 357, Enrollment Cards for the Five Civilized Tribes: Creek Freedmen, roll 85, M1186, OIA, RG75, NA; Bass, *Story of Tullahassee,* 131; William S. Robertson to parents, Oct. 22, 1849, file 7, box 2, and William Robertson to unidentified, ca. Sept. 1850, file 8, box 3, ARCOHS. Many thanks to William D. Welge, director of the archives at OHS, for providing material from the Robertson Collection.

15. James L. DeGroot, "Old Timer Article," n.d., file 3, box 1, series 1, ARCUT; Simon Brown, claim 58, LCC, OIA, RG75, NA.

16. Mary Ann Lilley autobiography 17–18; James Ross Ramsey autobiography, 21–22, 39, 59–60, WHC.

17. Lilas Marshall, claim 17, LCC, OIA, RG75, NA; G. Foreman, *The Five Civilized Tribes,* 195; C. T. Foreman, "North Fork Town," 81; Billy Hawkins, claim 228, LCC, OIA, RG75, NA. Southern Baptist missionary Henry Buckner proclaimed earlier that Hawkins should have been arrested and publicly whipped for preaching

the abolitionist message, to which one of the Creek town chiefs replied: "If they whip that little nigger they will have to whip me first!" Minges, *The Keetoowah Society*.

18. Gilbert Lewis, claim 86, Kizzie Sells, claim 43, LCC, OIA, RG75, NA.

19. Taylor, *In Search of*, 95–96; Cornish, *The Sable Arm*, 70–75.

20. D. N. McIntosh to John Drew, Sept. 11, 1861, folder 278, Drew Collection, GIAAH.

21. *Van Buren Press*, Nov. 11, 1861, 2:2; "Terms of Albert Pike to Hopothleyohola [Opothleyahola], Oct. 7, 1861," folder 1, box 15, Cate Papers, WHC; Stand Watie to Drew, Oct. 21, 1861, folder 290; Lt. Col. Samuel Checote by Sgt Maj. J. M. Perryman to Drew, Oct. 21, 1861, folder 289; D. H. Cooper to Motey Kanard, Oct. 21, 1861, folder 291; D. N. McIntosh to Cooper, Oct. 27, 1861, folder 296, Drew Collection, GIAAH; Ross to Motey Kennard, Oct. 8, 1861, 490; Ross to Opothleyahola, Oct. 8, 1861, 491; Ross to Opothleyahola, Oct. 11, 1861, 495; Motey Kennard and Echo Hacho to Ross, Oct. 18 and 20, 1861, and Ross to Motey Kennard and Echo Hacho, Oct. 20, 1861, in Moulton, *Papers of Chief John Ross*, 496–97. Interestingly, Pike's letter was found among items seized at Chitto Hacho's (called "Crazy Snake" by white news-papers) camp by U.S. marshals and Oklahoma militia men called out to put down the Smoked Meat Rebellion in 1909.

22. *Ft. Smith Tri-Weekly Herald*, Oct. 9, 1861, 2:1; *Van Buren Press*, Nov. 7, 1861, 2:2; D. N. McIntosh to Douglas Cooper, Oct. 27, 1861, folder 296, Drew Collection, GIAAH; Moty Kanard, Echo Harjo [Hacho] and Others to Col. D. H. Cooper, Oct. 31, 1861, and Cooper to Moty Kanard, Echo Harjo [Hacho], and Creek Chiefs, Oct. 31, 1861, Sam Checote's Book of Records, CRN 9. Opothleyahola was derisively nicknamed "Old Gouge" for his sharp trading practices. The white Arkansans who published the story were probably more relieved at the news than the Creek Indians the Texans were supposed to save, since Texans had a reputation for their brutal dealings with Indians as well as with fugitive slaves.

23. Sparks, *War Between the States*, 22.

24. OR series 1, 8:5, 26; *Van Buren Press*, Nov. 7, 1861, 2:2; Nov. 14, 1861, 3:2; M. H. Wright, "Colonel Cooper's Report," 375–76 n. 13, 387–88; Russell, "Ekvn-hv'lwuce"; Bearss, "The Civil War Comes," 13–14. E. H. Carruth, a former missionary and teacher among the Seminoles and Creeks before the war, was appointed as special commissioner to the Indians of the Indian Territory by Kansas senator Jim Lane to find out what was going on among the Indians after reports had filtered back to Kansas about the Confederate treaties. After meeting with Creek emissaries Micco Hutke, Joe Ellis, and Bob Deer, who had come to Kansas to deliver Opothleyahola and Sands's letter to the president, Carruth wrote a letter to Opothleyahola and Sands dated September 10 that promised federal troops would be sent to aid "your people who are true and loyal." The letter was found in the Loyal Creek camp following the Battle of Chustenahlah on December 26. Abel, *American Indian as Slaveholder*, 242–47, 245 n. 491.

25. OR, 8:6; Charles Anderson, claim 51; Jim Barnett, claim 296; Jacob Bernard,

claim 53; Simon Brown, claim 58; Harry Colonel, claim 44; Redmon Colonel, claim 211; Thomas Conner, claim 16; John Coulter, claim 13; Thomas Dobbins, claim 5; Monday Durant, claim 177; Jim Doyle, claim 4; Ned Doyle, claim 6; Joe Fife, claim 33; Billy Hawkins, claim 228; Gilbert Lewis, claim 86; Morris McIntosh, claim 20; Scipio Sancho, claim 204; Joe Sells, claim 27, LCC, OIA, RG75, NA; Littlefield, *Africans and Creeks*, 236; McReynolds, *The Seminoles*, 301–302. The First Louisiana Native Guard Regiment (Corps d'Afrique) was mustered into the Union army September 1862, making it the first all black Union regiment. However, it should be noted that the unit began as a Confederate militia regiment organized in September 1861 to defend New Orleans.

26. Griscom, *Fighting with Ross'*, 4–6; Lowe, *A Texas Cavalry Officer's*, 25–28; Sparks, *War Between the States*, 31–32; OR, series 1, 8:6–7; *Dallas Herald*, Dec. 12, 1861, 1:2–3; *New York Times*, Jan. 25, 1862, 2. The *New York Times* article is the account of the Loyal Creek exodus given to Senator Lane by Opothleyahola after the Loyal Creeks' arrival in Kansas. Opothleyahola's remarks were interpreted by Monday Durant. The battle report in the *Herald* listed 10 killed among the Texans and 126 enemy dead.

27. J. P. Evans to his wife, Dec. 5, 1861, folder 309, Drew Collection, GIAAH; OR, series 1, 8:27–32; Britton, *The Civil War on the Border*, 1:170–74; McReynolds, *The Seminoles*, 301–302; Abel, *American Indian in the Civil War*, 79–80; Trickett, "The Civil War in the Indian Territory, 1861," 275–76; Lowe, *A Texas Cavalry Officer's*, 39–40; Griscom, *Fighting with Ross'*, 8–9; McReynolds, *The Seminoles*, 298–300; OR, series 1, 8:10–16, 18–21.

28. Gen. David A. Hunter to Adj. Gen. Lorenzo Thomas, Jan. 15, 1862, fr. 1494, roll 834, M234, LR OIA, RG75, NA; *Leavenworth Conservative*, Jan. 18, 1862, Jan. 28, 1862, Feb. 8, 1862; *New York Times*, Jan. 25, 1862, 2.

29. Abel, *American Indian in the Civil War*, 81–83; "George Cutler Report," 283, and "W. G. Coffin Report," 289, 291, in COIA, 37th Cong., 3rd sess., 1862, H. Doc. 1.

30. "A. B. Campbell Report," 295, 298, and "George W. Collamore Report," 299–300, in COIA, 37th Cong., 3rd sess., 1862, H. Doc. 1; "A. V. Coffin Report," 307–309, in COIA, 38th Cong., 1st sess., 1863, H. Doc. 1; "W. G. Coffin Report," 485, in COIA, 39th Cong., 1st sess., 1864, H. Doc. 1.

31. W. G. Coffin, Southern Superintendent, Office of Indian Affairs, to W. P. Dole, Commissioner of Indian Affairs, Jan. 15, 1862; O. S. Coffin to W. G. Coffin, Jan. 26, 1862; J. W. Turner to Dole, Feb. 11, 1862, "Loyalty of Indians in the Southern Superintendency; Mustering of Indians into Military Service for the U.S.," fr. 1146, roll 59, M574, special file 201, OIA, RG75, NA.

32. COIA, 37th Cong., 3rd sess., 1862, H. Doc. 1, 286–87, 295–96; William Kile to William Dole, Feb. 21, 1862, fr. 1548, roll 834, M234, LR OIA, RG75, NA. The estimate in the number of African Creeks and African Seminoles is based on a count of the LCC, which listed 1861 as the date they left the Creek country combined with the numbers listed in Claims of the Loyal Seminoles, roll 11, M574, special file 87, OIA,

RG75, NA; Britton, *The Civil War On the Border*, 2:24–25; Baker and Baker, *WPA Oklahoma*, 84; *New York Times*, Jan. 12, 1862.

33. OR, series 1, 8:534.

34. Adj. Gen. Lorenzo Thomas to Col. Robert W. Furnas, Apr. 2, 1862, First Indian Home Guard Regimental Order and Letter Book, 1, AGO, RG94, NA; Gen. David A. Hunter to A.G. Lorenzo Thomas, Jan. 15, 1862, fr. 1494, roll 834, M234,LR OIA, RG75, NA; *Emporia News* (Emporia, Kansas), Feb. 8, 1862, 2.

35. Cos. A, C, E, G, H, and I, May 1862 and Aug. 1862, First Indian Home Guard Muster Rolls; First Indian Home Guard Descriptive Book, AGO, RG94, NA.

36. Cos. A, C, E, G, H, and I, May 1862 and Aug. 1862, Muster Rolls; Descriptive Book; Order Book, 1–2, AGO, RG94, NA.

37. Porter, "Billy Bowlegs in the Seminole Wars," 239–40; Russell, "Ekvn-hv'lwuce," 387; Regimental Officers, Muster Rolls and Order Book, 1–2, AGO, RG94, NA.

38. Farb, "The Military Career," 19–20; Albert Chapman Ellithorpe, biographical material, 1897–1907, folder 4, box 1, Ellithorpe Family Papers, KSHS. Abel, *American Indian in the Civil War*, 126 n. 135.

39. Hughes, "Nations Asunder"; OR, series 1, 13:452.

40. Tenney, *War Diary*, 16, 19; Britton, *Memoirs*, 141–42, *The Civil War on the Border*, 2:24–25; General Order 6, July 13, 1862, and General Order 7, July 14, 1862, Headquarters, Indian Expedition, Dept. of Missouri, book 971, RACC, J. L., NA; Lt. W. R. Shuarte to Col. Frederick Saloman, Plat of the Horse Creek Camp, and Various Lists Relating to Safeguards, Details and Other Lists, Dept. of Missouri, book 973, RACC, RG393, NA.

41. Farb, "The Military Career," 24–26; Ellithorpe diary, July 3, 1862, in the private collection of Dr. Tom Sweeney, on display at General Sweeny's: A Museum of Civil War History. COIA, 37th Cong., 3rd sess., 1862, H. Doc. 1, 306–308. After Holladay was wounded, Ellithorpe was detailed to escort him back to Kansas for medical care, a whirlwind round-trip journey that took Ellithorpe less than a week.

42. Ellithorpe Diary, July 4, 12, and 14, 1862; *Ft. Smith Bulletin*, July 17, 1862, 2:1, and October 30, 1862, 2:3; OR, series 1, 13:511–12; Tenney, *War Diary*, 20; Grause, *Four Years*, 84–85; Ellithorpe to Furnas, July 25, 1862, Ellithorpe Papers, KSHS; OR, series 1, 13:181–83, 511–12; Furnas to Phillips, July 30, 1862, fr. 11320, roll 11, Furnas Papers.

43. OR series 1, 13:511–12; Furnas to Stanton, Sept. 7, 1862, frs. 11324–27, roll 11, Furnas Papers. Furnas returned to Nebraska and raised the Second Nebraska Regiment, which was used during Sibley's campaign against the Dakota Sioux Indians in 1863–1864.

44. Ellithorpe Diary, July 12, 14, 1862; OR 13:181–83 (Phillips report on Bayou Menard); Maj. John Ritchie to Gen. James G. Blunt, Aug. 13, 1862, Dept. of Missouri 146:265–66, 1–5, RACC, RG393, NA; COIA, 37th Cong., 3rd sess., 1862, H. Doc. 1, 160–61.

45. Cutler to Coffin, Aug. 13, 1862, frs. 1263–65, roll 834, M234, LR OIA, RG75, NA.

46. Abel, *American Indian in the Civil War*, 195, 203; Opotheyohola [Opothleya-hola] to Coffin, Nov. 24, 1862, frs. 1437–39, Roll 834, M234, LR OIA, RG75, NA; All cos. (except D), Aug.–Oct. and Oct.–Dec. 1862, Muster Rolls, AGO, RG94, NA.

47. Order Book, 7, AGO, RG94, NA; Blunt to Smith, Nov. 21, 1862, fr. 1532, roll 834, M234, LR OIA, RG75, NA.

48. Lt. H. G. Loring to Blunt, Aug. 26, 1862, Dept. of Missouri, 146/265–66, 20–22, RACC, RG393, NA; cos. A, C, E, G, and I, Muster Rolls, AGO, RG94, NA.

49. Manning, *Biographical*, 48–49; Kitts, "Civil War Diary," 324.

50. Meserve, "The Perrymans," 177–78.

51. Richard Atkins interview, IPH 12:128–29; Simon McIntosh interview, IPH 35:241; Baker and Baker, *WPA Oklahoma*, 31, 172–74; Nancy Rose testimony, doc. 25107, Roda Cooks testimony, doc. 25094, Dina Wallace testimony, doc. 24967, Citizenship, CRN 3.

52. Baker and Baker, *WPA Oklahoma*, 31; Scott Waldo McIntosh interview, IPH 35:213; Siegal McIntosh interview, IPH 35:238; Paro Bruner statement, doc. 25414, CRN 3; Perry McIntosh, claim 45; Grace Colonel, claim 48; Willis Monday, claim 63; Jack Marshall, claim 77; George Abram, claim 87; Jacob Perryman, claim 91; Hector Perryman, claim 92; Dennis Marshall, claim 95; Manam Marshall, claim 96; Hunter Grayson, claim 97; Troy Steadham, claim 98; William McIntosh, claim 99; Nancy Marshall, claim 119; Tally Lewis, claim 135; Rachael Durant, claim 198, LCC, OIA, RG75, NA; William Bowlegs claim, Ben Bruner claim, Claims of the Loyal Semi-noles, frs. 1550, 1577, roll 11, M574, OIA, RG75, NA.

53. Scott Waldo McIntosh interview, 35:213, Siegal McIntosh interview, IPH 35:238; Parks, *Day Book*, Nov. 9, 1862; *Ft. Smith Bulletin*, Nov. 8, 1862, 2:1.

54. Parks, *Day Book*, Nov. 9, 1862; Tenney, *War Diary*, 44.

55. Cos. C and H, Oct.–Dec. 1862, Muster Rolls, and Co. D, Descriptive Book, AGO, RG94, NA.

56. Ellithorpe Diary, Nov. 17 and 18, 1862; cos. C and I, Oct.–Dec. 1862, Muster Rolls, AGO, RG94, NA; Richards, *The Forts*, 283.

57. OR, series 1, vol. 22, pt. 1, 48. Manning, *Biographical*, 48.

58. Manning, *Biographical*, 48; Ellithorpe diary, Nov. 29, 1862; OR, series 1, vol. 22, pt. 1, 48; Farlow and Barry, "Vincent B. Osborne's," 201–202.

59. OR, series 1, 22:62–63; cos. A, B, C, E, G, H, I, Oct.–Dec. 1862, Muster Rolls and Descriptive Book, AGO, RG94, NA.

60. Monaghan, *Civil War*, 269–70; Banasik, *Embattled Arkansas*, 427–31, 433, 436 (Confederate quote), 441–44; OR, series 1, 22:93–94; Hewett et al., *Supplement to the Official Records*, pt. 1, vol. 3, 46–48; cos. A, C, E, G, H, and I, Oct.–Dec. 1862, Muster Rolls and Descriptive Book, AGO, RG94, NA; *Arkansas Gazette*, Dec. 27, 1862, 1:1; *San Antonio Herald*, Jan. 10, 1863. The *San Antonio Herald* material is based on transcription generously provided by Michael E. Banasik. Wilson, *Black Phalanx*, 111, 226.

61. Britton, *Union Indian Brigade*, 163, 168–69, *Chicago Evening Journal*, Jan. 29, 1863, 2:3; cos. C and I, Oct.–Dec. 1862, Muster Rolls, AGO, RG94, NA; OR, series 1 vol. 22, pt. 1, 168, 873–74.

62. *Chicago Evening Journal*, Jan. 29, 1863.

63. Refugee Creek and Euchee Census, Sac-Fox Agency, Dec. 30, 1863, frs. 553–57, 565–88 (Esteluste Town frames 583–88), roll 835, M234, LR OIA, RG75, NA (courtesy of Lance Hall, "War Related Records," Creek Indian Researcher, http://freepages.genealogy.rootsweb.com/texlance/civilwar/1863censusindex.htm#towns). Benjamin F. Van Horn manuscript, 21–22, KSHS.

64. Long John to Lincoln, Mar. 10, 1864, S21, roll 803, M234, LR OIA, RG75, NA; OR, series 1, vol. 22, pt. 2, 162–63, 165–67, 282–83.

65. "Circular Declaring Ft. Blunt, May 16, 1863," General Orders 17, Headquarters, District of Western Arkansas, Army of the Frontier, GIAAH; Order Book, AGO, RG94, NA; Britton, *Memoirs*, 141–42; *The Civil War on the Border*, 2:24–25; *New York Times* Jan. 16, 1862; COIA, 38th Cong., 1st sess., 1863, H. Doc. 1, 307; COIA, 39th Cong., 1st sess., 1864, H. Doc. 1, 452; Hunter Grayson, claim 97, LCC, OIA, RG75, NA; Jake Simmons interview, IPH 9:355; Britton, *Union Indian Brigade*, 273; various cos., Apr. 1863–May 1865, Muster Rolls and Order Book, AGO, RG94, NA. From early 1863 until the unit was mustered out of service in May 1865, an overwhelming number of the orders issued in the First Indian involved assignments and reassignments for the African Creek soldiers; Scott Waldo McIntosh interview, IPH 35:216–18, 76:128; George McIntosh interview, IPH 7:74–76; William Marshall, claim 76; Robert Lewis, claim 83; George Abram, claim 87; John Jefferson, claim 130; Sam Prince, claim 122; Isaac Marshall, claim 137; Hackless Corbrey, claim 203, LCC, OIA, RG75, NA; Special Order 36, Aug. 8, 1863, p. 19, Order Book, AGO, RG94, NA.

66. Various cos., Apr. 1863–May 1865, Muster Rolls and Order Book, AGO, RG94, NA; Scott Waldo McIntosh interview, IPH 35:216–18, 76:128; George McIntosh interview, IPH 7:74–76; William Marshall, claim 76; Robert Lewis, claim 83; George Abram, claim 87; John Jefferson, claim 130; Sam Prince, claim 122; Isaac Marshall, claim 137; Hackless Corbrey, claim 203, LCC, OIA, RG75, NA.

67. Ellen Rentie Bruner interview, IPH 89:262; Baker and Baker, *WPA Oklahoma*, 32.

68. OR, series 1, vol. 22, pt. 1, 378–83.

69. Britton, *Union Indian Brigade*, 257–58; Cornish, *The Sable Arm*, 146–47; OR, series 1, vol. 22, pt. 1, 378–83; Benjamin F. Van Horn manuscript, 23–24, KSHS.

70. OR, book 1, vol. 22, pt. 1, 447 62; Benjamin F. Van Horn manuscript, 24–25, KSHS; all cos., June–Aug. 1863, Muster Rolls, AGO, RG94, NA; Britton, *The Union Indian Brigade*, 273–82.

71. COIA, 39th Cong., 1st sess., 1863, H. Doc. 1, 338–39, 341.

72. OR, series 1, vol. 22, pt. 1, 689, 701; Co. C, Aug.–Oct. 1863, Muster Rolls; Co. D, Descriptive Book, AGO, RG94, NA; Kansas Adjutant General, *Regimental Papers*, Company I; Cornish, *The Sable Arm*, 176–77; Wilson, *Black Phalanx*, 317–19, 236–38; OR, series 1, 41:771–72.

73. Co. H, Aug.–Oct., 1863, Muster Rolls and Descriptive Book, AGO, RG94, NA; Mary Ann Lilley autobiography 17–18, WHC; James Ross Ramsey autobiography, 21–22, 39, 59–60, WHC; Co. F, Descriptive Book, AGO, RG94, NA.

74. Co. H, Aug.–Oct. 1863, Muster Roll, AGO, RG94, NA; Kansas Adjutant General, *Regimental Papers*, Company G; Wilson, *Black Phalanx*, 241–45. "Circular, in the Field, Fort Blunt, July 13, 1863," Letters and Orders Received and Sent, RACC, RG393, NA.

75. Debo, *Disappearance*, 160–61; Creek Treaty Negotiations—Negroes, folder 11, box 38, roll 74, Debo Papers; William Dole to William Coffin, Mar. 22, 1863, frame 134, roll 835, M234, LR OIA, RG75, NA; *Annual Report of the Secretary of the Interior, 1866*, hereafter cited as *Interior Report*, 1866.

76. "Unratified Treaty of September 3, 1863, with the Creek Indians," *Documents Relating to the Negotiations*, roll 8, frs. 990–97, T494, OIA, RG75, NA; Abel, *The American Indian in the Civil War*, 234–35.

77. "Unratified Treaty of September 3, 1863, with the Creek Indians," *Documents Relating to the Negotiations*, roll 8, frs. 990–97, T494, OIA, RG75, NA; Abel, *The American Indian in the Civil War*, 234–35.

78. Monday Durant to Dole, Feb. 23, 1864, fr. 4, roll 231, M234, LR OIA, RG75, NA.

79. Debo, *Disappearance*, 160–61; Littlefield, *Africans and Creeks*, 239; "Senate Amendments to the Creek Treaty of 1863," *Documents Relating to the Negotiations*, frs. 985–87, roll 8, T494, OIA, RG75, NA. The amendment the Creeks objected to would have given the federal government the right to confiscate Confederate Creek property, an ironic twist given that the Confederate Creeks would later charge that the Loyal Creeks "gave away the store" in the treaty negotiations.

80. John Harrison interview, IPH 4:409–10; Richard Franklin interview, IPH 91:449, 451–52; Jack Marshall, claim 70; Fanny Steadham, claim 82, LCC, OIA, RG75, NA; Jim Tomm interview, IPH 112:282–85; George McIntosh interview, IPH 7:76; COIA, 39th Cong., 1st sess., 1864, H. Doc. 1, 488.

81. Debo, *Disappearance*, 156–57, Baker and Baker, *WPA Oklahoma*, 176; Littlefield, *Africans and Creeks*, 237; Abel, *American Indian in the Civil War*, 307–308; John Harrison interview, IPH 4:408.

82. Abel, *American Indian in the Civil War*, 322–23; OR, series 1, vol. 34, pt. 2, 272; cos. D, E, and I, Aug.–Oct. and Oct.–Dec. 1863, Muster Rolls and Descriptive Book, AGO, RG94, NA.

83. Co. H, Jan. 1864–May 1865, Muster Rolls; Special Order 88, May 3, 1864, 35, Order Book, AGO, RG94, NA.

84. Blunt to Phillips, Mar. 16, 1864, General and Special Orders, Department of Arkansas, 92:285, RACC, RG393, NA.

85. COIA, 39th Cong., 1st sess., 1864, H. Doc. 1 476; Blunt to Phillips, Mar. 11, 1864, General and Special Orders, Department of Arkansas, 92/285, RACC, RG393, NA; various companies, June–Sept. 1864, Muster Rolls, AGO, RG94, NA.

86. Abel, *American Indian and the End*, 272; *Leavenworth Daily Conservative*,

Feb. 2, 1864, 2:1; Feb. 5, 1864, 2:3; COIA, 39th Cong., 1st sess., 1864, H. Doc. 1, 476; Littlefield, *Africans and Creeks*, 240; J. B. Jones, chaplain in charge of refugees, to Lt. Col. Dole, Mar. 28, 1865, Register LR, p. 80, RACC, RG393, NA.

87. *Emporia News* (Kansas), Aug. 27, 1864, 2:5; Warde, "Now the Wolf," 72, 78; D. D. Hitchcock to Anna Elizabeth Worcester Robertson, June 2, 1864, folder 1, box 18, series II, ARCUT; cos. B, D, E, G, and H, Descriptive Book, AGO, RG94, NA; Tas-he-hia-e-ha, NN3397, and Sul-lik-koh-hih, NN3157, Court Martial Case Files, Records of the Army Judge Advocate, RG153, NA.

88. Jones to Dole, Mar. 28, 1865, Register LR, RACC, RG393, NA; Legus Perryman to W. S. Robertson, Apr. 17, 1864, file 8, box 2, Moore Papers, OHS; Abel, *American Indian and the End*, 272 n. 516.

89. Britton, *Union Indian Brigade*, 440–46; OR, series 1, 41:768–71, 775.

90. Various companies, June 1864–Apr. 1865, Muster Rolls, AGO, RG94, NA; OR, series 1, vol. 48, pt. 1, 143–45, 543–44, 1193; pt. 2, 89, 107–108, 265; Abel, *American Indian and the End*, 97. In chapter 3, "Cattle Driving in the Indian Country," 73–97, Abel provides a thorough look at the complexities and the scope of the rustling activities. Jacob Perryman, claim 91, LCC, OIA, RG75, NA; Daniel Childress affidavit, Fr. 1077, roll 836; Oc-ta-has-as-har-jo [Oktahasas Hacho] to Commissioner Dole, Jan. 11, 1865, Frs. 41–42, roll 231; Fred Crafts affidavit, frs. 1090–91, roll 836, M234, LR OIA, RG75, NA; OR, series 1, vol. 41, pt. 1, 605–606; COIA, 1865, 436–37, 447, 450–52, 455–56.

91. Cos. A, E, and I, Dec. 1864–Apr. 1865, Muster Rolls, AGO, RG94, NA; Phillips to Dole, Feb., 27, 1865, frs. 47–48, roll 231, M234, LR, OIA, RG75, NA; OR, series 1, vol. 48, pt. 2, 27, 136.

92. OR, series 1, vol. 48, pt. 2, 27, 136; cos. A, E, G, I, Feb.–Apr. 1865, Muster Rolls, AGO, RG94, NA.

93. The African Creek soldiers' identified graves at Fort Gibson National Cemetery include Book, Co. C, grave number 702, section 1; Peter Johnson, Co. C, grave 154, section 1; John Steadham, Co. C, grave 1239, section 2; and George, Co. D, grave 538, section 1. After the Civil War, the black soldiers buried at the Ft. Gibson Cemetery were interned in a segregated section of the cemetery.

Chapter 3

1. Foner, *Reconstruction*, 246. Unfortunately, Foner repeats the error made by many scholars of Reconstruction in the Indian Territory that the Creeks were "forced" to accept African Creeks as equal citizens. As will be seen, Loyal Creek representatives fought both President Johnson and Interior Department officials (some of whom were later classified as radical Republicans) over the issue and refused to abandon the promise of full equality made to African Creeks in the summer of 1861.

2. Debo, *Disappearance*, 167; IJ (Eufaula), Aug. 4, 1882, Emancipation Day extra.

3. Abel, *American Indian and the End*, 175–77; "Creek Credentials," *Documents Relating to the Negotiations*, frs. 1344, 1368–69, roll 8, T494, OIA, RG75, NA.

4. Abel, *American Indian and the End*, 188–89.

5. Debo, *Disappearance*, 168–69; D. F. Littlefield, *Africans and Creeks*, 242.

6. D. N. McIntosh and R. S. Smith to D. N. Cooley, Sept. 19, 1865, fr. 1196, roll 8, T494, OIA, RG75, NA.

7. Debo, *Disappearance*, 169.

8. Abel, *American Indian and the End*, 216–18; John B. Garrett to parents, Sept. 9, 1865, Garrett Papers; Miner, *The Corporation and the Indian*, 1–18. Redeemers were Southern Democrats who came to power in the Southern states after the Republican Reconstruction regimes fell in the 1870s. White Southerners credited the them with "redeeming" the South from the corrupt Republican governments who had used the newly enfranchised black voters to maintain Republican power. Among other things, the redeemers claimed that the Fourteenth and Fifteenth Amendments, which were supposed to protect African American civil rights and voting rights, were forced on them (they were) and used to subvert the rights of white Southerners (the Fourteenth Amendment contained provisions that denied citizenship rights to certain former Confederates or to Southerners who refused to take a loyalty oath to the Union). Creek redeemers, then, were Creek politicians who later claimed that radical Republican government officials forced the Creeks to accept African Creeks as equal citizens in the tribe, which was only true in the sense that former *Confederate* Creeks recoiled at the idea and were "forced" to accept it. But the federal government did not insist that the Creeks adopt the freed people and grant them equal rights in the tribe—the Loyal Creeks insisted that those provisions be incorporated into the treaty in spite of objections from the Confederate Creeks *and* the federal government's not-so-radical treaty commissioners.

9. Simon McIntosh interview, IPH 35:242–43.

10. Littlefield, *Africans and Creeks*, 242.

11. Baker and Baker, *WPA Oklahoma*, 227.

12. Ibid., 114–15. Lucinda Davis's narrative (pp. 107–17 in the Bakers' edited volume) is one of the most interesting of the narratives describing Creek life and cultural traditions. Davis describes foodways, death and funerary practices, folk beliefs, dance customs, and adultery punishment and interjects Creek-inflected idiomatic English phrases throughout in addition to explaining the English meaning for Creek words and phrases. For instance, Davis says that her father's name, Stephany, was derived from the Creek word Istifani, which means "skeleton"— because he was so skinny.

13. Baker and Baker, *WPA Oklahoma*, 176–77. Mose Perryman's behavior toward Mollie and her children, refusing to offer the slightest aid in returning them to the Creek country, seems particularly callous given the fact that Mose and Mollie had a daughter together, Louisa. Louisa was ten years old in 1865 and was raised as part of Jacob and Mollie's family. Mose Perryman had other children with women that he held as slaves.

14. Dunn to Elijah Sells, Jan. 9, 1866, fr. 159, roll 231, M234, LR OIA, RG75, NA.

15. George McIntosh interview, IPH 7:172; Jim Tomm interview, IPH 112:287.

16. Jim Tomm interview, IPH 112:286, 304; Debo, *Disappearance*, 170–71.

17. Hurt, *Indian Agriculture*, 67–68.

18. Debo, *Disappearance*, 169; Scipio Barnett, claim 966, LCC, OIA, RG75, NA. Checote would mention this meeting at Barnett's farm many times in the upcoming years of political strife as proof that not only had the former Confederate Creeks agreed to accept African Creeks as equal members of the tribe, but the Loyal Creeks had also agreed to come under one unified government under the Creek Constitution.

19. Debo, *Disappearance*, 171–72.

20. Harlan to D. N. Cooley, Jan. 15, 1866, frs. 211–12; Reynolds to Cooley, Jan. 15, 1866, frs. 213–14; W. P. Smith (Secretary of the Interior) [acting on behalf of Harlan] to J. W. Garrett, Feb. 12, 1866, frs. 203–204, roll 837, M234, LR OIA, RG75, NA.

21. Debo, *Disappearance*, 177, 171.

22. McIntosh and Smith to Andrew Johnson, Mar. 31, 1866, fr. 449, roll 1, M825, LR, RG48, NA; Debo, *Disappearance*, 171; Abel, *American Indian and the End*, 338 n. 607.

23. Abel, *American Indian and the End*, 338 n. 607; McIntosh and Smith to Cooley, Mar. 5, 1866, fr. 95; McIntosh and Smith to Cooley, Sells, and Parker, Mar. 18, 1866, frs. 98–99, roll 231, M234, LR OIA, RG75, NA.

24. McIntosh and Smith to Cooley, Sells and Parker, Mar. 18, 1866, frames 108–110, Roll 231, M234, LR OIA, RG75, NA.

25. Ibid.

26. Ibid.

27. McIntosh and Smith to Johnson, Mar. 31, 1866, frame 452–53, roll 1, M825, LR, RG48, NA; McIntosh and Smith to Cooley, May 9, 1866, fr. 131, roll 231, M234, LR OIA, RG75, NA.

28. Sands, Cochotche, and Cowetta Micco, translated by Harry Island, to Harlan, Apr. 16, 1866, fr. 29, roll 23, M825, LR, RG48, NA; McIntosh and Smith to Cooley, May 9, 1866, frs. 128–31, roll 231, M234, LR OIA, RG75, NA.

29. Littlefield, *Africans and Creeks*, 247–48; *Interior Report*, 1866, 10.

30. McIntosh and Smith to Cooley, May 26, 1866, fr. 125, roll 231, M234, LR OIA, RG75, NA; McKellop, *Constitution and Laws*, 198. Claudio Saunt suggests that the Southern Creeks were convinced to withdraw their objections after being offered a cash settlement for their losses in a "side deal" with the U.S. commissioners that was not part of the official treaty. See Saunt, "The Paradox of Freedom," 82.

31. McKellop, *Constitution and Laws*, 198–200; Abel, *American Indian and the End*, 270 n. 514; Debo, *Disappearance*, 175.

32. McKellop, *Constitution and Laws*, 198–200; Debo, *Disappearance*, 174–75.

33. McKellop, *Constitution and Laws*, 200–201; Miner, *The Corporation and the Indian*, 38–56.

34. McKellop, *Constitution and Laws*, 202–203; Debo, *Disappearance*, 175–76.

35. Littlefield, *Africans and Creeks*, 243–44; Gen. M. S. Sprague to Gen. O. O. Howard, Dec. 18, 1865, frs. 617–23, roll 22, M752, Registers and LR, RG105, NA; Chaplain Francis Springer to Sprague, Nov. 28, 1865, frs. 627–30; Springer to Sprague, Dec. 4, 1865, frs. 631–33; Gen. H. L. Hunt to Cooley, Nov. 28, 1865, fr. 282, roll 836, M234, LR, OIA, RG75, NA.

36. Littlefield, *Africans and Creeks*, 245–46; Sanborn to Harlan, Jan. 8, 1866, frs. 343–46; Sanborn to Harlan, Jan. 5, 1866, fr. 351; Sanborn to Cooley, Jan. 29, 1866, fr. 639, roll 837, M234, LR OIA, RG75, NA; Baker and Baker, *WPA Oklahoma*, 112; *Interior Report*, 1866, 283–86.

37. Littlefield, *Africans and Creeks*, 246.

38. "Circular #6 Headquarters," Mar. 26, 1866, frs. 762–68; Sanborn to Cooley, Apr. 10, 1866, frs. 771–74, roll 837, M234, LR OIA, RG75, NA; J. S. Atkinson to Sells, Mar. 30, 1866, frs. 211–12, roll 231, M234, LR, OIA, RG75, NA; *Interior Report*, 1866, 283–87.

39. Sanborn to Cooley, Jan. 29, 1866, fr. 639, roll 837, M234, LR, OIA, RG75, NA; *Interior Report*, 1866, 286; Littlefield, *Africans and Creeks*, 246; "Circular #6 Headquarters," Mar. 26, 1866, frs. 762–68; Sanborn to Cooley, Apr. 10, 1866, frs. 771–74, roll 837, M234, LR OIA, RG75, NA; J. S. Atkinson to Sells, Mar. 30, 1866, frs. 211–12, roll 231, M234, LR OIA, RG75, NA; *Interior Report*, 1866, 287.

40. Beadle, *The Undeveloped West*, 374–75; George McIntosh interview, IPH 7:85; Jake Simmons interview, IPH 9:386; Fanny Rentie Chapman interview, IPH 4:7–8; Jim Tomm interview, IPH 112:287–88; John Harrison interview, IPH 4:422.

41. Dunn to Cooley, Apr. 26, 1866, fr. 200; "Expense Account-Creek Agency 1867," fr. 358, roll 231, M234, LR OIA, RG75, NA; George McIntosh interview, IPH 71:172.

42. Jim Tomm interview, IPH 112:301; COIA, 1866, 319; Q. L. Littlejohn, "Notes on Cow Tom," 7, folder 5, box 1, OHS; George McIntosh interview, IPH 7:83; Neighborhood Schools, docs. 37634, 37744, 37751, and 37753, frs. 198, 320–21, CRN 48.

43. Dunn to Byers, Dec. 12, 1866, fr. 246, roll 231, M234, LR, OIA, RG75, NA.

44. Sameth, "Creek Negroes," 37–38; Siegal McIntosh interview, IPH 35:233; Jake Simmons interview, IPH 9:389; Sameth, "Creek Negroes," 35; *MP*, Oct. 30, 1890, 4:2.

45. *Creek Nation v. Louisa Pease*, Special Master's Report, 2, case 281, box 25, Citizenship Contest Cases, FCTR, OIA, RG75, NAFW; Crouch, *The Freedmen's Bureau*, 77; Hestor Murphy application, 3, Applications for Enrollment, roll 422, M1301, OIA, RG75, NA.

46. *Interior Report*, 1866, 318–19.

47. Debo, *Disappearance*, 180–81; Champagne, *Social Order*, 204–205, 228–30.

48. Debo, *Disappearance*, 179–82; Champagne, *Social Order*, 204–205; W. F. Jones, *Experience*, 30–31; "Alice Robertson Autobiography," 5–6, box 2, file 3, ARCOHS; Sam Checote's Book of Records, 36–38, CRN 9.

49. Sameth, "Creek Negroes," 32–33; Robert Grayson testimony, doc. 25411,

Citizenship, CRN 3; Siegal McIntosh interview, IPH 35:233; Jim Tomm interview, IPH 112:294; Island Smith interview, IPH 59:331; *Senate Committee on Territories*, 45th Cong., 3rd sess., S. Rep. 744, serial 1889, 695, 684, hereafter cited as S. Rep. 744.

50. Debo, *Disappearance*, 184; Minutes of the House of Warriors, Creek Nation, 130–33, CRN 7. George W. Stidham, in testimony before the Senate committee that visited the Indian Territory in 1878, said that the freedmen legislators could not be counted on to vote as a block on any given issue.

51. Debo, *Disappearance*, 184; Minutes of the House of Warriors, Creek Nation, 130–33, CRN 7.

52. Courts, Arkansas District, docs. 254??, 255??; Blacksmiths, docs. 24695–96, 24681, CRN 27; Courts, Misc., doc. 29227, CRN 33; Debo, *Disappearance*, 182, 253.

53. Dunn to Charles E. Mix, Acting Commissioner of Indian Affairs, Oct. 14, 1868, frs. 626–27, roll 232, M234, LR, OIA, RG75, NA; Paro Bruner testimony, Creek Freedmen application 1393, Louisa Olden, *Applications for Enrollment*, roll 422, M1301, OIA, RG75, NA.

54. Dunn to Mix, June 1, 1868, frs. 495–97; J. W. Wright [writing for Nero] to O. O. Howard, Feb. 10, 1867, frs. 344–45; Byers to Bogy, Jan. 1, 1867, frs. 256–57; Byers to Bogy, Feb. 9, 1867, fr. 1099, roll 231, M234, LR OIA, RG75, NA; Williamson Dunn to O. H. Browning, Apr. 25, 1868, frame numbers illegible, roll 24, M825 (registered in vol. C, 173), LR, RG48, NA.

55. Dunn to Mix, June 1, 1868, frs. 496–97, roll 231, M234, LR OIA, RG75, NA; Sands and Cotchoche (attested by Harry Island), Barnett and Cow Tom to Perry Fuller; Browning to Howard, Apr. 28, 1868; Mix to Browning, Nov. 16, 1867, roll 53, M752, Register I 10 and LR, RG105, NA; *Congressional Globe*, 40th Cong., 2nd sess., vol. 39, pt. 5, 4122; Ely Parker to L. N. Robinson, Apr. 19, 1869, p. 487, roll 89, M21, LS, OIA, RG75, NA; Browning to N. G. Taylor, Aug. 12, 1868, frs. 576–79, roll 24, M825, LR, RG48, NA.

56. Reynolds to Parker, Nov. 22, 1869, frs. 142–43, roll 233, M234, LR OIA, RG75, NA. Sands et al. to Parker, Oct. 26, 1869, frs. 144–49; Dunn to Taylor, Jan. 1, 1869, frs. 14–15; Sands and delegates to Taylor, Jan. 15, 1869, frs. 88–89; Robinson to Parker, Mar. 6, 1869, frs. 126–27; and July 7, 1869, fr. 135; Sands et al. to J. D. Cox, Apr. 3, 1869, frs. 172–74; F. A. Fields to Parker, Aug. 24, 1869, frs. 25–30, roll 232, M234, LR OIA, RG75, NA; Champagne, *Social Order*, 230–31; Bailey, *Reconstruction*, 112–13.

57. Fields to Parker, Aug. 24, 1869, frs. 25–30; Reynolds to Parker, Nov. 22, 1869, frs. 142–43, roll 232, M234, LR OIA, RG75, NA; Debo, *Disappearance*, 190.

58. Debo, *Disappearance*, 190.

59. Field to Parker, Sept. 5, 1870, frs. 414–17, and Checote to Island, Sept. 5, 1870, fr. 418, roll 232, M234, LR OIA, RG75, NA; Cady to Field, Sept. 10, 1870, p. 95, roll 98, M21, LS, OIA, RG75, NA.

60. Walter H. Smith to Parker, Apr. 4, 1871, frs. 71–72; Lyon to Parker, May 31, 1871, frs. 87–88; Checote to Lyon, May 1, 1871, frs. 89–90, roll 233, M234, LR OIA, RG75, NA.

61. Lyon to Parker, May 31, 1871, frs. 87–88; Checote to Lyon, May 1, 1871, frs. 89–

90; Cowen to Parker, July 24, 1871, fr. 81; Walter H. Smith to Parker, Apr. 4, 1871, frs. 71–72, roll 233, M234, LR OIA, RG75, NA; Debo, *Disappearance*, 228–30. Debo mentions that Checote was generally reluctant to allow the death penalty to be carried out, invariably pardoning those scheduled for execution.

62. Delano to Francis A. Walker, Feb. 2, 1872, frs. 667–770, roll 233, M234.

63. Lyon to Parker, Apr. 26, 1871, fr. 126, roll 233, *M234*, LR, OIA, RG75, NA.

64. "Report of Investigation viz: the Charges Against Agent Lyon preferred by Loyal Creeks," William McIntosh statement, frs. 484–85, roll 233, M234, LR OIA, RG75, NA, hereafter cited as "Investigation"; Sands to Parker, Sept. 9, 1871, frs. 220–23, roll 233, M234, LR OIA, RG75, NA; Debo, *Disappearance*, 192–93.

65. "Investigation," Chi Kee statement, frs. 472–75, Futchalike statement, frs. 477–78.

66. Creek Elections, doc. 29327-a, section X, vertical files, OHS, hereafter cited as section X.

67. Debo, *Disappearance*, 198–200; "Investigation," Hoag and Campbell Report, Dec. 1, 1872, frs. 445–59. Originally, Muskogee was called Rag Town because of its hastily built structures and numerous tents, which served as homes, stores, and offices. Jim Tomm interview, IPH 112:295–96.

68. "Investigation," Hoag and Campbell Report, frs. 459–60.

69. Debo, *Disappearance*, 200.

70. Charges against Sage Barnwell, John Cook, James Cornells, Ben Cornells and Pompey Perryman, June 7, 1871, and Charges against Jerry Steadham and George Barnwell, May 7, 1871, Arkansas District, frs. 23–24, CRN 18; William Graham to F. W. Walker, Sept. 3, 1872, frs. 594–97, roll 233, M234, LR OIA, RG75, NA. Although horse stealing was the mainstay of many a desperado's occupation throughout the tribal period, it is hard to imagine that nine hundred men were required to bring them under control.

71. "Investigation," Hoag and Campbell Report, frs. 449–59; Grierson telegrams to Hoag, Sept. 3 and 6, 1872, fr. 636; Graham to Walker, Sept. 3, 1872, frs. 584–85, 594–97, roll 233, M234, LR OIA, RG75, NA; *Cherokee Advocate*, Aug. 24, 1872, 2:7; *The Vindicator* (Choctaw Nation), Sept. 14, 1872, excerpted from Litton Creek Papers, 1870–1930, in Littlefield Research Files, file CF(b), box 12.

72. Debo, *Disappearance*, 201–202; Champagne, *Social Order*, 233; section X.

73. Debo, *Disappearance*, 200.

74. Cemeteries, IPH 55:342; Speck, "The Creek Indians," 99–164; COIA, 1872, 239.

75. Champagne, *Social Order*, 232; Debo, *Disappearance*, 214; 1875 Elections, frs. 748–51, 760–61, 841–44, CRN 33; Checote to National Council, Dec. 15, 1873, pp. 46, 66; Dec. 16, 1874, p. 84; May 3, 1876, p. 404, LS, 1873–1878, FCTR,OIA, RG75, NAFW; Courts, frs. 6, 12, 16 CRN 33.

76. Champagne, *Social Order*, 232; David Anderson affidavit, Mar. 9, 1877, frs. 174–78; "Petition of the Colored Citizens of Arkansas Town," frs. 158–60; Lochar Harjo [Locha Hacho] affidavit, Mar. 9, 1877, frs. 180–92; "Petition of Colored Citi-

zens of the Creek Nation," frs. 652–57, roll 867, M234, LR OIA, RG75, NA. Nearly every African Creek male enrolled in the three Colored towns signed the petition protesting Locha Hacho's impeachment.

77. Minute Book of the Joint Committee on Education, Oct. 26, 1878, p. 51, frs. 294–95, CIMA 2; Ward Coachman to Monday Durant, Feb. 11, 1878, Creek Executive Office, 1878–1881, p. 4, CRN 21; Durant et al. to Houses, Oct. 14, 1878, Schools— Misc., docs. 38465, 38576, CRN 49.

78. S. Rep. 744, 676, 679–80, 685; Debo, *Disappearance*, 237; George McIntosh interview, IPH 7:83; Ned Thompson interview, IPH 112:184; Jim Tomm interview, IPH 112:301; Neighborhood Schools, frs. 132, 198, 320–21, 366, 712, 717, 1016, CRN 48; *Condition of the Indians in the Indian Territory*, pt. 2, 361, 49th Cong., 1st sess., S. Rep. 1278, serial 2363, hereafter cited as S. Rep. 1278; Henry Myers interview, IPH 37:418.

79. James Ross Ramsey autobiography, 67–69, WHC; Anna Eliza Robertson to Ann Augusta Robertson, Apr. 8, 1868, file 17, box 3, ARCOHS; Alfred Barnett interview, IPH 13:412; Roley Canard, Aaron Grayson, Samuel Simmons interview, IPH 18:65–66; Ned Thompson interview, IPH 112:184; *IJ* (Eufaula), Dec. 14, 1876, 2; Mar. 19, 1877, 2; Minutes of the Freedmen's Baptist Association (Eufala: *IJ*, 1878), 1–3, and Minutes of the Second Annual Session of the Freedmen's Baptist Association (Muskogee: *IJ*, 1879), 1–4, GIAAH.

80. Louis Rentie interview, 70:474; Alex Blackston interview, 90:371–72; Lemuel Jackson interview, 31:33–34; Fred Johnson interview, 31:221; John Harrison interview, 4:412–13; Island Smith interview, 59:331; Richard Franklin interview, 91:450; Scott Waldo McIntosh interview, 35:221; Ned Thompson interview, 112:188–89, IPH; Littlejohn, "Notes on Cow Tom," 6–7; S. Rep. 744, 678, 722; S. Rep. 1278, 152, 201– 202; *Journal of the General Council*, 41–43; *Proceeding of the Fifth General Council*, 79–80; Loughridge, "Report on Cotton Production," 3, 18, U.S. Census Bureau, RG29, NA. Many of the white merchants and traders in the Creek country did "carry" African Creek farmers from one season to the next, extending them credit for seed and supplies. But, because African Creeks also received regular annuity payments as members of the tribe, and the land they farmed was inalienable (particularly to noncitizen merchants), they were in no danger of losing their land to satisfy debts owed to merchants. In any case, most merchants considered Creek freed people honest almost to a fault and had few problems with outstanding freed people's debts. See Robinson, "History of the Patterson Mercantile," 57, 61, 63–64.

81. James T. Spencer interview, 12:27; Jake Simmons interview, 9:351; Charles Brant interview, 16:183; William Bruner interview, 17:152, *IHP*; Littlejohn, "Notes on Cow Tom," 7; Fite, "Development of the Cotton Industry," 346–47; Loughridge, "Report on Cotton Production," 18, 22, U.S. Census Bureau, RG29, NA; Sameth, "Creek Negroes," 37.

82. Checote to Council, Feb. 1, 1874, p. 67; Feb. 28, 1874, p. 93; Apr. 9, 1874, p. 143; Aug. 19, 1874, p. 202, LS, 1873–1878, FCTR, OIA, RG75, NAFW; Debo, *Disappearance*, 243.

83. Champagne, *Social Order*, 232, 233; Debo, *Disappearance*, 247–48; Current-Garcia, *Shem, Ham, and Japheth*, 34.

Chapter 4

1. Patterson was known as Honest John in South Carolina for his coziness with railroad corporations and his liberal use of public monies to promote the same.

2. Debo, *Disappearance*, 235–37.

3. Ibid., 235–37; Durant et al. to the House of Kings and House of Warriors, Oct. 14, 1878, Schools, CRN 48; Durant et al. to S. W. Marston, July 2, 1878, frames 253–55, Roll 869, M234, LR OIA, RG75, NA.

4. S. Rep. 744, 680–81, 684–85, 687–88, 695–98.

5. S. Rep. 744, 680.

6. Ibid.

7. Ibid.

8. Current-Garcia, *Shem, Ham, and Japheth*, 104–105; S. Rep. 744, 696–97.

9. Current-Garcia, *Shem, Ham, and Japheth*, 105; Minutes of the Second Annual Session of the Freedmen's Baptist Association (Muskogee: *IJ*, 1879), 1, GIAAH.

10. Current-Garcia, *Shem, Ham, and Japheth*, 104; Robinson, "Indian International Fair," 416; Scruggs, ed., *Women of Distinction*, 247–49.

11. Minutes of the Second Annual Session of the Freedmen's Baptist Association (Muskogee: *IJ*, 1879), 2; Leslie to Coachman, May 3, 1879, Intruders, doc. 30950, CRN 3.

12. Durant et al. to S. W. Marston, July 2, 1878, frs. 253–55, roll 869, M234, LR OIA, RG75, NA; S. S. Cutting to E. A. Hayt, July 23, 1878, frs. 248–52, roll 869, M234, LR OIA, RG75, NA; Hayt to Cutting, Sept. 2, 1878, p. 145, roll 143, M21, LS, OIA, RG75, NA; *IJ* (Eufaula), Apr. 24, 1878, 5:1, 2.

13. *IJ* (Eufaula), Apr. 24, 1878, 5:1; William M. Leeds to S. W. Marston, Aug. 16, 1878, p. 80, roll 144, M21, LS, OIA, RG75, NA; Marston to S. S. Cutting, Sept. 9, 1878, fr. 330; Cutting to E. A. Hayt, Sept. 12, 1878, fr. 331; William Fisher to Hayt, Oct. 16, 1878, fr. 364; Ward Coachman to Hayt, Oct. 17, 1878, fr. 363, roll 869, M234, LR OIA, RG75, NA.

14. Terms of Agreement—Robert A. Leslie and the Baptist Home Mission Society and Pleasant Porter, Simon Brown, Ned Robbins, Sampson Grayson, and David Cummings (Committee on Education of the Creek National Council), Oct. 13, 1878, doc. 38468; Union Agency School Report, n.d., doc. 38850, Schools—Misc., CRN 49; Robinson, "Indian International Fair," 416. The Leslies reportedly ran their hotel and boarding house, known as the Green Hotel, as a "whites only" establishment.

15. Union Agency School Report, n.d., doc. 38850, CRN 49; Checote to H. C. Reed, Mar. 3, 1881, and Checote to Leslie, Mar. 10, 1881, Records of the Principal Chiefs, CRN 21.

16. Debo, *Disappearance*, 244; Goble, *Progressive Oklahoma*, 158.

17. Leslie to Coachman, May 3, 1879, doc. 30950, Intruders, CRN 39; Samuel Soloman, Lustre Foreman, and Governor McIntosh affidavit, July 31, 1879, frs. 336–38; A. R Griggs to R. A. Leslie, May 13, 1879, frs. 294–95; A. B. Meachum to A. E. Hayt, July 31, 1879, frs. 321–23; "Memorial of Members of the Muskogee Baptist Church," July 26, 1879, fr. 328; roll 872, M234, LR, OIA, RG75, NA. This memorial from the members of the church is actually signed only by Leslie and the church clerk, Ned Robbin[s]; *IJ* (Eufaula), Apr. 3, 1879, 3:2; June 5, 1879, 3:2. Campbellites were followers of Alexander Campbell, who for a time was associated with the Baptist Church and later went on to found the Church of Christ and the Disciples of Christ, calling for a return to simplicity in worship and the original teachings of the Bible.

18. Leslie to Coachman, May 3, 1879, Intruders, doc. 30950, CRN 39; George Allen et al. to Daniel Rogers, June 6, 1879, fr. 325; Anthony Boyd to Deacon of Muskogee Baptist Church, June 16, 1879, fr. 334; Joe Johnson and Bill Smith to members of the Muskogee Baptist Church, June 18, 1879, fr. 336, roll 872, M234, LR OIA, RG75, NA; Athearn, *In Search of Canaan*; Duncan later joined a Methodist church in Parsons, Kansas, where he organized relief efforts for Exodusters stranded in Kansas and reportedly ran afoul with his Texas persecutors once again.

19. Debo, *Disappearance*, 231–32, 243. There was a story told that when the railroad was being built, Muskogee had a graveyard "before the first street was laid out" because of the violence endemic in the railroad camps. E. King, *The Great South*, 207–208.

20. *BHMM* 6, no. 9 (Sept. 1884): 213–15; Marston to Lochar Harjo [Locha Hacho], Oct. 5, 1876, doc. 32288; Andrew Brady to Coachman, Apr. 2, 1879, doc. 32291; F. B. Severs to Checote, May 23, 1880, doc. 32294, Liquor and Gambling, CRN 38; Debo, *Disappearance*, 231–32; Jim Tomm interview, IPH 112:288; John Robinson interview, IPH 8:530. In the Severs letter cited above, Severs complained sharply to Checote about "shooting and drinking in our quiet little town [Okmulgee]." He said if something was not done soon, Okmulgee would have "as bad a name as Muskogee." While there is no statistical evidence available, Angie Debo has speculated from anecdotal evidence that homicide was one of the leading causes of death for adults in the region during this period. My own extensive reading of territorial newspapers from the period seems to bear this out.

21. Debo, *Disappearance*, 253; May, *African Americans*, 70–72; Grinde and Taylor, "Red vs. Black," 212, 214, 216; Taylor, *In Search of*, 118–20; "Second Annual Report of the Board of Indian Commissioners, 1870," 89–91; Samuel Brown to Coachman, Nov. 7, 1879, doc. 32396, CRN 23; "Notes and Documents," 1122–23; *Cherokee Advocate*, Oct. 24, 1877. The *Advocate* article, "Shooting Affray—A Darkey's Magnanimity," tells of a confrontation between one of the principal Cherokee figures in the border war, William Clingan, and an African Creek named Marshall (unfortunately no first name was given). After Clingan was wounded in the gunfight, Marshall went to Clingan's wife and told where Clingan could be found. The article describes

Clingan as a valuable member of society and Marshall decidedly less so, yet applauds Marshall for his "magnanimity." Which society Clingan was a "valuable" member of is open to interpretation; he was later charged with murder and larceny in the Western Arkansas Federal District Court and was one of the Cherokees charged with horse theft by the Creeks.

22. Debo, *Disappearance*, 253–54; C. T. Foreman, "Marshalltown," 52–57; Alfred Barnett interview, IPH 13:412; H. W. Hicks interview, IPH 19:181–83; John C. Robinson interview, IPH 8:530; Marshalltown School, doc. 37975, fr. 717, Neighborhood Schools, CRN 48. A settlement near Marshalltown was known as Sodom for the nefarious activities that went on there. The area was a location for drinking and gambling since chief Roley McIntosh built a racetrack there in the early years of settling down in the western Creek country.

23. Debo, *Disappearance*, 253–55; Edward Fleetwood deposition, July 27, 1881, Muskogee District Court, doc. 26326, frs. 210–11, CRN 29.

24. Debo, *Disappearance*, 253–54; I. G. Vore to Checote, Feb. 23, 1880, Lighthorse, doc. 31732, frs. 423–25, CRN 38; Fleetwood deposition; John Kernel, Jesse Franklin, Samuel Lowe et al. to Coachman, May 23, 1879, Foreign Relations, Cherokee, doc. 30444, CRN 36.

25. Fleetwood deposition; *IJ* (Eufaula), Aug. 7, 1879, 2:2; John C. Robinson interview, IPH 8:530.

26. Berryhill to Coachman, Aug. 8, 1879, Lighthorse, doc. 31689, frs. 380–81, CRN 38; Coachman to Council, Aug. 5, 1879, Lighthorse, doc. 31687, frs. 378–79, CRN 38.

27. Vore to Checote, Feb. 23, 1880, Lighthorse, doc. 31732, frs. 423–25, CRN 38; Joe Barnett, Ben Barnett, Mose Redmouth, William Peters arrest warrant, Aug. 29, 1879, doc. 26292, fr. 170; Reed to Checote, July 26, 1881, doc. 26325, frs. 207–208; George M. Hill and Reed to Checote, Nov. 29, 1881, doc. 26325, frs. 216–17, Muskogee District Court, CRN 29; William Peters Claim, n.d., Lighthorse, doc. 31686, fr. 376, CRN 38; Election Certificate, Sept. 20, 1881, Lighthorse, doc. 31828, fr. 593, CRN 38.

28. Debo, *Disappearance*, 222, 237; S. Rep. 1278, 152; Annual Message, 1878, 100–12, Principal Chief, CRN 21; Vore, "Levering," 204. The Civil Rights Act of 1875, which guaranteed equal treatment in public accommodations, was never enforced and was later stripped of any meaning by the Supreme Court in the *Civil Rights Cases* decision of 1883. As far as the Creek Nation was concerned, no comprehensive civil rights bill was ever passed because one was not needed. Attempts were made to restrict African Creek political rights and rights to an equal share in the Creek lands and tribal funds during the 1890s, but unlike the wave of disfranchisement and segregation that swept through the South during the same period, such efforts were ineffective in the Creek Council.

29. Debo, *Disappearance*, 245–46; Current-Garcia, *Shem, Ham, and Japheth*, 34.

30. *IJ* (Eufaula), May 1, 1879, 1:3; July 7, 1879, 5:3; July 31, 1879, 3:1; Current-Garcia, *Shem, Ham, and Japheth*, 47.

31. Debo, *Disappearance*, 246–48; Robinson, "History of the Patterson Mercan-

tile," 55; Fischer to Coachman, Sept. 5, 1879, Elections, doc. 29374, frs. 933–34, CRN 33; John Yargee deposition, Dec. 1, 1879, doc. 35585, and Charley Foster deposition, Dec. 2, 1879, doc. 35585b, Principal Chief; Samuel Brown to Coachman, Nov. 7, 1879, doc. 32396, CRN 23; Coachman to John Q. Tufts, Dec. 3, 1879, Elections, doc. 29377, fr. 942, CRN 33. Thomas Adams and G. W. Grayson were other major Constitutionalist figures who had African Creek blood.

32. Scipio Sango et al. to Checote, Feb. 23, 1880, Foreign Relations, Cherokee, doc. 30449, CRN 36.

33. Sango et al. to Checote, May 24, 1880, Muskogee District Court, doc. 26302; Muskogee District Court Journal, May 29, 1880, fr. 304; Reed to Checote, May 31, 1880, Muskogee District Court, doc. 26305, CRN 29. One prosecution witness who did testify, Edmund Fleetwood, should have been a defense witness instead. Fleetwood said he saw the four Cherokees involved in the shoot-out earlier "shooting at every colored man they saw." Fleetwood also said he saw Peters talking amicably with the Cherokees earlier in the day.

34. "Notes and Documents," 1122. Debo, *Disappearance*, 255–57; Teall, *Black History in Oklahoma*, 99–107. Teall's resource book is an excellent compilation of original documents dealing with the Cobb case and other Oklahoma African American history subjects. In citing the Cobb case, I will give the standard citation for the documents I reviewed and the page numbers from Teall's book. Teall, *Black History in Oklahoma*, 105–107; Glass to J. C. Atkins (Commissioner of Indian Affairs), Apr. 24, 1885, 1885-7756, LR, 1881–1907, OIA, RG75, NA.

35. H. W. Hicks interviews, IPH 19:181–83 and 29:69.

36. Joseph P. Davidson to Checote, Apr. 10, 1882, doc. 30558, and Dan Tucker to Checote, Apr. 9, 1882, doc. 30557, Foreign Relations, Cherokee, CRN 36. Interestingly, G. W. Grayson and G. W. Stidham were on the Creek commission and not only signed the protest but were probably responsible for drafting it. Grayson and Stidham were two of the leading critics of the "Negro influence" in Creek public affairs.

37. Debo, *Disappearance*, 228–29, 255–56.

38. Tucker to Checote, Apr. 9, 1882, Foreign Relations, Cherokee," 30557, CRN 36; Checote to Bushyhead, Apr. 17, 1882, fr. 496; Apr. 19, 1882, fr. 499; and May 10, 1882, frs. 525–26; Checote to James R. Gregory (Judge Coweta District), Apr. 4, 1882, fr. 489, and May 1, 1882, fr. 521, Letter Book of Principal Chief Samuel Checote, all on CIMA 2.

39. Teall, *Black History in Oklahoma*, 106–107; Robert Jones had earlier been charged with larceny, and Glass with stealing a saddle, in the Muskogee District Court, hardly the record of a "notorious outlaw." Still, it is possible that other arrests and convictions did not show up in the scattered Creek Court records. Doc. 26363 and p. 71, Muskogee District Court, frs. 296, 300, CRN 29; Glass to Atkins, Apr. 24, 1885, LR, 1881–1907, Creek, 1885-7756, OIA, RG75, NA.

40. Debo, *Disappearance*, 257.

41. "Notes and Documents," 1122–23.

42. Debo, *Disappearance*, 249; *IJ* (Eufaula), July 7, 1881, 5:1; Checote to Trufts, May 5, 1881, National Council Resolution, Apr. 5, 1881, file C, box 2, Blacks, FWP, OHS; Paro Burner to Checote, June 19, 1880, doc. 38504, CRN 48; *BHMM* 6, no. 9 (Sept. 1884): 214; Checote to D. M. Hodge, Mar. 22, 1882, fr. 473, CIMA 2.

43. Checote to Tufts, May 4, 1881, p. 781, and Checote to Durant and Kernel, Nov. 24, 1881, p. 959, CRN 21; National Council Resolution, Nov. 2, 1881, doc. 38544, CRN 48; Durant et al. to Checote, Dec. 27, 1881, Blacks, FWP, OHS; Durant et al. to Checote, Nov. 7, 1881, doc. 38541, CRN 48; Porter to A. E. W. Robertson, Feb. 11, 1882 and Nov. 29, 1882, box 3, file 24, ARCOHS. Note that Alice M. Robertson, William and Anna Eliza's daughter, taught for several years at the Tullahassee Colored Mission after it became an African Creek school and was remembered fondly by many of her former students in the Indian Pioneer History interviews. Later, when serving as the government-appointed supervisor for the Creek schools in the final years of tribal government (1900–1905), she worked assiduously to improve conditions at the African Creek schools through, among other things, distancing the schools as much as possible from corrupt politics. *Cimeter* (Muskogee), Sept. 29, 1904, 2:3.

44. *IJ* (Eufaula), Nov. 1, 1883, 5:2; Harry L. Moorehouse to J. M. Perryman, Oct. 13, 1883, Blacks, FWP, OHS; H. R. Price to Rev. Cain, May 9, 1884, 100–447A, and H. R. Price to Tufts, Aug. 16, 1881, 162–306, LS, OIA, RG75, NA; Students in Schools in the States, n.d., doc. 38576, CRN 48.

45. Debo, *Disappearance*, 268–69, Grayson and Creek Delegation to H. R. Price, July 6, 1883, folder 1, box 6, Grayson Family Papers, WHC.

46. Checote to Cochar Emarthla and Silas Jefferson, Sept. 1, 1880, and Mar. 31, 1881, CRN 21; Cochar Emarthla (Tiger) was Isparhecher's Creek name. In Checote's letter book, Silas Jefferson is also referred to by his Creek name, Ho-tul-ko-micco, although in his own letters, Jefferson always signs himself Silas Jefferson; Debo, *Disappearance*, 268–70. In spite of the growing tensions between the two parties, when the Loyal delegation was pressing its claims in Washington and was stranded there after its funds ran out, Pleasant Porter, the official delegate from the Creek Nation, loaned them $183 to get them back to the Creek country. However, when Porter applied to the nation for reimbursement, he was told he would have to collect from the insurgents, and Porter probably never got the money back. Checote to Porter, Apr. 17, 1882, p. 153, fr. 494, and Checote to Hon. Cochar Emarthla and Silas Jefferson, Apr. 17, 1882, p. 157, fr. 495, CIMA 2.

47. Alex Blackston interview, IPH 90:273–75; Fisk and Whittlesey, "Peace Ratified in the Creek Nation," 22, hereafter cited as Fisk Report; Checote to Tufts, July 26, 1882, frs. 607–609; Checote to Snow Sells, July 31, 1882, frs. 617–18; and Checote to H. C. Reed, Aug. 9, 1882, frs. 628–29, CIMA 2. There were no jails in the Creek nation before the federal government built one in Muskogee to service the federal district court established there in 1889. Those arrested by the Lighthorse were let go once the arrest warrant had been served and expected to show up at their court trial. More desperate criminals were boarded with the Lighthorse officers themselves, who kept an eye on them.

48. Fisk Report, 22; S. Rep. 1278, 151; Joe Barnett, claim 62, Capt. Sam Scott, claim 132, LCC, OIA, RG75, NA.

49. Champagne, *Social Order*, 233; Warde, *George Washington Grayson*, 138. The idea that the breakdown in Creek politics came between those wanting a more assertive role for the central government versus those in favor of local control comes directly from Champagne's important work. The struggle in the Creek Nation could be compared broadly to the conflict between the Hamiltonians and Jeffersonians over the powers of the federal government versus state and local control and national development issues. The conflict in the Creek Nation (as Champagne points out) can be traced directly to the establishment of the Creek National Council in 1797 under the aegis of Benjamin Hawkins' civilization program. Mary Jane Warde, in her superb study of one of the leading progressive Creek nationalists and the politics of the period, provides an incisive look into the progressive–traditionalist and mixed-blood–full-blood dichotomies, the political and cultural ramifications of the split between the two parties, and how development issues played into the equation; see especially 136–40. Although Creeks themselves used the term "mixed blood" to impugn the authority and criticize the actions of their opponents who were of mixed ancestry, as such, the term is loaded with racist implications that provide little insight into understanding the politics of the period. Both progressive and traditionalist Creeks had so-called "mixed-bloods" among them. As Theda Perdue has pointed out in her important work *"Mixed Blood" Indians*, people with Creek matrilineal kinship ties were considered Creeks—no matter how they dressed, how they acted, or what their skin color.

50. Checote to Sells, July 31, 1882, fr. 617, and Checote to Reed, Aug. 9, 1882, frs. 628–29, CIMA 2; Lighthorse, Coweta District, doc. 31930, frs. 717–18, CRN 38; Checote to Taylor Postoak, Aug. 10, 1882, frs. 631–33, CIMA 2.

51. Lighthorse Election, Wewoka District, Sept. 20, 1881, doc. 31828, fr. 593, CRN 38; Fisk Report, 22; One month after the Vann shooting in Muskogee, Barnett came within one vote of being elected to the Lighthorse in the Muskogee District.

52. Muskogee District Court, 51:22, frs. 174–75, CRN 18; Coweta District Court, 42:34–39, frs. 572–76, CRN 17; Checote to Reed, Aug. 12, 1882, frs. 641–42, and Checote to whom it may concern, Aug. 25, 1882, frs. 650–51, CIMA 2.

53. *IJ* (Eufaula), Aug. 24, 1884, 5:3; Checote to Sells, July 31, 1882, fr. 618; Checote to Reed, Aug. 9, 1882, frs. 628–29; Pardons, Eufaula District, frs. 635–37; Checote to Reed, Aug. 12, 1882, 641–43; Reply to Petition for Clemency, Aug. 22, 1882, frs. 650–53, CIMA 2; Coweta District Court, 42:34–39, frs. 572–76, CRN 17; George McIntosh interview, IPH 7:81–82; *IJ* (Eufaula), Oct. 19, 1882, 4:4; Petition for Pardon, n.d., doc. 32463, Principal Chief, Misc., CRN 23. The conflict was originally called the Corn Shuck War because the insurgents stuck corn shucks in their hats to identify themselves. The name was later humorously changed to the Green Peach War because the effects that unripe peaches had on the soldiers' digestion matched the ruinous effects that absurd claims for damages arising from the war had on Creek finances. Jake Simmons, a Creek citizen with white, Indian, and African Creek ancestors, and

who served with the insurgents, suggests the conflict got its name because white reporters misunderstood Isparhecher's name as Green Peach. Regarding the three men sentenced to death—two were executed by a firing squad, and the third was released after the first volley failed to kill him; Debo, *Disappearance*, 273.

54. Reed to Checote, Dec. 5, 1882, and Tufts to Checote, Dec. 21, 1882, Outbreaks, doc. 34252, frs. 438–39 and 443–44, CRN 40; Debo, *Disappearance*, 274–75; Checote to Reed, Dec. 16, 1882, frs. 802–803, CIMA 2; *IJ* (Eufaula), Dec. 21, 1882, 4:1.

55. *IJ* (Eufaula), Dec. 28, 1882, 5:3; Fisk Report, 25; George McIntosh interview, IPH 7:81–82; Jake Simmons interview, 9:291–92.

56. J. M. Perryman to G. W. Grayson and L. C. Perryman, Dec. 27, 1883, 5:2; Checote to Grayson, Feb. 21, 1883, 5:7; Checote to Grayson, July 11, 1883, 5:16, Grayson Family Papers, WHC; Scott Waldo McIntosh interview, IPH 35:275–76; Henry S. Myers interview, IPH 37:417–18; Richard Franklin interview, IPH 91:452–53; Burl Taylor interview, IPH 10:324; Jim Tomm interview, IPH 112:292; Jake Simmons interview, IPH 9:389–93; Checote to Callahan, Jan. 12, 1883; Checote to Tufts, Jan. 13 and 27, 1883; Checote to James McHenry, Jan. 13 and 16, 1883, frs. 843–49, 859–63, CIMA 2; *IJ* (Eufaula), Apr. 28, 1883, 5:4, May 10, 1883, 5:3.

57. Island Smith interview, IPH 59:338–39.

58. Fisk Report, 29–30; Debo, *Disappearance*, 279–81; Warde, *George Washington Grayson*, 146.

59. *IJ* (Eufaula), Aug. 30, 1883, 4:1–2; Sept. 6, 1883, 4:3, 4:2, 5:4; Sept. 13, 1883, 4:2–3, 4:1; Sept. 20, 1:1, 4:1, Sept. 27, 4:3; Warde, *George Washington Grayson*, 146–47; Debo, *Disappearance*, 281. Although it is difficult to say how such a family relationship would calculate into either political support or disdain, it was known throughout the Creek country that Joseph Perryman had a number of African Creek half sisters and half brothers from his father's "relationships" with slave women.

60. *IJ* (Eufaula), Sept. 6, 1883, 4:3, 4:2, 5:4; Sept. 13, 1883, 4:2; J. M. Perryman to Checote, Sept. 5, 1883, Elections, doc. 29382, frs. 950–51; Sells and A. P. M. McKellop to Checote, Sept. 3, 1883, doc. 29383, frs. 952–53, CRN 33; Sells to Checote, Sept. 12, 1883, doc. 29427, CRN 33; *IJ* (Eufaula), Sept. 27, 4:3; Kellop Murrell, Daniel Tucker, Robert Marshall to Checote, Sept. 17, 1883, doc. 29429, fr. 19, CRN 34; Reports of the Election Counts of Oct. 8 and 12, 1883, box 1, WHC. Thanks to Mary Jane Warde for providing access to 1883 election materials and for unstinting support, advice, and insight into the arcane workings of postwar Creek politics.

61. H. M. Teller to Hiram Price, Feb. 27, 1884, folder 8, box 6, Grayson Family Papers, WHC.

Chapter 5

1. S. Rep. 1278, 183–86, 145, 151–52, 158–59, 171–72, 200–204. Interestingly, when Pleasant Porter served as Creek delegate to Washington in the early 1870s, he wrote to his friends the Robertsons that it was ironic the federal government protected

freedmen's rights in the South while they refused to protect the Indian nations from intruders as promised repeatedly in treaties with Creeks. He also lamented that only the communists gave the Indians a sympathetic forum, but alas, "they were infidels." Porter to W. S. Robertson, Mar. 28, 1874, box 3, file 21, ARCOHS.

2. S. Rep. 1278, 181–84.

3. S. Rep. 1278, 151–52, 158–59.

4. S. Rep. 1278, 197–98.

5. Debo, *Disappearance*, 319.

6. H. C. Carter and R. M. Mitchell to the President (Chester Arthur), July 28, 1882, Creek 14395-1882, 1881–1907, OIA, RG75, NA; *Congressional Record* 47:1, 4994; Chapman, "Freedmen and the Oklahoma Lands," 155–56; As the first African American appointed to the United States Diplomatic Corps, Turner served as minister and general counsel to Liberia from 1871–1878. After his stint as ambassador, Turner used his political influence and his persuasive abilities to organize the black boomer movement. Grinde and Taylor, "Red vs. Black," 213–15; Goble, *Progressive Oklahoma*, 116–17; Tolson, *Black Oklahomans*, 41–42.

7. Debo, *Disappearance*, 332; S. Rep. 1278, 156–57, Martha Fele case, doc. 24985, frame 235, Citizenship, CRN 3.

8. Moocher Hardage claim, doc. 25382, frs. 24–25, CRN 3; Lipscomb McGilvary affidavit, Sept. 12, 1878, and McGilvary to Marston, Feb. 28, 1877, frs. 672–73, 622–23, roll 233, M234, LR, OIA, RG75, NA. Lipscomb McGilvray to Commissioner, Jan. 13, 1887, LR, OIA, RG75, NA. McGilvray African Creeks and Indians also spelled and pronounced their name McGilbra and probably derived the name from Lachlan and Alexander McGillivray. J. M. Perryman to Tufts, Sept. 5, 1884, Citizenship, doc. 24968, fr. 199, CRN 3; Nancy Wallace claim, doc. 25208, fr. 163, 172, Citizenship, CRN 4; Hestor Murphy application, 3, *Applications for Enrollment*, roll 422, M1301, OIA, RG75, NA; "Mike McIntosh, et al." Simon Brown testimony, Citizenship, doc. 24978, frs. 20–23, CRN 3.

9. Dinah Wallace, doc. 24967, frs. 197–98; Rose Mats, doc. 24987; Martha Fele, doc. 24985; Doctor Redmouth, doc. 24995; Nancy Rose, doc. 25107, Citizenship, CRN 3; Wickett, *Contested Territory*, 9; Nancy Wallace, doc. 25211, Citizenship, CRN 4. Wickett discusses the issues of race and identity among the Five Tribes and how white attitudes influenced decisions regarding citizenship rights at length in chapter 2, "The One Drop Rule," 15–41, in his fine study on the evolution of race relations in Oklahoma. Tufts' speculation was probably based on high-profile cases involving leading white merchants like F. B. Severs and S. B. Callahan, who had intermarried and were granted Creek citizenship. But as Angie Debo and others have pointed out, the Creeks, unlike the Cherokees, Choctaws, and Chickasaws, did not grant citizenship rights to intermarried white residents as a matter of course, and their number remained low, although their influence was much greater than their numbers indicated. While the citizenship standards tightened during this period, many non-citizen spouses (black and white) were allowed to stay under permits granted with a great deal of leniency.

10. Dinah Wallace, doc. 24967, frs. 197–98, Citizenship, CRN 3; Monday Durant to Checote, Mar. 9, 1881, doc. 24956, frs. 177–78, CRN 3; *Sarah Brown v. Jennie Morrison*, doc. 28958, Supreme Court, CRN 4.

11. Debo, *Disappearance*, 290; Taylor, *In Search of*, 117–20; S. Rep. 1278, 138, 156–57, 182–83, 186, 197, 356–57; Chapman, "Freedmen and the Oklahoma Lands," 153–55; Grinde and Taylor, "Red vs. Black," 212–13.

12. Debo, *Waters*, 11–12; Lipscomb McGilvary affidavit, Sept. 12, 1878, and McGilvary to Marston, Feb. 28, 1877, frs. 672–73, 622–23, roll 870, M234, LR, 1824–1880, OIA, RG75, NA; Lipscomb McGilvray to Commissioner, Jan. 13, 1887, LR, 1881–1907, OIA, RG75, NA; G. W. Stidham to Commissioner of Indian Affairs, Sept. 25, 1888, 1888-24216, LR, 1881–1907, OIA, RG75, NA; Claim of the Creek Nation for Reimbursement of Money Paid to non-Creek Freedmen, 1868–88, file 284, roll 76, M574, special files, 1807–1904, OIA, RG75, NA. Before the Creeks gave a conditional cession of their western lands under the 1866 treaty, they shared forty miles of their southern border along the Canadian River with the Chickasaw Nation.

13. Turner to James H. McLean, June 2, 1883, LR, Relating to Choctaw and Other Freedmen, 1878–1884, entry 604, OIA, RG75, NA; Mayes Berry et al. to Commissioner, May 19, 1883, 9841F-1883; Tufts to Commissioner of Indian Affairs, May 14, 1883, 8855F-1883; Cherokee Freedmen Petition, Feb. 12, 1884, 2873L-1884; J. M. Morris to Commissioner, May 27, 1885, 12219C-1885, LR, 1881–1907, OIA, RG75, NA. Booker T. Washington and other advocates of the Tuskegee ideology of community and racial "uplift" also decried the Indian influence on native freed people in the Indian Territory.

14. Baker and Baker, *WPA Oklahoma*, 83.

15. Ibid., 83–84, Sameth, "Creek Negroes," 54–55.

16. "Sutton's History of Creek Freedmen," CRN 4A; James A. Patterson and A. G. Myers, two leading licensed white traders who opened stores in the Creek country before the Civil War and who were active in the development of the Creek country in the postwar years, both had children with African Creek women. Patterson fathered James E. Patterson (Joseph P. Davison's half brother) with Julia Gibson, and Myers fathered John A. Myers, who was one of Isparhecher's lieutenants during the Green Peach War.

17. *Report on Alleged Frauds in Bounty and Back Pay for Certain Indian Soldiers in the Indian Territory*, 42nd Cong., 2nd sess. H. Rep. 96, serial 1543, 256; *Davis Heirs v. Millie Brown*, Muskogee District Court, frs. 334–35, 364–65, CRN 18; Current-Garcia, *Shem, Ham, and Japheth*, 99; George McIntosh interview, IPH 7:83; Miscellaneous, 1860–1880, vol. 96, box 43, Foreman Collection, GIAAH.

18. George McIntosh interview, 7:76–77; Burl Taylor interview, 10:9–10; Siegal McIntosh interview, 35:233, 236–37; Jim Tomm interview, IPH 112:296–98; *Sugar George v. Mary Escoe*, docs. 27042–44, Muskogee District Court, CRN 18; *MP*, Aug. 8, 1897, 3:2; Myers, *From Creek Freedmen*, 36–40; Okmulgee Historical Society, *History of Okmulgee*, 48, 52.

19. "Sutton's History of Creek Freedmen," CRN 2A; J. P. Davison, Creek freedman land allotment jacket 2004, RCFCT, RG75, NAFW.

20. J. P. Davison, Creek freedman land allotment jacket 2004; *J. P. Davison v. Edmund Gibson*, Allotment Contest Records (Creek Freedmen), RCFCT, RG75, NAFW; Henry Myers interview, IPH 37:419–20; Burl Taylor interview, IPH 10:310–11; "Sutton's History of Creek Freedmen," CRN 2A; Robinson, "Indian International Fair," 415; "Creek Nation, Indian Territory," roll 1853, T623, U.S. Census Bureau, RG29, NA.

21. Creek freedmen enrollment card 232, Warrior Rentie; Creek enrollment case 73, RCFCT, RG75, NAFW; *MP*, Mar. 14, 1888, 3:3; "Sutton's History of the Creek Freedmen," CRN 2A. Caroline McIntosh (or Rentie as she was later known) also had a child with Alex Weatherford, the grandson of Alexander McGillivray.

22. James Ross Ramsey autobiography, 19, 60, WHC; Mary Ann Lilley autobiography 18, WHC; J. Coody Johnson, Creek land enrollment field jacket 75, applications for enrollment; Elizabeth Johnson, Creek land enrollment field jacket 74, Applications for Enrollment, RCFCT, RG75, NAFW; *Cimeter*, Jan. 7, 1905, 2:1–2; *The Black Dispatch*, Mar. 3, 1927, 1:6–7, 3:1.

23. Debo, *Disappearance*, 290; Sameth, "Creek Negroes," 59.

24. *J. P. Davison v. Edward Gibson*, docs. 27389–99, 27404–05, 27440–42, Muskogee District Court, CRN 30, 31; *Edward Gibson v. J. P. Davison*, doc. 28947; *J. E. Patterson v. J. P. Davison*, doc. 28935, Supreme Court, CRN 32; *Dave Roberts v. W. A. Rentie*, doc. 26822; *W. A. Rentie v. Billy and George Island*, docs. 26958–60, 27035, Supreme Court, CRN 32; Warrior Rentie to Commissioner of Indian Affairs, Dec. 2, 1889, 1889-579, LR, 1881–1907, OIA, RG75, NA.

25. Warde, *George Washington Grayson*, 158–59; Champagne, *Social Order*, 235; Debo, *Disappearance*, 324–25.

26. 1887 Election Returns, Arkansas Colored, North Fork Colored, and Canadian Colored, frs. 72–85, 211–14,102–106, CRN 34.

27. Meserve, "The Perryman's," 177–78; Posey, *Fus Fixico Letters*, 109.

28. *MP*, Mar. 14, 1889, 1:5.

29. Ibid.; S. Rep. 1278, 9–10; The Evangel Mission was supported through private contributions collected by Simon Brown, Samuel Soloman, Monday Durant, and Jonathan Kernel. The Baptist Home Mission Society initially proposed that the funds earmarked for opening Tullahassee Mission as an African Creek school be split between the two schools. While it is clear that the Creek Nation provided no money for the Evangel School, it is not clear whether the BHMS provided any funding. *IJ* (Eufaula), Nov. 1, 1883, 5:2; Louis Rentie interview, IPH 70:479–80.

30. "First Superintendent's Report, Tullahassee Manual Labor School, Nov. 26, 1883," file C, box 2, Blacks, FWP, OHS; *BHMM* 6, no. 9 (Sept. 1884): 214–15; Tullahassee Manual Training School, "Catalogue," 1888–1889, 5–6, GIAAH.

31. *BHMM* 6, no. 9, (Sept. 1884): 214–15.

32. *BHMM* 7, no. 3, (Mar. 1885): 78, 83–85; Josiah C. Perryman and Education Committee, Oct. 23, 1884, National Council Appropriation for Tullahassee Manual Labor School, Oct. 24, 1884, Blacks, FWP, OHS.

33. *BHMM* 9, no. 3 (Mar. 1887): 69–70.

34. Ibid.

35. E. H. Rishell interview, IPH 69:6–7; *MP*, Feb. 27, 1890; *BHMM* 11, no. 8 (Aug. 1889); Tullahassee Manual Labor School, "Catalogue," 6.

36. E. H. Rishell interview, IPH 69:6–7.

37. *BHMM* 11, no. 8 (Aug. 1889); *MP*, Mar. 21, 1889, 1:5; Apr. 4, 1889, 1:5; May 23, 1889, 1:5; June 6, 1889, 1:5; July 11, 1889, 1:5.

38. E. H. Rishell interview, IPH 69:6–7; Phillip Lewis interview, IPH 6:220; George McIntosh interview, IPH 7:82–83; Alex Blackston interview, IPH 90:375; Henry Myers interview, IPH 37:418; Louis Rentie interview, IPH 70:474; A. W. Bruner application, *Applications for Enrollment,* roll 422, M1301, OIA, RG75, NA.

39. *MP*, Jan. 24, 1889, 1:4; BTWP, 2:190–91.

40. Booker T. Washington himself taught Creek Indian students at Hampton in the early 1880s and supervised the Indian boys' dormitory.

41. J. D. Anderson, *Education of Blacks,* 122–25, 240–43.

42. "Minutes of the Second Baptist Church of the Freedmen's Baptist Association held at the Old Creek Agency, Muskogee Nation, Nov. 22, 1877," (Eufaula: *IJ,* 1878), GIAAH; "Minutes of the Second Annual Session of the Freedmen's Baptist Association of the Muskogee Nation held at Blackjack Baptist Church, Thursday, Aug. 1, 1878," (Muskogee: *IJ,* 1879), GIAAH; Gaskin, *Black Baptists,* 94–95, 116–17, 119–20. In the years leading up to the Civil War, there was an intense and bitter doctrinal battle among the Baptist missionaries in the Indian Territory, most of whom were sent out by the Northern-based Baptist Missionary Society, who objected to baptizing slave owners. Both the Baptist Missionary Society and the Southern Baptist Convention were active in the Indian Territory after the Civil War. Henry F. Buckner was a leading missionary for the Southern Baptists in the Creek country, but Creek Indian Baptists also had strong ties to the Baptist Missionary Society, and John M. McIntosh, the son of chief Chilly McIntosh, served for many years as the moderator for the Baptist Missionary Society's activities in the Creek country.

43. "Minutes of the Ninth Annual Session of the Freedmen's Baptist Association held at the Second Baptist Church, Creek Nation, Aug. 19, 20, 21, 22, 1886" (Muskogee: *IJ,* 1887), GIAAH; Cemeteries, IPH 55:340, 200; *IJ* (Muskogee), June 6, 1881, 3:1; Mar. 19, 1885, 3:1–2; Aug. 13, 1885, 3:1, Aug. 20, 1885, 3:2, Aug. 27, 3:2, Nov. 5, 1885, 3:2; May 20, 1886, 3:2–3.

44. Alex Blackston interview, 90:372–73; Lemuel Jackson interview, 31:36; Fred Johnson interview, IPH 31:221. Jackson says in his interview that he attended both ball games *and* camp meetings with Creek Indians in the postwar period. Baker and Baker, *WPA Oklahoma,* 110–12, 498.

45. Margaret Bonds, "Five Creek Freedmen Spirituals"; Walker-Hill, *From Spir-*

ituals to Symphonies, 163–66. Margaret Bonds transcribed and arranged the music for "Five Creek Freedmen Spirituals" for Hortense Love's Town Hall debut performance in New York City in 1942. Bonds and Love's collaboration began while they were students at Northwestern University in Chicago in the 1930s. Hortense Love's family moved to Chicago from outside Muskogee when she was still a child. Love's grandmother was a Creek freedwoman and sang the songs in both Creek and English to Love from her early childhood. In arranging the songs, Love asked Bonds to pay special attention to the mixture of Creek and African American musical elements that gave the songs a particular emotive power. Bonds, with this composition, contributed to launching the movement to arrange and score African American spiritual music as "art songs" worthy of consideration and study as an indigenous art form.

46. Berens, "Old Campaigners," 53–55; Debo, *Waters*, 21–22.

47. Foner, *The Story of American Freedom*, 135; BTWP 3:43–44, 70 n. 1, 41. *Lake Mohonk Conference* (1890), 10, 13, 138; *Lake Mohonk Conference* (1891), 16, 103–104, 74, 59, 62, 91.

48. Gibson, "The Centennial Legacy," 232–33; Debo, *Waters*, 21–22.

49. Debo, *Disappearance*, 344; *And Still the Waters Run*, 12–13; Warde, *George Washington Grayson*, 159–60; Porter to G. W. Grayson, Jan. 1, 1889; Jan. 23, 1889; and Feb. 2, 1889, file 1, box G22, series I, Grayson Family Papers, WHC. Crawford commanded the Second Kansas Colored (83rd Infantry, U.S. Colored Troops) during the Civil War, with its company (G) of African Creeks.

50. Debo, *Disappearance*, 344, *Waters*, 12–13; Warde, *George Washington Grayson*, 159–60; COIA (1873), 211, (1889), 201, 211, 790; S. Rep. 1278, 138, 144; Grinde and Taylor, "Red vs. Black," 217; "Five Civilized Tribes," 4, U.S. Census Bureau, RG29, NA; "Population: Part I," 47, U.S. Census Bureau, RG29, NA; Goble, *Progressive Oklahoma*, 117–20, 143–46.

51. *MP*, Apr. 25, 1889, 4:3; May 16, 1889, 1:6; Oct. 31, 1889, 1:2; Sugar George to N. B. Moore, July 2, 1890, series II, box 6, folder 4, ARCUT.

52. Debo, *Disappearance*, 316, 326, 349–50; *MP*, Oct. 31, 1889, 1:2.

53. Debo, *Disappearance*, 316, 326, 349–50; *MP*, Oct. 31, 1889, 1:2.

54. James R. Gregory, another of the leading progressive Creek nationalists, became one of the first Creeks to accept the offer of U.S. citizenship in 1891; he claimed his rights as a Creek citizen as well, and then dared anyone "manly enough" to oppose him! James Gregory to Emmett Starr, Feb. 16, 1900, Gregory Papers, OHS; Leo Bennett to L. C. Perryman, Nov. 2, 1891, doc. 24994, Citizenship, CRN 3. In contrast, there was no mass defection of African Creeks to claim U.S. citizenship; they "contended to the last" and were the first to be cut adrift after restrictions on the sale of allotments were removed in 1904.

55. Debo, *Disappearance*, 351–52; Pecan Creek Colored School, Tullahassee School, Colored Orphan Asylum, file C, box 2, Blacks, FWP, OHS; Gregory to L.C. Perryman, Nov. 2, 1891, Citizenship, CRN 3; J.P. Davison to Commissioner of Indian Affairs, Apr. 5, 1890, 1890-11773, LR, 1881–1907, OIA, RG75, NA; *MP*, Oct. 8, 1891, 3:2.

56. *MP*, Oct. 8, 1891, 3:2; R. H. Rishell interview, IPH 69:6; Siegal McIntosh interview, IPH 35:234–35; Petition to Suspend G. H. Taylor, n.d., doc. 36801, Schools—Misc., CRN 48; Debo, *Disappearance*, 352; *MP*, Mar. 24, 1892, 5:2; D. F. Littlefield, Jr., *Alex Posey*, 102–103.

57. 1891 Elections, Arkansas Colored, frs. 341–43; Canadian Colored, frs. 393–95; North Fork Colored, frs. 418–20, CRN 34; Debo, *Disappearance*, 325.

58. *MP*, July 25, 1889, 1:4–5; Feb. 12, 1891, 1:2; Feb. 19, 1891, 1:2; Apr. 19, 1891, 1:2; *Afro-American Advocate*, Dec. 25, 1891, 4:1; Mar. 11, 1892, 1:3; Mar. 18, 1892, 4:1. There was indeed a significant immigration to Liberia during this period (the late 1880s and early 1890s) undertaken by blacks from the Cherokee and Creek nations. However, close scrutiny of the ship manifests, citizenship records, and American Colonization Society correspondence show that those immigrating were almost entirely "permit men," black noncitizen tenant farmers being squeezed out of the agricultural economy by the arrival of a host of white intruders. Charles Rentie and his family, African Creek citizens, were a notable and interesting exception.

59. Sameth, "Creek Negroes," 54, 53 n. 200. Watchina is a Muscogee version of the English word "Virginian," which had been used by Creeks to designate intruders as early as the eighteenth century. Although the eighteenth-century Creeks attached no racial connotation to the word—both white and black intruders were labeled "Watchina"—by the 1890s African Creeks were using the term exclusively to describe state freed people in a negative way (see Saunt, *New Order*, 115–16); Robert L. Littlejohn, telephone interview by the author, Apr. 17, 1999.

60. Sameth, "Creek Negroes," 56.

61. Ibid., 53–58.

62. *N. O. Perry et al. v. Creek Nation*, Special Master's Report, case 269, box 25, Citizenship Contest Cases, FCTA, RG75, NAFW; "Report of the Committee to Insure Fair and Honest Allotment of Lands," Apr. 1, 1899, folder 15, box 1, series I, ARCUT; *MP*, Oct. 13, 1892, 4:1; Nov. 17, 1892, 8:1.

63. *MP*, Oct. 13, 1892, 4:1; Nov. 17, 1892, 8:1; Pleasant Porter to T. J. Morgan, Jan. 28, 1893, 1893-IA 3814, LR, 1881–1907, OIA, RG75, NA. It was only shortly after the Court disclaimed jurisdiction in the Creek case that the famous *Plessy v. Ferguson* case came before the Court in 1893, although the decision, to allow racial segregation in public places, was not handed down until 1896.

64. Gregory to Starr, Feb. 1, 1900, Gregory Papers, OHS; *Muskogee Evening Times*, Jan. 20, 1898, 4:2–5; Pleasant Porter to T. J. Morgan, Jan. 28, 1893, 1893-IA 3814, LR, 1881–1907, OIA, RG75, NA.

65. *MP*, Oct. 31, 1892, 8:1; Nov. 7, 1892, 8:1–2.

Chapter 6

1. Carter, *The Dawes Commission*, 1–11; D. F. Littlefield, Jr., "Henry Dawes and the Commission to the Five Civilized Tribes," 2–3.

2. Debo, *Disappearance*, 346–47; Warde, *George Washington Grayson*, 179–80; *IJ* (Eufaula), Feb. 22, 1894, 2:2–3; Mar. 1, 1894, 1:2–6.

3. Debo, *Disappearance*, 347–48, *Waters*, 21–30; "Report of the Commission to the Five Civilized Tribes" (1894), 18–28, in *Annual Report of the Secretary of the Interior, 1894*, RG48, NA, hereafter cited as Five Tribes Commission Report; McAdam, "An Indian Commonwealth," 886–92, 895–97; "Education of White and Negro Children in the Indian Territory," 55th Cong., 2nd sess., H. Doc. 310, serial 3679, 1–8, hereafter cited as H. Doc. 310. McAdams's article is an example of the propaganda blitz unleashed to support the Dawes Commission's views that the Indian nations were monopolized by aristocratic mixed-bloods who oppressed their people and the U.S. citizens who were there legally as traders or laborers under permit.

4. *IJ* (Eufaula), Mar. 1, 1894, 1:6; Feb. 22, 1894, 1:6; Warde, *George Washington Grayson*, 181–83.

5. Henry Louden case, doc. 25034, Citizenship, CRN 3; *N. O. Perry et al. vs Creek Nation*, Special Master's Report, case 269, box 25, Citizenship Contest Cases, FCTR, OIA, RG75, NAFW; Coweta District Court Records, June 22, 1893, CRN 18.

6. *Annual Report of the Creek Supervisor for Education* (1902), 307, in Annual Reports, RG48, NA, hereafter cited as Education Report; Sameth, "Creek Negroes," 37–38 (quoted passage), 62.

7. Island Smith interview, IPH 59:331–32, 334–35, 337; Sonny Jackson interview, IPH 31:77; Lemuel Jackson interview, IPH 31:33–34; George McIntosh interview, 7:77–78; Simon McIntosh interview, IPH 112:303–304; Alex Blackston interview, IPH 90:333; Richard Franklin interview, IPH 91:450; Debo, *Disappearance*, 298. When Okmulgee was established as the Creek capital in 1868, most of its permanent residents were African Creek. Angie Debo described the town as actually "little more than a hamlet except when Council was in session" (200–400 inhabitants). Okmulgee and the surrounding area had a large African Creek population, and African Creeks built the first schools and churches there. Myers, *From Creek Freedmen*, 34–38.

8. Island Smith interview, IPH 59:331–32, 334–35; Alex Blackston interview, IPH 90:333; Sameth, "Creek Negroes," 62.

9. Island Smith interview, IPH 59:331–32, 334–35. When Smith gave his Indian Pioneer History interview in 1937, his mother was still alive and supposedly 114 years old. Many older African Creeks mention the "night when the stars fell" to determine dates, age, and so forth in the Indian Pioneer History interviews.

10. Ibid.

11. Debo, *Disappearance*, 353; Creek Elections, doc. 29541, CRN 43.

12. Citizenship, doc. 25177, CRN 4; Creek Supreme Court, May 8, 1894, fr. 269, CRN 17. Ned Robbins, the sole African Creek member of the court, resigned before the decision was announced, though it is unclear if he did so in protest; the timing of his resignation suggests it may have been.

13. Debo, *Disappearance*, 356–58, D. F. Littlefield, Jr., *Alex Posey*, 102–103.

14. National Council, doc. 33317, CRN 13; Carter, "Snakes and Scribes," 387–88.

15. National Council, doc. 33317, CRN 13; Carter, "Snakes and Scribes," 387–88.

16. Citizenship, docs. 24947, 24949, CRN 3, and 25216, 25411, 25413, CRN 4.

17. The Sandy Ross, Sandy Perryman, Nancy Wallace, Bettie Snowden, and Mary Escoe cases all bear testimony claiming Indian identity in Lists of Applicants and Docket Books of the Creek Citizenship Commission, roll 2, 7RA68, RCFCT, RG75, NAFW.

18. Citizenship, docs. 25394, 25414, CRN 4.

19. Warde, *George Washington Grayson*, 186–87; Debo, *Disappearance*, 361; Creek Elections, docs. 29604–06, CRN 34; National Council, doc. 33276, CRN 13.

20. Phillip Lewis interview, IPH 61:237–38.

21. Debo, *Disappearance*, 364–67; Muskogee District Court, docs. 27778–79, CRN 30; Isparhecher to H. C. Reed, Aug. 12, 1897, LS, 1897–1899, FCTR, OIA, RG75, NAFW; Goble, *Progressive Oklahoma*, 166.

22. Debo, *Disappearance*, 364–65; Warde, *George Washington Grayson*, 187; Carter, "Snakes and Scribes," 388.

23. Citizenship, doc. 25144, CRN 4; Debo, *Disappearance*, 369; Five Tribes Commission Report (1894), 28.

24. Citizenship, doc. 24933, CRN 3.

25. Debo, *Disappearance*, 369; Carter, "Snakes and Scribes," 392; 1896 Colbert Roll, M7RA-69, roll 1, FCTR, OIA, RG75, NAFW.

26. T. J. Adams to Isparhecher, Aug. 5, 1896, Supreme Court, CRN 17; Citizenship, docs. 25149, 25156–57, 25159, CRN 4; *Indian Chieftan* (Vinita, Cherokee Nation), Aug. 6, 1896, p. 1, col. 5; *Daily Oklahoman* (Oklahoma City), Aug. 4, 1896, p. 4, col. 3; Debo, *Disappearance*, 369; Family Trees, folder 8, box 7, Cate Collection, WHC; J. L. Wright, *Creeks and Seminoles*, 78–79; *N. O. Perry et al. vs Creek Nation*, Special Master's Report, case 269, box 25, and *Annie Bowlegs et al. v. Muskogee Nation*, case 20, Citizenship Contest Records, FCTR, OIA, RG75, NAFW; Benjamin T. Duval to Isparhecher, Sept. 25, 1899, Citizenship, doc. 25327, CRN 4; Five Tribes Commission Report (1899), 156–59. Enclosed with Duval's lengthy description of the cases being appealed by the Creek Nation is Judge William Springer's decision regarding the *Escoe* case, and in particular his 1897 ruling regarding the Creek Council's power to grant citizenship rights. Springer was the federal judge for the Northern District of the Indian Territory.

27. Benjamin T. Duval contract, doc. 25300, CRN 4.

28. *Ft. Smith Bulletin*, Oct. 30, 1862, 2:2; Porter, *Black Seminoles*, 115–25; William Duval met his end after an unsuccessful slave-hunting expedition in the Seminole and Creek country in 1851, where he attempted to capture some of "his" African Seminoles. He stopped at the Edward's Store trading settlement on the Little River in the western Creek country in a drunken stupor one evening and disrupted a prayer meeting there, saying (among other things), "if this is Christian religion; I give up." Duval harassed the preacher and his African Creek interpreter, Sambo Barnett, until they had to leave off the sermon. After stumbling from the meeting, Duval apparently continued his bender and was later found dead in the woods

outside Fort Smith. Ramsey autobiography, 19–20, WHC. *N. O. Perry et al. v. Creek Nation*, Special Master's Report, case 269, box 25, and *Creek Nation v. Louisa Pease*, Special Master's Report 2, case 281, Citizenship Contest Cases, FCTR, OIA, RG75, NAFW; Carter, "Snakes and Scribes," 392–93; Hawkins, doc. 25166; Nancy Wallace, docs. 25190 and 25211; Sandy Ross, doc. 25201; Jim Perryman, doc. 25208; Ben Reece, doc. 25181; B. T. Duval correspondence, docs. 25315 and 25327 (discussion of Mary Escoe's case begins p. 8 of doc. 25327), Citizenship Documents, CRN 4.

29. *MP*, Oct. 10, 1895, 4:2; National Council, doc. 33276, CRN 13.

30. National Council, doc. 32976, CRN 40; Rentie, *Acts and Resolutions*; Pecan Creek Colored School, file C, box 2, Blacks, FWP, OHS; bond of W. A. Rentie and Sugar George, Dec. 4, 1895, fr. 859, and First Quarterly Report, Mar. 3, 1896, frs. 860–890, Muskogee National High School (Pecan Creek Mission School), CRN 43; W. A. Rentie to Dawes Commission, Oct. 28, 1896, Dawes Commission Reference Documents, Miscellaneous, box 5, RCFCT, RG75, NAFW; Pecan Creek School, docs. 36734, 36741, CRN 46; Citizenship, docs. 25218–19, CRN 4. Rentie apparently had a cottage industry going in creating political enemies. He also earned the wrath of Alexander Posey, the Creek School superintendent, whom he charged with bribery and corruption. D. F. Littlefield, *Alex Posey*, 102–103.

31. Roley McIntosh to W. A. Rentie, Sept. 3, 1896, Reference Documents, Miscellaneous, box 5, RCFCT, RG75, NAFW; Pecan Creek School, docs. 36739–40, CRN 46; Muskogee District Court, docs. 27778–79, CRN 30. Rentie maintained that Isparhecher favored his appointment, and if the chief had not been debilitated by the stroke, he would not have let the campaign against Rentie succeed.

32. Burl Taylor interview, IPH 10:310–11; Elections, docs. 32936, 32976, 33441, CRN 21.

33. W. A. Rentie to Citizenship Commission, Sept. 6, 1896, Citizenship, docs. 25218–19, CRN 4; W. A. Rentie to Dawes Commission, Oct. 28, 1896, Reference Documents, Misc., box 5, RCFCT, RG75, NAFW.

34. H. Doc. 310, 3–5; *Report of the Superintendent of Schools for Indian Territory* (1899), 195–201 and (1900), 121, hereafter cited as School Superintendent Report, in *Report of the U.S. Indian Inspector for the Indian Territory*, Annual Reports, RG48, NA; D. F. Littlefield, Jr., *Alex Posey*, 102–103. Even a cursory comparison of the statistics found in the voluminous U.S. Department of Education's *Report of the Commissioner of Education*, with the numbers and the narratives in the Education Report, reveals what a startling exception African Creek schools were to the general trend for black education in the age of Jim Crow. For another case of alleged corruption, see Isparhecher to Dan Tucker, Jan. 20, 1897, LS, 1897–1899, FCTR, OIA, RG75, NAFW; Jane Hawkins to Isparhecher, Dec. 12, 1897, Miscellaneous, CRN 40. Many of the charges of corruption and misconduct against school officials were politically motivated, so it is hard to judge if they were actually true, as in the Dan Tucker case.

35. *Five Tribes Commission Report* (1896), 145–47, 153–55.

36. Ibid., 154.

37. Phillip Lewis interview, IPH 61:275–76; Debo, *Disappearance,* 370–73; Dawes to Secretary of the Interior, Feb. 9, 1899, and Feb. 10, 1899, file 127, box 2, Miscellaneous Documents, RCFCT, RG75, NAFW; Dawes Agreement Referendum, Election, CRN 34; Dawes to Tams Bixby, Oct. 21, 1897, roll 65, fr. 194, DC, OHS; Debo, *Waters,* 30–34; Carter, "Snakes and Scribes," 394–95, 403; *Five Tribes Commission Report* (1900), 21–23, 51–55; *Memorial Against Bill to Ratify the Creek Agreement,* 56th Cong., 1st sess., S. Doc. 443, serial 3878; *Petitions Supporting Bill to Ratify the Creek Agreement,* 56th Cong., 1st sess., H. Rep. 1762, serial 4027; *To Ratify Proposed Agreement Between Dawes Commission and Creek Indians,* 57th Cong., 1st sess., H. Rep. 2495, serial 4407.

38. Debo, *Disappearance,* 373, *Waters,* 33; Carter, "Snakes and Scribes," 394–95; *For the Protection of the People of the Indian Territory,* 55th Cong., 2nd sess., H. Rep. 593, serial 3719; *Congressional Record,* 31 (4): 4947–54.

39. *MP,* July 28, 1898, 4:3; Aug. 4, 1898, 5:2; Aug. 18, 1898, 4:3; Sept. 8, 1898, 1:5; *Muskogee Evening Times,* Jan. 20, 1898, 4:2–5; Bixby to Allison B. Aylesworth, Sept. 2, 1898, fr. 410, roll 65, DC, OHS; Gregory to Isparhecher, July 7, 1899, Citizenship, doc. 25321, CRN 4.

40. Robert Grayson to (Dawes) Commissioners, Oct. 14, 1898, Nov. 3, 1898; James Grayson to Commissioners, Nov. 3, 1898, frs. 468–71, roll 65, DC; Dawes, "The Indian Territory," *Report of the Board of Indian Commissioners,* 671–74, in Annual Reports, RG48, NA.

41. Andrew Sullivan application, *Applications for Enrollment,* roll 422, M1301, OIA, RG75, NA. The commissioners also misunderstood Sullivan when he said he "drove a train." Apparently they thought he meant "locomotive" instead of a wagon train and became suspicious.

42. Myers, *From Creek Freedmen,* 41; *Report of the Senate Select Committee to Investigate Affairs in the Indian Territory,* 59th Cong., 2nd sess., S. Rep. 5013, serials 5062–63, pt. I, 697–98, pt. II, 688, hereafter cited as S. Rep. 5013; Debo, *Waters,* 98.

43. *Muskogee Evening Times,* Jan. 20, 1898, 4:2–5; Gregory to Isparhecher, Sept. 28, 1899, docs. 25321–22, Citizenship, CRN 4; Gregory to Emmett Starr, Feb. 16, 1900, Gregory Papers, OHS. A proposal to sell the entire Creek domain to the U.S. government and use the proceeds to buy lands in Mexico reserved for Creek Indians had been in the air only since 1895. Gregory was a hearty supporter of the idea.

44. Abe Kernels to Isparhecher, Aug. 12, 1896, doc. 23559 Citizenship, CRN 3; docs. 25308, 25310, Citizenship, CRN 4; Isparhecher to Abe Kernels, June 8, 1899, LS, 1897–1899,, FCTR, OIA, RG75, NAFW; Abram Kernel (Colonel), claim 47, Paro Bruner, claim 923, LCC, OIA, RG75, NA; Kansas Adjutant General, Regimental Papers, Co. I; *Creek Nation v. Louisa Pease,* Special Master's Report 2, case 281, box 25, Citizenship Contest Cases, FCTR, OIA, RG75, NAFW; Baker and Baker, *WPA Oklahoma,* 112; Warrior Rentie enrollment jacket 73, RCFCT, RG75, NAFW; Miley Johnson application, Applications for Enrollment, roll 422, M1301, OIA, RG75, NA; Phillip Lewis interview, IPH 61:223; Scott Waldo McIntosh interview, IPH 35:222–23; Siegal McIntosh interview, IPH 35:237; Ned Thompson interview, IPH 112:187.

45. "List of Lost Creeks, Advertized June 13, 1904," folder 111, box 1,Reference Documents, RCFCT, RG75, NAFW. Carter, "Snakes and Scribes," 406; Citizenship, docs. 25394, 25414, CRN 4; Citizenship, docs. 25411 and 25413, CRN 3; Fannie Rentie Chapman interview, IPH 5:7–8; Rentie Kernel application, Jane Morris and Joanna Ford application, pp. 4–7, 15–17, 19; Joseph Harrison application, p. 2; Patsy Mc-Carty and James Barnet application, pp. 5–6, 16–17; Louisa Olden application, 1, Applications for Enrollment, roll 422, M1301, OIA, RG75, NA.

46. Baker and Baker, *WPA Oklahoma*, 112; "Sutton's History of Creek Freedmen," CRN 4; Sameth, "Creek Negroes," 56; Joe Harrison application, p. 2; Rentie Kernel application; Miley Johnson application, 1–5, Applications for Enrollment, roll 422, M1301, OIA, RG75, NA; *Creek Nation v. James Freeman*, case 8, box 1, and *Creek Nation v. Charly Corbray*, file 211, box 3, Citizenship Contest Records, FCTR, OIA, RG75, NAFW; Fannie Rentie Chapman interview, IPH 17:7–8; Ellen Rentie Bruner interview, IPH 89:262–64.

47. Goble, *Progressive Oklahoma*, 73–75; J. P. Davison, Creek Land Contest Case 20, RCFCT, RG75, NAFW; James Coody Johnson, jacket 75, and Elizabeth Johnson, jacket 74, RCFCT, RG75, NAFW; Batemen, " 'We're Still Here,' " Ph.D. diss., 54; James Coody Johnson to Commissioners, Jan. 27, 1900, "Seminole," roll 72, DC; Debo, *Waters*, 114.

48. Col. Bliss to A. S. McKennon, Aug. 10, 1898, frs. 340–41, roll 65, DC; Debo, *Waters*, 100–101; *Five Tribes Commission Report* (1900), 31–33; *Report of the U.S. Indian Inspector for the Indian Territory* (1900), 121, Annual Reports, RG 48, NA; *Leasing and Selling Lands by Creek Indians in the Indian Territory*, 57th Cong., 1st sess., S. Doc. 226, serial 4235; A. C. Tonner (Acting Commissioner of Indian Affairs) to Secretary of the Interior Ethan Allan Hitchcock, Apr. 6, 1899, Foreman Collection, 5:28–29, OHS; *Muskogee Evening Times*, Aug. 26, 1902, 2:4.

49. *J.P. Davison v. Edmund Gibson*, Creek land contest case 20; J. P. Davison land allotment jacket 2004, RCFCT, RG75, NAFW.

50. Debo, *Waters*, 98; Myers, *From Creek Freedmen*, 41; Besides the Rentie family, other cases included *Kate Bemo v. Tobe McIntosh*, Creek land contest case 385; *Edward Gibson v. Tobe McIntosh*, Case 460, RCFCT, RG75, NAFW. Under pressure from reform groups and the burdens of paperwork, the commission later reversed the policy of encouraging allottees to select their surplus allotments in separate locations from their homesteads.

51. *Caroline Rentie v. Dave Roberts*, docs. 26597, 26661, 26680, 26687, 26691, 26711; *Dave Roberts v. W. A. Rentie et al.*, doc. 26822, Muskogee District Courts, CRN 30; *Dave Roberts v. Island Rentie*, Creek Land Contest 531–3, 537, RCFCT, RG75, NAFW.

52. *Dave Roberts v. W. A. Rentie et al.*, doc. 26822, Muskogee District Courts, CRN 30; *Dave Roberts v. Island Rentie*, Creek land contest 531, 2–5, 7–10, RCFCT, RG75 NAFW.

53. *Dave Roberts v. W. A. Rentie et al.*, doc. 26822, Muskogee District Courts, CRN 30; *Dave Roberts v. Island Rentie*, Creek land contest 531, 2–5, 7–10, RCFCT, RG75 NAFW.

54. *Dave Roberts v. Island Rentie*, Creek land contest 531, 1, 5–6, *George Harvison v. Warrior Rentie*, Creek land contest 265; *Mary Escoe v. Caroline Rentie*, Creek land contest 405; *Louis Jobe v. Warrior Rentie*, Creek land contest 315, RCFCT, RG75, NAFW.

55. Creek enrollment jacket 73, RCFCT, RG75, NAFW. Warrior, Roy Bismark, Ina Victoria, Leopold Augustus, and George Washington Lubiture Rentie. *George Harvison v. Warrior Rentie*, Creek land contest 265; *Mary Escoe v. Caroline Rentie*, Creek land contest 405; *Louis Jobe v. Warrior Rentie*, Creek land contest 315, RCFCT, RG75, NAFW.

56. Warde, *George Washington Grayson*, 189–90; Debo, *Disappearance*, 376; Creek Elections, docs. 29640–42, 29652, CRN 34. Mary Ann Grayson, an elderly Creek freedwoman, interviewed in the 1930s, recalled when the Dawes commissioners asked all Creeks opposed to allotment to step to the right that day in Okmulgee in 1894—Tiger was left standing alone. Mary Ann Grayson interview, IPH 104:60. Mary Jane Warde also points out that Moty Tiger was both a nationalist and an early advocate of accommodation; Warde, *George Washington Grayson*, 212.

57. Debo, *Disappearance*, 272; Pleasant Porter to T. J. Morgan, Jan. 28, 1893, Creek 1893-IA 3814, LR, 1881–1907, OIA, RG75, NA; Warde, *George Washington Grayson*, 200.

58. *IJ* (Eufaula), May 1, 1879, 1:3; Current-Garcia, *Shem, Ham, and Japheth*, 47; A. H. Mike to Pleasant Porter, Oct. 19, 1900, file 5, box 2, Blacks, FWP, OHS.

59. Phillip Lewis interview, IPH 6:223; Scott Waldo McIntosh interview, IPH 35:222–23; Siegal McIntosh interview, IPH 35:237; Littlefield and Underhill, "Crazy Snake," 309.

60. Carter, "Snakes and Scribes,", 402–404; Warde, *George Washington Grayson*, 194–96; Debo, *Waters*, 53–56; Littlefield and Underhill, "Crazy Snake," 309; Littlefield and Underhill, "Negro Marshals," 86; Henry Jacobs interview, IPH 31:101–102; Sonny Jackson interview, IPH 31:74–75; Jim Tomm interview, IPH 112:305.

61. Debo, *Waters*, 88–89. Carter, 404–405.

62. Carter, 404–406; Tams Bixby to Ethan Allan Hitchcock (Secretary of the Interior), July 18, 1902, case 123, box 2, Reference Documents,; Bixby to Hitchcock (Secretary of the Interior), Aug. 5, 1902, case 120, box 2, Reference Documents, RCFCT, RG75, NAFW; Pleasant Porter to Charles Gibson, June 21, 1902, and Porter to Blair Schoenfield (Inspector for the Indian Territory), Aug. 29, 1903, LS, 1899–1906, FCTR, OIA, RG75, NAFW; Phillip Lewis interview, IPH 61:277–78.

63. Election returns, 1903, doc. 35680, Misc., CRN 23; Porter to Blair Schoenfield (Union Indian Agent), Aug., 29, 1903, LS 1899–1906, FCTR, OIA, RG75, NAFW; Warde, *George Washington Grayson*, 201–203. During the 1903 election campaign, Alexander Posey, the Creek journalist and writer, excoriated Legus Perryman mercilessly in his widely read Fus Fixico Letters column in the *Indian Journal*, hammering away with a racist satirizing of Perryman's African heritage. See Posey, *Fus Fixico Letters*, 131.

Chapter 7

1. Annual Reports (1903), 84–86, RG48, NA; Debo, *Waters Run*, 89, 126, 137; *Memorial and Petitions for the Removal of Restrictions on the Sale of Surplus Allotments in the Indian Territory*, 58th Cong., 2nd sess., S. Doc. 169, 2–4, 8–11, hereafter cited as S. Doc. 169; S. Rep. 5013, 2:2113.

2. Goble, *Progressive Oklahoma*, 128; Debo, *Waters*, 89; S. Rep. 5013, 1:413, 441; Sameth, "Creek Negroes," 45, 54–55; J. W. Adams to B. T. Washington, May 1, 1905, BTWP, 8:271–72; Hearings Before the Committee on Indian Affairs on HR 15641: Removal of Restrictions on Indian Lands in Oklahoma, 60th Cong., 1st sess., H.R. 15641, 8–9, hereafter cited as HR 15641 Hearings.

3. "Who Will Guard the Guardians?" *Outlook* 74, no. 8, (Aug. 29, 1903): 1–2; "The Indian Land Investigation," *Outlook* 75, no. 1, (Sept. 5, 1903): 1 (quoted passage); *New York Times*, Aug. 24, 1903, 1:4; Aug. 25, 1903, 1:3; Aug. 27, 1903, 1:1; Sept., 15, 1903, 7:2; Oct. 19, 1903, 2:3; Charles Bonaparte to Theodore Roosevelt, Dec. 6, 1903, p. 5, roll 39, series 1; Bonaparte to Roosevelt, Jan. 24, 1903, roll 42, series 1, Roosevelt Papers. Tams Bixby and his Canadian Valley Land and Trust Company (CVLT) were one of the targets of investigation. Bixby steadfastly denied any wrongdoing and found nothing wrong with the CVLT occupying the same office building as the Commission to the Five Civilized Tribes. In fact, the CVLT moved into the same office space used by the commission before it moved upstairs. As a result, applicants, supplicants, and whoever had business with the commission, routinely visited the CVLT office before heading upstairs.

4. *MP*, Jan. 8, 1904, 1:5; Jan. 18, 1904, 3:2; Jan. 20, 1904, 1:5.

5. *MP*, Jan. 19, 1:5; Jan. 20, 1904, 2:1; S. Rep. 5013, 1:413; Debo, *Waters*, 137, 99.

6. *MP*, Dec. 11, 1903, 1:5–6; Dec. 13, 1903, 8:2–3 (first Owen quotation); S. Rep. 5013, 2:1920–1922; *Investigation of Alleged Abuses of Interior Dept. Officials in the Indian Territory*, 58th Cong., 2nd sess., S. Doc. 189, serials 5062–63 16, 37, hereafter cited as S. Doc. 189; Debo, *Waters*, 136. Indeed, Bonaparte's comment came at a time when progressive reformers wanted to cut the last ties to racial justice the federal government had promised African Americans during Reconstruction and repeal the Fifteenth Amendment in order to "protect" them from racist political violence; *Current Literature*, July 1903, 9, and Aug. 1903, 134.

7. *Congressional Record*, 58th Cong., 2nd sess., 38(3): 2893–94; *Cherokee Advocate*, Mar. 4, 1904, 1:4; Mar. 12, 1904, 1:1–2; *Oklahoma Guide*, Feb. 11, 1904, 1:4; *MP*, Apr. 10, 1904, 1:4–5.

8. *Congressional Record*, 58th Cong., 2nd sess., 38 (3): 2893.

9. Goble, *Progressive Oklahoma*, 139–40; *Congressional Record*, 58th Cong., 2nd sess., 38 (3): 2894, *Cherokee Advocate*, Mar. 12, 1904, 1:1.

10. *MP*, Apr. 10, 1904, 1:5, 2:1; Apr. 21, 1904, extra edition; Goble, *Progressive Oklahoma*, 130; S. Rep. 5013, 1:441–42 (J. C. Johnson testimony), 592–93, 1264–65, 1268–69 (M. L. Mott testimony); HR 15641 Hearings, 11, 52–53 (M. L. Mott testi-

mony). In response to Owen's charge that freedmen were fraudulently selling the same allotment to multiple buyers, Mott reckoned that with prices being offered by the grafters, if a freedmen allottee was able to sell his allotment to twenty different grafters, he might then be getting a fair market price for the land.

11. *MP*, Apr. 23, 1904, 4:1; Apr. 24, 8:2–3; May 1, 1904, 8:2–3, May 5, 1;4–5; *Cherokee Advocate*, Mar. 12, 1904, 1:1–2; *Daily Oklahoman*, Apr. 26, 1904, 2:2–3; Posey, *Fus Fixico Letters*, , 31–32; *MP*, Apr. 17, 1904 (Fus Fixico story), Apr. 22, 1904, 1:3–4 (white man's country quote). Stories of improvident African Creeks trading their allotments for whiskey, trinkets, and other spurious commodities were still being told by the descendants of state freed people around Muskogee in the 1990s.

12. "Sutton's History of Creek Freedmen," CRN 4.

13. Batemen, " 'We're Still Here,' " 128; Goble, *Progressive Oklahoma*, 140; Shepard, "North to the Promised Land," 312–13; BTWP 8:271–72; *MP*, June 19, 1898, 4:3; Franklin, *Journey Towards Hope*, 42.

14. Daniel F. Littlefield, Jr., has several hundred pages of transcribed material from the *Cimeter* and other African American newspapers from the Indian Territory and Oklahoma in his research material and notes housed at the Native American Press Archives at the University of Arkansas-Little Rock, which he so generously shared. Newspaper material taken from his transcripts will be designated with LT. *Cimeter* (black-owned businesses mentioned continuously 1904–1910) LT; *Muskogee Comet*, June 16, 1904, 1:1. As late as the 1920s, the pull of the "promised land" in Indian Territory and Oklahoma was still etched in African American consciousness. Bessie Smith sang "Goin' to the Nation, Going to the Terr'tor' " in 1926, in which she is going to a place where she could enjoy the freedom to work things out. Charley Patton and other Delta Blues singers also mention the Indian Nations as a promised land and a destination for black people down on their luck. Ralph Ellison explores the theme of geography and freedom in the title essay in his collection *Going to the Territory*, about growing up on the racial frontier of Oklahoma.

15. Gaskin, *Black Baptists*, 271–73; *Cimeter*, Sept. 29, 1904; Porter to National Council, Oct. 27, 1904, LS, 1899–1906, FCTR, OIA, RG75, NAFW; *Western World*, Feb. 24, 1905, LT; C. O. Boothe to Roosevelt, Feb. 23, 1907, file 9, box 2, Indian Inspector, LR, FCTR, OIA, RG75, NAFW.

16. Goble, *Progressive Oklahoma*, 133–34; Franklin, *Journey Towards Hope*, 17–19; Abel, *The American Indian as Slaveholder*, 24. Abel's map facing p. 24 shows some "Creek Negro" settlements predating the Civil War; Wickett, *Contested Territory*, 33–34, 113; "Booker T. Washington Special," *Cimeter*, Nov. 16, 1905; BTWP 8:473–74 and 9:430–31. The material from volume 9 is from an article that Washington wrote about his visit to Boley and the Indian Territory, published in *Outlook* in Jan. 1908; Sameth, "Creek Negroes," 93; May, *African Americans*, 230–32; Taylor, *In Search of*, 148–51.

17. Goble, *Progressive Oklahoma*, 141–42. Goble gives an enlightening and succinct presentation on the politics of race in the rush toward Oklahoma statehood. Wickett expands on Goble's interpretation that Republicans lost the organizational

advantage they enjoyed in the territorial period because of Democrats' race-baiting and bulldozing tactics; Republicans then felt obliged to lily-white themselves. Wickett, *Contested Territory*, 168–87.

18. *Cimeter*, Mar. 2, 1905; *Daily Searchlight*, Apr. 18, 1905, LT. Unfortunately, black Republican faith in Roosevelt was misplaced, because Roosevelt cast loyal African American Republicans adrift during his second term.

19. *Cimeter*, Jan. 12, 1905, LT, and Feb. 9, 1905, 1:3–4; Feb. 23, 1905, 1:3–4, Mar. 2, 1905, 1:3–4; C. V. Woodward, *Origins of the New South*, 351–52.

20. Goble, *Progressive Oklahoma*, 189–90; *Cimeter*, June 26, July 13, 1905, LT.

21. Goble, *Progressive Oklahoma*, 192–93; *Cherokee Advocate*, Oct. 14, 1905, 2 :1; *Cimeter*, July 25, 1905, Oct. 26, 1905, Nov. 11, 1905, LT; Nesbit, "Governor Haskell," 195–96, 200.

22. Maxwell, "The Sequoyah Convention," 190–91; *Muskogee Pioneer*, Nov. 11, 1905, 1:2–3.

23. Baxley, "Democracy, Equality, Justice." The origin of the slogan can be traced to a small looking-glass campaign trinket that Col. Lem Reynolds had manufactured in Chicago when he was running for superintendent of public instruction in the Chickasaw Nation in the 1880s. On one side, a white man and an Indian are clasping hands with a slogan on the rim that reads: "Democracy. Equality. Justice. White man and Indian against negro and carpetbagger." The Chickasaw freed people were locked in battle at the time with the Chickasaw Nation over their claims to citizenship. The slogan reappeared during the rush to statehood; although the Chickasaw freedmen were allotted forty acres under the Chickasaw Agreement with the Dawes Commission, they were never adopted as Chickasaw citizens. *Oklahoman*, Sept. 4, 1910, 11; Oct. 27, 1904, 1; and see D. F. Littlefield, *The Chickasaw Freedmen*.

24. *Cleveland Gazette*, Mar. 5, 1904, 2.

25. *Cimeter*, Nov. 16, 1905, sec. 1, 1:1–5, Booker T. Washington special edition; West, *Muskogee*, 109.

26. *Cimeter*, Nov. 23, 1905, LT; BTWP 1:265–67, 8:449, 471–74, 9:430–35; *Muskogee Pioneer*, Dec. 2, 1905, 2:2. Taskigi, or Tuskegee, was originally one of the white, or peace, towns in the old Creek Nation associated with the Alabama Indians, who were drawn into the Creek political and cultural web in the early 1700s. The town was reestablished after the removal in the hinterlands northwest of Okmulgee. Silas Jefferson served as town chief there for many years and was also elected to the House of Warriors from Taskigi. Some Creeks refused to recognize Taskigi as an "Indian" town because of the predominant African Creek influence there.

27. BTWP 8:486, 501–502, 9:431.

28. *Cimeter*, Nov. 2, 1905, Nov. 9, 1905, Nov. 23, 1905, LT; *Muskogee Pioneer*, Dec. 2, 1905, 2:2; *Muskogee Times-Democrat*, Nov. 19, 1905, 1:6; *Daily Oklahoman*, Nov., 21, 1905, Sec. 2, 8:4. Washington refused to comment on political matters in public, but as Louis Harlan and others have pointed out, he was busy behind the scenes arranging political matters with Roosevelt and other leading Republican politicians.

The B. T. Washington and Roosevelt Papers are full of letters and notes between Washington and Roosevelt concerning political matters, but unfortunately I could find no direct reference to the Quay amendment.

29. Chief Pleasant Porter's Message to Creek Council, Mar. 8, 1906, file 300, box 5, and file 315, box 3, Porter Papers, WHC.

30. *Cimeter*, Jan. 7, 1905, LT; *Tahlequah Arrow*, Apr. 12, 1902, 2:4–5; Chief Porter's Message on Protecting Allotments and Schools, Oct. 4, 1905, file 266, box 4, Porter Papers, WHC; *Cimeter*, July 21, 1904, 6:1; Nov. 9, 1905, 6:2–3; Samuel Tucker to Secretary of the Interior, Mar. 20, 1907, 17287, file 13, box 3, Misc., LR, FCTR, OIA, RG75, NAFW; C. F. Larrabee to Neal Trotter, July 17, 1907, 1907-60723, LR, 1881–1907, OIA, RG75, NA; Agnes Cyrus to E. A. Hitchcock, July 25, 1906, roll 72, DC.

31. Violet Crain to Secretary, May 5, 1906, roll 72, DC. Crain is also quoted in McReynolds, *The Seminoles*, 345–46.

32. Porter to Bradley Real Estate Company, July 7, 1903; Porter to Mott, Apr. 13, 1905, LS, 1900–1907 FCTR, OIA, RG75, NAFW; *Muskogee Pioneer*, Nov. 11, 1905, 2:1–2.

33. *Territorial Enterprise*, Oct. 20, 1905, 2:2–3; *School Superintendent I. T.* (1899), 212–13; (1900), 154–56, 160–61; *Creek Supervisor for Education* (1900), 161–65, both reports in Annual Reports, RG48, NA. Apparently, Benedict was more concerned with his real-estate investments than with looking after the schools.

34. G. Foreman, "The Hon. Alice M. Robertson," 14–15. Alice Mary Robertson, *Biographical Directory of the United States Congress*: http://bioguide.congress.gove/scripts/biodisplay.pl?index=R000318; Robertson began her teaching career in early childhood at Tullahassee. Between 1871 and 1873, she attended Elmira College in New York. She then spent seven years as the first woman clerk at the Office of Indian Affairs in Washington from 1873–1880. From 1880–1882 she was the private secretary to R. H. Pratt at the Carlisle Indian School in Pennsylvania. She returned to teach at Tullahassee after the mission was turned over to the African Creeks and helped found Nuyuka Mission School in 1883 (another Creek Indian boarding school) with her sister Ann Augusta. She then taught for several more years at a Creek school in Okmulgee before the Presbyterian Mission Board asked her to superintend a boarding school for young women of the Five Tribes in Muskogee in 1885, which later became Henry Kendall College, then, after moving to Tulsa, the University of Tulsa. While the Robertsons were dedicated Presbyterian missionaries, unlike some of those involved in Indian education during the period, they did not work to extinguish Indian identity. In fact, they encouraged pride in Creek heritage, collected tribal stories and songs, and recorded traditional ceremonies. They also endorsed teaching beginning students in the Creek language until they became proficient in English. From the Robertson missionary correspondence, one gets the impression that they were probably more concerned about their charges becoming Baptists than they were about them reverting to paganism through attending a poskita ceremony.

35. Phillip Lewis interview, IPH 61:277–78; BTWP 6:27–28; *Creek Supervisor for Education* (1903), 260.

36. BTWP 6:28.

37. *Creek Supervisor for Education* (1901), 307–308.

38. Ibid. (1903), 259–60; (1901), 307–308; (1904), 278–79; *Annual Reports* (1900–1901) 2:2306–2307, 2310–12.

39. *Creek Supervisor for Education* (1905), 752–53; (1906), 161–62; (1907), 184; *School Superintendent I. T.* (1905), 745–46; (1907), 350–53.

40. (Muskogee) *Cimeter,* Feb. 1, 1906; Feb. 22, 1906; Mar. 8, 1906; Apr. 5, 1906; Apr. 26, 1806; Sept. 13, 1906; Sept. 27, 1906, LT.

41. Goble, *Progressive Oklahoma,* 142–43, 219, 230; *Daily Oklahoman,* Oct. 27, 1906, 3:3–4; Wickett, *Contested Territory,* 182–83, 191–200; *Guthrie Daily Leader,* Nov. 28, 1906, 6:1, transcribed in Blacks, FWP, OHS.

42. Wickett, *Contested Territory,* 196.

43. Goble, *Progressive Oklahoma,* 219–20; African Creek informant Robert L. Littlejohn recounted a case from the 1920s when a student was refused admittance to a Tulsa school because of suspected African descent. The student was later admitted after the parents threatened to expose some of the Perryman family's African descent in open court.

44. *Cimeter,* Sept. 27, 1907, 1:1–3; *MP,* Oct. 3, 1907, 1:1–3; *Cimeter* Aug. 23, 1907, Aug. 30, 1907, Sept. 20, 1907, Nov. 1, 1907, Nov. 8, 1907, LT; Wickett, *Contested Territory,* 195 (Roosevelt quote); Bateman, "'We're Still Here,'" 136. Roosevelt felt the constitution was the work of wild-eyed radicals, socialists, anarchists, and worse because of its strong anticorporation and proconsumer provisions.

45. *Muskogee Times Democrat,* Dec. 3, 1907, 8:4; Jan. 8, 1908, 8:3; Feb. 15, 1908, 1:2; Feb. 18, 1908, 6:3; Feb. 22, 1908, 8:2–3; Wickett, *Contested Territory,* 197–98; *Cimeter* Jan. 17, 1908, Jan. 24, 1908, May 15, 1908, Sept. 25, 1908, LT; *Indian Chieftan,* Feb. 3, 1911, 6:3; Nov. 22, 1912, 1:4.

46. *Cimeter,* July 31, 1908; Sept. 18, 1908; Nov. 8, 1908; Jan. 15, 1909; Jan. 29, 1909, LT; *Daily Oklahoman,* Sept. 4, 1910, 11; Goble, *Progressive Oklahoma,* 257 n. 31; Wickett, *Contested Territory,* 199–201; Lawson, *Black Ballots,* 17–19. The *Guinn v. United States* case originated in Oklahoma, but as Lawson points out, African American Oklahomans were "franchised" for only a brief time before the Oklahoma legislature enacted an even more byzantine statute, which was not challenged and overturned until 1939.

47. S. Rep. 5013.

48. Debo, *Waters,* 142–43; S. Rep. 5013, 1245–55, 1258–59 (Chitto Hacho), 650–72 (Bradley statement), 1263–83, (M. L. Mott), 431–35(Creek Council), 437–39 (Ellis-Chiders); Debo, *Waters,* 145 (Murrow quote); HR 15641 Hearings, 162–65 (Creek Memorial), 10–12.

49. HR 15641 Hearings, 162–65; Debo, *Waters,* 179–80.

50. HR 15641 Hearings, 54–55.

51. Debo, *Waters*, 179–80; Gibson, "The Centennial Legacy," 246; Mott, *A National Blunder*, 2–3, box 109, RG46, NA.; *Five Tribes Commissioner Report* (1908), 192; Annual Report (1908), 349–50, RG48, NA.

52. *Oklahoma News*, Aug. 20, 1908, 1:1, transcribed in Blacks, FWP, OHS; *Oklahoma Guide*, July 28 1908, 1:1–2; Sameth, "Creek Negroes," 92.

53. *Cimeter*, May 29, 1908, 1:1; West, *Muskogee*, 137; *Tulsa Daily World*, July 28, 1908, 1:2; Debo, *Waters*, 200–201, 232–35.

54. Debo, *Waters*, 182–83; Morehead, *Our National Problem*, 5–6; *Lake Mohonk Conference*, 1912, 246–47; 1913, 44; 1915, 177–83; "Agriculture" 5(1): 79, U.S. Census Bureau, RG29, NA; "Historical Census Data," Geospatial and Statistical Data Center, University of Virginia, Fisher Library, http:///fisher.lib.virginia.edu/collections/stats/histcensus/php/county.php. In contrast, of the white farmers in the Creek country in 1900, 90 percent were sharecroppers or tenants. By 1910, 54 percent of farm owners in the former Creek Nation (Creek, Hughes, McIntosh, Muskogee, Okfuskee, Okmulgee, Tulsa, and Wagoner counties) were white. In 1920 the number had grown to 69 percent. The figures in the published census reports for 1900 are for Negro and other nonwhite farmers and do not distinguish between African Creeks and state freed people. African Creek farm ownership would no doubt be closer to 90 percent.

55. *Creek Supervisor for Education* (1909), 455–56; *Five Tribes Commissioner Report* (1911), 464–65; *School Superintendent I. T.* (1908), 109; (1909), 115; *Daily Oklahoman*, Feb. 10, 1907, 3:2; Pecan Creek Mission, Tullahassee, Colored Orphan's Home, file 3, box 2, Blacks, FWP, OHS; Pecan Creek School, docs. 36793–94, 36798, CRN 46.

56. Bateman, " 'We're Still Here,' " 177.

57. Sameth, "Creek Negroes," 62.

Bibliography

Manuscripts

American Colonization Society Collection. Library of Congress, Washington, D.C.

American Baptist Foreign Mission Society Records, 1817–1959. "Missionary Correspondence." In Correspondence, 1800–1900, American Indian Baptist Missions. Valley Forge, Pa.: American Baptist Historical Society Microfilm Publication, 1966.

> Lee Compere letters, 1826–1828, and journal entries, December 1826–November 1828
> Charles R. Kellum letters, 1836–1842, and journal entries, February 1836–November 1839
> David Lewis letters, 1832–1836

American Missionary Society Papers. Amistad Research Center, Tulane University, New Orleans.

Bonds, Margaret. "Five Creek Freedmen Spirituals." Introductory notes by Hortense Love. Manuscript and score. American Music Research Center. University of Colorado at Boulder.

Creek Indian Memorial Association Archives. Okmulgee: Oklahoma Historical Society Microfilm Publication, 1980. Creek Council House Museum.

> Council Minutes of the Creek Nation West, 1831–1835
> Index of Creek Land Transactions, 1833–1876
> Letter Book of Principal Chief Samuel Checote, 1882–1883
> Minute Book of the Joint Committee on Education, 1874–1881

Crowell, John. Journal. Alabama Department of Archives and History, Montgomery.

Debo, Angie. Papers. Special Collections. Oklahoma State University Library, Stillwater. Oklahoma State University Library Microfilm Publication, 1996.

Ellithorpe, A. C. Diary. General Sweeney's: A Museum of Civil War History, Republic, Missouri.

Furnas, Robert W., Papers. Archives and Manuscripts Division. Lincoln: Nebraska Historical Society Microfilm Publication, 1951.

Garrett, John B., Papers. The Quaker Collection. Haverford College Library, Haverford, Pennsylvania.

George, David Lloyd. "An Account of the Life of Mr. David George." Black Loyalists, n.d. http://collections.ic.gc.ca/blackloyalists/documents/diaries/george_a_life.htm.

Gilcrease, Thomas, Institute of American Art and History. Manuscripts Division. Tulsa, Oklahoma.

    Gilcrease-Hargrett Collection

    John Drew Collection

    Grant Foreman Collection

    Freedmen's Baptist Association Minutes, 1877–1878, 1886

    Hall-Pennant Document, 1775

    Tullahassee Manual Labor School, "Catalogue," 1889

Jones, William Frank. "The Experience of a Deputy United States Marshall of the Indian Territory." S.l.: n.p., 1937.

Kansas State Historical Society, Manuscript Collections, Topeka.

    Ellithorpe Family Papers

    Isaac McCoy Papers

    Military History Collection

    Benjamin Van Horne manuscript

Knapp, Seaman. Papers. Southwest Collection. Special Collections Library. Texas Tech University, Lubbock.

Littlefield, Daniel F., Jr. Research Files. Creek Freedmen. Native American Press Archives. University of Arkansas, Little Rock.

Oklahoma Historical Society. Archives and Manuscripts Division. Oklahoma City.

    Creek Nation Records

    Dawes Commission Records—Creek

    Federal Works Project Papers

    Grant Foreman Collection

    James R. Gregory Papers

    Q. L. Littlejohn Papers

    Augusta Robertson Moore Collection

    Alice Robertson Collection

Robertson, Alice. Collection. Special Collections. McFarlin Library, University of Tulsa, Oklahoma.

Roosevelt, Theodore. Papers. Washington, D.C.: Library of Congress Microfilm Publication.

Washington, Booker T. Papers. 13 vols. Louis R. Harlan, ed. Champaign and Urbana: University of Illinois Press, 1972–1984. Online publication at University of Illinois, The History Cooperative, http://www.historycooperative.org/btw/index.html.

Western History Collection. University of Oklahoma Library, Norman.

    Roscoe Simmons Cate Papers

    Samuel Checote Papers

Creek Nation Collection
Doris Duke Indian Oral History Collection
Alan W. Farley Papers
Foreman Transcripts
Grayson Family Papers
Isparhecher Papers
Mary Ann Lilley autobiography
Pleasant Porter Papers
James Ross Ramsey Papers
Sac and Fox Collection
James Andrew Slover Collection
Moty Tiger Collection

Government Documents

National Archives, Washington D.C.
Record Group 29. Records of the Bureau of the Census.
"Agriculture." *Manuscript Schedules of the Twelfth Census of the United States: 1900.* Microfilm publication T623, rolls 1853–54.
"Creek Nation, Indian Territory." *Manuscript Schedules of the Twelfth Census of the United States: 1900.* Microfilm publication T623, rolls 1853–54.
Eighth Census of the U.S.: 1860. Microfilm publication M653, roll 54.
"Five Civilized Tribes in the Indian Territory." *Eleventh Census of the United States: 1890.* Washington, D.C.: GPO, 1890.
Loughridge, R. H. "Report on Cotton Production in the Indian Territory." *Census Reports, Tenth Census,* vol. 5. Washington, D.C.: GPO, 1884.
"Non-Citizens, Creek Nation." Arkansas and Indian Lands. *Population Schedules of the Eighth Census of the U.S.: 1860.* Microfilm publication M653, roll 52.
"Oklahoma." *Manuscript Schedules of the Thirteenth Census of the United States: 1910.* Microfilm publication T624, rolls 1244, 1246, 1254–55, 1260, 1263–65, 1267, 1274–75, 1277.
"Population: Part I." *Manuscript Schedules of the Twelfth Census of the United States: 1900.* Microfilm publication T623, rolls 1853–54.
"Slave Schedules, Creek Nation." Arkansas and Indian Lands. *Population Schedules of the Eighth Census of the U.S.: 1860.* Microfilm publication M653, roll 52.
Record Group 46. Records of the United States Senate, Committee on Interior and Insular Affairs.
Oklahoma—Five Civilized Tribes
Record Group 48. Records of the Office of the Secretary of the Interior.
Annual Reports of the Secretary of the Interior. 1845–1909.

Letters Received by the Indian Division of the Office of the Secretary of the Interior. 1849–1880. National Archives Microfilm Publication M825. Rolls 1, 24.

Record Group 75. Office of Indian Affairs.

Creek Freedmen and Newborns. Applications for Enrollment to the Commissioner of the Five Civilized Tribes: 1898–1914. M1301. Roll 422.

Documents Relating to the Negotiations of Ratified and Unratified Treaties with the Various Tribes of Indians, 1801–1869. T494.

Enrollment Cards for the Five Civilized Tribes: Creek Freedmen. M1186. Rolls 85–91.

Letters Received by the Office of Indian Affairs: 1824–1880. M234.

Creek Agency. Rolls 230–35.

Sac and Fox Agency. Roll 735.

Seminole Agency. Roll 803.

Southern Superintendency. Rolls 833–39.

Union Agency. Rolls 865–75.

Western Superintendency. Roll 923.

Letters Received by the Office of Indian Affairs: 1881– 1907.

Letters Received Relating to Choctaw and Other Freedmen: 1878–1884.

Letters Sent by the Office of Indian Affairs: 1824–1880. M21. Rolls 92, 94, 96, 98, 100, 102–103, 106, 108, 110, 112, 114, 116, 118, 120, 122.

Records Relating to the Loyal Creek Claims.

Report of the Commissioner to the Five Civilized Tribes: 1893/4–1919/20. Washington, D.C.: GPO, 1894–1920.

Special Files: 1807–1904. M574.

File 87. Claims of the Loyal Seminole for Losses Suffered During the Civil War. Roll 11.

File 201. Loyalty of the Indians in the Southern Superintendency and Assistance to Refugee Indians. Roll 59.

File 207. Creek Claims for Property Left in the East and Lost During Removal, 1827–1838. Roll 61.

File 284. Claim of the Creek Nation for Reimbursement of Money Paid to Non-Creek Freedmen, 1868–88. Roll 76.

Record Group 94, Records of the Office of the Adjutant General.

First Indian Home Guard:

Muster Rolls

Regimental Descriptive Book

Regimental Order and Letter Book

Volunteer Service Files

Pension Records

Record Group 105. Records of the Bureau of Refugees, Freedmen and Abandoned Lands.

Registers and Letters Received by the Commissioner of the Bureau of Refugees. Freedmen and Abandoned Lands: 1865–1872. M752. Rolls 22, 53.
Record Group 153. Records of the Army Judge Advocate.
Court-Martial Case Files
Record Group 393. Records of U.S. Army Continental Commands.
    Army of the Frontier
    Department of Arkansas
    Department of Kansas
    Department of Missouri
    Indian Expedition to South Kansas-1862
    Post of Fort Gibson and Fort Blunt, Creek Nation, 1863–1865
    Letters and Orders Received and Sent, Rosters and Other Records, 1863–1865, Indian Brigade, Department of Arkansas
    Register Letters Received, February 1864–May 1865, Headquarters Indian Brigade, vol. 92/284, Department of Arkansas
    Provost Marshall's Field Organizations: Arkansas, Kansas, Missouri.
    Recruitment in Volunteer Organizations: District of South Kansas.

National Archives, Fort Worth, Texas
Record Group 75. Records of the Office of Indian Affairs.
    Dunn Roll, Creek Freedmen and Index, 1869. 7RA-44.
    List of Applicants and Docket Books of the Creek Citizenship Commission, 1888–1896. 7RA68, Rolls 1–2.
    Records of the Commissioner to the Five Civilized Tribes
    Allotment Contest Records
    Applications for Enrollment
    Records Relating to Creek Citizenship
    Records Relating to Creek Allotments
    Allotment Jackets
    Reference Documents
Records of the Five Civilized Tribes Agency
    1896 Colbert Roll.
    Citizenship Contest Cases heard in the United States Court in the Indian Territory, Northern District at Muskogee.
    Letters Received, Indian Inspector.
    Letters Sent by the Chief of the Creek Nation: 1873–1878, 1897–1899, 1900–1907
Records Relating to the Sale of Allotted Land.
    Sales Under the Act of April 21, 1904
    Sales Under the Act of May 27, 1908

United States Congress

House. *Commissioner of Indian Affairs Report.* 37th Cong., 3rd sess., 1862. H. Doc. 1.
——. *Commissioner of Indian Affairs Report.* 38th Cong., 1st sess., 1863. H. Doc. 1.
——. *Commissioner of Indian Affairs Report.* 38th Cong., 1st sess., 1864. H. Doc. 1.
——. *Commissioner of Indian Affairs Report.* 39th Cong., 1st sess., 1865. H. Doc. 1.
——. *Commissioner of Indian Affairs Report.* 39th Cong., 2nd sess., 1866. H. Doc. 1.
——. *Commissioner of Indian Affairs Report.* 42nd Cong., 3rd sess., 1872. H. Doc. 1.
——. *Commissioner of Indian Affairs Report.* 43rd Cong., 1st sess., 1873. H. Doc. 1.
——. *Commissioner of Indian Affairs Report.* 51st Cong., 1st sess., 1889. H. Doc. 1.
——. *Complicity of William P. Ross in Alleged Bounty Frauds of John W. Wright.* 44th Cong., 1st sess., 1876. H. Doc. 132, serial 1689.
——. *Education of White and Negro Children in the Indian Territory.* 55th Cong., 2nd sess., 1898. H. Doc. 310, serial 3679.
——. *For the Protection of the People of the Indian Territory.* 55th Cong., 2nd Sess., 1898. H. Rep. 593, serial 3719.
——. *Hearings Before the Committee On Indian Affairs on HR 15641: Removal of Restrictions on Indian Lands in Oklahoma.* 60th Cong., 1st sess. Washington, D.C.: GPO, 1908.
——. *To Ratify Proposed Agreement Between Dawes Commission and Creek Indians.* 56th Cong., 1st sess., 1900. H. Rep. 1762, serial 4027.
——. *Removal of Restrictions from Part of the Lands of the Five Civilized Tribes.* 60th Cong., 1st sess., 1908. H. Rep. 1454, serial 5226.
——. *Report on Alleged Frauds in Bounty and Back Pay for Certain Indian Soldiers in the Indian Territory.* 42nd Cong., 2nd sess., 1872. H. Rep. 96, serial 1543.
——. *To Ratify Proposed Agreement Between Dawes Commission and Creek Indians.* 56th Cong., 1st sess., 1900. H. Rep. 1762, serial 4027.
——. *To Ratify Proposed Agreement Between Dawes Commission and Creek Indians.* 57th Cong., 1st sess., 1902. H. Rep. 2495, serial 4407.
Senate. *Conditions of the Indians and Freedmen in the Indian Territory.* 49th Cong., 2nd sess., 1887. S. Rep. 1278, serial 2363.
——. *Lands Available in the Indian Territory for Settlement by Colored People.* 47th Cong., 2nd sess., 1882. S. Doc. 117, serial 1996.
——. *Leasing and Selling Lands by Creek Indians in the Indian Territory.* 57th Cong., 1st sess., 1902. S. Doc. 226, serial 4235.
——. *Memorial Against Bill to Ratify the Creek Agreement.* 56th Cong., 1st sess., 1900. S. Doc. 443, serial 3878.
——. *Memorial and Petitions for the Removal of Restrictions on the Sale of Surplus Allotments in the Indian Territory.* 58th Cong., 2nd sess., 1904. S. Doc. 169, serial 4590.
——. *Investigation of Alleged Abuses of Interior Dept. Officials in the Indian Territory.* [Report of Charles Bonaparte.] 58th Cong., 2nd sess., 1904. S. Doc. 189, serial 4491.
——. *Report of the Senate Select Committee to Investigate Affairs in the Indian Terri-*

tory, Nov. 11, 1906–Jan. 9, 1907. 59th Cong., 2nd sess., 1907 S. Rep. 5013, serials 5062–63.

——. *Senate Committee on the Territories Investigation into Sentiments in the Indian Territory Regarding Establishment of a Territorial Government, etc.* 45th Cong., 3rd sess., 1879. S. Rep. 744, Serial 1889.

Published Primary Sources

African Methodist Episcopal Church. *The Budget, 1881–1884.* Philadelphia: A.M.E, 1885. Special Collections. Newton Grisham Library, Sam Houston State University, Huntsville.

Beadle, J. H. *The Undeveloped West.* 1873. Reprint, New York: Arno Press, 1973.

Bibb, Henry. *Narrative of the Life and Adventures of Henry Bibb, an American Slave, Written by Himself.* 1850. Reprint, Miami, Fla.: Mnemosyne, 1969.

de Biedma, Luys Hernandez. "Relation of the Island of Florida." Ed. and trans. John E. Worth. In *The De Soto Chronicles: The Expedition of Hernando de Soto to North America in 1539–1543*, vol. 1, ed. Lawrence A. Clayton, Vernon James Knight, Jr., and Edward C. Moore, 221–46. Tuscaloosa: University of Alabama Press, 1993.

Blunt, James G. *Report of James G. Blunt Relative to Alleged Frauds on Payments of Pensions Bounties and Back Pay.* Washington: Gibson Brothers Printers, 1869. Gilcrease-Hargrett Collection, Manuscripts Division, GIAAH.

Britton, Wiley. *The Civil War on the Border.* 2 vols. 1899. Reprint, Ottawa: Kansas Heritage Press, 1994.

——. *Memoirs of the Rebellion on the Border.* Lincoln: University of Nebraska Press, 1993.

——. *The Union Indian Brigade in the Civil War.* 1922. Reprint, Ottawa: Kansas Heritage Press, 1994.

Capers, William. *Report Before the Bishops and South Carolina Conference of the Methodist Episcopal Church: Feb. 21, 1822.* Georgetown: Wiayan Intelligencer, 1822. Gilcrease-Hargrett Collection, Manuscripts Division, GIAAH.

——. *Second Annual Report of the Missionary Commission of the South Carolina Conference: Feb. 26, 1823.* Midgeville, Ga.: Grantland and Orme, 1823. Gilcrease-Hargrett Collection, Manuscripts Division, GIAAH.

Carroll, Bartholomew R., ed. *Historical Collections of South Carolina.* Vol. 2. New York: Harper and Bros., 1836.

The Christian Index. *History of the Baptist Denomination in Georgia.* Atlanta: James P. Harrison, 1881.

Clayton, Lawrence A., Vernon James Knight, Jr., and Edward C. Moore, eds. *The De Soto Chronicles: The Expedition of Hernando de Soto to North America in 1539–1543.* 2 vols. Tuscaloosa: University of Alabama Press, 1996.

Fisk, Clinton, and E. Whittlesey. *Peace Ratified in the Creek Nation.* Washington: GPO, 1883.

Gazetteer and Business Directory of the Indian Territory: 1901. Buffalo, N.Y.: McMaster, 1901.

Grause, Isaac. *Four Years with Five Armies, the Army of the Frontier, the Army of the Potomac, the Army of the Ohio, and the Army of the Shenandoah*. New York: Neale, 1908.

Hawkins, Benjamin. *Letters of Benjamin Hawkins, 1796–1806*. Collections of the Georgia Historical Society, vol. 9. Savannah: The Morning News, 1916.

Hitchcock, Ethan Allan. *A Traveler in Indian Territory*. Ed. Grant Foreman. Cedar Rapids, Iowa: Torch Press, 1930.

Journal of the General Council of the Indian Territory. 1870. Lawrence Kans.: Excelsior Printing, 1871. Manuscripts Division. Thomas Gilcrease Institute of American Art and History. Tulsa, Oklahoma.

Kansas Adjutant General. *Regimental Papers, First and Second Kansas Colored*. Topeka: KSHS Microfilm Publication, 1967.

King, Edward. *The Great South: A Record of Journeys in Louisiana, Texas, Indian Territory, Missouri, Arkansas, Mississippi, Florida, North Carolina, South Carolina, Alabama, Georgia, Kentucky, Tennessee, Virginia, West Virginia and Maryland*. Hartford, Conn.: American Publishing, 1875. Electronic edition at Documenting the American South, University of North Carolina at Chapel Hill Libraries, http://docsouth.unc.edu/nc/king/menu.html.

Kitts, John Howard. "The Civil War Diary of John Howard Kitts." In *Kansas State Historical Collections*, vol. 14, 318–332. Topeka: KSHS, 1918.

Lake Mohonk Conference on the Negro Proceedings: 1890–1891. Boston: G.H. Ellis, 1890–1891. Reprint edited by I. G. Barrows. New York: Negro Universities Press, 1969.

Lake Mohonk Conference Proceedings, 1883–1929. Microfiche. New York: Clearwater Publishing, 1974.

Lyon, Eugene, ed. "The Cañete Fragment: Another Narrative of Hernando de Soto." In *The De Soto Chronicles: The Expedition of Hernando de Soto to North America in 1539–1543*, vol. 1, ed. Lawrence A. Clayton, Vernon James Knight, Jr., and Edward C. Moore, 307–310. Tuscaloosa: University of Alabama Press, 1993.

Manning, Edwin C. *Biographical, Historical and Miscellaneous Selections*. Cedar Rapids, Iowa: n.p., 1911.

Mayo, A. D. "The Work of Certain Northern Churches in the Education of Freedmen." In *Report of the Commissioner of Education 1900–1901*, vol. 1., 285–307. Washington, D.C.: GPO, 1903.

McAdam, Rezin W. "An Indian Commonwealth." *Harper's New Monthly Magazine* 87, no. 522 (November, 1893): 884–98.

McCoy, Isaac. *Periodical Account of the Baptist Missions Within the Indian Territory*. Shawnee Mission: Isaac McCoy, 1836. Special Collections. Mullins Library. University of Arkansas-Fayetteville.

——. *Annual Register of Indian Affairs Within the Indian Territory*. Shawnee Mission: Isaac McCoy, 1835–1838. In *Western Americana: History of the Trans-*

Mississippi West: 1500–1900, microfilm ed., reel 12. New Haven, Conn.: Research Pub., 1975.

McDowell, William L., Jr., ed. *Documents Relating to Indian Affairs.* Vol. 2. Columbia, S.C.: Archives Department, 1958.

Morehead, Warren. *Our National Problem: The Sad Condition of Oklahoma's Indians.* 1913. Reprint, Indian Rights Association Papers, Historical Society of Pennsylvania Microfilm Publication. Wilmington, Del.: Scholarly Resources, 1974.

Payne, Daniel Alexander. *History of the African Methodist Episcopal Church.* Nashville, Tenn.: A.M.E. Sunday School Union, 1891.

Peterson, Burkhard, and Johann Christian Karsten. *Partners in the Lord's Work: The Diary of Two Moravian Missionaries in the Creek Indian Country, 1807–1813.* Research Paper 21, trans. and ed. C. Mauelshagen and G. H. Davis. Atlanta: Georgia State College, 1969.

Pope, John A. *A Tour Through the Southern and Western Territories of the United States of North America: the Spanish Dominions, on the River Mississippi and the Floridas; the Countries of the Creek Nation and Many Other Uninhabited Parts.* 1791. Reprint, New York: Charles L. Woodward, 1888.

Proceeding of the Fifth General Council of the Indian Territory, 1875. Muskogee: Indian Journal, 1876. Manuscripts Division, GIAAH.

Proceedings of the Eighth Annual Meeting of the American Indian Mission Association. Louisville: Hulls and Shannon, 1851. Manuscripts Division, GIAAH.

Proceedings of the Fifth Annual Meeting of the American Indian Mission Association. Louisville: Monsaratt, 1847. Manuscripts Division, GIAAH.

Proceedings of the First Annual Meeting of the American Indian Mission Association. Louisville: Buck's Steam Power Press, 1843. Manuscripts Division, GIAAH.

Proceedings of the Fourth Annual Meeting of the American Indian Mission Association. Louisville: Monsaratt, 1846. Manuscripts Division, GIAAH.

Proceedings of the Second Annual Meeting of the American Indian Mission Association. Louisville: Buck's Steam Power Press, 1844. Manuscripts Division, GIAAH.

Proceedings of the Semi-Annual Meeting of the American Indian Mission Association. Louisville: Monsaratt's Steam Power Press, 1845. Manuscripts Division, GIAAH.

Proceedings of the Seventh Annual Meeting of the American Indian Mission Association. Louisville: Hull and Brother, 1849. Manuscripts Division, GIAAH.

Proceedings of the Sixth Annual Meeting of the American Indian Mission Association. Louisville: The Baptist Banner, 1848. Manuscripts Division, GIAAH

Proceedings of the Third Annual Meeting of the American Indian Mission Association. Louisville: Monsaratt's Steam Power Press, 1845. Manuscripts Division, GIAAH.

Rangel, Rodrigo. "Account of the Northern Conquest and Discovery of Hernando De Soto." Ed. and trans. John E. Worth. In *The De Soto Chronicles: The Expedition of Hernando de Soto to North America in 1539–1543*, vol. 1, ed. Lawrence A. Clayton, Vernon James Knight, Jr., and Edward C. Moore, 247–306. Tuscaloosa: University of Alabama Press, 1993.

Robertson, James Alexander, ed. and trans. "The Account by a Gentleman From Elvas." Notes by John H. Hahn. In *The De Soto Chronicles: The Expedition of Hernando de Soto to North America in 1539–1543*, vol. 1, ed. Lawrence A. Clayton, Vernon James Knight, Jr., and Edward C. Moore, 19–220. Tuscaloosa: University of Alabama Press, 1993.

"Second Annual Report of the Board of Indian Commissioners, 1870." *Chronicles of Oklahoma* 5, no. 1 (March 1927): 89–91.

Sparks, A. W. *The War Between the States As I Saw It: Reminiscent, Historical, and Personal.* Tyler, Tex.: Lee and Burnet, 1901.

Stanton, F. P. *Argument of F. P. Stanton on the Indian Frauds of Judge J. W. Wright.* Washington: McGill and Witherow, 1872. Manuscripts Division, Minnesota Historical Society, Minneapolis.

Stiggins, George. *Creek Indian History: A Historical Narrative of the Genealogy, Traditions, and Downfall of the Ispocoga or Creek Indians.* Introduction and notes by William Stokes Wyman; edited by Virginia Pounds Brown. Birmingham: Birmingham Public Library Press, 1989.

Tenney, Harris Luman. *War Diary of Harris Luman Tenney.* Cleveland: Evangelical Pub., 1914.

United States Department of Education. *Report of the Commissioner of Education, 1902.* 2 vols. Washington, D.C.: GPO, 1903.

United States Department of War. *The War of the Rebellion: A Compilation of the Official Records of the Union and Confederate Armies.* 70 vols. Washington, D.C.: GOP, 1880–1901.

de la Vega, Garcilaso. "Florida of the Inca." Trans. Charmion Shelby, ed. David Bost, with notes by Vernon James Knight, Jr. In *The De Soto Chronicles: The Expedition of Hernando de Soto to North America in 1539–1543*, vol. 2, ed. Lawrence A. Clayton, Vernon James Knight, Jr., and Edward C. Moore, 25-560. Tuscaloosa: University of Alabama Press, 1993.

Wright, John W. *Reply of John W. Wright to Certain Libelous Statements Published in the New York Tribune and in a Certain Pamphlet signed by James G. Blunt.* Washington: H. Polkinhorn and Co., 1869. In *Pamphlets in American History: Indians*, microfilm publication I 778. Glen Rock, N.J.: State Historical Society of Wisconsin, 1978.

Secondary Sources

Abel, Annie Heloise. *The American Indian as Slaveholder and Secessionist.* Lincoln: University of Nebraska Press, 1992.

——. *The American Indian and the End of the Confederacy: 1863–1865.* Lincoln: University of Nebraska Press, 1992.

——. *The American Indian in the Civil War: 1862–1865.* Lincoln: University of Nebraska Press, 1992.

Akers, Donna L. *Living in the Land of Death: The Choctaw Nation, 1830–1860.* East Lansing: Michigan State University Press, 2004.

Anderson, James D. *The Education of Blacks in the South: 1860–1935.* Chapel Hill: University of North Carolina Press, 1988.

Anderson, James G. "The Fluctuations Between Simple and Complex Chiefdoms: Cycling in the Late Prehistoric Southeast." In *Political Structure and Change in the Prehistoric Southeastern United States.* Ed. J. F. Scarry, 231–52. Gainesville: University Press of Florida, 1996.

Andrews, Thomas F. "Freedmen in the Indian Territory: A Post–Civil War Dilemma." *Journal of the West* 4, no. 3 (July 1965): 367–76.

Athearn, Robert. *In Search of Canaan: Black Migration to Kansas, 1879–80.* Lawrence: Regents Press of Kansas, 1978.

Bailey, M. Thomas. *Reconstruction in the Indian Territory: A Story of Avarice, Discrimination and Opportunism.* Port Washington, N.Y.: Kennikut Press, 1972.

Baker, T. Lindsay, and Julie Baker. *The WPA Oklahoma Slave Narratives.* Norman: University of Oklahoma Press, 1996.

Banasik, Michael E. *Embattled Arkansas: The Prairie Grove Campaign of 1862.* Wilmington, N.C.: Broadfoot Publishing, 1996.

Bartram, William. *Travels of William Bartram.* Ed. Mark Van Doren. 1928. Reprint, New York: Dover Publications, 1955.

Bass, Althea. *The Story of Tullahassee.* Oklahoma City: Semco Color Press, 1960.

Bateman, Rebecca Belle. " 'We're Still Here:' History, Kinship and Group Identity Among the Seminole Freedmen of Oklahoma." Ph.D. diss., The Johns Hopkins University, 1991.

Baxley, Steve. "Democracy, Equality, Justice: A New Deal, Let the People Rule." http://members.cts.com/crash/b/baxley/okie.html (accessed March 15, 2002).

Beard, Charles. "The Constitution of Oklahoma." *Political Science Quarterly* 24, no. 2 (March 1909): 95–114.

Bearss, Edwin C. "The Civil War Comes to Indian Territory, 1861: The Flight of Opothleyoholo." *Journal of the West* 11, no. 1 (Spring 1972): 9–42.

Berens John F. "Old Campaigners, New Realities: Indian Policy Reform during the Progressive Era, 1900–1912." *Mid-America* 59 (January 1977): 53–55.

Berlin, Ira. *Slaves Without Masters: The Free Negro in the Antebellum South.* New York: The New Press, 1974.

Billington, Monroe. "Black Slavery in the Indian Territory." *Chronicles of Oklahoma* 40, no. 1 (Spring 1982): 56–65.

Bourne, Edward Gaylord, ed. *Narrative of the Career of Hernando de Soto in the Conquest of Florida.* 2 vols. New York: Allerton Book, 1922

Braund, Kathryn E. Holland. "The Creek Indians, Blacks and Slavery." *Journal of Southern History* 57, no. 4 (November 1991): 601–36.

——. *Deerskins and Duffels: The Creek Indian Trade with Anglo-America, 1685–1815.* Lincoln: University of Nebraska Press, 1993.

Brooks, James F. *Captives and Cousins: Slavery, Kinship, and Community in the Southwest Borderlands*. Chapel Hill: University of North Carolina Press, 2002.

———, ed. *Confounding the Color Line: The Indian-Black Experience in North America*. Lincoln: University of Nebraska Press, 2002.

Brooks, Walter H. *The Silver Bluff Church: A History of Negro Baptist Churches in America*. Washington, D.C.: R. C. Pendleton Press, 1910. Electronic edition, University of North Carolina at Chapel Hill Libraries, Documenting the American South, http://docsouth.unc.edu/church/brooks/brooks.htm.

Bullock, Henry Allen. *A History of Negro Education in the South from 1619 to the Present*. Cambridge: Harvard University Press, 1967.

Carter, Kent. *The Dawes Commission and the Allotment of the Five Civilized Tribes, 1893–1914*. Salt Lake City, Utah: Ancestry, 1999.

———. "Snakes and Scribes: The Dawes Commission and the Enrollment of the Creeks." *The Chronicles of Oklahoma* 75, no. 4 (Winter 1997–1998): 384–413.

Castel, Albert. *A Frontier State at War: Kansas, 1861–1865*. Ithaca, N.Y.: Cornell University Press, 1958.

Champagne, Duane. *Social Order and Political Change: Constitutional Government among the Cherokee, Choctaw, Chickasaw, and the Creek*. Stanford, Calif.: Stanford University Press, 1992.

Chapman, Berlin B. "Freedmen and the Oklahoma Lands." *Southwestern Social Science Quarterly* 29, no. 2 (September 1948): 150–59.

Chaudhuri, Joan, and Joyotpaul Chaudhuri. *A Sacred Path: The Way of the Muscogee Creeks*. Los Angeles: UCLA Indian Studies Center, 2001.

Christensen, Laurence O. "J. Milton Turner: An Appraisal." *Missouri Historical Quarterly* 70, no. 1 (1975): 1–19.

Clark, Carter Blue. "Opothleyohola and the Creeks during the Civil War." In *Indian Leaders: Oklahoma's First Statesmen*, ed. H. G. Jordan and T. M. Holm, 49–64. Oklahoma City: OHS, 1979.

Cornish, Dudley Taylor. "Kansas Negro Regiments in the Civil War." *Kansas Historical Quarterly* 20 (May 1953): 417–429.

———. *The Sable Arm: Black Troops in the Union Army, 1861–1865*. Lawrence: University Press of Kansas, 1987.

Crawford, Samuel J. *Kansas in the Sixties*. Chicago: A. C. McClurg and Co., 1911.

Crocket, Norman L. "Witness to History: Booker T. Washington Visits Boley." *Chronicles of Oklahoma* 67, no. 4 (1989): 382–91.

Crouch, Barry A. *The Freedmen's Bureau and Black Texans*. Austin: University of Texas Press, 1992.

Current-Garcia, Eugene, with Dorothy B. Hatfield, eds. *Shem, Ham, and Japheth: The Papers of W. O. Tuggle, Comprising His Indian Diary, Sketches and Observations, Myths and Washington Journal in the Territory and at the Capital, 1879–1882*. Athens: University of Georgia Press, 1973.

Cutler, William G. *History of the State of Kansas*. Chicago, Ill.: A. T. Andreas, 1883.

Davis, Karl. "'Remember Fort Mims': Reinterpreting the Origins of the Creek War." *Journal of the Early Republic* 22 no. 4 (Winter 2002): 611–37.

Debo, Angie. *And Still the Waters Run: The Betrayal of the Five Civilized Tribes.* Princeton, N.J.: Princeton University Press, 1940.

——. *The Road to Disappearance: A History of the Creek Indians.* Norman: University of Oklahoma Press, 1941.

Denison, W. W. "Battle of Prairie Grove." *Kansas Historical Collections* 16 (1925): 586–90.

Dickerman, George. "History of Negro Education in the United States." In *Negro Education: A Study of Private and Higher Schools for Colored People in the United States.* Ed. T. J. Jones, 244–68. Washington, D.C.: GPO, 1917.

Doran, Michael F. "Antebellum Cattle Herding in the Indian Territory." *Geographical Review* 66 (1976): 48–58.

——. "Negro Slaves of the Five Civilized Tribes." *Annals of the Association of American Geographers* 68, no. 3 (September 1978): 335–51.

Duncan, Otis D. "The Fusion of White, Negro and Indian Cultures at the Converging of the New South and the West." *Southwestern Social Science Quarterly* 14 (March 1934): 357–69.

Dundes, Alan. "African Tales among the North American Indians." *Southern Folklore Quarterly* 29, no. 3 (September 1965): 207–19.

Ellison, Ralph. *Going to the Territory.* New York: Random House, 1986.

Ethridge, Robbie. *Creek Country: Creek Indians and Their World.* Chapel Hill: University of North Carolina Press, 2003.

Farb, Robert C. "The Military Career of Robert W. Furnas." *Nebraska History* 32, no. 1 (March 1951): 18–41.

Farlow, Joyce, and Louise Barry, eds. "Vincent B. Osborne's Civil War Experiences: Part 2." *Kansas Historical Quarterly* 20, no. 3 (August 1952): 187–223.

Fite, Gilbert. "Development of the Cotton Industry by the Five Civilized Tribes in Indian Territory." *Journal of Southern History* 15 (August 1949): 346–47.

Foner, Eric. *Reconstruction: America's Unfinished Revolution, 1863–1877.* New York: Harper Row, 1988.

——. *The Story of American Freedom.* New York: W. W. Norton, 1998.

Forbes, Jack D. *Africans and Native Americans: The Language of Race and the Evolution of Red-Black Peoples.* Champaign: University of Illinois Press, 1993.

Foreman, Carolyn Thomas. "Marshalltown, Creek Nation." *Chronicles of Oklahoma* 32, no. 1 (Spring 1954): 51–58.

——. "North Fork Town." *Chronicles of Oklahoma* 29, no. 1 (Spring 1951): 79–111.

Foreman, Carolyn Thomas, ed. "Journal of a Tour in the Indian Territory by N. Sayre Harris." *Chronicles of Oklahoma* 10, no. 2 (June 1932): 219–40.

Foreman, Grant. *Advancing the Frontier, 1830–1860.* Norman: University of Oklahoma Press, 1933.

——. *The Five Civilized Tribes: Cherokee, Chickasaw, Choctaw, Creek Seminole.* Norman: University of Oklahoma Press, 1934.

——. "The Hon. Alice M. Robertson." *Chronicles of Oklahoma* 10, no. 1 (March 1932): 13–17.

——. *Indians and Pioneers; The Story of the American Southwest Before 1830.* New Haven: Yale University Press, 1930.

——. *The Indian Removal: the Immigration of the Five Civilized Tribes.* Norman: University of Oklahoma Press, 1972.

——. *Muskogee, The Biography of an Oklahoma Town.* St. Louis: Blackwell Weelandy Company, 1947, privately printed for Grant Foreman.

——. *Pioneer Days in the Early Southwest.* Lincoln: University of Nebraska Press, 1994.

Franklin, Jimmie Lewis. *Journey Towards Hope: A History of Blacks in Oklahoma.* Norman: University of Oklahoma Press, 1982.

Gaines, Craig W. *The Confederate Cherokees: John Drew's Regiment of Mounted Rifles.* Baton Rouge: Louisiana State University Press, 1989.

Gallay, Alan. *The Indian Slave Trade: The Rise of the English Empire in the American South.* New Haven, Conn.: Yale University Press, 2002.

Gaskin, J. M. *Black Baptists in Oklahoma.* Oklahoma City: Messenger Press, 1992.

Gibson, Arrell Morgan. "The Centennial Legacy of the General Allotment Act." *Chronicles of Oklahoma* 65, no. 3 (Fall 1987): 228–51.

Goble, Danny. *Progressive Oklahoma: The Making of a New Kind of State.* Norman: University of Oklahoma Press, 1980.

Graebner, Norman A. "Pioneer Indian Agriculture in Oklahoma." *Chronicles of Oklahoma* 23, no. 3 (1945): 232–48.

——. "Provincial Indian Society in Oklahoma." *Chronicles of Oklahoma* 23, no. 4 (1945): 323–37.

——. "The Public Land Policy of the Five Civilized Tribes." *Chronicles of Oklahoma* 23, no. 2 (1945): 97–118.

Green, Michael. *The Politics of Indian Removal: Creek Government and Society in Crisis.* Lincoln: University of Nebraska Press, 1993.

Greene, Albert Robinson. "Campaigning in the Army of the Frontier." *Kansas Historical Collections* 14 (1918): 283–310.

Grinde, Donald A., Jr., and Quintard Taylor. "Red vs. Black: Conflict and Accommodation in the Post–Civil War Indian Territory, 1865–1907." *American Indian Quarterly* 8, no. 3 (Summer 1984): 211–29.

Griscom, George L. *Fighting with Ross' Texas Brigade, C.S.A: Diary of Lieut. George L. Griscom, Adjutant, 9th Texas Cavalry Regiment.* Ed. H. Kerr. Hillsborough, Tex.: Hillsborough Junior College Press, 1976.

Grow, Stewart. "The Blacks of Amber Valley: Negro Pioneering in Northern Alberta." *Canadian Ethnic Studies* 6, nos. 1/2 (1974): 17–39.

Hahn, Steven C. *The Invention of the Creek Nation, 1670–1763.* Lincoln: University of Nebraska Press, 2004.

Hailliburton, Janet. "Black Slavery in the Creek Nation." *Chronicles of Oklahoma* 56, no. 3 (Fall 1978): 298–314.

Hall, Lance. Creek Indian Researcher website. http://freepages.genealogy.rootsweb
.com/texlance/main.htm (accessed March 15, 2002).

Halley, David J., Marvin T. Smith, and James B. Langford. "Archaeological Reality of
de Soto's Coosa." In *Columbian Consequences*, vol. 2, ed. D. Hurst Thomas, 121–
38. Washington, D.C.: Smithsonian Institution Press, 1990.

Herzog, George. "African Influences in North American Indian Music." In *Papers
Read at the International Congress of Musicology Read at New York City, September 11–16, 1939*, 130–43. New York: The Congress, 1944.

Hewett, Janet B., et al., eds. *Supplement to the Official Records of the Union and Confederate Armies*. Pt. 1, vols. 3–4. Wilmington, N.C.: Broadfoot Publishing, 1994.

Hudson, Charles. *Conversations with the High Priest of Coosa*. Chapel Hill: University of North Carolina Press, 2003.

——. "Coosa: A Chiefdom in the Sixteenth Century Southeastern United States."
American Anthropologist 50, no. 4 (Winter 1985): 723–37.

——. *Knights of Spain, Warriors of the Sun: Hernando de Soto and the South's Ancient
Chiefdoms*. Athens: University of Georgia Press, 1997.

——. *The Southeastern Indians*. Knoxville: University of Tennessee Press, 1976.

Hughes, Michael A. "Nations Asunder, Part II: Reservation and Eastern Indians
during the American Civil War, 1861–1865." *Journal of the Indian Wars* 1, no. 4
(2000): 21–50.

Hurt, R. Douglas. *Indian Agriculture in America: Prehistory to the Present*. Lawrence:
University of Kansas Press, 1987.

Johnston, James H. "Documentary Evidence of Relations Between Negroes and
Indians." *Journal of Negro History* 14, no. 1 (January 1929): 21–43.

Jones, Warrick Lane. "A Lettered Portrait of William McIntosh, Leader of the Creek
Nation." *Chronicles of Oklahoma* 64, no. 1 (Spring 1996): 76–95.

Jordan, H. Glenn, and Thomas M. Holm, eds. *Indian Leaders, Oklahoma's First
Statesmen*. Oklahoma City: Oklahoma Historical Society, 1979.

Kerr, Homer, ed. *Fighting with Ross' Texas Brigade, C.S.A: Diary of Lieut. George L.
Griscom, Adjutant, 9th Texas cavalry Regiment*. Hillsborough, Tex.: Hillsborough
Junior College Press, 1976.

King, Adam. "Creek Chiefdoms at the Temporal Edge of the Mississippian World."
Southeastern Archaeology 21, no. 2 (Winter 2002): 221–32.

——. "De Soto's Itaba and the Nature of Sixteenth Century Paramount Chiefdoms."
Southeastern Archaeology 18, no. 2 (Winter 1999): 110–33.

Klein, Herbert S. *The Atlantic Slave Trade*. Cambridge, U.K.: Cambridge University
Press, 1999.

Knight, Vernon James, Jr. "Symbolism of the Mississippian Mounds." In *Powhatan's
Mantle: Indians in the Colonial South*, ed. P. H. Wood, G. A. Waselkov, and M. T.
Hatley, 279–91. Lincoln: University of Nebraska Press, 1989.

Knight, Vernon James, Jr., James A. Brown, and George E. Lankford. "On the
Subject Matter of Southeastern Ceremonial Complex Art." *Southeastern Archaeology* 20, no. 2 (Winter 2001): 120–41.

Krauthamer, Barbara. "Kinship and Freedom: Fugitive Slave Women's Incorporation into Creek Society." In *New Studies in the History of American Slavery*. Ed. E. E. Baptist and S. M. H. Camp, 148–65. Athens: University of Georgia Press, 2006.

Landers, Jane. "Spanish Sanctuary: Fugitive Slaves in Florida, 1687–1790." *Florida Historical Quarterly* 62, no. 3 (January 1984): 296–313.

Lauber, Almon Wheeler. *Indian Slavery in Colonial Times Within the Present Limits of the United States.* New York: Columbia University Press, 1913.

Lawson, Steven F. *Black Ballots: Voting Rights in the South, 1944–1969.* New York: Columbia University Press, 1976.

Littlefield, Daniel C. *Rice and Slaves: Ethnicity and the Slave Trade in Colonial South Carolina.* Baton Rouge: Louisiana State University Press, 1981.

Littlefield, Daniel F., Jr. *Africans and Creeks: From the Colonial Period to the Civil War.* Westport, Conn.: Greenwood Press, 1979.

———. *Africans and Seminoles: From Removal to Emancipation.* Westport, Conn.: Greenwood Press, 1977.

———. *Alex Posey: Creek Poet, Journalist, and Humorist.* Lincoln: University of Nebraska Press, 1992.

———. *The Cherokee Freedmen: From Emancipation to American Citizenship.* Westport, Conn.: Greenwood Press, 1978.

———. *The Chickasaw Freedmen: A People Without a Country.* Westport, Conn.: Greenwood Press, 1980.

———. "Henry Dawes and the Commission to the Five Civilized Tribes." Paper presented to the Mid-America Conference, Stillwater, Oklahoma, April 1998.

———. *Seminole Burning: A Story of Racial Vengeance.* Jackson: University of Mississippi Press, 1997.

Littlefield, Daniel F., Jr., and Mary Ann Littlefield. "The Beams Family: Free Blacks in the Indian Territory." *Journal of Negro History* 61, no. 1 (January 1976): 17–35.

Littlefield, Daniel F., Jr., and Lonnie E. Underhill. "Black Dreams and 'Free' Homes: The Oklahoma Territory, 1891–1894." *Phylon* 34, no. 4 (December 1973): 342–57.

———. "The Crazy Snake Uprising of 1909: A Red, Black or White Affair?" *Arizona and the West* 20, no. 4 (Winter 1978): 307–24.

———. "Negro Marshals in the Indian Territory." *The Journal of Negro History* 56, no. 2 (April 1971): 77–87.

Lowe, Richard, ed. *A Texas Cavalry Officer's Civil War: The Diary and Letters of James C. Bates.* Baton Rouge: Louisiana State University Press, 1999.

Majors, M. A. *Noted Negro Women: Their Triumphs and Activities.* Chicago: Donohue and Henneberry, 1893.

Martin, Joel W. *Sacred Revolt: The Muskogee's Struggle for a New World.* Boston: Beacon Press, 1991.

Maxwell, Amos. "The Sequoyah Convention: Part I." *Chronicles of Oklahoma* 28, no. 2 (1950): 161–92.

May, Katja. *African Americans and Native Americans in the Creek and Cherokee Nations, 1830's to 1920's: Collusion and Collision.* New York: Garland Press, 1996.

McEwan, Bonnie G., ed. *Indians of the Greater Southeast: Historical Archaeology and Ethnohistory.* Gainesville: University Press of Florida, 2000.

McKellop, A. P. *Constitution and Laws of the Muskogee Nation.* 1893. Reprint, Wilmington, Del.: Scholarly Resources, 1973.

McMillan, Joseph Turner, Jr. "The Development of Higher Education for Blacks During the Late Nineteenth Century: A Study of the African Methodist Episcopal Church; Wilberforce University; The American Missionary Association; Hampton Institute; and Fisk University." Ed.D. diss., Columbia University, 1985.

McReynolds, Edwin C. *The Seminoles.* Norman: University of Oklahoma Press, 1957.

Meserve, John Bartlett. "Chief Opothle Yahola." *Chronicles of Oklahoma* 9, no. 4 (December 1931): 439–53.

———. "The Perrymans." *Chronicles of Oklahoma* 15, no. 2 (June 1937): 166–84.

Miles, Tiya. *Ties That Bind: The Story of an Afro-Cherokee Family in Slavery and Freedom.* Berkeley: University of California Press, 2005.

Miner, H. Craig. *The Corporation and the Indian: Tribal Sovereignty and Industrial Civilization in Indian Territory, 1865–1907.* Columbia: University of Missouri Press, 1976.

Minges, Patrick. *The Keetoowah Society and the Civil War in the Indian Territory.* http://www.people.virginia.edu/pnm3r/kituwah/Chapter%203-02.htm#P149_48969 (accessed November 21, 2004).

Monaghan, Jay. *Civil War on the Western Border: 1854–1865.* 1955. Reprint, Lincoln: University of Nebraska Press, 1992.

Morris, Michael. "Emerging Gender Roles for Southeastern Indian Women: The Mary Musgrove Story Reconsidered." *Georgia Historical Quarterly* 89, no. 1 (Spring 2005): 1–24.

Mott, M. L. *A National Blunder.* Washington: M. L. Mott, 1924.

Moulton, Gary E., ed. *The Papers of Chief John Ross,* vol. 2, 1840–1866. Norman: University of Oklahoma Press, 1985.

Muffly-Kipp, Laurie F. "Introduction to the Church in the Southern Black Community." http://docsouth.unc.edu (accessed March 15, 2002).

Mulroy, Kevin. *Freedom on the Border: The Seminole Maroons in Florida, the Indian Territory, Coahuila and Texas.* Lubbock: Texas Tech Press, 1993.

Myers, Terri. *From Creek Freedmen to Oklahoma Oil Men: The Black Heritage and Architectural Legacy of Okmulgee: 1878–1929.* Okmulgee, Okla.: City of Okmulgee Historic Preservation Committee, 1991.

Naylor-Ojurongbe, Celia E. "Born and Raised among These People, I Don't Want No Other." In *Confounding the Color Line: The Indian-Black Experience in North America,* ed. J. F. Brooks, 161–91. Lincoln: University of Nebraska Press, 2002.

Nesbit, Paul, ed. "Governor Haskell Tells of Two Conventions." *Chronicles of Oklahoma* 14, no. 2 (June 1936): 189–217.

"Notes and Documents." *Chronicles of Oklahoma* 11, no. 4 (December 1933): 1122–24.

Ohadike, Don C. *Anioma: A Social History of the Western Igbo People.* Athens: Ohio University Press, 1994.

Okmulgee Historical Society. *History of Okmulgee County, Oklahoma.* Okmulgee: Okmulgee Historical Society, 1985.

Opler, Morris Edward. "The Creek 'Town' and the Problem of Creek Political Organization." In *Human Problems in Technological Change: A Casebook,* ed. E. Spicer. New York: Russell Sage Foundation, 1952.

Parks, R. C. *Day Book, First Cherokee Regiment* [Confederate]. Topeka, KSHS Microfilm Publication, 1994.

Perdue, Theda. *"Mixed Blood" Indians: Racial Construction in the Early South.* Athens: University of Georgia Press, 2003.

——. *Slavery and the Evolution of Cherokee Society.* Knoxville: University of Tennessee Press, 1979.

Pierson, William D. *From Africa to America: African American History from the Colonial Era to the Early Republic, 1520–1790.* New York: Twayne, 1996.

Piker, Joshua. *Okfuskee: A Creek Indian Town in Colonial America.* Cambridge, Mass.: Harvard University Press, 2004.

Porter, Kenneth W. "After Removal to the West." *The Journal of Negro History* 17, no. 3 (July 1932): 351–58.

——. "Billy Bowlegs (Holuta Micco) in the Seminole Wars (Part I)." *Florida Historical Quarterly* 45, no. 1 (January 1967): 219–42.

——. "Billy Bowlegs in the Civil War (Part II)." *Florida Historical Quarterly* 45, no. 2 (April 1967): 391–401.

——. *The Black Seminoles: History of a Freedom Loving People.* Ed. A. M. Amos and T. P. Senter. Gainesville: University of Florida Press, 1996.

——. "The Hawkins' Negroes Go to Mexico." *The Chronicles of Oklahoma* 24 (1946): 55–58.

——. "Negro Guides and Interpreters in the Early Stages of the Seminole War, 28 December 1835–6 March 1937." *Journal of Negro History* 35, no. 2 (April 1950): 174–82.

——. *The Negro on the American Frontier.* New York: Arno Press, 1971.

——. "Negroes and the East Florida Annexation Plot, 1811–1813." *The Journal of Negro History* 30, no. 1 (January 1945): 9–29.

——. "Negroes on the Southern Frontier." *Journal of Negro History* 33, no. 1 (January 1948): 53–78.

——. "Notes Supplementary to 'Relations Between Negroes and Indians.'" *The Journal of Negro History* 18, no. 3 (July 1933): 282–321.

Posey, Alexander. *The Fus Fixico Letters.* Ed. D. F. Littlefield, Jr., and C. A. Petty Hunter. Lincoln: University of Nebraska Press, 1993.

Prantle, Alberta, ed. "The Story of a Kansas Freedmen." *Kansas Historical Quarterly* 11, no. 4 (November 1942): 341–61.

Rawick, George, ed. *The American Slave: A Composite Autobiography.* Supplement Series 1, vol. 12, Oklahoma. Westport, Conn.: Greenwood Press, 1977.

Rentie, W. A., ed. *Acts and Resolutions of the National Council of the Muskogee*

Nation of 1893: English and Creek. 1893. Reprint, Wilmington, Del.: Scholarly Resources, 1975.

Richards, Ralph. *The Forts of Fort Scott and the Fateful Borderland.* Kansas City, Mo.: The Lowell Press, 1976.

Robinson, Ella. "History of the Patterson Mercantile Company." *Chronicles of Oklahoma* 36, no. 1 (Spring 1958): 38–51.

———. "Indian International Fair." *Chronicles of Oklahoma* 17, no. 4 (December 1939): 413–16.

Rough, E. C. "Henry Frieland Buckner." *Chronicles of Oklahoma* 14, no. 4 (December 1936): 456–66.

Russell, Orpha. "Ekvn-hv'lwuce: Site of Oklahoma's First Civil War Battle." *Chronicles of Oklahoma* 29, no. 4 (Winter 1951–52): 401–407.

Sameth, Sigmund. "Creek Negroes: A Study in Race Relations." Master's thesis, University of Oklahoma, 1941.

Saunt, Claudio. *Black, White, and Indian: Race and the Unmaking of an American Family.* New York: Oxford University Press, 2005.

———. "'The English Has Now a Mind to Make Slaves of Them All,' Creeks, Seminoles and the Problem of Slavery." *American Indian Quarterly* 22, no. 1/2 (Winter 1998): 157–81.

———. *A New Order of Things: Property, Power, and the Transformation of the Creek Indians.* New York: Cambridge University Press, 1999.

———. "The Paradox of Freedom: Tribal Sovereignty and Emancipation during the Reconstruction of Indian Territory." *The Journal of Southern History* 19, no. 1 (January 2004): 61–94.

Scarry, John F. *Political Structure and Change in the Prehistoric Southeastern United States.* Gainesville: University Press of Florida, 1996.

Schultz, Jack M. *The Seminole Baptist Churches of Oklahoma: Maintaining a Traditional Community.* Norman: University of Oklahoma Press, 1999.

Scruggs, Lawson A. *Women of Distinction: Remarkable in Works and Invincible in Character.* Raleigh: L. A. Scruggs, 1892.

Searcy, Martha Condray. "The Introduction of African Slavery into the Creek Indian Nation." *Georgia Historical Quarterly* 66, no. 1 (Spring 1982): 21–33.

Shepard, R. Bruce. "North to the Promised Land: Black Migration to the Canadian Plains." *Chronicles of Oklahoma* 66, no. 3 (Fall 1988): 312–13.

Smith, Buckingham, trans. *Narratives of the Career of Hernando de Soto in the Conquest of Florida as told by a Knight of Elvas and in a Relation by Luys Hernandez a Biedma, Factor of the Expedition in The Hernando de Soto Expedition.* Ed. and with an introduction by J. T. Milanich. New York: Garland, 1991.

Smith, Marvin T. *Coosa: The Rise and Fall of a Southeastern Chiefdom.* Gainesville: University Press of Florida, 2000.

Speck, Frank G. "The Creek Indians of Taskigi Town." *Memoirs of the American Anthropological Association* 2 (1907): 99–164.

——. "The Negroes of the Creek Nation." *The Southern Workman* 37, no. 2 (February 1908): 106–10.

Sturm, Circe. *Blood Politics: Race, Culture, and Identity in the Cherokee Nation of Oklahoma.* Berkeley: University of California Press, 2002.

Swanton, John R. *The Indians of the Southeastern United States.* Bureau of American Ethnology Bulletin 137. Washington, D.C.: Smithsonian Institution Press, 1979.

Taylor, Quintard. *In Search of the Racial Frontier: African Americans in the American West, 1542–1990.* New York: W. W. Norton, 1998.

Teall, Kaye M. *Black History in Oklahoma: A Resource Book.* Oklahoma City: Oklahoma City Public Schools, 1971.

Tolson, Arthur L. *Black Oklahomans: A History, 1541–1972.* New Orleans: Edwards Printing, 1974.

Trickett, Dean. "The Civil War in the Indian Territory, 1861." *Chronicles of Oklahoma* 17, no. 3, (September 1939): 315–27; 17, no. 4 (December 1939): 410–12; 18, no. 2 (June 1940): 142–53; 18, no. 3 (September 1940): 266–80.

——. "The Civil War in the Indian Territory, 1862." *Chronicles of Oklahoma* 19, no. 1, (March 1941): 55–69; 19, no. 4 (December 1941): 381–96.

Troper, Harold Martin. "The Creek-Negroes and Canadian Immigration, 1909–1911." *The Canadian Historical Review* 53, no. 3 (September, 1972): 272–88.

de la Vega, Garcilaso. *Florida of the Inca.* Ed. and trans. J. G. Varner and J. J. Varner, Austin: University of Texas Press, 1951.

Underhill, Lonnie E. "Hamlin Garland and the Final Council of the Creek Nation." *Journal of the West* 10 (1971): 511–20.

Van Sertima, Ivan. *They Came Before Columbus: The African Presence in Ancient America.* New York: Random House, 1976.

Vest, Jay Hansford C. "From Bobtail to Brer Rabbit: Native American Influences on Uncle Remus." *American Indian Quarterly* 24, no. 1 (Winter 2000): 19–43.

Vore, Israel. "Levering Manual Labor School." *Chronicles of Oklahoma* 25, no. 3 (Autumn 1947): 201–208.

Walker-Hill, Helen. *From Spirituals to Symphonies: African American Women Composers and Their Music.* Westport, Conn.: Greenwood Press, 2002.

Warde, Mary Jane. "Fight for Survival: The Indian Response to the Boomer Movement." *Chronicles of Oklahoma* 67, no. 1 (Spring 1989): 30–49.

——. *George Washington Grayson and the Creek Nation: 1843–1920.* Norman: Oklahoma University Press, 2000.

——. "Now the Wolf Has Come: The Civilian Civil War in the Indian Territory." *Chronicles of Oklahoma* 74, no. 3 (Summer 1993): 70–88.

Waring, Antonio J., ed. *Laws of the Creek Nation.* University of Georgia Libraries Miscellaneous Publication 1. Athens: University of Georgia Press, 1960.

Waselkov, Gregory A., and Marvin T. Smith. "Upper Creek Archaeology." In *Indians of the Greater Southeast: Historical Archaeology and Ethnohistory,* ed. B. G. McEwan, 242–64. Gainesville: University Press of Florida, 2000.

Welch, Paul. "Control Over Goods and Political Stability of the Moundville Kingdom." In *Political Structure and Change in the Prehistoric Southeastern United States*. Ed. J. F. Scarry, 69–91. Gainesville: University Press of Florida, 1996.

Wells, Mary Ann. *Searching for Red Eagle: A Personal Journey Into the Spirit World of Native America*. Jackson: University Press of Mississippi, 1998.

West, C. W. *Muskogee, I. T.: Queen City of the Southwest*. Muskogee, Okla.: Muskogee Pub., 1972.

White, Christine Schultz, and Benton R. White. *Now the Wolf Has Come: The Creek Nation in the Civil War*. College Station: Texas A&M University Press, 1996.

Wickett, Murray. *Contested Territory: Whites, Native Americans, and African Americans in Oklahoma, 1865–1907*. Baton Rouge: Louisiana State University Press, 2000.

Wickman, Patricia Riles. *A Tree That Bends: Discourse, Power, and the Survival of the Maskókii People*. Tuscaloosa: The University of Alabama Press, 1999.

Williams, Nudie. "Black Men Who Wore the Star." *Chronicles of Oklahoma* 59, no. 1 (Spring 1981): 83–89.

———. "The Black Press in Oklahoma: The Formative Years." *Chronicles of Oklahoma* 61, no. 3 (Fall 1983): 308–18.

Willis, William S. "Anthropology and Negroes on the Southern Frontier." In *The Black Experience in America*, ed. J. C. Curtis and L. L. Gould, 33–49. Austin: University of Texas Press, 1970.

———. "Divide and Rule: Red, White and Black in the Southeast." *Journal of Negro History* 48, no. 2 (July 1963): 157–63.

Wilson, Joseph T. *The Black Phalanx: African American Soldiers in the War of Independence, the War of 1812, and the Civil War*. 1890. Reprint, New York: Da Capo Press, 1994.

Wood, Peter. *Black Majority: Negroes in Colonial South Carolina from 1670 through the Stono Rebellion*. New York: W. W. Norton, 1974.

———. "The Changing Population of the Colonial South: An Overview by Race and Region." In *Powhatan's Mantle: Indians in the Colonial South*, 1st ed., ed. P. H. Wood, G. A. Waselkov, and M. T. Hatley, 434–43. Lincoln: University of Nebraska Press, 1989.

Woodward, C. Vann. *Origins of the New South, 1877–1913*. Baton Rouge: Louisiana State University Press, 1951.

Woodward, Thomas S. *Woodward's Reminiscences of the Creek, or Muscogee Indians*. 1859. Reprint, Tuscaloosa and Birmingham: Alabama Bookstore and Birmingham Book Exchange, 1939.

Worth, John E. "The Lower Creeks: Origin and Early History." In *Indians of the Greater Southeast: Historical Archaeology and Ethnohistory*. Ed. B. G. McEwan, 265–98, Gainesville: University Press of Florida, 2000.

Wright, J. Leitch, Jr. "Blacks in British East Florida." *Florida Historical Quarterly* 54 no. 3 (1976): 425–42.

———. *Creeks and Seminoles: The Destruction and Regeneration of the Muscoculge People*. Lincoln: University of Nebraska Press, 1986.

——. "A Note on the First Seminole War as Seen by the Indians, Negroes and Their British Advisors." *Journal of Southern History* 34, no. 2 (July 1968): 565–75.

——. *The Only Land They Knew: The Tragic Story of the American Indians of the Old South.* New York: The Free Press, 1981.

Wright, Muriel H. "Colonel Cooper's Report on the Battle of Round Mountain." *Chronicles of Oklahoma* 39, no. 4 (Winter 1961–1962): 352–97.

Zellar, Gary. "The First to Fight for Freedom: African Creek Soldiers Enter the Civil War." *Journal of the Indian Wars* 1, no. 4 (2000): 1–20.

——. "Occupying the Middle Ground: African Creeks in the First Indian Home Guard, 1862–1865." *Chronicles of Oklahoma* 76, no. 1 (Spring 1998): 48–71.

Index

References to illustrations are in italics.

1860 Census, 42
Abram, George, 65
Adams, Cully, 59
Adams, John, 59
Adams, Thomas Jefferson (T. J.), 206–207
Adkins, Thomas, 78
Africa, West: cultures of and similarities with southeastern American Indians, 11, 263n16; pre-Columbian contact with America, 3, 261n1; kinship slavery in, 15
African Americans. *See* African Creeks: African Americans
African Seminoles, 39, 245; among Opothleyahola's Loyal Creeks, 45, 51; among refugees in Kansas, 53–54; in First Indian Home Guard, 55
African Creeks: and 1904 land sales, 235–37; and 1908 land sales, 254–56; and adoption, 10, 14, 15, 36, 65, 84, 91, 99, 117, 186, 196, 202, 206, 210, 212, 221, 227; and African Americans, 112, 118, 163, 164, 168–69, 181, 189, 190–91, 237, 248–49, 292–93n45, 302n11; and African Indian intruders, 162, 163, 165–67, 217, 231; and agriculture, 13–14, 22, 34–35, 36, 38, 112–14, 117, 169,

181, 197, 212, 234, 306n54; and allotment, 24–25, 115–17, 192–93, 195–96, 198–99, 212–13, 216, 220–26, 231–34, 252–53, 255; and allotment restrictions, 231–34, 252–56; in border race war with Cherokees, 123–27, 130–35; and Christianity, 20–23, 30–32, 74, 111–12, 181–83; and Creek citizenship rights, 65, 103, 144, 163, 164, 165, 171, 174, 186, 187, 191–92, 201–202, 205–208, 213, 216–17, 219–20, 226–28, 293n54; and Creek politics (*see also* Creek elections), 98, 109–10, 129, 172, 176; as cultural brokers, 11, 31–32, 44, 54, 75, 111, 116, 125, 129, 173; and disfranchisement, 191–92, 200, 240–41, 242–44, 284n28; as entrepreneurs, 169–70, 173–74, 237–38; free blacks among, 25, 32, 36–38, 40, 42; and Green Peach War, 136–43; identity and, 32, 104, 114, 118, 161, 163, 168, 186, 219–20; as interpreters, 16, 35–36, 169, 173; and kinship ties with Creek Indians, 10, 15–16, 163, 164, 167, 169, 202, 219, 257, 263n16, 265n56, 266n75, 290n13; and land, 34–35, 36–37, 75, 77, 82, 84, 85, 93, 95–96, 112, 113–14, 116, 168–69, 197–98, 199, 212–13, 215, 220–21, 224–25, 245, 249–52, 253; and padding town rolls, 196–97, 201, and

African Creeks (*continued*)
  politics of Oklahoma statehood, 230, 237–44, 249–51; population of, 25, 42, 201, 217, 218–19; as preachers, 27–30, 36, 112, 119, 122, 182–83; as refugees in Choctaw and Chickasaw nations, 60, 72, 86, 93, 96; as refugees at Ft. Gibson, 73–74; as refugees in Kansas, 52–54, 81, 96, 168; as refugees in Texas, 60, 81, 72, 96; representatives on Creek Council, 98–99, 101, 109, 116, 126, 175, 195, 199, 201; schools and education, 110–11, 117, 118–20, 135–36, *151, 152, 153, 154, 157*, 171, 172, 176, 177–81, 188–89, 209–10, 227, 238, 246–49, 256–57, 297n34; as slaves, 11–12, 15–16, 32–36, 38–40, 267n79; and white intruders, 120–21, 163–64, 169, 170, 190, 231
African Baptist Church (Silver Bluff church), 13–14
Afro-American League, 237
All-black towns, 238–39
Allotment, 116, 119, 131, 173, 183, 185, 193, 194–95, 198–99, 203, 205–206; in the Creek Nation East, 24–25; and African Creeks, 215, 217–18, 219–220, 226; African Creek opposition to, 118, 163, 183, 199, 203; contest cases, 221–26; leasing of, 220; restrictions on sale of, 231–36, 252–53, sale of, 1904, 234–37; sale of, 1908, 254–56. *See also* Dawes Commission
American Revolution, 11, 17; and slavery among Creeks, 14–15
American Missionary Society Freedmen Relief Association, 74
Anderson, Charles, 51
Arkansas Colored Town, 97, 98, 104, 106, 117, 126, 140, 163, 171, 174, 189, 194, 191, 201, 203, 208, 209, 213, 230; and 1879 election irregularities, 144–45; and 1883 election irregularities, 175–76; creation of, 97–98; Creek council representatives from, 99, 106, 126, 203
Arkansas District, pre–Civil War, 25; after Civil War, 99. *See also* Muskogee District
Arkansas River, 27, 33, 35, 36, 46, 50, 56, 58, 60, 68, 70, 88, 101, 163, 170, 215, 218, 235, 237, 255
Arkansas-Verdigris River valley, 24, 26, 47, 81–82, 84, 91, 95
Army of the Frontier, 61, 63
Asbury Mission: in old Creek Nation, 22; in the West, 26, 31

Baptist Board of Foreign Missions, 21, 28
Baptist Church: African American church at Silver Bluff, Georgia, 13–14; and African Creek preachers, 21, 26, 27–29, 31–32, 112, 119, 122, 182–83; and establishment of 2nd Baptist Church (Muskogee), 111; and establishment of Muskogee Baptist Church, 118–19; and establishment of Creek African Church, 21; and establishment of Muscogee Baptist Church, 27; missionaries in the East, 20–21, 22, 23; missionaries in the West, 26–31
Baptist Home Mission Society, 120–21, 177, 292n42
Barnard, Jacob, 51
Barnard (also Barnett), Timothy, 17, 68
Barnett, Ben, 130
Barnett, Jim, 59
Barnett, Joe, in First Indian Home Guard, 59, 62; and Green Peach War, 139–40, 141; and John Vann shooting, 126–27
Barnett, Ketch, 69, 111
Barnett, Scipio, 37, 78, 86, 277n18
Beautiful Indian Territory, 189–90, 239, 240, 250, 257

Benedict, Leo, 246, 304n33
Big Warrior (Tustenuggee Thlocco), 21
Biscayan, Johann, 5
Bixby, Tams, 211, 221, 301n3
Black flag policy, 67
Blackjack Grove, 96
Blacksmith Jack (African Creek preacher), 27–28
Blue Salt King, 13
Blunt, (Gen.) James G., 59, 61, 62, 63, 64, 66, 74; orders to First Indian at Prairie Grove, 62; orders African Creeks to join U.S. Colored Troops regiments, 73
Board of Indian Commissioners, 124, 232; and mediation of Green Peach War, 138–42
Bogy, Lewis V., 100
Bonaparte, Charles, investigation, 232–34; as U.S. attorney general, 245–46
Boomers, 121–22, 163; African American, 164
Border Race War: African Creeks and Cherokee vigilantes, 123–27, 130–35
Boston Mountains, 61
Bowlegs, Billy, 55, 62
Bradley, C. M., 252
Braund, Kathryn Holland, 10, 15
Brown, Simon, 94, 144; and 2nd Baptist Church, 110; as business owner, 139, 165; on Creek Citizenship Committee, 164–65; in Creek politics, 98–99, 101–102, 106, 109, 110, 116, 139; and Evangel Mission school, 136; in First Indian Home Guard regiment, 61; flees to Opothleyahola's camp, 45–46; joins Loyal Creeks, 51; and Tullahassee as African Creek boarding school, 135; at Tullahassee mission, 44–45
Brown, Jack, 78
Brown, Jake, 37
Brown, Hannah, 45

Bruner, Paro, 98, 135, *159*, 172, 202, 217, 218, 237; and allotment, 199; in Creek politics, 98, 109–10; and Dawes Commission, 202, 217; establishes Prairie Edge community, 98
Bruner, Thomas, 99
Bruner, Richard, 62
Buckner, Henry (Baptist minister), 265n56, 268-69n17
Bushyhead, Jesse, 131–32, 133, 134
Byers, William, 100.

Camp Babcock, 60–61
Campbell, A. B., 52–53
Campbell, (Lt. Col.) William T., 67
Campbellites, 122, 283n17
Canadian Colored Town, 128, 174, 199, 201, 218, 219, 230; and 1879 election irregularities, 129, creation of, 97–98; Creek council representatives from, 99, 106, 109, 202
Canadian District: in pre–Civil War Creek Nation, 31, 37
Canadian River, 29, 36, 44, 67, 71, 82, 85, 95, 97, 176, 181, 197–98
Cane Creek, 95
Cannan (settlement), 95
Cannard, Sophia, 94
Capers, William, 22
Cattle ranching: early Creek involvement in, 12–14; in pre–Civil War Creek Nation West, 35; and African Creek slaves and free blacks, 34–35, 36, 37–38, 45
Charles (pastor, Creek African Church), 21
Chattahoochie River, 17
Checote, Samuel, 166; and 1867 payment, 100; and 1869 disturbances, 102; and 1875 election, 109; and 1883 election, 143–45; and 1887 election, 174; actions during Green Peach War, 137–38, 140–41, 280–81n61; and

Checote, Samuel (*continued*)
African Creek citizenship, 103; as
early Methodist convert, 26; as Confederate Creek, 87; actions in Cobb
case, 132–34; elected principal chief
(1867) 101–102, (1871) 105–106, (1879)
129–30; and Vann case, 131
Cherokee Indians, 48, 86, 163, 207, in
Confederate service, 47, 48, 51–52, 57,
58, 60, 66, 67, 172; and Border Race
War, 115, 123–27, 130–35; Cherokee
freed people, 93; race relations in
Cherokee nation, 93, 124, 134; and
Reconstruction, 93; Loyal Cherokee,
51, 58
Childers, R. C.: as Coweta District
judge, 132; actions in Cobb case, 132
Chitto Hacho (Crazy Snake), 228–29,
252
Choctaw Nation: and missionairies, 27;
slavery in, 33; Confederate troops of,
51, 68
Civil War, impact in Indian Territory,
41–42. *See also* First Indian Home
Guard regiment
Clarkson, (Col.) J. J., 57
Clay, Henry (African American), 168
Clinging, Billy, 134, 283–84n21
Co-so-gee, (Lt.), 72
Coachman, Ward, 116, 119, 122, 128, 209;
and 1875 election, 109; and 1879 elec-
tion, 128–30; and African Creek sup-
port, 110, 127–28; and Cherokee vig-
ilante violence, 126; and formation of
Muskogee Party, 114; installed as
principal chief, 110; and John Vann
killing, 126–27
Coalescent societies, 6; impact of dis-
ease in forming, 6
Cobb, William (Billy), killing of, 132;
Cherokee reaction to shooting, 132;
Cherokee reward for African Creeks
involved in shooting, 133, trial of

African Creeks involved in shooting,
133–34
Cobrey, Hackless, 65
Coffin, A. V., 53
Coffin, William, 52–53
Colbert Committee, 201–202, 206
Colonel, Harry, 51
Colonel, Redmon, 51
Colonels, Fanny, 38
Colonels, Alexander, 17–18
Colored Orphan's Home school, 188,
189, 247, 256
Committee of Eighteen, 201, 208
Compere, Rev. Lee, 22–23
Confederate Creeks, alliance with Con-
federacy, 42; treaty negotiated 43;
regiments of, 43, 51–52, 57, 66–67;
Opothleyahola's opposition to, 43–
44
Conner, Thomas, 51
Constitutionalist Party, 99, 102, 104–
107, 117, 128, 133, 134, 138–39, 143–45;
and 1879 election controversy, 128–
30; and African Creek support for,
102, 109, 131, 135, 139, 142
Cooper, Douglas C.: as Choctaw agent,
47; as Confederate commander, 47,
67; and defense of Beams family,
267n.80
Coosa chiefdom, 3–5, 6; corn cultivation in, 4; slavery in, 4–5; de Soto
expedition and, 5–6; African slaves
escape in, 5–7
Cotchoche (Loyal Creek), 78, 86, 90; as
Loyal candidate for principal chief,
104–106
Cotton production, beginnings of in
Creek Nation, 35, 69; post–Civil War,
112, 112–13; African Creeks and, 112–
13, 197, 197, 212
Coulter, John, 51
Council Hill (High Springs), 26, 37, 77,
97

Cow Tom, 24, 69, 78, 85, 95, 101; background of, 37–38, builds school near Cane Creek, 95; on Creek Council, 106; death of, 109

Cowen, Alexander, 132–34

Cowen, B. R., 103

Coweta District, 95, 99, 132, 140, 163, 176, 191

Coweta Micco, 43

Cox, John T., 73

Crawford, Samuel J., 69

Crazy Snake Rebellion, 228–29

Creek Agency: in the East, 17; in the West, 1851–1875, 35; 1876–1878, 67, 94

Creek Agency settlement, 35, 37, 46, 65, 68, 75, 94, 100, 171, 172, 221, 222, 225

Creek Citizenship Committee (1883), 164, 196, 289n9

Creek Confederacy, formation of, 6–7, 262n12

Creek Constitution (1867): adoption of, 97; and referendum election, 199–200

Creek Council: adoption legislation, 103, 116; African Creek representatives on, 98–99, 101, 109, 116, 126, 175, 195, 199, 201; and establishing African Creek schools, 110, 116, 165, 176, 178, 185, 188; and restricting African Creek rights, 191–92, 284n28

Creek courts, 107, 116–17, 124, 127, 131, 132, 208, 209, 221, 222, 224; and Supreme Court decisions regarding African Creek citizenship, 191, 200, 206–207

Creek cultural practices, 7–8, 114, 98, 219, 276n12

Creek elections, of 1867, 101–102; of 1871, 104–106; of 1875, 108–109, 174; of 1879, 119, 122, 127–30; of 1883, 143–45, 165; of 1887, 174–76, 185; of 1891, 189; of 1895, 200, 203; of 1899, 226–27; of 1903, 230

Creek freed people. *See* African Creeks

Creek Indian Baptist Association, 111, 181

Creek kinship practices, 4, 9–10, 15, 97, 167; and Dawes Commission, 213

Creek laws, 77; in the East, 21–22; in the West, 32–33, 39–40; fencing law, 204–205; permit law, 113–14, 120, 164, 204; slave codes; 22, 77

Creek Lighthorse, 43, 93, 97, 102, 107, 124, 127, 134, 137–38, 142, 175, 204, 209, 280n70, 286n47; African Creeks in, 99, 109, 124, 125–27, 130, 144, 189

Creek National Council: in the East, 22; in the West 97, 109, 164, 200–201. *See also* Creek laws and elections

Creek Nation v. Mary Escoe, 207

Creek political structure: after removal, 26; in the East, 6; under the 1867 Constitution, 96–98

Creek redeemers, 80, 81, 210, 276n8

Creek religion and Christianity, 18, 23, 29, 30–31, 182, 265n55

Creek removal: and 1832 census, 25; Upper Creeks, 25; Lower Creeks, 25; McIntosh Creeks, 24

Creek slavery, 8–9, 15; beginnings of, 8, 10; and kinship slavery, 11, 15–16; slave traders and, 14–16, 39; manumissions, 22; patron-client slavery, 15, 34; slave codes, 21–22, 35, 36, 39–40; in the West, 32–36

Creek treaties: of Ft. Jackson, 20; of 1832 (removal treaty), 24; of 1863 (unratified), 69–71, 77

Creek treaties: Agreement of 1899 (unratified), 210–11; Agreement of 1901, 229; Supplemental Agreement of 1902, 228–30, 236; opposition to, 229–30

Creek treaties of 1866, 77, 100–103, 104, 106, 120, 121, 164, 175, 185, 196, 200, 202, 207, 210, 210, 212; and 1867

Creek treaties of 1866 (*continued*)
payment, 101; and African Creek citizenship rights 103, 110, 112, 116–17, 174, 191, 192, 197, 199, 206–207, 213, 227, 232; and Article II, 65, 89, 90–92, 100, 104, 112, 128, 137, 164, 165, 191, 192, 207, 210, 212, 227; compared to Seminole 1866 treaty, 101; Confederate delegates, 87–88; Loyal Creek delegates, 86; negotiation of, 87–90, 277n30; provisions of 90–92

Crowell, John, 23

Curtis Act (1898), 194, 211–12, 246

Cutler, George, A., 71

Davis (Johnson), Elizabeth, 37, 68, 172, 266n75

Davis, Lucinda, 38, 82, 276n12

Davis, John, 23, 26

Davis, Benjamin, 21

Davis (Gibson), Julia, 37, 221, 266n75

Davis, Sarah, 68, 94, 113, 172, 171, 174, 218, 221, 266n75; background of, 36–37

Davison, George, 237, 239

Davison, Joseph P. (Buzz Hawkins), 37, 94, 266n75, 290n16; and allotment, 221, 222; background of, 171; in business, 174, 234, 237; conflict with Warrior Rentie, 208–209; in Creek politics, 171, 208–209; and Pecan Creek Boarding School, 171, 188, 208–209, 256; and politics of statehood, 237, 239, 240–41, 251, 256; shooting of John Island, 209

Dawes, (Sen.) Henry L.: and 1885 investigating committee, 162; and General Allotment Act (Dawes Act), 183; head of Dawes Commission, 195, 211

Dawes Commission, 194–97, 198, 199, 200, 202, 203, 205, 207, 210, 217–18, 232, 254, 258, 295n3, 300n56; and African Creek allotment, 215, 217–18,

219–21, 224–26, 299n50; and African Creek citizenship, 205–206, 207, 209, 211–12, 219–20; and African Creek enrollment, 205–207, 213–14; 215–19; and corruption charges, 232; and Creek Agreement of 1899, 211; and Creek Agreement of 1901, 228; and Supplemental Agreement of 1902, 226, 228–29; and survey of Creek lands, 205

De Soto, Hernando, expedition, 3–5; slaves on, 5

De Luna, Tristan, 5

Debo, Angie, 99, 102, 174

Deep Fork, Canadian River, 44, 47, 48, 50, 84, 95, 98, 102

Deerskin trade, 6–8, 10, 12, 14–15

Delano, Columbus, 104

Democratic party, 239; and race issue in Indian Territory politics, 240–41; and Sequoyah movement, 241–42; and race issue in statehood politics, 249–50, 251, 254

Derrisaw, Jacob, 42

Disease, impact on Mississippian chiefdoms, 6

Doaks, Ben, 132, 133

Dole, (Lt. Col.) George, 64, 65

Dole, William P., 70

Doyle, Ned, 51

Doyle, Jim, 51

Drew, John, 48

Duncan, Turner, 122–23, 283n18

Dunn, J. W., 88, 93, 94, 95, 99, 100, 202; and 1867 payment, 100–101; creation of Dunn roll census, 100; distributes aid to refugees, 84; and moving Creek Agency, 95; report on African Creeks (1866), 96

Dunn roll, 100, 102, 202–203, 211, 212, 213; problems with, 217–18

Durant, Monday, 36, 51, 140, 270n26; and 1863 treaty negotiations, 69–70;

and African Creek schools, 110, 121, 135; appointed judge, 99; background of, 36; as Baptist preacher and missionary, 36, 74, 111, 182; as Constitutionalist in Green Peach War, 139–40; death of, 182; describes citizenship rights as free black, 165; petition for family's adoption, 166; as council representative, 98, 109, 110

DuVal, Benjamin T., 207–208

Ebeneezer Station, 28
Echo Hacho, 43, 48
Eleventh U.S. Colored Troops, 73
Ellithorpe, (Maj.) Albert Chapman, 55, 57, 58, 61, 62; description of African Creek refugees, 62–63
Emancipation Day (August 4), 77
Esteluste Town, 71
Evangel Mission, 136, 177, 291n29

Federal courts. *See* U.S. courts
Fields, Franklin A., 102, 103
Fife, Joe, 51
First Indian Home Guard regiment: African Creeks as first black soldiers in Union army, 55; African Creek duties in, 56, 58, 59, 64–66, 75, 273n65; African Creek soldiers and Confederate black flag policy, 67–68; African Creek soldiers promoted in, 72–73; establishes outposts in Creek country, 75; first attempts to organize, 54–55; organization of, 55; at Battle of (First) Cabin Creek, 66–67; at Battle of (Second) Cabin Creek, 74; at Battle of Cane Hill, 61; at Battle of Greenleaf Prairie, 66; at Battle of Honey Springs, 66–69; at Battle of Locust Grove, 57, 207; at Battle of Maysville (Fort Wayne), 59; at Battle of Prairie Grove, 61, 62–63; at Bayou Menard skirmish, 58; on Indian Expedition, 56–58; operations during fall–winter 1863–1864, 71–72; and operations against cattle rustlers, 75; supply and subsistence, 65, 75; violence in, 74

First Kansas Colored (79th U.S. Colored Troops): Company I organized, 64; at the Battle of (First) Cabin Creek, 66; at the Battle of Honey Springs, 67; and Poison Springs massacre, 67–68; contributions of, 76

Flint River, Ga., 17

Florida: Redsticks and African Creeks flee to, 20; under British, 12, 13, 14; under Spanish, as refuge for runaway slaves, 8, 20

Foner, Eric, 77, 275n1
Fourth (Ninth) Texas Cavalry, 50
Francis, Henry, 14
Franklin, Jesse, 94, 99; as Creek Supreme Court judge, 116
Freedmen Baptist Association, 111, 118, 181; separates from Creek Indian Baptist Association, 181
Freedmen's Oklahoma Immigration Association, 164
Frontier exchange economy, 12
Ft. Arbuckle, 50
Ft. Blunt. *See* Ft. Gibson
Ft. Davis, 63
Ft. Gibson, 51, 58, 63, 64, 66, 67, 68, 69, 71, 74, 94, 95, 102, 132, 171; Civil War refugees at, 73–74, renamed Ft. Blunt, 64; reoccupied by Union forces, 64
Ft. Leavenworth, Kansas, 53
Ft. Mims, 20, 264n34
Ft. Scott, Kansas, 58, 61, 64, 68, 171; supply trains from, 65
Ft. Smith Council (1865), 78–81, 84; African Creek delegation at, 78, Creek redeemers' view of, 80–81; results of, 80
Ft. Washita, 60

Furnas, (Col.) Robert W.: appointed commander, First Indian, 55, 58; organizes 2nd Nebraska regiment, 271n43

Gallay, Alan, 8
Galphin, George, 13
George (African Creek soldier), 67
George, David, 13–14; and establishment of African Baptist Church, 13
Gibson, Edward (Ned), 221–22
George, Sugar T., 187, 201, 208; in First Indian, 68, 72–73; Creek politics and, 94, 99, 102, 106, 109; Green Peach War and, 139; involvement in business and real estate, 170, 174, 177
Glass, Dick: arrest record of, 285n39; in Cobb shooting, 132–34; in Green Peach War, 141; death of, 134
Goble, Danney, 250, 302–303n17
Grafters, 233, 234, 252
Grayson, George Washington (G. W.), 186–87, 191; and allotment, 196; and African Creek citizenship rights, 162, 191, 285n36; and testimony at 1885 hearings, 162; and 1899 election, 226–27
Grayson, Bob, 67
Grayson, Mary, 60
Grayson, Robert, 62
Green Peach War, 115, 134, 136–42, 143, 161, 162, 175, 197; African Creek role in, 138–39; causes of, 136–38, 287n49; negotiations to end, 142–43; origin of name for, 140, 287–88n53; results of, 143
Gregory, James Roane, 220
Guinn v. Oklahoma (1915), 252, 305n46

Halleck Tustenuggee, 54–55
Harlan, James B., 78, 101
Harris, John H.: and testimony at 1885 hearings, 163
Haskell, Charles, 241

Hastings, William W., 241
Hawkins, Ben (William McIntosh's son-in-law), 37
Hawkins, Benjamin (Creek agent), 17, and civilization program, 17–19
Hawkins, Billy, 30, 46, 51
Hawkins, Jane, 27
Haynes, Charly, 134
Henry (African Creek Baptist), 26
Herrod, Cyrus, 130
Hes-siah-hupt-keh (African Creek soldier), 59
Hicks, Hannah Worchester, 74
High Springs (Council Hill), 96
Hindmann, (Gen.) Thomas, 61
Hinton, Richard J., 54
Hitchcock, (Gen.) Ethan Allan, 30–31
Hitchcock, Laura, 94
Holdenville, Okla., 98
Holladay, Andrew, 55, 57
Hopkins's Battery, 63
House of Kings, 97
House of Warriors, 97
Howard, Oliver O., 100
Hunter, (Gen.) David A., 52, 54

Independent Party, the, 175
Indian Brigade, 63, 64, 71
Indian trade: English and Scottish traders, 12–13; slaves involved in, 12–14; trade goods, 8
Indian slave trade, 6–7
Indian Expedition, 1862: 41, 56–58, 66; Battle of Locust Grove, 57; skirmish at Bayou Menard, 58; results of, 58
Indian Territory Baptist Association, 111
Intruders, 24, 91, 92, 114, 121, 123, 138, 161–63, 168, 174–75, 191, 203, 204, 205, 206, 219, 231; African Americans as, 163–64, 169, 189–90, 195; Oklahoma land run and, 185; permit system and, 113; railroad construction and, 113; white, 120–21, 169, 190, 195

Island, Harry, 34, 36, 94; at 1866 treaty negotiations, 86, 90; as Chief Sand's interpreter at 1863 treaty negotiations, 69, 70; converts to Christianity, 29–30; in Creek politics, 99, 102, 103, 106; death of, 109; as delegate and interpreter at Ft. Smith Council, 78, 81; as delegate to Washington to protest 1867 payment, 101; as North Fork representative on Creek Council, 99, 106; as merchant's interpreter, 37

Isparhecher (Spahecha), 128, 134, 165, 174, 175, 176, 208, 209, 210, 215, 286n46; and 1883 election, 143–45; and 1887 election, 174–76; and 1891 election, 189; and 1895 election, 203; in Green Peach War, 136–42; as Loyal Creek party leader, 128, 136–37; as principal chief, 204, 205–206, 208; retires from politics, 226

Jackson, Lizzie, 38
Jackson, Andrew, 19, 23
Jake (African Creek Baptist), 26, 28
Jamison, Gabriel, 196, 201
Jefferson, John, 65
Jefferson, Silas, 144, *146, 147*, 202, 286n46, 303n26; background of, 108–109; and Green Peach war, 140, 142; and Loyal Party, 128, 136, 137
Jesse (African Creek preacher), 29–30
Jessup, (Gen.) Thomas S., 39
Jim Boy (Tustenuggee Emarthla), 20
Johnson, Andrew: and negotiation of 1866 treaty, 78
Johnson, Nellie, 33
Johnson, James Coody: and allotment, 220, 222, 235, 253; background of, 172–73; in Creek politics, 244; as entrepreneur, 173, 234; in Oklahoma statehood politics, 237, 240, 241, 249

Johnson, Peter, 60, 62, 66
Johnson, Robert; 172, 173, 202; as interpreter for Presbyterian missionaries, 31; escapes to Union lines and enlists in First Indian, 68; father of James Coody Johnson, 172; returned to slavery, 46; as Seminole interpreter at 1866 treaty negotiations, 86; as Seminole interpreter at Ft. Smith Council, 78
Joneh (Keptene Uchee or Little Captain), 55, 62
Jones, Evan, 46
Jones, Robert, 131
Juba (African Creek), 30
Jumper, John, 46, 68

Kansas: African Creek refugees in, 52–54, 81, 96, 81, 168; as destination for Loyal Creeks, 51, 52
Kansas Jayhawkers, 48
Karsten, Johann Christian, 17–19
Kellum, Charles, 27–29
Kernel, (Rev.) Jonathan: as Baptist minister, 111; and Evangel School, 135–36; and Freedmen's Baptist Association, 181–82; as Tullahassee trustee, 177
Kernels, Abe, 201, 216, 217
Kennard, Motey, 43, 48
Ketch (Galphin's slave), 13
King's Gifts, 14

Lady of Cofitachequi, 5
Lake Mohonk Conference on the Negro Question, 183–85
Lane, (Sen.) James H., 48, 64
Lee, David, 95
Lee, settlement of, 95, 171, 173
Lewis, Phillip, 203–204, 247
LeRoy, Kans., 53, 58–59, 61, 63.; Creek refugee camp outside, 58–59
Leslie, Nellie Ann (Coles), 118–19, 188, 283n17

Leslie, Robert, 118, 283n17, 283n18; as boarding school superintendent, 119–21; and Coachman's Muskogee Party, 122; as minister at Muskogee Baptist Church, 122–23
Lewis, Tally, 71
Lewis, Robert, 65
Lewis, Kendle, 47
Lewis, Gilbert, 47, 51
Lewis, David, 26–27
Liberia: immigration to, 190, 294n58
Liele, George, 14
Lilley missionary family, 68
Lincoln, Abraham: Emancipation Proclamation, 69; Loyal Creek letter to, 45; Opothleyohola and Halleck Tustenuggee letter to, 55
Little, John Sebastian, 234
Little Prince (of Broken Arrow), 18
Littlefield, Daniel F., 38, 267n80 and n81
Locha Hacho, 78; death of, 128; elected principal chief, 109; impeachment of, 109–10, 116; as leader of Loyal Creek party, 108
Logan, James, 29–30
Loughridge, Robert H., 46
Lower Creeks, 6, 13, 21, 22, 25, 43; Confederate sympathizers among, 43; free blacks among, 25; and removal, 25; settlements of in the West, 25; slavery among in the West, 33
Loyal Creeks: and African Creeks, 44–50, 101, 104–106, 114, 128, 140; and Battle of Chusto Talasah, 41, 51–52; and Battle of Chustenalah, 41, 51–52, 66; and Battle of Round Mountain, 41, 65; defined, 268n7; and exodus to Kansas, 51–52; at Ft. Smith Conference, 78–81; as opposition party, 77, 101, 104–109, 114, 128, 136–38, 142, 144, 175; and opposition to Confederate treaty, 43; refugees in Kansas, 52–53; refugees at Ft. Gibson, 73–74

Luckey, Daniel, 133–34
Lyons, F. S., 103; and 1871 election dispute; 104–106, 108; Creek agent, 103; and jurisdiction over Creek freedmen; 103–104

Manning, (Lt.) E. C., 59; opinion of African Creek interpreters, 61
Marshall, Abe, 132
Marshall, Benjamin, 29, 33, 35; and selling slaves in the West, 38
Marshall, Isaac, 65
Marshall, Monday, 99
Marshall, William, 65
Marshalltown, 99, 124–25, 131, 284n22
Master of Breath, 30
McCoy, Isaac, 26
McGillivray, Alexander, 15
McGilvray, Lipscomb, 165, 167
McGilvray family (African Creeks), 165, 167
McHenry, James: as Coweta District judge in Cobb case, 132–33
McIntosh Creeks: immigration to the West, 24–26; settlements in the West, 24–25; slaves immigrating with, 24
McIntosh (Rentie), Caroline, 172, 291n21
McIntosh, Chilly, 30
McIntosh, Daniel Newnan (D. N.), 187; and 1866 Treaty negotiations, 87–90; as commander of Confederate Creek regiment, 48; as Confederate treaty supporter, 37, 43, 47; fathers Joseph P. Davison, 266n75; at Ft. Smith Peace Conference, 79; objections to African Creek citizenship, 79, 88–89; orders attack on Loyal Creeks, 50; plantation of, 34; slaves of, 37
McIntosh, Jackson, 81
McIntosh, John, 27
McIntosh, Morris, 51
McIntosh, Rentie, 172

McIntosh, Rebecca, 37

McIntosh, Roley (Creek chief), 24, 26, 28; death of, 81; lands of, 81; objection to missionaries, 30; slaves of, 24, 33, 75, 162

McIntosh, Tobe: as free black wagon train operator, 37; in business, 171; in supply service during Civil War, 65; as representative in Creek Council, 98, 99

McIntosh, William (Creek chief), 15, 17, 21; death of, 24, 27; Indian Springs Treaty and, 23–24; slaves of, 22

McIntosh, William (African Creek), 24, 69, 164, 171, 196, 218; charges of corruption against, 191, 196–97, 216; and citizenship commissions, 196–97, 201–202; Civil War service, 65–66; in Creek politics, 99, 105, 109, 191; flight to Union lines, 60; and Green Peach War 142, slave life of, 33–34

McQueen, Ben, 99

McQueen, Peter, 17

Mercer, Thomas, 21

Methodist Church: missionary activities with the Creeks, 22; missionary activities in the West, 26

Micco Hutke, 78, 102

Mike, Alexander, 247

Miller, Daniel, 96, 125, 144; and 1883 election disputes, 144; in Green Peach War, 133; political offices held, 109

Minnack, Alec, 62

Missionaries: and African Creeks, 18–19, 22–23, 26–32; and Creek Indians, 17–18, 22–23, 29, 30, 31; Creek objections to, 23, 28, 29–30. *See also* Baptist Church; Methodist Church; Presbyterian Church

Mississippian Indian cultures, 3; corn and, 4; men's roles, 4; women's roles, 4; similarity with West African cultures, 4–5; slavery in, 4–5; survival of cultural practices of, 7

Mohonk Conference on the Negro Question, 191

Moore, N. B., 40

Mott, M. L.(Creek National Attorney), 235, 245–46, 254, 255, 301–302n10

Moravian missionaries, 17–19; and black prophet Phil, 18–19; impact on Creek Indians, 17–18; and success with African Creeks, 17–19

Murray, William F. (Alfalfa Bill), 241

Murrell (African Creek Baptist), 26

Muscogee Baptist Church, 27

Muskogean languages, 7

Muskogee, Okla., 106, 109, 111, 112, 115, 116, 119, 120, 121, 125, 126, 127, 128, 130, 135, 162, 170, 171, 173–74, 182, 188, 213, 214–15, 216, 220, 221, 222, 228, 237; and African American businesses, 123, 173–74, 237–38; and African Creek businesses, 123, 174, 237–38; African Creek population of, 123; Booker T. Washington visits, 243, 247–48; as development center for Indian Territory, 123, 173–74; educational opportunities in, 238; establishment of, 123; intruders at, 189; politics in, 237–38, 239, 240, 241; 240–50; violence in, 123, 124, 137–38, 175, 283n19, 283n20

Muskogee Baptist Church, 27, 122

Muskogee District, 99, 109, 127, 131, 104, 171, 196, 204, 209

Muskogee Party, the, 114, 119, 143–44, 175; and African Creek support, 114

Nashville Institute, 172

Negro Fort, 20

Nero, William, 37, 99, 100

North Fork Colored Town, 129, 143, 165, 174, 175–76, 219, 230; creation of 97–98; representatives on Creek Council, 99, 106, 109

North Fork settlement, 25, 27, 29, 37, 50, 68, 71, 82, 85, 95, 100, 102

Oktahasas Hacho (Sands), 69, 70, 75, 77, 78, 99, 128; and 1866 treaty negotiations, 88–90; and 1867 election, 101–102; and 1871 election dispute, 104–107; death of, 108; as Loyal Creek leader, 43, 45, 69–70
Old Fountain Church (Ebeneezer Station), 111, 125
Oklahoma Territory, 164, 185
Oklahoma (state of): Constitutional Convention, 249–50; and grandfather clause, 252, 305n46; and Hamilton statehood bill, 244; legislature and disfranchisement, 251–52; legislature and segregation, 250–51; and segregated schools, 256–57; and single state politics, 241, 243–45
Okmulgee, Okla., 95, 96, 97, 170, 197; African Creek residents, 295n7
Opothleyahola, 23, 25, alliance with African Creeks, 45–47; death of, 69, 70; and exodus to Kansas, 41, 50–52; free blacks and, 25; letters to Abraham Lincoln, 45, 54; Loyal Creek camp on Deep Fork, 45, 48; opposition to Confederate treaty, 43; opposition to missionaries, 23, 30–31; and removal, 24–25; slaves of 24, 25, 268n9
Owen, Robert L., 233, 241

Parker, Ely, 101
Parker, (Judge) Isaac, 172–73
Parks, (Lt. Col.) R. C., 60, 133
Payne, David, 163; and boomer movement, 164
Pecan Creek Boarding School, 171, 188, 208, 209, 256
Perdue, Theda, 287n49
Perryman, Hector, 60

Perryman, Jacob, 140, 213; flight to Union lines, 60–61; service in First Indian 66, 67; slave life of, 35
Perryman, Joseph, M., 175, 288n59; in 1883 election, 143–44; declared chief by U.S. officials, 145
Perryman, Legus C. (L. C.), 175, 187, 208; African ancestry of, 176, 300n63, 305n43; African Creek political support for, 176; African Creek rights and, 162; in Creek politics 174; as Creek principal chief, 175, 185; impeachment of, 200
Perryman, Mollie, 60, 82–84, 96
Perryman, Mose, 33–34, 60, 276n13
Perryman, Pompey, 62
Perryman, Sanford, 78
Peter (Galphin), Jesse, 14
Peterson, Burkhard, 17–19
Phil (Benjamin Hawkins's slave), 18–19, 21
Phillips, (Col.) William A., 57, 58, 64, 66, 71, 75; and 1864 expedition, 72; details First Indian soldiers in planting and repair, 1865, 75–76; commander, Third Indian, 58; commander, Indian Brigade, 63; as officer in First Indian, 56–58
Pike, Albert: as Confederate District commander, 58; negotiates Confederate treaties, 48, 58; offers amnesty to Loyal Creeks, 48
Plessy v. Ferguson, 294n63
Point, the (peninsula between Arkansas and Verdigris rivers), 47, 84, 95, 107
Poison Springs Massacre, 67–68
Pope, John, 18
Posey, Alexander, 236, 297n30, 300n63
Porter, Pleasant, 105, 118, 129, 135, 162, 185, 187, 196, 204, 211, 244, 245, 249, 286n46, 288–89n1; African ancestry, 129, 216, 226, African Creek support of, 226, 227, 228; as Creek principal

chief, 226–27, 230–33, 244; and limiting African Creek citizenship rights, 162, 191, 196, 227; and restrictions on African Creek allotments, 233, 245–46; support for allotment, 196, 210, 227–29

Poskita (busk, or green corn ceremony), 6, 28, 29, 30, 97, 182

Post Oak settlement, 46

Prairie Edge (Paro Bruner settlement), 98, 172, 173, 176

Presbyterian Church: and Coweta mission, 31, 46; and Tullahassee, 31; and Union mission (Cherokee), 26

Prince, Sam, 65

Quay, (Sen.) Matthew, 242

Quay amendment, 242–43, 249

Quantrill, William, 67–68, 71

Queensbury, William, 33

Railroads, 88, 92, 163–64, 174: construction through Creek Nation, 123, 127–28; impact of, 106–107, 113–16, 127–28, 136

Red Fork, Arkansas River (Cimarron), 50

Redmon, Mose, 71

Redstick War, 165; African Creek role in, 19–20, 41; outbreak of, 19

Reed, H. C.: in business, 170–71, 174; in Creek politics, 77, 177, 201, 204, 208, 216; and Green Peach War, 139, 141–42; as judge in Vann case, 131; in statehood politics, 250–51

Reed's Mountain, skirmish at, 62

Rentie, Ellen, 95

Rentie, Island, and allotment contest case against Dave Roberts, 222–25

Rentie, Pickett, 66, 212

Rentie, Warrior, 191–92, 239, 297n30, 297n31; and allotment, 220, 222–26; background of, 171–72; in business,

174, 234; in Creek politics, 172, 200–201, 204, 208; opposition to Sequoyah constitution, 242; in politics of Oklahoma statehood, 237, 240–42, 251

Republican Party, 232, 237; and race issue in Indian Territory, 239–41; and race issue in statehood movement, 249–50, 251, 254; splits off into lily-white faction, 250

Rhea's Mill, Ark., 63

Ritchie, (Maj.) John, 58

Robbins, Ned, 99, 295n12

Roberts, Monday, 131

Robertson, Alice Mary, 256, 286n43, 304n34; as Creek school supervisor, 246–48

Robinson, William, 78

Robles (runaway slave from De Soto expedition), 5–6

Roosevelt, Theodore, 232, 239–40, 245, 303n18, 305n44; extends Creek tribal government operations, 244; receives African Creek/African American delegation protesting Oklahoma constitution, 251; signs Oklahoma Enabling Act, 249; visits Indian Territory and Oklahoma Territory, 241

Ross, John, 48

Sac-Fox Agency, 64, 69, 70, 71, 75

Sampson, James, 132–33

Sanborn, (Gen.) John B., 92–93

Sango, Alexander, G. W.: as business leader in Muskogee, 237–38; founder of Sango Baptist College, 238; in municipal and statehood politics, 239, 240, 249, 251; as superintendent at Tullahassee, 243, 247

Sango Baptist College and Industrial Institute, 238, 247

Sango, Scipio, 51, 94, 125, 237; and Freedmen's Baptist Association, 182;

Sango, Scipio (*continued*)
    as representative on Creek Council,
    99, 106; as school trustee, 121
Sands. *See* Oktahasas Hacho
Saunt, Claudio, 10, 261n3, 263n4,
    277n30, 287n49
Schofield, (Gen.) John M., 63
Second Baptist Church (Muskogee), 170
Second Great Awakening, 20–21
Second Indian Home Guard, 56, 58
Second Kansas Colored (83rd U.S.C.T.):
    Company G, 68–69, 76
Second Ohio Cavalry, 56
Sells, Elijah, 78
Sells, John (Creek slaveholder), 47
Sells, Joe, 51
Sells, Kizzie, 47
Sells, Snow: and 1879 election contro-
    versy, 129; and 1883 election contro-
    versy, 144; as Arkansas Colored
    leader, 109, 121, 125, 129; support for
    Constitutionalists in Green Peach
    War, 131, 135, 139; and Tullahassee,
    140, 177, 178
Seminole Indians, 20, 207
Seminole War (First), 20, 22
Sequoyah statehood movement, 241–
    42; and African Creeks, 242
Silver Bluff Baptist Church, 13–14; and
    connection with African American
    slaves in Indian trade, 13
Sixth Kansas Cavalry, 63, 67
Smith, Island, 158, 295n9; background
    of, 197–98, and Green Peach War;
    142; native healing and, 257
Smith, James M. C., 43, 47
Snow, G. C., 53–54
Soloman, Samuel, 136, 182
South Carolina, 6, 12, 13, 14; and colo-
    nial Indian trade, 5, 7–8; and Indian
    slave trade, 16; runaway slaves from,
    7, 12, 14
Southern Baptist Convention, 111

Stanton, Edwin, 58
Steadham, John, 67
Steadham, Troy, 35
Stidham, George Washington (G. W.),
    43, 167, 187; African Creek citizenship
    rights and, 163, 164, 167, 191, 196,
    285n36
Suffrage League, 237; convention at
    Muskogee (1906), 249
Sullivan, Andrew, 214–15, 298n41

Tapping, (Capt.) J., 69
Taskigi town, 303n26
Taylor, George, 188
Tenney, (Lt.) Luman, 56
Texas, Confederate troops from, 67
Third Indian Home Guard, 58
Thomas, (Judge) John R., 229, 233
Tomm, Jim, 71, 229
Treaty of Ft. Jackson, 20
Treaty of Paris (1763), 12
Treaty with the Creeks, of 1832 (removal
    treaty), 24
Treaty of 1863 (unratified). *See* Creek
    treaties
Treaty of 1866. *See* Creek treaties of 1866
Tuckabatchee Hacho, 55
Tuckabatchee Micco, 30, 43
Tuckabatchee (Upper Creek town), 21,
    22, 30
Tuckabatchee Baptist Church, 30
Tuggle, William O., 129, 257, 258
Tufts, John Q., 132
Tullahassee Mission, 107, 153, 154; estab-
    lishment of, 31; Simon Brown and,
    46; Robertson missionary family
    and, 45–46; as African Creek school,
    135–36, 177–81, 188, 204, 243, 256
Tulsey Fixico, 55
Turner, James Milton, 164, 167, 289n6
Tuskaya-hiniha (Upper Creek slave
    owner), 38
Tuskeneehau (Upper Creek chief), 23

Tuste nup-chup-ko (Creek), 62
Twine, William H., 237, 239, 240, 250
Tyler (deacon, Creek African Church), 21

U.S. courts, 103, 164, 173, 205, 207, 206n26; established for Indian Territory, 183; and jurisdiction over African Creeks, 103–104, 186
U.S. Senate: and 1878 hearings 115–19; and 1885 hearings, 162–63; and 1906–1907 hearings, 252–53; and 1908 hearings, 253
Unassigned Lands, 164, 174, 185
Union Indian Agency, 132, 135; established, 170
Union party, the, 174–75, 203; and African Creek support, 175
Upper Creeks, 6, 22, 25, 43; free blacks among, 25; removal and, 25; settlements of 25, 29; slave holders among, 25; traditional culture among, 30

Van Sertima, Ivan, 261n1
Van Horne, (Capt.) Benjamin, 64, 67
Vann, Dick, and shootout in Muskogee, 125; revenge raids of, 130
Vann, John, 139; African Creeks stand trial for, 127, 285n33; Cherokee

revenge raids, 130; death of, 126; and shootout in Muskogee, 125
Vann, Joseph, 48
Waite, (Gen.) Stand, 57, 58, 60
Warde, Mary Jane, 196, 287n49, 288n60, 300n56
Washington, Booker T., 232, 238, 247, 303–304n28; and Quay amendment, 244; visits Boley, 239; visits Indian Territory, 243–44
"Watchina," 190
Wattles, (Col.) Stephen H., 55, 64; appointed lt. col. in First Indian, 55; appointed commander First Indian, 59; at Prairie Grove, 62
Weer, (Col.) William: arrest of, 57; commander of Indian Expedition, 56; at Locust Grove, 57
Wellington (Lee), 95, 98
Whatley (Capt.), 50
Wickett, Murray, 289n9, 302–303n17
William (African Creek preacher), 21
Withington Mission, 22.
Wright, J. Leitch, 16, 265n55
Wright, John W., 170

Ya-fa-la-mart-la (Creek interpreter), 59
Yuchi Indians: as part of Creek Confederacy, 7; in First Indian, 55